ZINN & THE ART OF
TRIATHLON
BIKES

$3–

ZINN & THE ART OF
TRIATHLON BIKES

AERODYNAMICS,
BIKE FIT, SPEED TUNING,
AND MAINTENANCE

LENNARD ZINN

Illustrated by Todd Telander

VELO press

BOULDER, COLORADO

Printed in the United States of America

10 9 8 7 6 5 4 3 2 1

Distributed in the United States and Canada by Publishers Group West

Library of Congress Cataloging-in-Publication Data

Zinn, Lennard.

  Zinn & the art of triathlon bikes / Lennard Zinn.

    p. cm.

  Includes bibliographical references and index.

  ISBN-13: 978-1-931382-97-7 (pbk. : alk. paper)

  ISBN-10: 1-931382-97-2 (pbk. : alk. paper)

  1. Bicycles—Maintenance and repair. 2. Bicycle racing. 3. Triathlon.

  I. Title. II. Title: Zinn and the art of triathlon bikes.

  TL430.Z568 2007

  629.28'772—dc22

                                          2007012108

VeloPress®, a division of Inside Communications, Inc.
1830 N. 55th Street
Boulder, Colorado 80301–2700 USA
303/440-0601; Fax 303/444-6788; E-mail velopress@insideinc.com

To purchase additional copies of this book or other VeloPress books,
call 800/234-8356 or visit us at www.velopress.com.

Cover and interior design by Erin Johnson
Composition by Pauline Brown
Cover photo by Don Karle; tri bike built by Lennard Zinn.
Author photo by Brad Kaminski
Interior photography credits: photo 2.1, Dr. Kim Blair, MIT;
photos 2.2 and 2.3, Cor Vos; photo 3.1, Delly Carr; photo 3.2, Timothy Carlson;
photo 3.3, Getty Images; and photo 3.4, Graham Watson.

To Ted, Lodema, and Chama

CONTENTS

A TIP OF THE HELMET TO . . .

Todd Telander. A picture is worth a thousand words, adding up to hundreds of thousands of illustrative "words" from Todd's capable hand. Todd's drawings make my written words more intelligible and this book more useful and beautiful.

Thanks to Steve Hed, John Cobb, and Boone Lennon for the good times at the Texas A&M wind tunnel and for teaching me almost everything I know about aerodynamics. Thanks also to Mark Allen, Scott Tinley, Scott Molina, Tim DeBoom, Greg LeMond, Lance Armstrong, and the many other athletes who so generously gave us the opportunity to work with them in the wind tunnel. For their direct additions to this book, I want to express my deep gratitude to Gale Bernhardt, Kim Blair, Len Brownlie, Todd Carver, John Cobb, Joe Friel, Steve Hed, Dan Heil, Neal Henderson, Hunter Allen, Chris Kautz, Chet Kyle, Morgan Nicol, Andy Pruitt, Paul Swift, Max Testa, and Kraig Willett.

I appreciate and have incorporated suggestions from Scott Adlfinger, Paul Ahart, Saul Danoff, Skip Howat, Calvin Jones, Paul Morningstar, Wayne Stetina, the late Bill Woodul, and many others too numerous to mention, including countless readers of my Q&A column on www.velonews.com and www.insidetri.com who have written me with great tips.

My undying appreciation goes to Dave Trendler, Jen Soulé, Ted Costantino, and Renee Jardine for keeping the fires burning under this book and for their contributions to making VeloPress such a fine organization to work with, and to Nick Wigston and J. P. Burow for assisting in every way possible with this book and for taking the load off of me at Zinn Cycles so that I could work on it. Thanks to Ted, Chrisona Schmidt, Jade Hays, Kevin Edwards, and Iris Llewellyn for their fine editing and insightful suggestions, to Iris, Renee, and Liza Campbell for keeping everything moving smoothly through the editorial process, and to Charles Pelkey for his editing contributions and content suggestions.

Thanks to Felix Magowan and John Wilcockson for creating VeloPress in the first place.

And, lastly, thanks to my family for providing support and a wonderful environment at home for me to work in and the freedom to work away from it as well.

Exploded view of tri bike

INTRODUCTION

First things first, but not necessarily in that order.
—Doctor Who

Triathletes have a strong, fiercely independent spirit, sometimes to the point of being stubborn. That mentality may be what leads them to the sport, which in turn reinforces it. It takes a certain type of person to train incredibly hard in three disparate disciplines simultaneously with the intent of eliminating weaknesses in any one. While admirable and likely to produce an amazing body, those demands may not be conducive to keeping a bike in top working condition or ensuring that the setup of the bike to its rider is ideal.

Unlike elite bike racers, most elite triathletes do not have bike mechanics who travel with them. And age-group triathletes also tend to devote less attention to the maintenance of their bike than do average bike racers. After all, the bike is only a tool for one of a triathlete's three sports, and with all of that time spent training, who has time to fuss over the bike when there are immediate issues to attend to like dialing in the shape of new orthotics to combat tendon pain from running, or physical therapy to deal with a shoulder sore from swimming? And for that matter, who even has time to take the bike to be serviced in a bike shop, especially during the height of the season when you have to schedule an appointment a week or three out? And how about finding the opportunity and the right person to make sure you are positioned efficiently? Heck, just setting aside the time to get your bike out of the bike case, reassembled, and back on the road after flying to a race can be challenge enough!

Triathletes often train alone on the bike. Makes sense; triathlons are largely solitary events. It's also hard to schedule rides with others when you have another workout or two to fit in every day, as well as work and home life. However, you don't get comments like, "Hey, your seat is too low," "Your stem is too long," "Dude, that bike's too big for you," or, "What's up with your handlebar tilt?" if you don't go on large group rides with fellow racers.

I.1 Complete tri bike with parts labeled

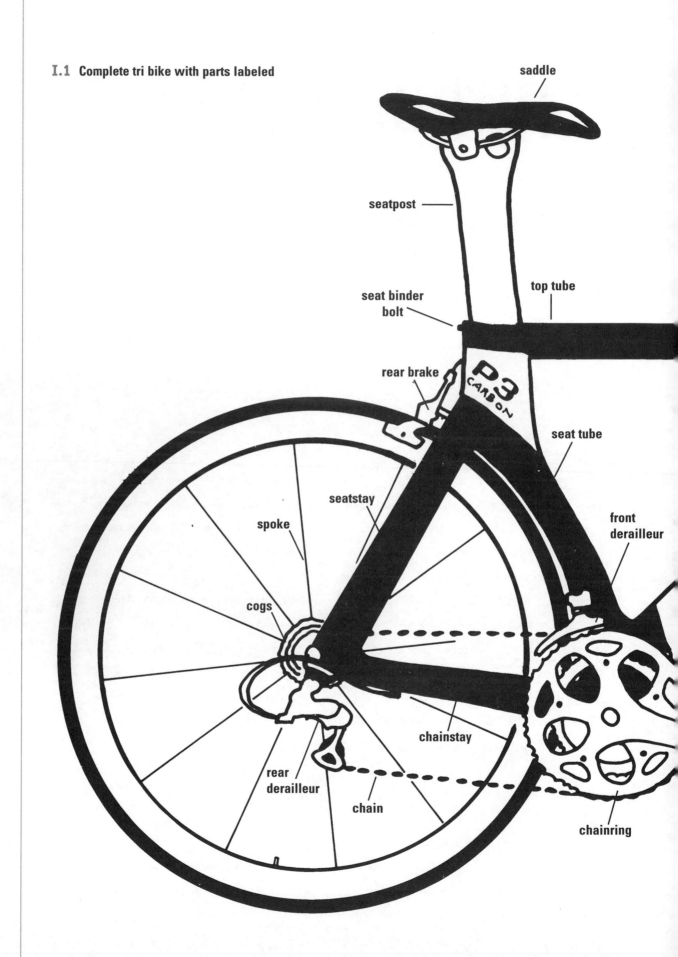

saddle

seatpost

seat binder
bolt

top tube

rear brake

seat tube

seatstay

spoke

front
derailleur

cogs

chainstay

rear
derailleur

chain

chainring

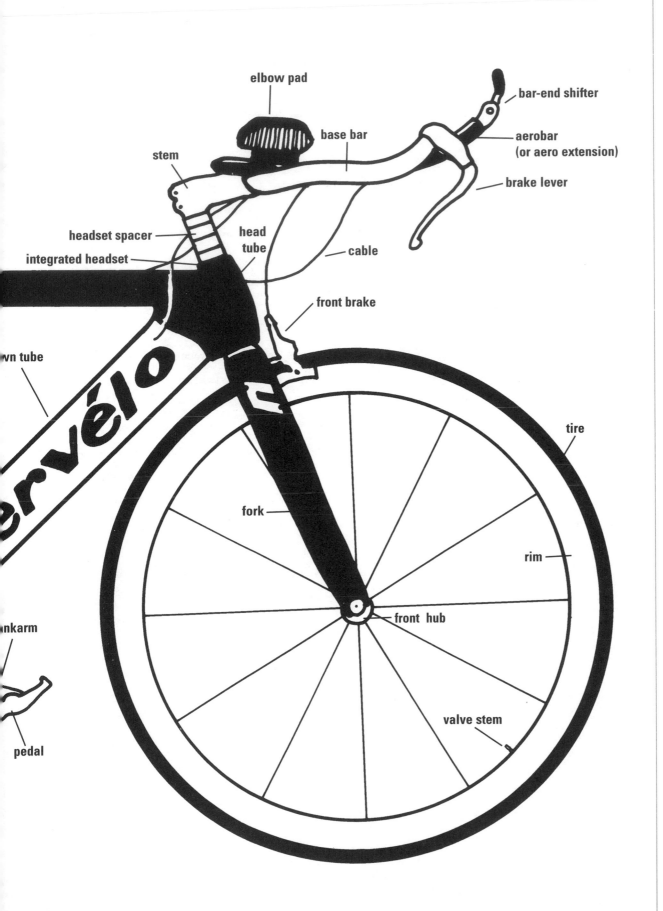

elbow pad

bar-end shifter

base bar

aerobar
(or aero extension)

stem

brake lever

headset spacer

head
tube

integrated headset

cable

wn tube

front brake

tire

fork

rim

front hub

nkarm

valve stem

pedal

All of the way up to the elite level, you see variations in positioning of triathletes (and duathletes) on their bikes that can be mind-boggling when looking from the perspective of what is efficient biomechanically and aerodynamically. You don't find that kind of variation in positioning among bike racers; even down to a club level, they receive coaching or peer input that smoothes out those aberrations. But triathletes, particularly those juggling their sport with career and family concerns, have limited time for those kinds of details.

ASSISTANCE IS ON THE WAY

So what is the answer? Well, making it a habit to pay some attention to your bike on a regular basis is sure to improve your racing and training. As is knowing what to do when something breaks. As is knowing how to set yourself up in an efficient pedaling position, or knowing how to pack and unpack your bike for air travel quickly and properly. Every triathlete or duathlete would like more efficiency, comfort, safety, and enjoyment on the bike. And this book is designed to teach you how to attain it yourself.

This book is for that triathlete who spends enough time, money, and effort on the sport that he or she sees no point in being held back by a bike that is not working ideally. And by working ideally, I am referring not only to the mechanical operation of the bicycle, but also to the setup of the bike to the individual athlete, to the selection of the appropriate bike and components to the individual athlete's application, and even to the ease of getting it packed and unpacked—without damage—when traveling to distant races.

You find time to take a shower after workouts. But do you take five minutes after every ride to wipe down and lube your drivetrain? You probably get occasional (or frequent) massages, but do you occasionally tune up your bike or regularly inspect your tires, chain, cogs, brake pads, and shoe cleats for wear? You change your socks daily, but do you change your handlebar tape and elbow pads even semiannually (and inspect for damage hidden by them)? Every now and then, you may get a physical or an ECG or Max VO$_2$ test, but when do you check that your position on your bike supports your body in an inefficient pedaling position that doesn't compromise your run? All of these things are simple enough, if you know how and can find a way to incorporate them into your schedule.

HOW THIS BOOK IS LAID OUT

This book begins with traveling with your bike, since if you can't get to your triathlons (or duathlons) with an intact and fully functional bike, much of your hard work has been for naught. And given that there are lots of things that can happen to a bike in transit, including to carbon fiber parts, which are good at masking internal damage, this chapter describes how to inspect your bike to make sure it's safe.

Choosing equipment is the next chapter (2). How do you know what type of bike to buy or what wheels and handlebars to get? And what about if you do both short- and long-course events? How about hilly races? Or windy races? This chapter will provide you with the tools you need to choose.

Everybody has had experience with a bad riding position, which can be downright painful. And you know you can pay dearly for an un-aerodynamic position, especially on a windy day. Positioning yourself on the bike is something you may be the most qualified person for, given that you know your body better than anybody else. You just need the tools to do it, and the third chapter of this book gives you those.

Chapter 3 is probably the most extensive triathlon-positioning treatment in print anywhere.

Not maintaining your bike means that minor problems eventually become emergencies. And you know how hard it is to find somebody in August to fix your bike right away when it breaks down! I've seen things like rusted-through handlebars on bikes shipped ahead to a Kona bike shop for the Ironman. Believe me, leaving it up to a bike shop a few thousand miles away to fix problems at the last minute before the most important event of the year is not the way to a relaxed, successful race. The following 11 chapters of this book explain in detail and show you visually exactly how to find and repair whatever ails your trusty steed. Each task carries a rating of how much mechanical proficiency is required, and a list of required tools accompanies every chapter.

In an effort to keep this book to a manageable size, and to maintain its focus on the primary tasks most triathletes will take on, I have omitted some maintenance and repair jobs. For instance, since so many triathletes use bar-end shifters, I have not included overhaul procedures for integrated shift/brake levers, although replacing cables in them and adjusting their feathering is covered. Checking and adjusting frame and fork alignment is also omitted, because on the carbon and aluminum frames prevalent in triathlon there is virtually nothing that can be adjusted or corrected at home. Similarly, removal and installation of headset cups is not covered; the prevalence of integrated headsets is making this procedure irrelevant (though headset service, even including threaded headsets, is covered). I've eliminated discussion of toeclip-style pedals and old, obsolete bottom brackets and brakes, and I've also omitted the procedures for working with separate freewheels and thread-on hubs, since few

triathletes will ever see these items. Finally, I have not included wheel building, as I doubt many triathletes would choose to give up a dozen hours of valuable training time to learn this increasingly arcane art, especially with the widespread availability today of very fast and very aerodynamic prebuilt wheels. All of these topics, however, are covered in my book *Zinn and the Art of Road Bike Maintenance*; if you are a die-hard do-it-yourselfer, I recommend that book to you.

Exploded diagrams are used to show more clearly than a photograph could how parts go together. Nevertheless, the first time you go through a procedure, you may find it easier to have a friend read the instructions out loud as you perform the steps.

Obviously some maintenance tasks are more complicated than others. I am convinced that anyone with an opposable thumb can perform any repair on a bike. Still, it pays to spend some time getting familiar with simple tasks before throwing yourself into complex jobs.

Tasks and tools required are divided into three levels indicating their complexity or your proficiency.

Level 1 tasks need level 1 tools and require only an eagerness to learn. Level 2 and level 3 tasks have corresponding tool sets and are progressively more difficult. All tools required are shown in Chapter 4, and all repairs described in this book are classified as level 1 unless otherwise indicated. At the end of Chapter 5 is the must-read section "A General Guide to Performing Mechanical Work" (§v-16); it states general policies and approaches that apply to all mechanical work. Note that the symbol § denotes the section in the book.

Each maintenance chapter starts with a list of required tools in the margin. If a section involves more than basic experience and tools, there will be an icon designating the difficulty. Tasks and illustrations are numbered for easy reference.

A troubleshooting section is included at the end of some chapters. This is the place to go to identify the source of a certain noise or particular malfunction in the bike. There is also a comprehensive troubleshooting guide in Appendix A.

The appendixes contain other valuable information as well. Many tasks will be simplified or improved by using the information presented in the appendixes. Appendix B is a complete gear chart and includes instructions on how to calculate your gear with non-standard-size wheels. Appendix C lists the tightening (torque) specifications of almost every bolt on the bike. I can't emphasize enough how useful it is to use a torque wrench to tighten bolts as tightly as the component manufacturer intended, but no tighter. Flag Appendix C so you can flip to it easily whenever you work on your bike. Appendix D, the glossary, is an inclusive dictionary of triathlon-related bicycle technical terminology.

The Internet can be a useful supplement to the maintenance section of this book. For instance, exploded views of some parts can be found on component manufacturers' websites, such as www.campagnolo.com, www.shimano.com, and www.mavic.com.

Peppered throughout the book are tips for speed, safety, or comfort, many of which are from top triathletes and equipment gurus. Compassion for you in caring for yourself and your bike is also built in.

When talking with triathlon mechanics or equipment sponsors about what I am including in this book, I've been told often that educating triathletes about working on their bikes is a humanitarian pursuit. So be it! If writing this book prevents one avoidable crash, it will have been worth it. With this book, I intend to reduce the danger and the frustration of this sport, and increase the enjoyment. Have fun!

I

Travel, Fit & Aerodynamics

TRAVELING WITH A BIKE

The saying "Getting there is half the fun" became obsolete with the advent of commercial airlines.
—Henry J. Tillman

He who would travel happily must travel light.
—Antoine de Saint-Exupery

Triathletes and duathletes probably rack up as many flight miles as training miles with their bikes. Races take place all over the globe, with some of the best held on islands. The only way to get to these races is to fly. But flying with a bike, or even shipping it ahead to a bike shop so that it's ready to go when you arrive, can be traumatic.

This chapter and this book are designed to take as much of the worry out of travel as possible. You'll need mechanical abilities to pack your bike; the information here will guide you through the process. You'll also need to make a checklist of everything that needs to get done; for example, you'll need to take assembly tools with you to put your bike together at the other end, and you will need to buy CO_2 cartridges for your tires when you arrive, since you can't fly with them. I suggest you read through this chapter and collect the tips you'll need for your own mode of travel, and then write them down so you don't forget anything in the rush of preparation. This book can't do much about the high cost of transport and the problem of dealing with your bike container at the other end of your flight, but you'll find suggestions here on ways to minimize the expense and inconvenience.

The first rule for taking the worry out of travel is to schedule enough time to pack your bike properly in a suitable protective container that you know how to use. This requires planning ahead, acquiring a container if you don't have one, and allowing enough time to pack without rushing. In addition, if you are shipping the bike ahead, you need to allow time for it to arrive (and to be assembled by the shop on the other end, if that's how you're doing it).

If you don't travel often with a bike, you may be able to rent a bike case from your local shop, saving the $300–$800 that a good case can cost. Also, some shops will pack your bike and even ship it to your destination.

There are other challenges, of course.

i-1 GENERAL SUGGESTIONS FOR ANY BIKE CONTAINER

1. When in doubt, take parts off. If you are having trouble getting everything to fit, you will probably cause less damage to the bike, and take less time packing too, if you simply remove more parts from the bike. Instead of struggling to wedge something in when the water bottle cage is in the way, for example, just remove the cage.

2. Unless you have to deflate the tires to fit your bike in the container, leave them inflated to 75–80psi to protect them from impact. The maximum tire pressure increase due to altitude is less than one bar (14psi), so even if you leave the tires at 100psi, you'll have no worries about a blowout. A bigger concern might be ground shipping, where your bike could sit in a big brown truck in the sun. But if the temperature in the truck is bearable for the driver, it should not be hot enough to blow a tire that started the trip at 75–80psi.

3. Put spacers between the front (Fig. 1.1) and rear dropouts (Fig. 1.2) to avoid damage to the bike if it gets buried under piles of luggage. For this purpose, you can use (1) the plastic spacers new bikes come shipped with (Fig. 1.1), (2) pieces of dowel cut to length taped into the dropouts, (3) hollow axles (with nuts at the correct spacing) held in place by your quick-release skewers (Fig. 1.2; you must always remove your skewers from your wheels anyway), (4) separate front and rear hubs tightened into the dropouts, or (5) long pieces of threaded rod with pairs of nuts and washers near each end to establish the right spacing and wing nuts to clamp them in place. Soft cases with wheels may have built-in mounts to clamp the front and rear ends, eliminating the need for spacers.

4. If you have slotted cable stops on the frame, pull all cable housings out of them (Fig. 1.3A; no need to disconnect the cables) to avoid kinking and damaging the cables or housings when moving the handlebars around during packing. Pulling the housing out of the cable stop requires some cable slack, so first remove the rear wheel (Chap. 5, §v-9)and shift the rear derailleur to the smallest cog position. To remove the rear derailleur housing, push the rear derailleur inward toward larger cogs with one hand to create slack in the cable while you pull the housing out of the chainstay cable stop with the other hand (Fig. 1.3A). To remove the rear brake housing, squeeze the brake pads together with one hand (with the rear wheel removed) while you pull the cable housing ends out of the cable stops on either end of the top tube (Fig. 1.3B). Internal cable routing prevents you from doing this.

1.1 Spacers between front dropouts

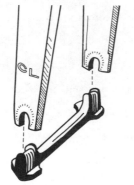

1.2 Spacers between rear dropouts

1.3A **Shift cable housing pulled from slotted cable stop on chainstay**

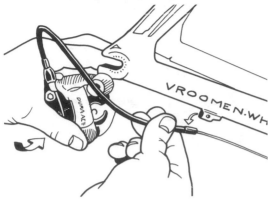

1.3B **Brake cable housing pulled from stop on top tube**

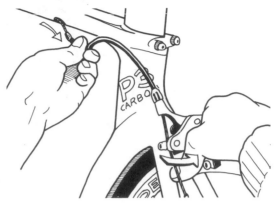

5. Unscrew the rear derailleur from the derailleur hanger (Fig. 1.4). If left on, it is vulnerable to damage, not only to itself but also to its hanger. If the derailleur hanger is bent or the cable barrel adjuster on the back of the derailleur is broken or bent when you arrive, you will have a heck of a time getting your shifting to work properly again. Once the derailleur is unscrewed, you can let it hang by the chain and the cable, though it's a good idea to wrap all three in a rag so they don't bang around and get twisted.

6. A front-opening stem cap (Fig. 1.5) at the handlebar, rather than a stem with a single-bolt bar clamp (Figs. 14.2, 14.4–6) or a one-piece bar/stem, will make frequent flying easier, due to ease of removing the handlebar. And a threadless headset system (Figs. 14.18–20) with a threadless stem (Figs. 14.2–4) will be a lot easier to deal with than a threaded headset (Fig. 14.21) and quill stem (Figs. 14.5–7).

7. Before you remove the handlebar or twist it down in the stem clamp, mark its position. You can put tape around the bar on either side of the stem and mark with a pen where it lines up with the slot in the stem clamp (Fig. 1.6) so that you'll be able to

1.4 **Rear derailleur hanging free**

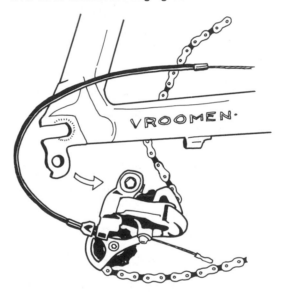

1.5 **Front-opening stem with front cap and bolts exploded open**

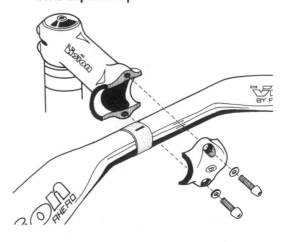

TRAVELING WITH A BIKE

1.6 Base handlebar marked with tape

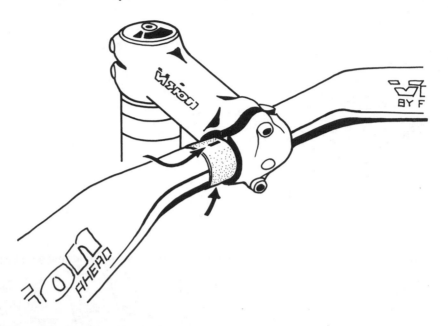

return your handlebar to its familiar position prior to your next ride. The same goes for your seatpost; mark its position either with a piece of tape or a scratch mark before removing it or shoving it in farther. You don't want to spend your first ride readjusting things that would not have needed re-adjusting if you had marked them properly.

8. If you discover something damaged, about to fail, or in any way questionable as you're packing, fix it before you go rather than leaving it to deal with at your destination or hoping that it does not plague you once there. View disassembling your bike for travel as an opportunity to inspect it closely for cracks, corrosion, and other damage.

9. Replace the nuts and bolts (and stem caps and skewer springs, oriented properly) on any parts you disassemble so that you can find them at your destination.

10. Leave CO_2 inflation cartridges (Fig. 4.4) and foam fix-a-flat inflators at home if you're flying, as they are prohibited on commercial airplanes. Of course,

what do you think inflates that life vest under your seat if you pull the tab? You guessed it . . ., a CO_2 cartridge! But, as with every airline security rule, ours is not to question why, ours is but to smile and comply. Arguing will get you nowhere, and it will annoy other passengers in line.

11. Remove your bike computer head and put it in a padded bag or in your other luggage.

12. Do not lock your bike container before flying unless you have TSA-approved locks.

13. Weigh your bags at home. You need to know the weight for ground shipping. For flying, the stan-dard guidelines these days allow two checked pieces of 50 pounds maximum apiece, and one carry-on piece. Know your airline's weight limits ahead of time. Frequent flyers are sometimes allo-cated more, such as three checked pieces of 70 pounds maximum each. It can be hard to stay within 50 pounds per piece with a bike, even if you have a superlight one. Some travel cases alone weigh 30 pounds! Add tools, floor pump, spare

tires, tubes and parts, helmet, shoes, and bike clothes and you'll be paying some extra overweight charges, unless your frequent flyer status gets you a more generous allowance. If you've weighed your bags at home, you'll either know you're underweight or you'll be prepared to pay the excess baggage charge; you won't be pulling everything out of your bags at the counter and repacking in order to avoid getting charged.

14. Don't pack bike tools in your carry-on luggage, since they could be confiscated.

15. Seek out vouchers from your triathlon federation, friends, or employer that allow your bike to fly free. You'll need one for each direction.

16. Finally, clearly label your bike container with your name, address, phone number, and e-mail address.

i-2 TRAVEL CONTAINER SELECTION

The container you choose depends on the size and type of your bike, whether you are flying with it or shipping it, how much of the bike you are willing to disassemble, how much time you are willing to devote to packing, and how much money you are willing to spend on the container. The following instructions describe how to pack each type.

i-3 HARD CASE

Generally, a hard case offers your bicycle the best protection but requires a lot of disassembly. Most hard cases consist of two clamshell halves of flexible plastic containing three separate layers of foam an inch or two thick whose outside dimensions are the same as the inside dimensions of the case. Others have one side padded for the frame, while the other side has built-in compartments for the wheels. Tie-downs to hold the frame and parts in place may or may not be integral

to the case. The case usually has wide straps or latches to hold it closed, wheels on one end, and a handle to drag it around.

i-3a Packing a Hard Case

Since the case is flat and narrow, the bike must become as two-dimensional as possible to fit in (Fig. 1.7).

1. Remove the pedals.

2. Remove the wheels from the bike; they usually go in a pair of foam layers separate from the frame and fork to avoid scratches.

3. Place the frame in the case atop a layer of padding to see how it fits, and to judge what other parts need to be removed.

4. Remove the seatpost if needed; mark it first (see §i-1, step 7, Fig. 1.6). The seatpost and saddle can remain in the bike on small frames and must be removed on bigger ones. Really big frames may require removal of the right crankarm and perhaps even the fork.

5. Deal with the handlebar and aero extensions. Fitting in the handlebar is the hardest part with almost any type of case. You are limited in where it can be positioned, either attached to the stem or dangling from the cables once removed from the stem. Not being flat, a drop bar, particularly one with an aero clip-on bar attached, is tall for a narrow case. Some cases, particularly with small bikes with short stems, will allow you to fit the bike simply by removing or rotating the clip-on and then rotating the base bar downward in the stem clamp with the fork turned 90 degrees from straight ahead. This works better with drop bars than with cowhorns. Being flat, a cowhorn bar with a clip-on, or an integrated aero bar and flat base bar, will fit better in a hard case once the bar has been removed from the bike.

1.7 Exploded view of bike in Trico hard case

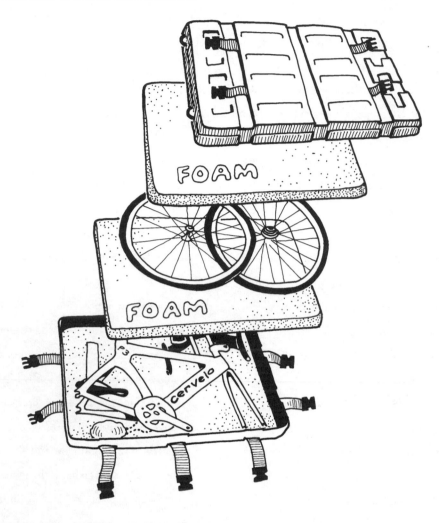

A front-opening stem (§i-1, step 6, Fig. 1.5) is a great help in disassembly. As described in §i-1, step 7, mark the position of the stem slot on the handlebar (Fig. 1.6).

6. It's not a necessity, but if possible turn your fork 90 degrees so that it can lie flat in the case, reducing its vulnerability to side impacts. If you do this and have removed the base bar from the stem, everything will fit flat if you loosen the bolts that clamp the stem to the fork and rotate the stem flat with the case as well. Don't loosen the headset top cap (see Fig. 14.8), though, or you will have to readjust the headset upon arrival.

7. If you have an old-style quill-type stem with a threaded fork and your bike can't be fit simply by rotating the base bar, you'll need to remove the stem. Loosen (but do not remove) the expander bolt and smack it with a hammer to free its expander wedge (see Fig. 14.11) in order to pull the stem out of the steering tube.

8. Place the wheels in the case, either atop a large foam rectangle placed over the frame, or in their dedicated wheel compartments.

9. Place the third and final layer of foam over the wheels, if applicable to your bike case.

10. Latch or buckle the case together.

i-4 SOFT-SIDED WHEELED BAG

Packing up and getting out of Dodge is fastest when you have a padded bag with a hard base on four wheels (Fig. 1.8); the front two wheels are steerable swivel casters. This bag type also folds down to a more compact size than a hard case for storage at your destination. It does not protect the bike as well and cannot be considered for shipping the bike with a carrier like UPS or FedEx; the shipping label won't stick to it, and it can't have other packages stacked on top. That said, professional cycling teams almost universally fly with this type of container and rarely suffer damage.

i-4a Packing a Soft-sided Wheeled Bag

Remove the wheels and remove the skewers from the wheels, plugging plastic protectors for wheel shipping into the axle ends (available, usually for free, from your local bike shop).

1. Clamp the frame and fork into the bike-securing system. Wheeled bike bags generally have one of two likely clamping systems. All of them clamp the fork with a skewer into a fork mount. In the rear, some clamp the rear dropouts with a skewer in a wider version of the front fork mount. These bags have a pivoting or sliding system between the front and rear mounts to adjust for wheelbase differences. Other systems employ a platform supporting the bottom bracket, and a J-bolt hooked over the chainstay, which is secured with a wing nut. You still need a spacer between the rear dropouts, and if you don't tighten the J-bolt enough, you'll find when you arrive that your frame has been damaged from slapping around in the bag and banging on the bottom bracket platform. It's worth adding a supplemental strap to hold the bottom bracket down. The front fork mount on some soft-sided bags is turned at 90 degrees, so that the fork and handlebar are turned to the side to fit better; with one of these and a small to medium-size bike, you can just rotate the handlebar down and be done with it. Mark its position first as in §i-1, step 7, Figure 1.6.

2. Once you have both the frame and fork clamped in, the bag's support base makes a convenient bike stand for the bike's disassembly and reassembly. Look at how the pedals will be located relative to the wheels, and remove one or both if they hit. Many bags have enough room to leave the pedals on.

3. Insert the wheels into the internal pockets for them in the bag's sides, or strap the wheels to either side of the frame if there are no wheel pockets. Pad the frame wherever there is contact; foam tubes used to insulate water pipes, available in hardware stores, work well for this. Things can move around in soft bike containers, so frame padding is a good idea.

4. Try zipping the bag closed from the back end. If the zipper won't go over the saddle, pull out the seatpost.

1.8 **View of bike in Sci-Con soft case with wheels**

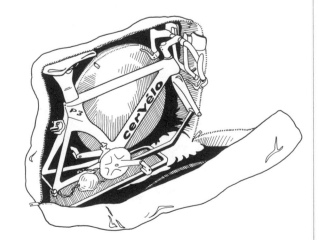

TRAVELING WITH A BIKE

PRO TIP

GALE BERNHARDT'S FLIGHT PACKING TIPS

I use pipe insulation cut to the specific length of each part of the frame. I write the bike part directly on the insulation (top tube, left rear stay, etc.) for quick packing. I then wrap stretchable bandages, such as Ace, around the insulation to hold it on. The insulation keeps the frame from getting damaged, and the Ace bandage can be used to hold ice packs on damaged body parts.

To stay within the airline 50-pound weight limit, I pack a high-volume frame pump rather than a floor pump and wrap it in pipe insulation in case it comes loose and bounces around in the box.

I pack Pledge Wipes to give my bike the final pre-event wipe down. They clean the bike and give it a great shine and good smell too!

—*Gale Bernhardt*

USA Olympic Triathlon and World Championship Coach, and author of Triathlon Training Basics, Training Plans for Multisport Athletes, *and* The Female Cyclist: Gearing Up a Level

5. Now start closing the front zipper. Your aero extensions will stick out too far to close the bag, but look to see what else needs to come off or be moved. If the zipper will close over the base bar, rotate the clip-ons down, first marking their position so that you can return them to their correct angle on arrival. Or, if you have aero extensions that can slide straight out, mark their positions, pull them out, pad them, and strap them to the frame. If your base bar/aero extensions are one piece, you'll likely need to open the stem cap and remove the whole bar (mark it as in §i-1, step 7, Fig. 1.6), padding it and strapping it to the frame. With a big bike, you may even need to do this with a drop bar. If your bike has a one-piece stem/bar, you'll need to remove it from the fork and attach it alongside the frame. To hold the now loose fork in, put in a spacer or a hose clamp where the stem clamp was, and tighten the headset top cap back in place.

6. Unless your bag already holds the fork turned at 90 degrees, you may want to try loosening the stem clamp at the fork (don't loosen the headset top cap!) and turning the stem 90 degrees, rotating the handlebar down (mark it as in §i-1, step 7, Fig. 1.6). Be aware of how vulnerable your brake levers are, and if one (or both) seems to be hard against the side of the bag, begging to be broken, reposition the handlebar. If the zipper won't close over the base bar, even when it's been rotated to the side and down or back, remove it (mark it as in §i-1, step 7, Fig. 1.6) and strap it alongside the frame.

7. Since you already did this step in §i-1, step 4, your cable housings should be freed from their slotted cable stops (Fig. 1.3A) to allow the handlebar and extensions to get the freedom they need for rotation or removal. Internal cables can create a problem if they are cut short; you won't be able to place the bar where you need it. But you also don't want to have to fish the cables back through on your arrival. So do what you can without disconnecting the cables to turn and/or detach the bar however necessary.

8. Consider wrapping computer wires differently so they do not impede putting your bike in the bag.

9. If you are putting a floor pump or tools in the bag, pad them or secure them in place.

10. Zip up the bag and fly!

i-5 SOFT CONTAINER WITHOUT WHEELS

Apart from flying with a collapsible bike in a suitcase, a soft-sided, padded bag with a shoulder strap is the most likely container to avoid scrutiny at check-in and thus avoid the usual bike charge. It also is the lightest and easiest to store when you arrive. But since it lacks wheels, you have to lug it around on your shoulder, which can be painful and awkward.

i-5a Packing a Soft-sided, Nonrolling Bag

Putting your bike in a soft case may only require removing the wheels and turning the handlebars with the aero extension removed or tipped down. Or it may require similar disassembly as a soft-sided bag with wheels (§i-4) or as a hard case (§i-3). Strap the wheels securely to either side of the (padded) frame to protect the tubes from being dented if the soft edge of the bag gets dropped on an edge of a cart or shelf.

i-6 CARDBOARD BOX

As long as you pack it well, a cardboard box is a good container for shipping ahead to a bike shop. It's cheap (usually free), and the shop can use it to ship the bike back to you after the race. For flying, it is also fine, but it can be damaged more easily, it's bulky to store, it can fall apart if it gets wet, and it requires you to have a lot of tape. It can require more bike disassembly than other containers, depending on the size of your bike.

i-6a Packing a Cardboard Box

1. To select the box (usually at a bike shop or at the recycling container behind the bike shop), remove your bike's front wheel and lay your bike on the side of the box to see whether it is large enough. A small bike will often fit with its rear wheel in place. A big bike may be a different story; see step 4.

2. Open the stem front cap and remove the handlebar (mark its position first as in §i-1, step 7, Fig. 1.6), padding it and strapping it to the frame. You may fit really small bikes by simply turning the fork 90 degrees and rotating the handlebar and aero extensions down (mark as in §i-1, step 7, Fig. 1.6).

3. Remove the front wheel (and its skewer). Pad the axle ends and the frame and fork. Remove the pedals and the seatpost (mark it as in §i-1, step 7, Fig. 1.6), and then pad them. Drop the bike into the box and slide the front wheel in alongside the front triangle. Slip the pedals and seatpost in alongside the bike.

4. If your bike is too big to fit in the box with the rear wheel in, remove it. It's then a good idea to remove the right crank as well, so the chainrings don't punch through the bottom of the box. It's pretty tough to fit two wheels alongside the frame, so if you had to remove both of them, it's a better idea to ship the wheels in a separate box, so they don't damage the frame and fork and get damaged themselves.

5. Wrap up and tape in extra parts you removed from the bike.

6. Tape up and label the box. Make sure the bottom and edges of the box are taped up well too. Your bike would not be the first to fall out of the bottom of a box.

i-7 COUPLED BIKE IN A SUITCASE OR SMALL HARD- OR SOFT-SIDED CASE

Couplers made by S&S Machine or Ritchey installed into a bike frame allow separating the front and rear

1.9 **X-ray-style view of coupled bike in bike case**

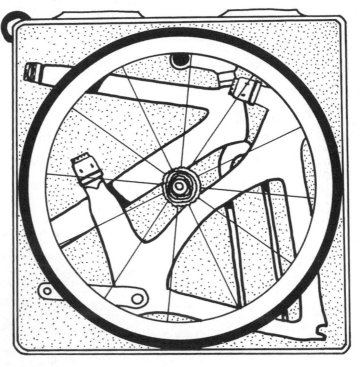

frame triangles. The shift cables and rear brake cable usually have threaded cable splitters so they can be separated as well. The entire bike can then be fit inside a hard or soft case whose inner linear dimensions are the same as the diameters of 700C wheels with the tires deflated (Fig 1.9). The bike may then not incur an extra charge from the airlines, since the case not only looks like a suitcase, but a 28×28×10-inch-deep case is within the standard dimensions for airline checked bags. At your destination, the case will easily fit into a taxi and will take less room to store during your stay.

There are also folding bikes with small wheels on the market that fit into standard suitcases, but the small wheel size and gearing and handling issues preclude them from being highly competitive triathlon bikes.

S&S couplers and the Ritchey down tube coupler are round in cross-section, which means that the top tube and down tube, or just the down tube in the case of Ritchey, must be cylindrical in the area of the cou-

plers, precluding aero tube shapes in those places. The Ritchey system separates at the top of the seat tube instead of within the top tube. The seatpost holds the frame sections together by means of two slotted seat-binders, one attached to the top tube and one to the seat tube, seatstays, and bottom bracket, thus mandating a cylindrical, rather than aero-shaped, seatpost and seat tube.

I recommend taking along photos of the assembly sequence (or maybe even a DVD of the procedure) for your particular bike to speed things up and simplify packing when you're in a hurry before your flight.

i-7a Packing a Coupled-bike Hard Case

1. Remove the pedals, handlebar, and seatpost (mark them as in §i-1, step 7, Fig. 1.6). You can generally leave the stem attached and turn it (and the fork) around backward. If you remove the stem and are not removing the fork (which is only required on very tall bikes), put a spacer or hose

clamp where the stem was (assuming yours is a threadless fork) and replace the headset top cap to retain the fork.

2. Remove the rear derailleur (Fig. 1.4). No need to disconnect the cable.

3. A chain with a master link (Figs. 7.21–23) is nice for this kind of bike. If you have one, open the link and remove the chain. Otherwise, wrap or pad the chain so it does not bang around in transit. Note that SRAM 10-speed master links are not openable.

4. Remove the front brake. No need to disconnect the cable.

5. Remove the wheels (§v-2–§v-4 and §v-9 or §v-10) and the skewers from the wheels. You may wish to plug the axle ends with hub protectors.

6. Separate the cables by means of the cable splitters.

7. Separate the front and rear halves of the frame with the appropriate wrench for the couplers.

8. Wrap the frame and fork tubes with padding (not imperative, but advisable). Wrapping the chainrings and the rear cogs in padding is a good idea too. The padding cannot be thick or it will make packing difficult. I recommend using thin, reusable pads with Velcro closures that you label for each tube or part (with white paint pen marker if black) to speed up the process.

9. If you have a TSA net system, place one net into the bottom of one clamshell half of the case, and place the other net into the other half. A TSA net is a two-part net with Velcro straps to connect both halves together. It holds all of your carefully packed stuff together, should TSA security at an airport open your bike case. You don't want to depend on security agents to recreate your intricate packing job!

10. Place the front frame section (usually with the fork attached) into one clamshell half of the case (atop the TSA net). Medium-size or smaller coupled bikes fit into a 28×28×10-inch case just fine like this. Large bikes may require removal of the fork and even of the right crankarm and may require a deeper case. The fork has to come out if it is taller from end to end than the 27-inch internal dimension along one side of the case, thus rotating the front end of the bike with it so that the end of the top tube or down tube sticks out of the case. And if the fork is so long that it has to fit diagonally across the middle of the case or close to it, the case will need to be deeper. This is because the lengths of the front and rear axles, placed end to end, add up to 10 inches (112mm + 142mm = 254mm = 10 inches). So if the fork has to go between the axle ends, the case must be wider to allow it.

11. Place the rear wheel atop the front frame section, cogs down (toward the outside of the case).

12. Place the rear frame half over the rear wheel (Fig. 1.9). Tilt the wheel to make room for the wide rear end (a spacer between the dropouts is still a good idea).

13. Weave the handlebar through the wheel in a way that it won't preclude the case's top from closing with the front wheel in it.

14. Place the pedals, seat and seatpost, and any other miscellaneous parts around the case where they fit.

15. If your case has separate support members to prevent crushing of the case, stand them up through the parts lying in the case. Slide the support bases through the spokes first so they sit on the bottom.

16. Place the front wheel in the opposite clamshell half (atop the other TSA net).

COUPLED BIKE IN A SUITCASE OR SMALL HARD- OR SOFT-SIDED CASE

TRAVELING WITH A BIKE

COUPLED BIKE IN
A SUITCASE OR
SMALL HARD- OR
SOFT-SIDED CASE

·

WHEEL
CONTAINERS

·

AT THE AIRLINE
COUNTER

17. Close the case half with the front wheel in it over the other half, and stick the Velcro TSA net straps together. If you have case supports, thread them up through the front wheel's spokes and put their top caps on. If the case closes and latches, great. If not, rearrange things until it does. I hope you allowed enough time for this.

i-7b Packing a Coupled-bike Soft Case

1. Follow steps 1–9 above in §i-7a.

2. If this is a square soft case, follow the remainder of the steps above in §i-7a.

3. If the soft case is rectangular and has a domed plastic protrusion on the deeper side (Ritchey), prop the edge of the case up so that the cogset can drop into it while the rear wheel sits flat in the bottom.

4. Place the rear wheel in the bottom of the case, cogs down into the domed plastic protrusion.

5. Place the front wheel on top of the rear wheel, offset to the longer side of the case.

6. Lay the separator pad over the wheels.

7. Place the rear end of the frame on top of the pad, rear derailleur down, if you have not removed it.

8. Place the front end over it (unless the fork is too long, it will have the fork attached), looking for space to overlap them where possible.

9. Weave the handlebar around/through the wheel in a way that it won't preclude the top from closing with the front wheel in it.

10. Place the pedals, seat and seatpost, and any other miscellaneous parts around the case where they fit.

11. Zip the case closed.

i-8 WHEEL CONTAINERS

Hard cases or wheel bags to carry from one to three wheels are a must for the triathlete who wants to be prepared for any conditions on race day. It's pretty obvious how to load a zippered, soft wheel bag or a hard, clamshell wheel case, but if the wheels have their own quick-release skewers, remember to remove them from the wheels and then rescrew the end with the springs held captive on the skewer before packing.

i-9 AT THE AIRLINE COUNTER

Most airlines charge for bikes on domestic flights, around $100 each way. This is one of the primary reasons for a coupled bike (§i-7a–b). Most carriers do not charge for bikes on international flights, however, as long as you stay within the weight limits.

If you are traveling with a full-size bike case, particularly if it has bike-related logos and writing, don't expect to be able to pass your bike off as something else and avoid being charged. If you are traveling with a coupled bike (§i-7a–b), the case should be within the airline size guidelines for normal checked baggage. You will probably not even be asked what's in it, as long as it's not overweight.

1. Remember to remove any CO_2 cartridges from your luggage (§i-1, step 10).

2. If you have a voucher that allows your bike to fly free, use it. Some cycling and multisport federations have deals with certain carriers to provide their members with vouchers. Again, if you are flying internationally, most carriers (Delta is an unfortunate exception) will not charge you for your bike.

3. Since you've weighed your bags at home and know your airline's weight limits (§i-1, step 13), you won't be unpacking and repacking at the counter to escape an excess-baggage charge. If you know your bag is overweight, pay the charge and move on.

4. Be aware that airlines have limited liability for damage to your bike (they will generally replace

lost bikes), and will likely have you sign a release to that effect.

i-10 SHIPPING YOUR BIKE AHEAD OF TIME

A shipping carrier like UPS, FedEx, DHL, or even the post office may be easier on your bike than the airlines. For international shipping, the cost is prohibitive. For domestic flights, shipping your bike may be cheaper than paying the charge to fly with it, but that's only if you ship it via ground a week or so ahead—which also means you need to have a second bike to train on while your race bike is in transit. You also need to have an address at your destination for a friend, hotel, or bike shop that has agreed to receive your bike. You can have a bike shop or shipping store pack and ship your bike, or you can do it yourself as below:

1. Pack the bike in a hard case (§i-3) or in a cardboard box (§i-6).

2. Print a shipping label online if your carrier allows it and drop it off at an authorized location, or take it to a shipping store or an outlet of the shipping carrier for labeling.

3. Insure it fully.

4. Ship it to a street address (not a P.O. box), and if you want to make sure someone is there to sign for it, specify that at the time of shipping.

i-11 UPON ARRIVAL

Even though it's often difficult in airports or in transit, open your bike container as soon as you can after arrival and inspect your bike and accessories for damage. When your bike is disassembled for travel, you can inspect areas you normally cannot see.

In metal parts, look for cracks, dents, gouges, surface waviness, corrosion, and stretched or cracked paint. Replace anything that you have a question about; your life is worth far more than the replacement cost of some bike parts.

In carbon fiber parts, look for the same indications as in metal ones, but be aware that carbon can mask damage, since the surface layer can spring back to its original position while deeper layers can be broken or delaminated. The top layer of carbon is often primarily cosmetic, and damage in that thin surface layer may not be cause for concern. But if damage goes deep into the fibers, you need to replace the part.

To find carbon problems, you don't have to be an expert or have a high-tech lab; there are simple, low-tech methods of determining damage. If you see a surface indication of any kind of an impact, check it out using the following tests:

• Tap on the carbon with a coin all along the part, listening for telltale differences in pitch alerting you to failed layers below.

• Does it feel soft?

• Look for signs of delamination (separation of layers). A surface crack that follows the carbon fibers is a red flag. So are cracks in the surface coating.

• Inspect bonded edges for cracks and signs of separation.

• Check for movement between adjoining members by twisting and pulling on them.

• Listen for noise while riding.

Replace or repair any damage right away and file a claim if necessary. Reassemble the bike as soon as you can and take it out for a test ride, adjusting anything that needs it.

TRIATHLON EQUIPMENT SELECTION

Sports serve society by providing vivid examples of excellence.
—George F. Will

Triathletes and duathletes often make equipment choices based on weight and aerodynamics, since reducing the weight and aerodynamic drag of your bike lets you go faster with no extra work. For an athlete who is already fit and fast, little can be done to reduce the rider's weight or aero drag without significantly affecting performance. Not so with equipment. If the lighter or more aerodynamic equipment is as stiff, strong, and safe as what it replaced, then there is only an upside.

In bicycle circles, aerodynamics is often called "free speed," since you can go faster without pedaling any harder if you can drop your aerodynamic drag. The same can be said for reducing weight, bearing friction, or rolling resistance, but these effects are much smaller than aerodynamics, since aerodynamic drag increases as the cube of the velocity. While you may be able to ignore wind drag at 3mph on a calm day, the air drag on you and your bike at 30mph is 1,000 times as high. So, except in the case of a race that requires a lot of climbing and little descending, the first place to look for speed improvements with your equipment is in aerodynamics.

PRO TIP

STEVE HED'S COURSE EVALUATION TIP

When you are a novice triathlete, getting faster comes quickly. Training, aerobars, and other aero equipment can drop minutes off your bike split. As you get faster, however, dropping time becomes harder, since you are now on the course for less time than when you were slower, and you already have aero equipment. You can continue to save time, but it takes thinking, not just equipment and more training. Knowing and evaluating the course is the top time saver there is.

—*Steve Hed*

Founder, HED Cycling Products

Becoming familiar with an upcoming race course, either by seeing it in person, talking with others, or watching a video, gives you an advantage by enabling you to select the most appropriate equipment. HED Cycling Products, a maker of aero wheels, has a computer program that allows you to choose the ideal equipment once you have input the course terrain, wind speed, and direction, as well as the weight and power output of the rider. There is a similar program on the Web at http://www.analyticcycling.com.

ii-1 THE WIND TUNNEL AS ARBITER OF EQUIPMENT CHOICE

A wind tunnel is a glorified bathroom scale in a windstorm. The tunnel itself is nothing more than a tube bent into a ring to recirculate the air driven by a pro-

peller. In a wind tunnel that tests bicycles and riders, the tube is tall enough to stand inside (Photo 2.1), and the propeller is correspondingly huge. The walls, ceiling, and floor are straight and smooth where the item to be tested is mounted, to make the driven air as smooth and uniform in speed and direction as possible. The test object is affixed to a sensitive balance the equivalent of a bath scale held against the wind; it measures the force applied on the object by the wind, just as a bath scale measures the force applied on an object by gravity.

Changing the rotational speed and pitch of the propeller varies the wind speed inside the tunnel. Rotating the fixture to which the test subject is mounted simulates changes in wind direction, or yaw angle. The balance measures the total drag force on

Photo 2.1 A bike and a rider in a wind tunnel

THE WIND
TUNNEL AS
ARBITER OF
EQUIPMENT
CHOICE
·
FRAME CHOICE

PRO TIP

KIM BLAIR'S EQUIPMENT TIPS

An aerodynamic wheel set consisting of a deep rim, low spoke count front wheel, and a disc rear wheel can save 40 seconds over a 40K race, about the same as smoothing out details like cable routing and other protruding items on the front of the bike. Make the cable runs as short as possible, try to hide them behind bars, internally route through aerobars if possible, hide computer wires at the trailing edge of the frame, and so on. If it is flapping in the breeze, it's creating drag.

Substituting a standard round tube frame with a frame consisting of aerodynamic tubing may save over one minute in that 40K race. While the results vary from helmet to helmet, wearing an aerodynamic helmet can save up to 90 seconds over a 40K race. In terms of cost per second saved, hiding cables or wearing an aero helmet (and improving your body position) is well under $5/second, while replacing the frame or the wheels is up around $50/second.

—*Kim B. Blair, PhD*
Founder, Sports Innovation Group

the subject at the given wind speed and direction. The objective of aerodynamic research is to reduce the force required by the balance to hold the subject in place against the wind. In the case of a triathlete and bike, this can be done by making changes to equipment or rider position, or both. As long as the wind speed and direction simulated are representative of those experienced in competition, with every improvement in the aerodynamics of the bike and rider you can expect to see a commensurate reduction in power output required by the rider to maintain that bike speed during the race.

ii-2 FRAME CHOICE

The ideal is to choose a bike frame based on the conditions under which you will race it. Frames for different applications vary, as do wheels, aerobars, and tires.

ii-2a Aero or Standard Road Bike?

I recognize the allure of a sleek, aero-shaped bike (Fig. 2.1), and I've made plenty of them in my years as a frame builder (like the one on the cover). But keep

in mind that the aerodynamic drag of the rider accounts for over 80 percent of the drag of the bike and rider, with the drag of the frame accounting for, at most, 5 percent of the total drag. Aero tubes make little difference until speeds get very high and small time differences become extremely important.

For professionals competing in nondrafting (draft-illegal) events, an aero-shaped frame is a smart choice. Keep in mind, though, that professionals, unlike most triathletes, usually have more than one race bike and choose their weapon for each battle. In a draft-legal triathlon, pros generally use standard road-racing bikes and may or may not have aerobars. And in a mountainous triathlon, a pro may pull a superlight climbing bike out of his quiver. But age-group triathletes often only have one race bike, and it must be versatile enough for all types of events.

When considering an aero bike, note that aero tubing is less stiff than round tubing. If you twist and laterally flex a toilet paper tube, you will notice that it is quite stiff against both lateral deflection and torsion.

2.1 Steep-seat-angle, aero-tube tri bike with two-position seatpost, yielding two possible seat angles

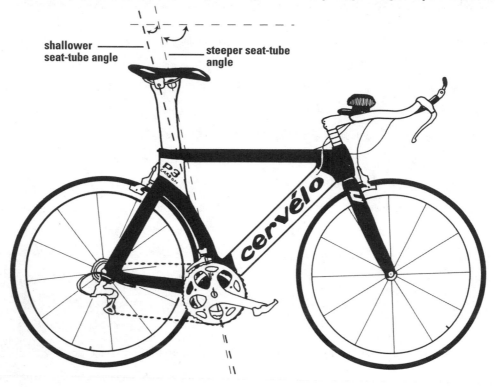

2.2 Standard road-racing bike

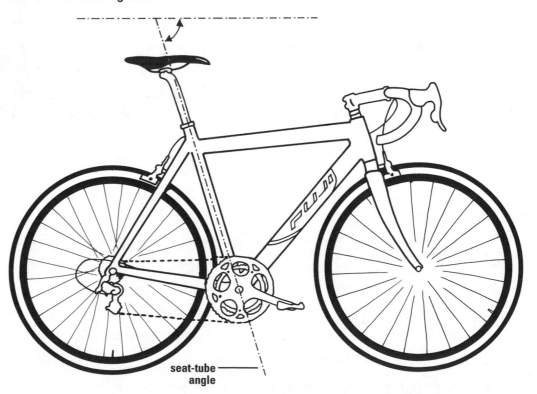

Now flatten the toilet paper tube and notice how easily it twists and how easily it flexes laterally along its flat sides. A stock frame with aero tubes is not a great choice for a tall, heavy rider. A custom aero frame designed by a knowledgeable frame builder may deliver acceptable rigidity for a Clydesdale, but that frame will be heavier than an equally stiff frame with round tubes of the same material.

Before you choose a frame, think about the course profiles of your important events as well as your personal strengths. If you are a fast rider on the flats and draft-prohibited events are your bag, then by all means get an aero frame (Fig. 2.1). But if you favor mountainous events, it probably makes more sense to go with a light, stiff, nonaero frame (Fig. 2.2). An aero frame with reduced stiffness and added weight will be a liability on climbs. You won't make up for those detriments on descents, and the round tubes will cost you little in flat races.

ii-2b Seat-tube Angle

The best seat-tube angle range for you depends as much on course type as it does on riding style. In general, triathlon bikes have steep seat angles (Fig. 2.1), which move the saddle forward relative to the bottom bracket. On a bike with a curved seat tube, the seat angle is a virtual measurement—it's the angle, relative to horizontal, of the line connecting the bottom bracket with the center of the saddle (Fig. 2.1). A bike with a two-position seatpost has two possible seat-tube angles, one less steep than the other (also Fig. 2.1).

The reason for the steeper seat angle has to do with the fact that it is easier to pedal in the lower shoulder position demanded for aerodynamic efficiency with the saddle farther forward, not because a steeper tube or a more forward rider is in itself more aerodynamic.

Photo 2.2 **Chris Boardman from the side on a road-racing bike**

Photo 2.3 **Chris Boardman from the side on a time trial bike with aerobars**

2.3 How seat angle (or moving the seat fore–aft on an offset seatpost) affects top-tube length

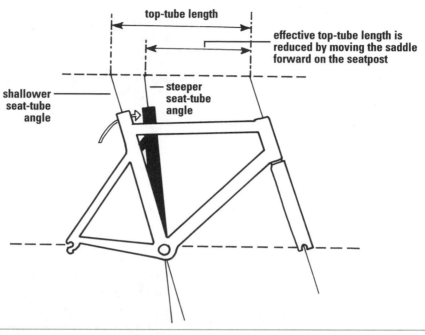

Consider World Hour Record holder Chris Boardman (Photos 2.2 and 2.3), who in 1996 set the mark of more than 56km in an hour on a track at sea level in Manchester, England, before aerobars were banned for the hour record. At this speed, low aerodynamic drag is paramount, yet obviously power output cannot be compromised. Also an accomplished road racer, Boardman raced road stages of the Tour de France in a classic seat-back position on his road bike and also set a World Hour Record in 2000 in this classic position (Photo 2.2) after aerobars were banned from the event. But when racing on aerobars, he rotated his entire road position (which was set up with his knee slightly aft of the pedal center) forward around the crank center (Photo 2.3). Thus his shoulders came forward and down and his butt came forward and slightly up, to bring his back to a level, aerodynamic position. He applied power lower and farther back around the stroke than when riding his standard road bike, but the distance from his saddle to his pedals and the relative positions of his chest, feet, and knees and the angles of his

torso relative to his legs and arms were unchanged. This is the idea of a forward seat position: to maintain a powerful riding position while getting the body more out of the wind with lower shoulders and head, a level back, and narrow arms.

For draft-prohibited triathlons and duathlons on flat or rolling terrain, especially in windy conditions, this position makes lots of sense, and the frame must support it. In the bygone days of triathlon, forward-position seatposts were used to achieve a forward position on a standard road bike. This was an expedient solution but not a good one, because of course the top-tube length did not change, leading to either an uncomfortable and inefficient foreshortened riding position (Fig. 2.3) or, if a superlong stem and aerobar were added, bad weight distribution over the wheels. Since then, bikes have been designed for this position, so if you will ride this way, get a bike with a steep seat angle (76 degrees or more) so that the top-tube length will be appropriate and the wheels will be properly positioned under you (Fig. 2.1). Some bikes, like the super-popular Cervélo P3C (Fig. 2.1), have two-position seat-posts (Fig. 13.6) that allow you to change your fore–aft setup for a particular course.

Again, draft-legal triathlons demand standard road bikes and geometry (Fig. 2.2). A conventional road position gives you more flexibility to jump, sprint, close gaps, climb, and sit in within the group than does an aero position. Wind cheating is not as critical, because you are trying to conserve energy by hiding in the slipstream of others rather than breaking the wind yourself.

The same goes for a straight-up hill climb; a road position will work better. And of course an off-road triathlon will demand a cross-country mountain bike.

The influence of bike position on the transition from cycling to running used to be controversial. The forward position was thought to be kinder to running legs than the standard road setup. However, triathletes have shown they can run fast whether coming off a standard road bike in a draft-legal race or off an aero position in an Ironman, so this should not be a fundamental concern.

ii-2c Wheel Size

Before selecting a frame, you will have to choose the wheel size you intend to use. In the 1980s and 1990s, 26-inch (650C) wheels were very popular among triathletes, and they, along with a steep seat angle, were what partially comprised a triathlon bike. Smaller riders even had success on 24-inch wheels; Paula Newby-Fraser won a number of Ironman World Championships in Kona on them. Nowadays, however, most triathlons are won on standard, 700C wheels, and most rank-and-file triathletes have embraced them as well.

So why pick one wheel size over another? As you may know from pushing a wheelbarrow or shopping carts with various wheel sizes, the rolling resistance of a taller wheel is generally lower, all other things being equal. On a larger wheel, the contact patch on the ground is longer, distributing pressure more evenly, and the contact angle of the tire with the road is lower. On the other hand, a taller wheel, if it is to be as strong, will be heavier. The smaller wheel should be more efficient aerodynamically, but that is counterbalanced by the fact that on a bike designed around smaller wheels, the front of the frame, specifically the head tube—the first frame tube the wind hits—will be taller to get the handlebars up to the right height, and thus will create more aerodynamic drag. At high speeds (i.e., descending), the smaller wheel will have less gyroscopic stability. Finally, since road bike gearing is generally designed for 700C wheels, having sufficiently high gears for fast courses (and gears that shift well) can be problematic with 650C wheels.

Setting aside concerns like availability of wheels and tires and gears, here are some general guidelines for wheel size.

If your races involve a lot of climbing but not high-speed descending, the lighter 650C wheels will be an advantage. Power to weight is everything when climbing, and not having high gearing won't be an issue.

Larger wheels will penalize short riders in flat races as well as hilly ones. The taller wheel means that once the head tube, headset, and stem are all stacked atop the fork, the rider's handlebars will be so high that a low, aero position is impossible. So, for riders shorter than 5'6" or so, 650C wheels make sense, and below 5'2" or so, 24-inch wheels may be the ticket. And of course, lighter bikes and wheels will make a difference for small, light riders who do not have as much power to heft a heavy bike up the hills. In Appendix B, there are gear charts for both 700C and 650C wheels.

ii-2d Frame Composition

Good bicycle frames can be made from a number of different materials. That said, some materials are better suited to certain applications due to considerations of weight, strength, formability, and cost.

Carbon fiber is the star of the moment, and the massive shift among top triathletes to this material has inspired consumers to buy similar bikes with confidence in their safety and performance.

Carbon fibers are light and extremely strong in tension, and with the right resin matrix they can be made into stiff, strong frames of very low weight. Carbon requires molding under pressure to optimize its characteristics, and the molding process conveniently lends itself to smooth, aerodynamic shapes. Carbon is also easy to add to areas where it is needed for strength in a frame while leaving other areas thin and light, a specificity that is harder to achieve with metal tubes. Done properly, carbon is a great material for a triathlon frame—light, stiff, strong, and aerodynamically shaped.

On the downside, carbon requires a lot of manual labor to lay it into molds, and sticking it together and applying a finish involves toxic resins and clear coats. And while continuous tubes are strong, stiff, and light, problems can arise at joints or where carbon tubes are bonded to metal inserts for the head-tube bottom bracket shell or dropouts, and thick resin areas caused by improper molding can be brittle. Carbon also masks damage better than the telltale ripples, kinks, or cracks in a damaged metal frame. A flexible carbon top layer can conceal damage to the underlying layers in a carbon construction, which can be cracked or delaminated and consequently dangerous. See Chapter 1, §i-11 for ways to locate hidden damage in carbon structures.

Carbon can be molded as a monocoque (one-piece) complete frame or as series of smaller subassemblies that are glued together. Successful bikes are made with both methods, so the type of construction should not be a primary consideration. Carbon tubes can also be bonded into lugs made of titanium, steel, or aluminum. Ride characteristics like stiffness or shock damping can be designed into the frame with tube shapes and carbon layup.

Aluminum is a low-density metal that can be made into lightweight bicycle frames. It is soft and ductile and can be shaped and machined easily. Welding it is straightforward, although the welds are large and unattractive unless subjected to time-consuming grinding and smoothing. Extruded like pasta through dies far more easily than other metals, aluminum can be formed into aerodynamic tubes or large, superstiff round tubes. Because of its wide presence in the earth's crust and the relatively modest energy requirements to process it and recycle it, it is an inexpensive material for bike frames.

Aluminum's main downside is that it fatigues easily and eventually cracks under hard use, so frames are generally made very rigid to minimize flexure and thus fatigue. That's fine, but the stiffness can transfer road shock to the rider, creating an uncomfortable ride. Corrosion can also be a problem if aluminum is not properly painted, powder coated, or anodized.

Aluminum is nearly always alloyed with other elements (common ones like iron, silicon, copper, magnesium, zinc, chromium, and manganese as well as exotics like scandium) and heat treated to improve its strength and durability. Aluminum metal-matrix composites are made by forcing other compounds into the crystal structure to boost their mechanical properties; welding becomes problematic because of these impurities introduced into the aluminum, but the metal-matrix materials are invariably stronger than standard aluminum alloys.

Titanium used in bicycles is usually alloyed with aluminum and vanadium, either in percentages of 3 percent aluminum, 2.5 percent vanadium (3/2.5), or 6 percent and 4 percent (6/4), to strengthen the titanium. The 6/4 alloy is particularly tough, but it is more difficult to draw into tubing, so seamless 6/4 tubing is rare; most 6/4 tubes are formed from sheet and welded down their length. Titanium is much stronger than aluminum, is immune to corrosion at normal temperatures (and thus requires no paint or other coating), and is less dense than steel. It can make a strong, light, and durable bike that is also gentle on the rider over the long haul.

Titanium's main drawback is cost. It's one of the most common elements on earth, so finding it is no problem, but every process associated with it—refining, cutting, machining, welding, and so on—requires an enormous amount of energy and other processing materials, highly skilled labor, or both. And the difficulty of working with titanium limits the sizes, shapes, and thicknesses of available tubing, making custom work even more costly.

But if you can afford it, titanium has many benefits. Given that so many triathlons are located in coastal areas, titanium's corrosion resistance is a plus. So is its longevity and its comfortable ride character. Another advantage is that, unpainted, it cannot get chipped when traveling in a bike case the way carbon or painted or powder-coated bikes can.

Steel used in bike frames is generally cro-moly, a high-strength blend of steel alloyed with chromium and molybdenum. It is stiff, strong, and durable. It can be welded, brazed, or silver-soldered, and machining

it and drawing it is straightforward. On the downside, its high density means that making a lightweight frame from it is difficult, and it lacks corrosion resistance (has a tendency to rust). Steel frames have long been praised for ride quality, but they're rarely used in triathlons today, primarily due to their high weight and lack of glamour.

Magnesium (as in the bike on the cover) has lower density than aluminum and considerably higher strength. It is also easy to draw into different tube shapes with varying wall thicknesses. Welding it is not difficult, but the welds tend to be large and bumpy. One of its chief attributes is its ability to dissipate vibration. It can be built into extremely light, stiff, strong, and durable bike frames that pamper riders on long rides.

Magnesium is highly flammable, so machining it requires generous dousing with coolants. It also is highly susceptible to corrosion, so it requires a chromate or phosphate dip prior to painting.

ii-2e Compact Versus Standard Geometry Frames

Compact or sloping frames have an up-sloping top tube (Fig. 2.2). Aero bikes generally have level top tubes (Fig. 2.1) except in really small sizes where there is no other way to accommodate a short rider if the front wheel's size lifts the front end too high for stand-over clearance. A level top tube is obviously more aerodynamic than a sloping one because it is parallel to the wind, so it makes sense for flatter, higher-speed courses.

For a climbing bike or draft-legal bike, either configuration makes sense. Sloping frames are generally lighter than standard frames of the same construction, but they require longer, heavier seatposts, so weight may be a wash. Sloping geometry is used by some frame manufacturers as a means to offer fewer frame sizes, so be wary of this tactic, and make sure that the top-tube length (the *effective* top-tube length, measured horizontally; see Fig. 3.16B), and the height of the front end (to get proper handlebar height) are appropriate for you.

ii-2f Bike Fit and Custom Frames

Bike fit is paramount to comfort and performance in the bike leg (and perhaps in the run as well; you don't want your back to be sore when you start pounding the pavement). Chapter 3 of this book covers positioning on the bike, and proper positioning is only possible if the frame fits the rider.

Average-size riders will be able to find stock bikes to fit them, unless they have disproportionately long or short legs, arms, or torsos. A custom frame may be more suitable for a particular condition, like a fused vertebra in the back or neck, different-length legs, or the like. It may also be a way to achieve a particular frame weight, frame stiffness, or frame durability goal given a particular rider's weight, power, or riding style.

ii-2g Fork Choice

Generally you will stick with the fork that comes with your frame. In some cases, you will get a choice from the frame manufacturer, or you will decide to upgrade your existing fork. Forks for triathlon and road bikes these days are almost universally made out of carbon fiber, a material that affords the possibility of many fork shapes.

The most likely reason to spend the extra money for a fork upgrade is aerodynamic. Arguably the fork alone makes as much difference aerodynamically as the entire frame, since it is out in front of the bike and hitting air that is less turbulent, before being churned up by wheels, turning legs, and other components. Most fork manufacturers stick within UCI (International Cycling Union) guidelines that dictate fork specifications, but there are many different fork shapes and variations that meet these standards. If you are really looking for aerodynamics, then look at wind tunnel

results comparing various forks under simulated real-world conditions—with the front wheel spinning to simulate its added drag coupled with the fork's effect. Some forks actually seem to reduce the drag of the front wheel, so testing them together is important.

ii-3 WHEEL CHOICE

Your choices range from standard aluminum clincher rims to full-carbon disc wheels. In between these are clincher and tubular wheels of various depths made from aluminum, carbon, or carbon-capped aluminum.

ii-3a Wheel Size

See §ii-2c.

ii-3b Aero or Lightweight Wheels?

To choose the best wheels for a race, you must know something about the course. In general, except perhaps in the case of draft-legal races, err on the side of aerodynamic wheels. Heavier weight is not a significant issue unless the course involves a lot of climbing or has many sharp turns that require you to accelerate and decelerate the wheels repeatedly. Otherwise, a more aerodynamic wheel will almost always be an advantage.

ii-3c Wind Direction

Crosswinds require different wheel choices than headwinds. A wheel with a lot of side surface area that is very fast in a headwind (or no wind) can be problematic in a crosswind. In addition to often being slower than a standard spoked wheel in a strong crosswind, the tall sides of the aero wheel can cause serious handling problems when the wind hits them. This will cause you to slow down, since you will not pedal as hard when you are concentrating on keeping your bike going straight or worrying about getting blown over.

The slower you are, the greater the problem you have with crosswinds. The "relative wind" is the wind

2.4 Vector illustration of relative wind

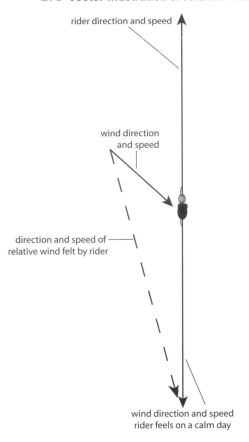

rider direction and speed

wind direction
and speed

direction and speed of
relative wind felt by rider

wind direction and speed
rider feels on a calm day

that you feel on the bike, and it is the vector sum of your speed and direction with the speed and direction of the wind (Fig. 2.4). So in a 30mph wind at 90 degrees from the side, the relative wind will be 42mph at 45 degrees if you are riding 30mph. But if you are riding 15mph, the relative wind will be 33.5mph at 63.4 degrees. The greater the crosswind and the lower your speed, the more deep-section or disc wheels cost you in handling difficulty and instability.

In general, a wheel with a few aerodynamic composite spokes and a relatively shallow aerodynamic rim shape will give you good performance in headwinds and crosswinds. The performance straight into a headwind is dependent on the wheel's shape and surface area. With good aero shapes and the same total side surface area, the composite-spoke wheel (Fig. 2.5,

left) can have the same performance as a deep-section spoked wheel (Fig. 2.5, right) in a headwind. In a crosswind, however, the fact that the side surface area of the composite-spoke wheel is distributed over the spokes and relatively shallow rims, yet neither in itself is very broad, allows the wind to blow through more easily than the large side surface area the wind encounters hitting the deep-section wheel. It's like the difference between the wind hitting a fence with gaps between staves and hitting a solid wall.

Lance Armstrong and his team sometimes used Hed's software to determine wheel selection for a given Tour de France time trial course. They first went out on the course to measure the average wind speeds, and then combined that information with Armstrong's known power output and wind drag, the course profile, the wheel weights, and wheel drag coefficients (the latter available on the Hed website). The software delivered accurate predictions of how various wheel choices would affect the total time. Admittedly, few athletes have the resources to go to that much trouble, but Hed's software is still a useful source of information for wheel selection (see the introduction to this chapter).

2.5 A deep-section spoked wheel (right) next to a composite-spoke wheel (left)

ii-3d Clincher or Tubular?

Any discussion of wheel type must also involve a consideration of tire type, so you'll have to review the pros and cons of tubular and clincher tires as well (read §ii-7 first). When looking strictly at wheels, however, you'll find that tubular wheels are almost always lighter because the simple concave top surface to which the tire is glued is structurally strong without a lot of material. Tubular rim stress is not affected by tire pressure, either.

A clincher rim, on the other hand, must have hooked vertical walls to constrain the tire beads, as on the rim in Figure 9.17, and those walls must be strong enough to contain enormous burst pressures when the tire is pumped up to high figures. Those same rim walls also form the braking surface, so they must be thick enough to prevent the rim from bursting due to tire pressure as the rim becomes worn from the brake pads rubbing it thinner with road grit.

Tubular rim materials can also be lighter. The tubular rim can be made completely out of carbon fiber. While carbon clincher rims do exist, carbon is not an ideal material for making these rim walls since it is strong in tension but not in compression. In fact, it requires so much material for strength that often there ends up being little or no weight advantage in carbon versus aluminum clincher rims.

ii-3e Braking Performance

Braking is consistent and predictable with aluminum rims. Carbon rims, however, can be grabby, and finding a brake pad that stops well but does not wear away rapidly is often difficult. Unlike aluminum, carbon does not dissipate heat well; carbon rims can get very hot and melt the brake pads, even carbon-specific ones. This is especially true under heavy riders. The high heat can also melt tubular rim cement, allowing tubular tires to roll off after heavy braking on an extended descent.

Poor or inconsistent braking is the biggest drawback to superlight all-carbon wheels. On a course with little braking the wheels can be a plus. But on a technical course with lots of high-speed turns, they may not be worth the weight advantage. This is especially true in draft-legal races, since riding at high speed in big groups requires precise, consistent braking.

ii-4 HANDLEBAR CHOICE

Handlebar questions are like Russian nesting dolls—decide the first one, and it reveals another question, which, when answered, reveals yet another.

In broad strokes, the first question is whether to use aero extensions or not. The only time that it makes sense to ride a drop bar with no aero extensions is in a draft-legal race or in a straight-up hill climb. In the first case, your aerodynamic riding advantage lies in drafting behind other riders, and riding aero extensions simply reduces your steering control and keeps you farther from your brakes, both of which are no good when riding in a pack. In the second instance, you are moving so slowly uphill that aerodynamics has little impact, and you have more effective positions for climbing with a drop bar and no elbow pads in the way. In any kind of race other than these two, though, the aerodynamic body position on the elbow pads and aero extensions is such a huge advantage that it makes no sense to race without them.

Choosing to use aero extensions clears the way for the next nested question, What kind of base bar to use? For flat or rolling courses, it makes sense to have a lower overall position for the elbow pads and aero extensions, so mounting them on a cowhorn bar makes

PRO TIP

MORGAN NICOL'S EXTENSION SELECTION TIPS

TT riders or short-course triathletes are more likely to use straight or S-bend extensions to get more leverage (power).

Long-course and Ironman triathletes will more likely use single or multibend extensions for a more comfortable hand position.

—Morgan Nicol
President, Oval Concepts,
maker of aerodynamic forks,
stems, and handlebars

the most sense (Fig. 14.14). If you were to mount them on a low drop bar (Fig. 14.15), the drops would be too low to use practically, so why have them at all?

On a course with a lot of climbing, but also flats and descents, a drop bar set in a normal road position is the way to go. The clip-ons mounted on them will make a huge difference on the descents and the flats, but you will not compromise your climbing by having only a cowhorn bar set low. Note that not all carbon drop bars are designed to accept classic clip-ons; in fact, most are not, so check with your dealer or the manufacturer. However, some new clip-ons load the stem or the stem cap and not the handlebar, allowing the use of any bar, and some newer carbon bars are designed to handle classic clip-on clamps.

Once the base bar has been determined, it's time to move on to which aero extensions to use. Looks, price, length, and availability will help you determine which brand is for you, but consider also the curvature of the extensions. When Lance Armstrong switched over to straight and low S-bend extensions

(Figs. 2.6A and 2.6B), there was a massive shift to that choice in triathlon as well, at least among top pros. But you may do better with a different setup.

The most critical component of the aero extensions is fit. This generally requires adjustability in the extensions and in their elbow pad shape and position. Different bodies and different frames require adjustability in the bar and stem to compensate for the industry's building bikes for some average Joe to the detriment of many other Joes and Josephines. The stem should not be integrated with the handlebar in order to achieve the proper position. The only place for an integrated system is on a bike that has been completely dialed in for the rider, and an integrated stem/bar can be found (or specially made) to achieve the same desired position, which has been experimented with using adjustable components and has been ridden and raced on.

The traditional upturned aerobar offers comfort, control, and the ability to yank on it pretty hard. S-curved bars come with large S-curves and the more recent very low S-bends that are not much different from a straight extension.

Rather than following fashion, you should choose the extension shape based on your comfort and feeling of speed and power. Some people can pull best with an upturned bar (Figs. 2.6C and 2.6D), some with a straight one (Fig. 2.6A), and some with an S-curved one (Fig. 2.6B). Others yet may prefer a "slam position" (see §iii-13) and a slam bar (Fig. 2.6E). There is no single answer for a shape that works for everyone.

The straight bar in itself is lighter and more aerodynamic, but once the rider's hands are on it, the air encounters similar resistance around the hands. Of course, the more parallel to the wind the forearms are,

2.6A–E Illustrations of various bends of aero handlebar extensions

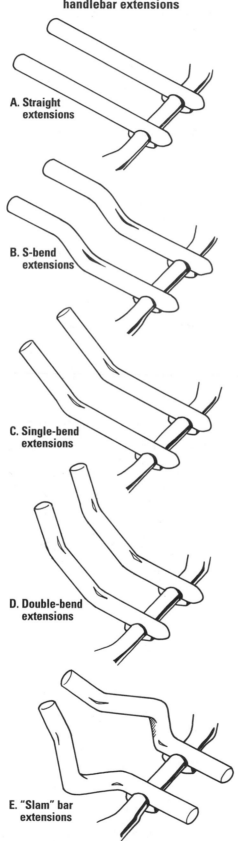

A. Straight
extensions

B. S-bend
extensions

C. Single-bend
extensions

D. Double-bend
extensions

E. "Slam" bar
extensions

the less drag they create, but on the other hand, they block less air directed at the chest. It's impossible to be certain which creates the lowest overall drag without monitoring the individual athlete in a wind tunnel. So it is probably best to choose your shape according to comfort and not worry whether you are giving away a few grams of drag.

One-piece or "wing" bars, which have a base bar and extensions as a single unit, come in flat or drop style to the base bar. Drop wings seem more used in short courses, while flat bars seem more used in long courses where riders want to recover while accelerating or climbing while gripping the wings.

ii-5 SHIFTER CHOICE

Once you have decided on aero extensions, you discover another nested question. Do you want to run bar-end shifters at their tips (Fig. 2.7) or standard dual control brake/shift levers (Figs. 8.18–19) on the base bar?

Make your choice based on how much time you spend in each position. If you are on the aerobars constantly, then shifters at the ends of the extensions make sense. Draft-legal races require standard dual control levers, since it's too precarious to reach out and shift at the end of the aerobars when riding in a pack. And since you shift the front derailleur infrequently in most events, and in many cases only when you are moving slower with your hands gripping the base bar, you may want to connect your front derailleur to your left brake/shift lever, while using a bar-end shifter for the rear derailleur.

ii-6 SADDLE CHOICE

All cyclists who spend a lot of time in the saddle have to deal with at least occasional saddle pain, but multisport athletes are more prone to it, since the pressure point on the saddle is farther forward with aero

2.7 An aerobar with bar-end shifters installed

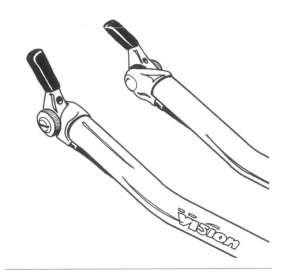

Photo 2.4 **Selle San Marco Aspide Triathgel saddle**

handlebars than with standard drop bars or on a mountain bike. A forward riding position exacerbates this, as rotating the hips and shoulders about the bottom bracket (described in §ii-2b) puts the saddle contact area directly below the genitals, with virtually no weight being borne on the sit bones. In addition, the pressure is directed onto the saddle nose, rather than being shared in a triangular pattern over the rear of the saddle as well as the nose.

Saddle preference is a personal decision, but given the pressure concentrated on the saddle nose when riding in a forward position, the rear section of the saddle is of little importance. Accordingly, some way

must be found to spread that saddle-nose load over as broad an area as possible. Triathlon saddles with a tall, broad, gel-filled nose may be the answer many triathletes seek (Photo 2.4). The larger platform distributes the stress, and the gel damps vibration and offers support that conforms to your shape.

Concerns over impotence have resulted in a generation of saddles with cutouts, but a saddle with a split nose is less likely to work for most triathletes using a forward position. An indentation may work, but an open split, while reducing the pressure on the soft tissue down the center of the perineum, may afford too little total saddle surface to spread the pressure when the pelvis is tipped forward. The reduced contact area, while less sensitive, may bear too much weight to avoid cutting off blood or nerve flow.

In general, the fitter and stronger the athlete, the firmer the saddle he or she can tolerate, or will prefer over time. With fitness comes reduced body weight, and with strength comes harder pedaling, both of which reduce pressure on the saddle and make a firmer saddle more comfortable.

Triathletes using traditional road racing positions (favored for climbing and draft-legal events), as well as the slam position (see §iii-13), probably will find comfort on road-racing saddles, with or without cutouts, of which there are thousands from which to choose.

ii-7 TIRE CHOICE

So, which will you ride, clinchers or tubulars? How will you choose?

A tubular tire's casing—the body of the tire—wraps all around the inner tube and is stitched together on the bottom (Fig. 2.8). It is glued to a rim whose outer edge is concave to match the tire's shape.

In contrast, a clincher tire's casing is C-shaped in cross-section (Fig. 2.9) with a rubber-covered bead along each edge made of steel, Kevlar, or carbon fiber. The bead hooks into a rim that's U-shaped in cross-section, as on the rim in Figure 9.17. The inner tube is separate.

A new breed of road clincher tire is tubeless with (obviously) no inner tube. Tubeless clinchers are lined with an airtight rubber layer, have lip seals on the inside of the bead, and have a square edge above the bead on the outside to lock into the rim. As of this writing, only Hutchinson offers tubeless road clinchers, and only Shimano makes a wheel to go with them, and only one model at that.

In general, a racing tubular tire is lighter than a clincher plus its inner tube, since the casing is similar to that of a clincher except without the beads; the tubular's inner tube is thinner and lighter, as it need not be tough enough to handle being installed into the tire and rim. Tubular rims are also lighter than clincher rims, and their closed-box shape is structurally stronger than the C-shape of a clincher rim.

Tubulars, being sewn together, can be made to hold tremendously high air pressure. In contrast, a clincher constrains air pressure with a combination of a tire bead that must stay locked to the rim with friction, and a separate rim whose walls must be strong enough to contain the pressure.

A tubular is round in cross-section, so as the wheel tips from side to side during cornering, the transi-tions are smooth from edge to edge and grip is con-sistent. A clincher, on the other hand, is more verti-cally oblong in cross section, so the transitions and grip along the tire vary as the wheel tips from side to side.

Tire casings are made of rubber-coated fabric. In general, tires with thin casing threads and thus high thread counts (threads per inch, or TPI) roll faster because thinner, more supple threads conform to vari-ations in the road surface better than fatter, stiffer threads. Both clinchers and tubulars can be purchased with thin, supple casings of up to 300 TPI.

Flat tires are another issue. Clinchers can come dis-lodged from the rim when ridden flat, whereas tubu-lars lose air less rapidly when punctured, and they stay glued to the rim, making them safer in the case of a blowout. This is one advantage of the new tubeless road clinchers over standard clinchers, since they tend to stay locked to the rim in case of a blowout and hence may be safer than standard clinchers.

Tubulars are more of a hassle to mount on the rim, requiring a multistep gluing process (see §ix-8). If glued well, they are extremely difficult to remove from the rim, making them hard to change during a race. How-ever, latex-foam canisters like the Vittoria Pit Stop can be injected into the tire to fix small punctures perma-nently. That's a good thing, because patching a tubular is a pain (and throwing out an expensive tubular with only a small leak is disheartening). Patching a tubular

2.8 Tubular tire cross-section

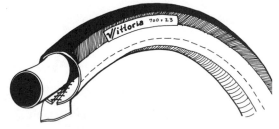

2.9 Clincher tire cross-section

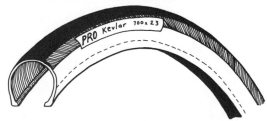

requires finding the precise location of the air leak, removing the base tape in that area, and opening the stitching underneath. The tube must then be pulled out, patched and stuffed back inside, and the tire must then be resewn to contain it (§ix-10). For most triathletes, clinchers make more sense, since they are much simpler to install and remove than tubulars and are generally less expensive, especially when you consider that a clincher's inner tube can be easily patched or replaced after a puncture, if the tire itself is undamaged.

Most high-end tubulars have a latex inner tube, which is very supple and resists punctures but unfortunately bleeds air constantly. When you leave latex tubulars overnight in the transition zone at a major event, you may end up on a bike whose tires are too soft to ride fast the next day. But that is changing. The sub-200 gram Vittoria Triathlon EVO CS tubular has a superlight butyl tube that does not bleed air like a latex tube. So a triathlete required to leave his or her bike overnight in a transition zone will not exit the swim to find soft tires.

Tire hoop diameter is discussed with regard to wheel size in §ii-2c. Tire width, however, is a more personal preference. In terms of aerodynamics, the ideal is to have a tire just slightly wider or narrower than the rim. Some tires even have a molded-in gradual transition to fair them into the rim, smoothing the wind blowing over them.

On the other hand, big riders should not ride on narrow 19mm tires because of the dangers of pinch flatting on a sharp impact. Wider (fatter) tires make sense for heavier riders.

One thing that must be driven home with many triathletes is that the maximum inflation pressure printed on the side of the tire is *not* compulsory! Triathletes are notorious for pumping their tires up to incredibly high pressures on the assumption that a hard tire has less rolling resistance. However, except on the very smoothest of surfaces (i.e., on a smooth wood-surfaced track), a really hard tire will be slower, not faster. Yes, the tire feels fast because you are being bounced all over the place, but the bouncing costs more energy than a softer tire that can absorb small surface imperfections without popping the whole bike and rider up in the air. You want the tire hard enough to protect against pinch flats, so the heavier you are, the higher the pressure you must run. But if you want to be fast, keep the tires inflated to well below the maximum rated pressure. A softer tire will also grip better on corners and will be more comfortable to ride.

ii-8 COMPONENT CHOICE

Deciding between components like Shimano Dura-Ace and Ultegra or 105, or Campagnolo Record, Chorus, Centaur, Veloce or Mirage, or SRAM Force or Rival may not be easy. Obviously price will affect your decision and may be your deciding factor. Components from Shimano, Campagnolo, and SRAM will generally perform well, especially when new. In general, as you move down a product line, you pay less because the materials are cheaper (and heavier, usually, as well as often more flexible), the mechanisms are simpler (and often wear more easily or don't spin with as little friction), and the finishing is less expensive (generally only an aesthetic concern). Performance of lower-end components will drop off faster over time, due to lower-quality materials and construction (like plastic derailleur-pivot bushings rather than metal ones). With higher-end components, you pay for lower weight, increased stiffness and precision, longer-lasting performance, and improved looks.

ii-9 CLOTHING AND HELMET CHOICE

Comfort should be your first priority when shopping for triathlon apparel. That said, the next most important aspect is aerodynamics. Your clothing should fit tightly, even if unzipped for ventilation, or you will pay a high price in increased drag and elapsed time over the bike leg. If you will be riding in the same outfit you swim in, this will already be handled, since your swim clothes should fit tightly.

Your helmet should also be comfortable. Some aero helmets do offer a speed advantage (see Kraig Willett's Pro Tip in Chap. 3), but their benefits depend on how fast you ride. At 20mph, the difference will be very slight, unlike at 30mph. However, especially for slower riders, over whom air passes more slowly, helmet aerodynamics should not be pursued at the expense of ventilation when the temperature is high. If the helmet gives you an aero edge, if you can ride in it comfortably under race conditions, and if you are good keeping your head still and not flipping the helmet tail up into the wind, then by all means, get an aero helmet. But if it is not comfortable or you constantly drop your head and lift it back up as you ride (see Len Brownlie's Pro Tip in Chap. 3), select a standard helmet with as much ventilation as you can get.

ii-10 POWER METERS

A power meter measures your effort in watts and is the most accurate way to gauge your overall fitness, not only in training but also during a race. There are many brands available today; choose one based on features and price. Keep in mind that the more directly the meter measures power, the more accurate it will be. Calculating power from your body weight and speed, for example, is less accurate than measuring torque directly.

As for what to do with the power data you obtain, I recommend that you read *Training and Racing with a Power Meter*, by Hunter Allen and Andrew Coggan. It contains recommendations for the various types of meters available, as well as clear guidelines on how to interpret the data and get the most from these amazing training tools.

POSITIONING ON THE BIKE

*All we actually have is our body and its muscles
that allow us to be under our own power.*
—Allegra Kent

The most important components of bike speed in a draft-prohibited triathlon or duathlon are power output, aerodynamic efficiency, biomechanical efficiency (which is also reflected in power output), and comfort. It is intuitively obvious that power output, biomechanical efficiency, and comfort go hand in hand. Many multisport athletes and time trialists have misunderstood at their peril that if you sacrifice power output to get aerodynamic efficiency (and one way to do that is to sacrifice comfort), you will go slower. Remember:

Speed = Comfort + Power + Aerodynamics

It is possible to make aerodynamic improvements on the order of 10 percent, as Kim Blair's Pro Tip indicates. Certainly you should strive for this and then some, but even if you can actually make such a huge gain, it does not guarantee you will be faster. If, as Hunter Allen suggests in his Pro Tip on the next page, you can now ride at 26mph putting out 270 watts where it used to take 300 watts with your old position and equipment, that's great. But if with your new position and equipment you can only maintain 270 watts for the duration of the event, and you used to be able to maintain 300 watts, how are you better off? If you have to sacrifice *any* power output for lower aerodynamic drag, it's a Faustian bargain (see Max Testa's Pro Tip).

Of course, we cannot always know these things. If you can go to a wind tunnel and simultaneously have your aerodynamic drag, power output, and blood lactate measured, you can know precisely whether you will be faster in a given position. But few athletes can do this. As a substitute, you can ride a course you are familiar with using a power meter to see if you can maintain the same or higher power in your new position and also see a reduction in your time. Without power measurement, you will have to ride a familiar course many times in both positions. With enough repetitions of the effort to smooth out environmental and fitness differences, you can know

PRO TIP

HUNTER ALLEN'S AERO TIP

The more "aero" you can get, the less wattage you need to produce for a given speed. It's possible with a good aerodynamic position, aero bike, and aero wheels that you can gain 30 watts of power by only having to put out 270 watts in order to go 26mph, instead of 300 watts.

Wattage is the power required by you, the rider, to overcome the forces opposing you, and it is measured with a power meter. Some of these forces are wind resistance, rolling resistance, mechanical friction, and gravity. By adopting a more aerodynamic position and choosing aerodynamic parts for your bike, you give yourself the best shot at producing the highest speed for the least effort.

—Hunter Allen
Founder/owner, Peaks Coaching Group,
cofounder, CyclingPeaks Software,
USA Cycling Level 1 cycling coach,
coauthor of Training and Racing with a
Power Meter, *and former professional cyclist*

PRO TIP

KIM BLAIR'S AERO TIP

Approximately 90 percent of a rider's energy goes into overcoming aerodynamic drag, with over 60 percent of that total drag due to the rider. Thus rider positioning is of utmost importance. Our wind tunnel testing program has typically resulted in a 5 percent reduction in drag for professional cyclists who already had a decent time-trial position. For a competitive age-group triathlete, that 5 percent improvement can mean a two-minute savings over a 40K time trial.

—Kim B. Blair, PhD
Founder, Sports Innovation Group

with a fair amount of certainty whether your racing will improve.

The positioning options available to you with adjustments to your bike are not just to find the most aerodynamic position. While you can adapt to and eventually become comfortable in new aero positions and produce more power in them, you still must respect fundamental requirements of your body. All of those bike adjustments are equally important for creating more comfort and more power. We are no longer limited to saddle height adjustments, a little bit of saddle fore–aft adjustment, and stem length changes. We are fortunate now to have seatposts with multiple fore–aft positions, and handlebars with myriad options of handlebar extension length, bend shape, angle, and width coupled to elbow pads adjustable for length, width, rotation, height, pad firmness, and shape.

SEAT POSITION

There are many formulas for determining seat height, and most of them are useful. However, these calculations only provide a starting point. Because a formula may not work for your unique anatomy, you should also seek an anatomical determination of your saddle height, fore–aft position, and tilt.

PRO TIP

MAX TESTA'S KEEP PERSPECTIVE TIP

When deciding how aerodynamic you want your position to be, you need to look at the whole picture. Keep in mind what you can actually produce and what is realistic for you in your racing, rather than getting carried away with aerodynamics. There are two components of bike speed in a triathlon: power output and aerodynamic drag; reducing air drag is not as critical for a recreational Ironman athlete riding at 18–23mph as it is for an elite athlete riding 30mph. At that recreational power level, like 220–240 watts, you don't need to be so low and so forward; you need your position to

not injure you and to allow you to run afterward. Take advantage of the science of biomechanics too. Runners coming to triathlon need to go forward just because they can't tilt their pelvis and don't really use their hamstrings and glutes, but they need not be so far forward if they are not trying to drop their shoulders so low.

—*Dr. Max Testa, Sports Science and Medicine Department TOSH (The Orthopedic Specialty Hospital), Salt Lake City, UT, former 7-Eleven and Motorola team doctor*

---

iii-1 SADDLE HEIGHT

a. Two inseam formulas

To use a formula, you need to measure your inseam, and you may need an assistant to help you. The idea is to compress a horizontal straightedge firmly up into your crotch with as much pressure as you'd have sitting on a saddle, and measure from it to the floor.

For the straightedge, try a three-quarter-inch dowel rod with a bubble level taped atop it and notched at the end for a tape measure hook. Stand with your bare feet placed two inches apart. Pull the dowel rod up firmly from both ends into your crotch while your assistant measures from the floor to the top of the dowel rod (Fig. 3.1). A three-foot carpenter's level can be used in a similar manner.

You can also stand against a wall and pull a large book up into your crotch, making sure that you have one edge of the book against the wall to keep the book level. (Pull hard to fully compress the soft tissue!) Mark the height of the top of the book on the wall

---

PRO TIP

GALE BERNHARDT'S BIKE POSITIONING TIP

The "best" aero position is worthless if you're uncomfortable. You will produce more power for a sustained period if you are not squirming around on the bike. Dial in your best aero position and then make reasonable adjustments for comfort. Every body is different.

—*Gale Bernhardt USA Triathlon Men's and Women's coach for the 2004 Olympics and 2003 Pan Am Games, author of* Training Plans for Multisport Athletes, Triathlon Training Basics, *and* The Female Cyclist: Gearing Up a Level

and measure from it to the floor. Whether using a book or a level, make sure you add in the width of the tape measure body. Now you're ready to try the two inseam formulas.

A 1970s study of Eddy Merckx and other riders of his day established that multiplying the inseam measurement by 1.09 determines the distance from the top of the saddle to the center of the bottom pedal spindle when the crank is aligned with the seat-tube.

The LeMond method, based on a 1987 study with Greg LeMond, instead multiplies the inseam measurement by 0.883 to find the distance from the center of the crank to the top of the saddle along the seat tube.

3.1　Measuring inseam using a bubble level on a dowel

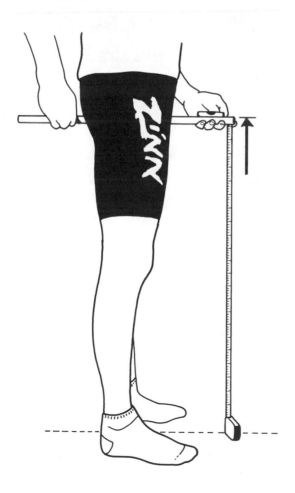

The trick with both methods is the difficulty of eyeballing the height of the top of the saddle with the tape measure. Look straight across the saddle, measuring to the point where the sit bones touch the saddle.

b. Problems with these formulas

Neither method above takes into consideration the angle of your ankle while pedaling, which is a personal thing. Neither method takes into account the length of the foot, which, if abnormally short or long, effectively shortens or lengthens the leg. Nor do these methods consider variations in shoe-sole thickness under the ball of the foot and height of the shoe above the pedal spindle when clipped in.

The LeMond method does not account for crank length, which, if not in the same proportion to leg length from person to person (and it won't be with stock cranks for a short or tall rider), will give a saddle position that's too low or too high. For instance, a 6'6" rider with a 97.3cm inseam gets a predicted crank length of 210mm using a constant of proportionality of 0.216 between leg length and crank length (see §iii-26 on crank length). The LeMond method seat-to-bottom-bracket distance of 85.9cm added to a 210mm crank length gives a distance from the pedal to the top of the saddle of 106.9cm, which is close to the 106cm obtained by multiplying the 97.3cm inseam by 1.09. However, using the longest stock crank, 180mm, the LeMond method would place the seat height at 103.9cm, 2–3cm closer to the pedal, which would be hard to tolerate.

Neither inseam formula accounts for abnormally thick tissue under the crotch that can compress over time (resulting in a saddle that's too low) or for wearing extra thick padding, like layers of tights in the winter (resulting in a saddle that's too high).

c. Simple on-bike seat height methods

After warming up on a stationary trainer, clip in and slowly pedal backward until you lock your knee without rocking your hips. Adjust the seat up or down until the bottom of the foot is level when your knee is locked at the bottom of the stroke, with the crank lined up with the seat tube (Fig. 3.2).

Another method is to set your heel (while wearing your shoes) on top of the pedal and slowly pedal backward. Again, adjust the seat up or down until the heel just barely maintains contact with the pedal as you straighten your leg at the bottom of the stroke without your hips rocking. This method only works when wearing road cycling shoes with thin soles at the heel.

d. Detailed anatomical seat height method

A goniometer is a long-armed protractor for measuring joint angles. If you can get your hands on one, place its pivot adjacent the center of the knee joint, one end centered on the top of the femur and the other end centered on the ankle joint (see Fig. 3.3). At the bottom of the pedal stroke and with your foot in its normal pedaling position, your knee angle should measure between 25 and 30 degrees. This measurement holds for either an aero position or a road position.

Be aware that it is hard to measure accurately with a goniometer, even for an experienced fitter. One way to improve accuracy is to use a photo of yourself pedaling from the side. Draw a line down the centerline of the thigh and another down the centerline of the calf and measure your knee angle with your leg at the bottom of the stroke, as shown in Photo 3.1. If you are calling up your photo on a computer, use a transparent overlay—something like a stiff plastic bag—as a surface to draw on, or print your photo onto a sheet of paper.

3.2 Set the seat height so the foot is level when the knee is locked

3.3 Measuring knee flexion with a goniometer

POSITIONING ON THE BIKE

Photo 3.1 Measuring knee flexion on a photo (in this case, Michellie Jones in the 2006 Ford Ironman World Championships)

knee flexion
angle

PRO TIP

CHRIS KAUTZ'S SEAT HEIGHT TIP

Tight hamstrings can limit performance, and a forward seat position can improve it by putting less stress on the hamstrings. Although I believe you should start with a forward seat position (see §iii-2), if you still need to remove more stress from tight hamstrings, the rider could be faster simply by lowering the saddle, rather than moving the rider farther up and forward. If the hamstrings are tight and the seat is high, the athlete may tilt the pelvis backward to reduce the pull on the hamstrings, which collapses the diaphragm and inhibits breathing, puts strain on the lower back, and prevents the quads

from getting up over the pedal and pushing harder. However, simply lowering the saddle so that the knee bend at bottom dead center is 30–35 degrees rather than 25–30 degrees could reduce the pull on the hamstrings enough that none of this rotation occurs.

Remember also not to open the hip angle too much with any forward position; the hip angle still has to be tight enough for the gluteus muscles to fire, just as a basketball player has to compress his hip angle in order to jump.

—*Chris Kautz, MA*
Owner, PK Racing, Fairfax, CA

SADDLE HEIGHT

SADDLE
FORE–AFT
POSITION FOR
AERODYNAMIC
EFFICIENCY

Measuring the angles is easier if, before you take the photos, you mark dots on your ankle bone, knee center, and center of rotation at the hip (top of the femur; anatomists call it the "head of the greater trochanter").

You will probably find the level-foot method described in §iii-1c to be a simple and fast way to the same end. It usually yields about 30 degrees of knee flexion at the bottom of the stroke.

Your power drops off with higher seat height. At less than 25 degrees of knee bend at bottom dead center, the kneecap, the fulcrum for the leg lever, loses contact with the joint, and you cannot push as hard without the fulcrum.

Conversely, power output goes up with a lower saddle, up to a knee angle of 40 degrees at bottom dead center, since the quadriceps muscles are working in the midrange of their contraction. However, the risk of injury goes up as well due to high pressure inside the knee joint. Track sprinters seek absolute power and tend to ride with a minimum knee flexion of about 35 degrees. The knee strain is high but of low duration, since the races require only short, explosive bursts of power.

iii-2 SADDLE FORE–AFT POSITION FOR AERODYNAMIC EFFICIENCY

In an ideal aerodynamic setup, the rider will be farther forward of the crank than in a standard road position. This allows riding with the shoulders lower, approaching being horizontal with the hips, without closing up the hip angle uncomfortably at the top of the stroke or causing the knees to hit the chest.

To avoid bunching up at the hips when the torso is horizontal, most riders must bring the saddle forward 3–6cm from the knee over pedal standard road position (Photo 3.1). Saddle height from the center

PRO TIP

ANDY PRUITT'S RULE OF THUMB ON KNEE PAIN

If your knee hurts in the front, raise the saddle; if it hurts in the back, lower it. If you are hurting on a ride, raising or lowering the saddle with this rule of thumb will get you home; don't leave it in that position forever.

—Andy Pruitt, EdD

Director and founder of the Boulder Center for Sports Medicine and expert on bike fit and cycling-related injuries who pioneered the use of 3-D computer video analysis of pedaling

of the bottom bracket should remain the same, so the seatpost moves up a bit as the saddle moves forward.

Keep in mind that every rider pulls forward onto the nose of the saddle during hard efforts (Photos 3.1, 3.2, 3.3, and 3.4), making this effective position perhaps as much as 12cm farther forward. (On the other hand, a rider going hard on drop bars in a standard road position, as when closing a gap to a group of riders up ahead, will also pull out onto the saddle nose, so the relative difference in the fore–aft position when comparing hard efforts stays in the 3–6cm range found at low power output on a stationary trainer.)

Do not be tempted to keep moving the saddle forward if you only move forward on it when pedaling hard. Riders pull forward onto the saddle nose during hard efforts for a number of reasons, and doing so may not indicate that anything needs to change with the current setup. In seeking more speed, the body automatically moves out onto the nose, but if you keep moving the saddle forward, you will just keep pulling forward onto the nose anyway.

SADDLE
FORE–AFT
POSITION FOR
AERODYNAMIC
EFFICIENCY

∘

SADDLE
FORE–AFT FOR
DRAFT-LEGAL AND
MOUNTAINOUS
RACING

Photo 3.2 **Luke Bell pulling forward on the saddle nose during the 2006 Ford Ironman World Championships**

You will need to revisit the fore–aft adjustment after working on your handlebar position. Since the whole purpose of moving the saddle forward is to allow the shoulders to move down and bring the torso as close to horizontal as possible, you will want to set an initial saddle height and fore–aft position, and then set your elbow pad and bar position, check your hip angle, and continue to adjust both seat and bar until you find the ideal setup.

iii-3 SADDLE FORE–AFT FOR DRAFT-LEGAL AND MOUNTAINOUS RACING

While only pro triathletes participate in draft-legal racing, many triathletes focus on mountainous races or live in areas where they climb often while training. For climbing or draft-legal triathlon, the best setup is a road bike with standard road positioning. This is almost mandated by the International Triathlon Union (ITU), the sanctioning body of draft-legal

PRO TIP

DAN HEIL'S ADAPTATION TIP

Start with a conservative position. Your search for an optimal position should start with a more shallow seat-tube angle (STA) of 76–78 degrees and torso angle (TA) of 15–20 degrees. The conservative approach allows you to become accustomed to the change in handling of the steep geometry (versus road bike geometry), which makes you safer on the road. A properly sized frame will allow you to adopt a more aggressive position (steeper STA and lower TA) when you are ready.

—*Dan Heil, PhD*
Associate professor
of exercise physiology,
Montana State University–Bozeman

triathlon, whose rulebook reads, "The front-most point of the saddle will be no more than 5cm in front of and no more than 15cm behind a vertical line passing through the center of the chain wheel axle, and a competitor must not have the capability of adjusting the saddle beyond these lines during competition." This rule effectively eliminates the forward position otherwise so prevalent in triathlon.

Furthermore, drafting and the low speeds of climbing largely eliminate the advantage of an aerobar, while safely drafting, braking, shifting, and steering in a group is best done with a drop bar, which the ITU requires anyway. The ITU does permit a clip-on aero extension in draft-legal races, but it must be very short because the rules mandate that the end of the aerobars shall not extend beyond the brake levers (and no more than 15cm beyond the front wheel axle).

Ideal positioning for climbing or draft-legal racing is with the center of rotation of the knee directly over or slightly behind the pedal axle. But the knee does not have a center of rotation as if there were a pivot bolt through it; the two sliding surfaces on the end of the femur are elliptical, and the two ellipses are not even the same. So, we must approximate it.

Before trying to find the knee center, first warm up on the bike for at least 10 minutes and then level your bike on a stationary trainer or stand. Sit as normally as possible on your saddle and reach forward to grasp your brake levers. Spin the cranks so they are horizontal and hold the position; ideally, your ankle angle will be the same as when you are pedaling through this point. Have an assistant drop a plumb line from the front of your kneecap; it should line up with the end of the crankarm (Fig. 3.4). This puts the center of rotation of the knee over or slightly behind the pedal axle.

iii-4 SADDLE TILT

Set the saddle so that it is entirely level from nose to tail. Doing so will support as much weight as possible on the sit bones (ischial tuberosities) and will reduce pressure on the perineum. Use a carpenter's three-foot level (Fig. 3.5), or eyeball it using a windowsill for reference.

3.4 Dropping a plumb bob from the kneecap over the end of the crankarm

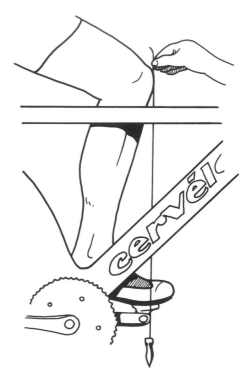

3.5 Checking saddle angle with a 3-foot level

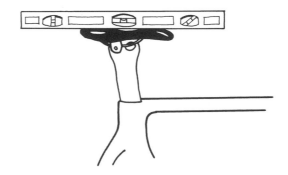

SADDLE
FORE-AFT FOR
DRAFT-LEGAL AND
MOUNTAINOUS
RACING
∘
SADDLE TILT

If the saddle nose is tipped upward, the pelvis tends to roll back, which creates more curvature and pain in the lower back, confines the diaphragm and constricts breathing, and increases pressure on the perineum. Perineum compression can cause pain and even long-term injury (in both men and women). Backward tilt can also lead to less bike control. One exception may be a very slight upward tilt when using the "Slam Position" (see §iii-13).

A downward or forward tilt is no better. If your seat is tipped down, it will throw you against the bars and put too much strain on your arms. If you tip your saddle up or down for reasons of comfort, there is a problem with your bike position or your saddle choice. If you still feel the need to tilt the saddle after leveling it and going through the steps here that address saddle position and bar position, perhaps a different saddle is in order.

iii-5 RECHECK SADDLE HEIGHT

Whenever you shift your saddle fore or aft or change its tilt, double-check your saddle height (§iii-1) using a tape measure (Fig. 3.6). In general, for every centimeter the saddle goes forward, the distance from the top of the saddle to the bottom bracket decreases by a half centimeter, so you must raise it to compensate. Obviously, leveling a formerly downward-tipped saddle raises its nose and drops its tail.

HANDLEBAR POSITION

Now that you have your saddle position and handlebar height in the ballpark, you can find your proper handlebar position. You can expect to go back and forth a bit between bar and saddle adjustments as you fine-tune your position.

3.6 Measuring saddle height with a tape measure

Handlebar positioning, more than any other fit variable, depends on personal preference. It is also the least exact, having to do with the number of years you've been riding, your hamstring and lumbar flexibility and strength, the degree of pelvic rotation with which you ride, any back or neck problems you may have, and your torso length and arm length.

Air drag is your enemy on the bike in a triathlon, and handlebar and elbow pad positioning are the primary determinants of your aerodynamic drag, provided your saddle position allows you to pedal freely when on your bars. Since aerodynamic drag from the bike itself accounts for less than a quarter of the total drag force opposing you and the bike together, and because there is not much you can do to change the shape of your body, you must reduce its drag primarily by riding in a lower, narrower position.

iii-6 HANDLEBAR HEIGHT

Short-course racers will generally want their bars lower than Ironman athletes do. But it takes time to work down to a low, aero position; don't expect to be able to ride hard that way immediately.

Position your elbow pads so that your funny bones (tips of your elbows) are directly under the tops of your shoulders, and the angle between your torso and your upper arms is about 90 degrees. With this fore–aft elbow pad position established, you'll get best aerodynamic results if your handlebar is at such a height that your chest is horizontal. If you go lower than this, drag goes back up (see Chester Kyle's Pro Tip). To achieve a horizontal chest, the line from the center of rotation of your hip (top of your femur) to the center of rotation of your shoulder (top of your humerus) will be 6–8 degrees above horizontal. Again, you can check this with a goniometer or on photos of yourself.

For many triathletes, particularly those new to the sport or not as thin as they used to be, this may be an unattainable position. But for anybody, including extremely thin professional racers, this will still be unattainable if the saddle is not forward enough to

PRO TIP

CHESTER KYLE'S BAR HEIGHT TIP

Ride with aerobars and the forearms horizontal with hands together and elbows just inside the frontal area projection of the body. The height of the bars can make an enormous difference. The back should be flat or gently arched, shoulders even with or lower than the top of the back. University of Washington wind tunnel tests at 30mph conducted in 2006 illustrate this:

Tests	Total Drag (Gms)	Drag Diff. (Gms)
Normal bar position	2,805	0
Lower bars 1 inch	2,766	-39
Lower bars 1–1¾ inches	2,718	-87
Lower bars 2 inches	2,694	-111
Lower bars 2–2¼ inches	2,684	-121
Lower bars 3 inches	2,723	-82

If you can ride efficiently in a lower position, try it. A drop of 120 grams can mean 56 seconds in a 40km TT at 30mph.

—Chester R. Kyle, PhD
Chief aerodynamicist for USA Cycling's
1984 and 1996 Olympic projects
Research director,
Sports Equipment Research Associates

PRO TIP

CHRIS KAUTZ'S AEROBAR TIP

To ride an Ironman, you want an aerobar position to support the skeletal structure, rather than being positioned like a TT rider to generate power by pulling hard on the bars. Most people simply cannot pull hard like that for 112 miles.

—Chris Kautz, MA
Owner, PK Racing, Fairfax, CA

POSITIONING ON THE BIKE

open the hip angle sufficiently. The most acute hip angle any rider can use successfully is about 30 degrees, measured between the lines formed by the center of the knee when at its highest point in the pedal stroke, the center of rotation of the hip, and the center of rotation of the shoulder. Any less than 30 degrees (check it with a goniometer or on a photo), and the knees may hit the chest, breathing will be constricted, and the gluteus and hip flexor muscles will be too extended to work properly.

The hip angle need not be this acute to be aerodynamic, and tight hamstrings will prevent many riders from achieving it anyway. Tim DeBoom won two Ironman titles at Kona with a hip angle of about 40 degrees (Photo 3.3), and David Zabriskie beat Lance Armstrong in the 19km time trial at the beginning of the 2005 Tour de France (and grabbed the yellow jersey) with

a similar position (Photo 3.4). Zabriskie's chest is completely level, and his position is extremely aerodynamic, but his hips, like DeBoom's, are far enough forward that his hip angle stays quite open, allowing pedaling freedom and preventing his knees from hitting his chest.

PRO TIP

NEAL HENDERSON'S HIP ANGLE TIP

When the angle (between the thigh and the torso) is less than 30 degrees, a rider will often have impairment in breathing and the glute and hip flexor muscles will be outside of their optimal force-producing ranges.

—*Neal Henderson, MS, CSCS*
Coordinator of sports science,
Boulder Center for Sports Medicine

Photo 3.3 **Tim DeBoom racing**

Riders outside the bell curve of average height, body proportions, or flexibility require special handlebar height measurements. For instance, people shorter than 5'3" usually tolerate less drop to their bars, largely because stock crankarms are relatively long in proportion to their legs. Whereas an average person's crankarm length might be 21–22 percent of inseam length, the 165mm or 170mm cranks of a person with a 65cm inseam will be more than 25 percent of leg length. This means that relative to the "average size" rider, the shorter rider's knees will come up higher and constrict to a greater degree the angle between the torso and the thigh at the top of the stroke. So if your thighs hit your chest, raise your bar. (See §iii-26 on selecting crank length.)

The converse is true with tall riders, as 175 or 180mm cranks are only 17.5–18 percent of the length of the legs of someone with a 100cm inseam. The knee will be bent less sharply at the top of the stroke, and the angle between the torso and thigh will be wider, so they will prefer a lower bar if using stock cranks.

The role of body proportions and flexibility cannot be underestimated. Some great champions who ride with their backs close to horizontal have longer thighs relative to their lower legs. A long thigh means a short lower leg, so the knees do not come up as high and constrict the hips or hit the chest.

If a rider tips his pelvis forward, he compresses the iliac arteries (the main source of oxygenated blood to the legs) less than someone whose lower back is rolled back. Thus a lower, longer position is not only possible but also more efficient for the more flexible person. Riders will inevitably prefer a higher bar as they age; our bodies become more sensitive to a lower

Photo 3.4 David Zabriskie time trialing

POSITIONING ON THE BIKE

bar than when we are racing at age 20. The bottom line is to fine-tune the bar height, listen to your body's feedback and not to your buddies who think your bars should be positioned as low as a world champion's.

A separate drop issue is whether to use a base bar that is flat or that has a drop to it. Since you are generally only in this position for cornering and perhaps climbing, it will not make a big difference in your total energy loss over the race due to aerodynamic drag. Just pick the bar that's most comfortable for climbing and cornering.

Draft-legal racers and those who do lots of hill climbing will like a drop bar better than a cowhorn bar, and they should set it with perhaps 3–8cm of drop from the top of the saddle to the top of the handlebar; try a ballpark height difference equal to the width of your clenched fist. Look again at what Chester Kyle says in his Pro Tip. Measure the drop from saddle to bar by placing a long straightedge with a level on the saddle (see Fig. 3.7). Extend the straightedge forward horizontally and measure down from its underside to the top of the bar.

PRO TIP

ANDY PRUITT'S FORWARD SADDLE VERSUS BAR HEIGHT TIP

The most common positioning mistake I see at the Boulder Center for Sports Medicine is that the athlete tries to get too aerodynamic and forsakes comfort to a point of diminished returns. Trying to get too low without coming far enough forward is the worst, commonly seen when riders try to use one bike for both regular road riding and triathlon, and they just put clip-on bars without adjusting the seat. Ouch! A common rule we use is that for every centimeter riders move forward compared to their road position they can have an equal centimeter of drop from the top on the saddle to the top of their forearm pads.

—Andrew Pruitt, EdD
Director and founder of the
Boulder Center for Sports Medicine
and author of Andy Pruitt's Complete
Medical Guide for Cyclists

3.7 Measuring saddle-to-bar drop

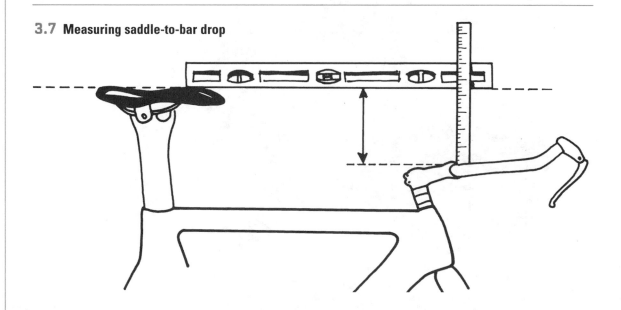

3.8 Stem flipped up or down

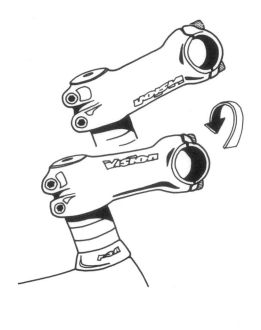

3.9A–B Aerobar adjustments

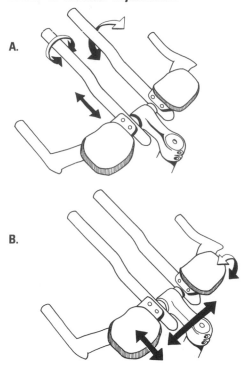

A.

B.

iii-7 HOW TO RAISE OR LOWER THE BAR

If you have an old bike with a quill stem and threaded headset (see Fig. 14.7), loosen the vertical bolt, smack it with a hammer (a rubber mallet or plastic-faced hammer, if you have one) to free the wedge, slide the stem up or down, and retighten the bolt.

Raising or lowering a stem for a threadless headset requires removing the stem from the fork steering tube and adding or removing spacers below it (see §xiv-2). The other way to raise or lower a threadless-style stem is to change its angle, either by flipping it over (Fig. 3.8, provided it is not a "zero-degree" stem, that is, 90 degrees from the steering tube) or by replacing it. You can consult the stem size tool on my website, www.zinncycles.com, to assist in choosing the dimensions of a different stem to get you where you want to be.

You will have to readjust the headset when you install a stem. For instructions, see Chapter 14, §xiv-2.

iii-8 ELBOW PAD WIDTH

For optimal aerodynamics, you want to bring your arms close together, which reduces the frontal area of your body and directs more of the wind around it. When your elbows are on pads placed at shoulder width or wider, it's easier to control the bike and support the body, so you will have less control as you move your elbows together. Consequently, move the elbow pads and extensions (Figs. 3.9A–B) inward gradually rather than all at once. Get comfortable with the control you have at each setting before making the next adjustment. If you have a power meter, check that you can produce as much power at each new arm position as you did in your previous position before going still narrower. Be patient. This may take several weeks or even months, but the gains in speed could be significant.

How far inward your elbows should be is a matter of debate. Ideally, you want them positioned as narrow as your knees (which should also be narrow; read

POSITIONING ON THE BIKE

> ## PRO TIP
>
> ### JOHN COBB'S ELBOW PAD POSITIONING TIP
>
> Elbows positioned wider increase power and oxygen uptake because in narrow positions the lateralis (lat) muscles alongside the chest overpower the diaphragm and reduce breathing space. Furthermore, wider elbows result in an aerodynamic cost in a straight-on headwind of less than 0.1 pound of drag at 30mph, and no difference in sidewinds.
>
> —*John Cobb*
> *Chief designer, Blackwell Research,*
> *and bicycle aerodynamics guru*

on). If you can bring your elbows in until your forearms touch, you will have closed (as much as you can) the hole that lets air in under your chest. However, such a narrow arm position makes it considerably harder to breathe and to steer, and you may be causing air that comes around your elbows to bang into or get scooped in between your knees. So, unless you have gone to a wind tunnel and have data on yourself to back it up, don't bring your elbows in closer than knee width apart.

Body shape and pedaling style play a role, and you will not know precisely your best elbow position without being tested in a wind tunnel. However, if you set yourself up on your bike in front of a large mirror, you can see yourself as the wind "sees" you and you may find ways to improve your position.

iii-9 PEDAL WITH NARROW KNEES

It may seem weird to discuss knee position within the handlebar positioning section, but your arms and knees affect each other aerodynamically. The farther inboard your knees are without losing pedaling efficiency or creating knee injury, the more they hide behind the arms and the more aerodynamic you become. The legs are large objects, and pedaling with them pointed outward scoops a lot of air and slows you

down. Bringing in the knees makes at least as much difference as bringing in the arms. This is something to do consciously, and it is great to do on a trainer facing a large mirror as well as looking down at your legs while riding on the road.

If you find that one knee swings out with each pedal stroke, you may have a leg-length discrepancy and should consider corrective methods; see *Zinn's Cycling Primer* (VeloPress) for ways to deal with this. If you pedal with both knees out and are not naturally bowlegged, then your hip angle may be too constricted (§iii-2) or your foot position on the pedal (see §iii-18–§iii-25) could be corrected.

If your knees swing outward to avoid hitting your chest, there are three ways to correct the situation. First, move your seat forward (see §iii-2). To maintain the same distance to the pedals, it will need to come up as well—about half the distance you moved it forward. You will also need to move your handlebars correspondingly farther forward. Second, you can raise your handlebar to get your chest higher and out of the way, although this move comes at some aerodynamic cost. Third, you can reduce your crank length (see §iii-26) to keep your knees from coming up as high; this may be great for short riders but a poor idea for tall riders.

iii-10 HANDLEBAR REACH

In §iii-6 you worked on lowering your shoulders, which reduces frontal drag. But to be aerodynamically efficient and to breathe most easily, you want your torso fairly straight, not arched up like an angry cat, and you want your arms supporting you effectively.

Reducing the arch in your back requires rotating your pelvis forward. Moving your seat forward as discussed above, increasing your hamstring flexibility, and consciously bringing your belly button closer to the top tube (see Photo 3.4) will all flatten your back. A flat back requires that you have enough reach from the seat to the handlebar to stretch out properly while not being so stretched out that you cannot support your weight efficiently on your elbows. With your back flat, you want the angle between your torso and upper arm to be 90 degrees, which you can measure on a photo of yourself or with a goniometer. Another way to get at this is with a plumb line; if you drop it from the front of your shoulder, it should come out

at the back of your elbow (Photos 3.1, 3.3, 3.4). In that position, you won't be reaching too far, you will support your weight well, and you should have enough extension.

Adjust reach by changing stem length, length of your aero extensions, and fore–aft positioning of your elbow pads (Fig. 3.9).

iii-11 FOREARM ANGLE AND ELBOW PAD FORE–AFT

Triathlon has moved from the upward-angled forearm position of its early years of aerobars to a flat position with arms level. Obviously the flat position creates the least added drag, especially if your aero extensions go straight out from your elbow pads so that your hands are not in closer than your elbows, meaning that your forearms are not cutting across the wind in either the horizontal or vertical planes. However, if you find that tilting the bar up works better for you, the aerodynamic cost is not large and is obviously worth it if your power output increases. Floyd

---

PRO TIP

KIM BLAIR'S AERO POSITIONING TIP

As you move forward with a steeper seat angle to flatten your back while still maintaining the angles between the torso and legs required for breathing, bring your arms forward as well, which can help to round and lower your shoulders. Narrowing the arms on the aerobars can help round the shoulders and make them appear narrower to the oncoming air.

—*Kim B. Blair, PhD*

Founder, Sports Innovation Group

PRO TIP

KIM BLAIR'S BAR-ANGLE TIP

Your body type and flexibility give some indication of how to adjust your forearm angle. If you ride with a relatively flat back and narrow arms, your forearms can be flat to tilting toward the ground to improve your aerodynamics. If you have a more arched riding position, you may be able to reduce your drag by angling your forearms up to shield your torso from the oncoming wind.

—*Kim B. Blair, PhD*

Founder, Sports Innovation Group

Landis won a lot of big stage races in 2006 using this arm position; he did it to take pressure off his deteriorating hip, but his times did not suffer from any compromise in aerodynamics.

Your elbow pads should be positioned somewhere between your elbow and the middle of your forearm. This too may be personal preference. The world's fastest time trialists in 2006 had the elbow pads just forward of the elbow, while the fastest triathletes of 2006 were mixed, some of the best having the pads at midforearm, others just forward of the elbow, and others between the two.

PRO TIP

MORGAN NICOL'S ELBOW PAD ADJUSTMENT AND EXTENSION LENGTH TIPS

- Short-course triathletes are more likely to place the arm rests in the middle of their forearms for more leverage (power).
- Long-course and Ironman triathletes are more likely to place the arm rests close to their elbows for greater comfort.
- The bigger your arms the more important your hands are in front of your elbows to help guide the wind up your arms.
- Wider shoulders require wider elbow positioning for better breathing.
- Courses with short hills you do not need to stand to attack are best ridden by shortening your reach on the extensions to get more leverage (power).

—Morgan Nicol
President, Oval Concepts, maker of
aerodynamic forks, stems, and handlebars

Having the pads at the elbow is an obvious way to efficiently support the weight of the upper body. John Cobb makes the argument for moving the elbow pads away from the elbow and closer to the wrist, believing that power output is enhanced. To illustrate, he suggests placing your left elbow and forearm lying on a desk or flat surface. With your right hand, hold the left hand down on the desk as you try to lever your left hand up off the desk. Notice what your left upper arm and shoulder muscles are doing. Now slide the left elbow back off the desk so the desk edge is closer to the wrist than to the elbow, and push up against the right hand. See how much better your left shoulder is engaged and how much more power you can get from it. "You will be instantly aware of a speed increase with the elbow pads up there," says Cobb.

iii-12 LOW CHIN

One last way to gain aerodynamic efficiency is to drop your chin. You want to be comfortable looking ahead down the road with your chin low, to block air flowing under your chest and to keep your head from sticking up and increasing your frontal area. Look at Photo 3.4 as compared to Photo 3.1. Without bobbing your head or otherwise squirming around, which is aerodynamically inefficient, keeping your head down will block air from filling under your chest. But if you tip your face down, you won't be able to see ahead.

Keeping your head down is great, but modern aero helmets smooth the air over the head only when your eyes are forward; putting your face down sticks the tail up in the wind. So keep your eyes forward and your chin low for the best combination of aerodynamics and safety. You may find that a change in eyewear is necessary so that the top rim of your glasses does not obscure your vision.

iii-13 THE SLAM POSITION

Cobb has worked at matching the joint angles of triathletes between running and cycling. On the bike, he duplicates the running position of their legs— freeze-framed from running on a treadmill. Elite runners run with far more knee bend than average runners; they use hip rotation to get more stride length, and more knee bend keeps them from bouncing up and down. Matching this on the bike dictates a saddle set relatively low and positioned far back to optimize efficiency. The average triathlete, however, has slower foot speed and less knee bend, and the high, forward position on the bike comes closest to matching those angles and will improve pedaling power as well as ease the transition from cycling to running.

In Cobb's slam position, the rider is much farther back and lower than in conventional triathlon positioning. Cobb claims that mimicking the deep knee angles of elite runners has dramatically reduced the bike times of many elite triathletes. Slam positioned, the saddle nose of a 5'9" athlete would end up 8.5 to 9cm behind the bottom bracket center, and the knee could easily end up 5cm behind the pedal spindle when the crank is horizontally forward. A shorter clip-on aerobar (Fig. 3.10), such as the Cobb-designed Oval A700 Slam or Blackwell Research Performer, or the Profile Jammer GT or Syntace XXS, is required to work with this position, because having the saddle so far back mandates it. I'll let Cobb himself describe it:

The Slam Position was developed as an alternative to the more traditional "forward" Triathlon or TT positions. The Slam Position has consistently shown to offer equal or better aerodynamics, higher cadence potential and generally improved crotch pressure relief. I started researching this position more as racers would come to me for positioning and complain about being on a plateau for their speed. It's very common for a racer to "plateau" where adding more training miles or more intense workouts does not give a noticeable increase in speed. I found that by completely changing the rider positions and having them use all new muscle firing points they could easily break through these flat times and move to the next measurable speed improvement. Bringing in more muscle groups and making them work at different workloads gives the rider the ability to do more power work without paying a higher cardiovascular price. Several things had to be considered in this development—primarily, can you "run" off the bike, and was there an aero penalty? There have been a couple of studies showing that the selected group of athletes could turn in a faster first mile run time when coming off a "forward" position compared to a traditional road bike. The overall run time has stayed about the same but there was a gain in the first mile. (Looking at Ironman history showed that the early racers, using traditional road positions, also ran very well off the bikes.) By setting up the racer in an even more rearward position (Fig. 3.11), we were able to bring in more of the running muscles, using the glutes, hamstrings and femora muscles more, to overcome the "dead leg" feel on the first mile of the run.

Is there an aero penalty? This was easy; take many racers to a wind tunnel and collect data on these racers in both positions. After a couple of years with approxi-

mately 30 racers for comparisons, I can say that there is never an aero loss. The more rearward Slam Position puts the rider in more of an Egg position which seems to easily direct air around and off the rider. What the Slam Position definitely offers is much improved seat comfort. Riding out on the nose of a bicycle seat generally cuts off up to 90 percent of all blood flow to the crotch. This results in numbness sometimes lasting for several days—not a desirable result.

I still set up many racers in a forward position, probably 60 percent. For sprint and Olympic races it works very well. By working with the rider on small but specific changes to the saddle location we can achieve very good comfort. If your bike splits have not improved over the last couple of seasons, however, you might look into a totally different and proven position.

How do you get there? Here is a guide for this new position:

Rider inseam	Nose of saddle behind bottom bracket center
27–29 in	7–8cm
29–31 in	8–9.5cm
31–32 in	9.5–11cm
32–34 in	11–12cm
34–36 in	12–14cm

If the rider's upper leg is shorter compared to the lower leg (knee to floor) then generally go toward the smaller seat offset.

Next will be saddle height. Generally I will lower the saddle from 1–1.5cm from the forward position height.

Cockpit length will sometimes be more challenging. If your bike frame has a long top tube then you will find that you have to use a very short stem, often in the 40–60mm range. As a note, the Slam Position rarely can be set up correctly on a forward-position frame that uses a 76 degree or steeper seat angle. When setting the cockpit length, generally measure from the back of your elbow out to the tip of your middle finger with your hand fully opened. Then use this number (example, 18.5 inches) and set the back edge of the base handlebar that distance from the nose of the saddle. I have also found it very common to have the nose of the saddle 5mm–15mm higher than the rear of the saddle. By using the saddle rotation to either the right or left side you will put the riding pressure on the adductor muscles instead of the prostate or soft tissue. On the aerobars, I generally start with the elbow pads level with or up to 2 inches below the saddle height. You do not

3.10 "Slam" aerobar

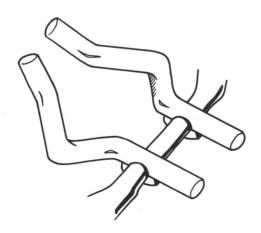

3.11 **Forward position (solid line) compared to slam position (dotted line)**

generally want to get the bars too low; it will not properly block the airflow through the rider's chest area, resulting in poor aerodynamics. Then after setting all the perameters, go out and enjoy newfound higher cadence and comfort.

Cobb states that the slam position is particularly good for athletes with long femurs, crotch pain, hand problems, or chronic hamstring soreness. And deeper knee bends have always been associated with higher power outputs (§iii-1d); the downside is higher stress on the knees.

iii-14 IRONMAN-DISTANCE VERSUS SHORT-COURSE EVENTS

Whether you are using a forward position or one that's farther back, you should raise your aerobars slightly when adjusting the bike for a long event such as an Ironman. When you sit up more, your diaphragm stays more open, there is less tension on the hamstrings, the lower back is less strained, and the pressure on the nose of the saddle is reduced. Greater

> **PRO TIP**
>
> ### TODD CARVER'S GOLDEN RULE OF TRI FITTING
>
> If comfort and aero profile conflict, always choose comfort.
>
> *—Todd Carver*
>
> *Biomechanist,*
>
> *Boulder Center for Sports Medicine*

> **PRO TIP**
>
> ### LEN BROWNLIE'S COASTING POSITION TIP
>
> Which position creates less drag when you are coasting downhill: cranks horizontal with knees squeezed together, or cranks vertical with one leg down? In 2005, wind tunnel testing with the Discovery Channel Professional Cycling Team confirmed that the cranks horizontal/knees together position provides 150–300 grams less drag. Coasting downhill at round 30mph/ 50km/hr. for 4K, this position would save 7–13 seconds.
>
> *—Len Brownlie, PhD*
>
> *Sports aerodynamicist,*
>
> *www.aerosportsresearch.com*

comfort adds up to greater speed when you are on the bike for so many hours.

And don't forget in an Ironman to use any opportunity to rest when it costs you no time. Coasting down from the turnaround at Hawi at the Ironman Kona is a good example.

Conversely, the higher speeds and shorter length of time you spend on the bike for short-course triathlons make it worthwhile to have the bars a bit lower. That said, not everybody makes the change, particularly elite competitors. Two-time Ironman World Champion Tim DeBoom says, "I don't really change my bike set up. I set it at the beginning of the year and it sticks."

It's okay to make adjustments and equipment switches for a course, but test your new position thoroughly beforehand and give yourself time to adapt to it. You don't want to be doubled over with back cramps in your most important race of the year because you changed your position the night before. Never change anything on or close to race day.

iii-15 REACH WITH STANDARD ROAD DROP BARS

When using standard road drop bars for draft-legal racing and mountainous triathlons, one reliable on-bike method is to look at your back relative to your arms, and also relative to horizontal when you are sitting up holding the bars on top, adjacent the stem. The angle of your back relative to your arms (a straight line from shoulder to wrist) should be about 90 degrees, and your back (a straight line from top of femur to top of shoulder) should be about 45 degrees above horizontal (Fig. 3.12)—slightly less for faster riding in groups and perhaps slightly more for climbing.

Another technique is to position yourself on the bike with your hands in the drops, elbows comfortably bent (15 degrees), and your eyes looking ahead. Then have an assistant drop a plumb bob from the end of your nose. Look for it to drop over the center of the handlebar (Fig. 3.13) or up to an inch behind it (and never ahead of it).

Listen to your body. According to former U.S. National Cycling Team coach Eddie Borysewicz, "If

3.12 **When holding the top of the bars, the torso and arms form a 90 degree angle, and the torso is just below 45 degrees from horizontal**

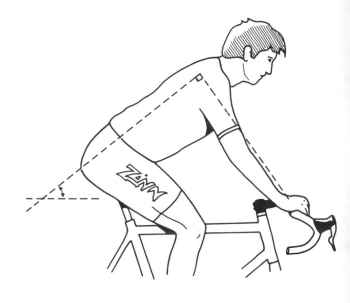

you develop soreness in your trapezius muscle [upper back], the stem is too short; when your deltoids and triceps [front of shoulder and back of arm] hurt, it is too long."

iii-16 OTHER REACH FACTORS

Reach also depends on your degree of pelvic rotation. You can have reduced pedaling efficiency, collapsed breathing space, and lower back pain if you sit on the saddle as if sitting in a chair and then bend forward at the waist. On the other hand, if you rotate your pelvis forward and down so you roll forward on the front part of your crotch, you can pedal and breathe more effectively, and your back will have less of the detrimental reverse curvature. You will need to position the bar farther away, since you will be extending your torso farther forward. Your saddle choice will be critical for comfort.

3.13 **With the hands in the drops, the end of the nose is directly above the center of the bar, or up to an inch behind it**

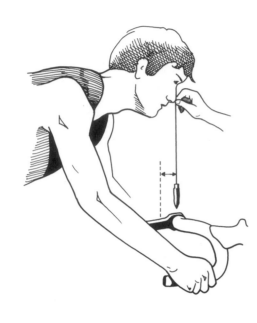

Your choices for bar reach and drop also depend on the kind of events you are doing. Events of relatively short duration are more forgiving of a low, aerodynamic position that delivers the most outright speed, while an Ironman-distance event requires a more comfortable setup. Indeed, the speed required in a short-distance event demands attention to aerodynamics, since drag increases as the square of the bike speed relative to the air. In a long event, a comfortable, efficient position that allows you to reach the run transition in good condition is paramount.

iii-17 HOW TO CHANGE REACH

Because you have already set your seat position, change the reach by changing stems, changing aero extension length (by length adjustment or by buying a different length extension; Fig. 3.9A), and changing elbow pad fore–aft position.

Most stems come with a removable front faceplate these days (Fig. 1.5), making it easier to change stems than before, when you had to remove the clip-ons, handlebar tape, and levers. Stem choice will be dictated by the change in length and height that you want. On my website, www.zinncycles.com, I have a stem calculator page that you can refer to. To use it, put in your frame's head angle and the dimensions of your current stem to find its current rise and reach. To these numbers, add or subtract how much longer or shorter and higher or lower you want your bar to be. Then plug in dimensions of possible stems and spacers to see which combination brings you closest to your desired position.

You switch the stem by first removing the handlebar and the headset top cap and loosening the clamp bolts clamping the stem to the steering tube (Fig. 14.1). Then, assuming you've got a threadless headset (Fig. 14.3), slide the stem up and off of the steering tube (see §xiv-1). You will have to readjust the headset when you replace the stem; for instructions, see Chapter 14, §xiv-14. On a new bike or fork, it behooves you to leave the steering tube long and use lots of spacers to support the stem until you determine the final stem height, at which point you can cut the steering tube to length (see §xiv-2) and discard the extra spacers.

FOOT POSITION

iii-18 CLEAT POSITION

For comfort and efficiency, it is critical that your physical effort be transmitted directly onto your pedals. If one or both of your feet roll to either side, if their placement on the pedals forces the knees to twist or move laterally, or if your feet hurt when riding, you will pedal ineffectively and develop injuries. These

OTHER REACH FACTORS

HOW TO CHANGE REACH

CLEAT POSITION

POSITIONING ON THE BIKE

3.14 Cleat positioning on the shoe

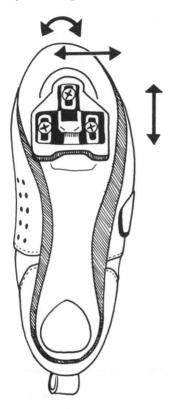

PRO TIP

PAUL SWIFT'S FEET TIP

A Tri Fit is probably the one bike fit with the most possibilities, options, and variables, but the most important connection to the bike remains the foot/pedal interface. Starting at this interface identifies a stable datum from which to work. Often the foot/pedal connection is overlooked or underestimated in its importance. My advice is get your feet handled first and then work your way up the fit.

—*Paul Swift*

Designer of the

Bicycle Fitting System and the Wedge;

eight-time Elite National Champion

---

issues may be addressed by changing the position of your cleats (Fig. 3.14) and/or shimming them. Sometimes, however, these measures are insufficient. If pain or other problems persist after you've followed the cleat-adjustment instructions in sections §iii-18 to §iii-24, proceed to §iii-25, which explains how to customize your shoes.

iii-19 INITIAL FORE–AFT CLEAT POSITION

In the neutral fore–aft foot position, the ball of the foot is over the pedal axle when the foot is level. However, many riders, particularly those with big feet, will want the cleats farther back. Bike fit guru Andy Pruitt explains that "a cycling shoe becomes an orthotic (that is, a corrective device) by taking a flexible foot and making it into a rigid lever," which makes cycling more efficient. Pruitt says that if the shoe size is larger than 42, the lever is too long (and often flexible) with the ball of the foot over the pedal. Greater efficiency is achieved by shortening the lever—sliding the cleat back so that the pedal axle is behind the ball of the foot.

In my work building bikes for big, heavy riders with big feet, I also find that moving the cleat behind the ball of the foot spreads the force of pedaling better and eliminates the pain caused by too much pressure concentrated on the metatarsals.

iii-20 ROTATIONAL CLEAT POSITION

Your foot should sit on the pedal the way it wants to, not how somebody else's feet are angled. Do you walk duck-footed, straight, or pigeon-toed? Expect your shoe to rotate similarly when pedaling.

You want to have at least 3–6 degrees of float from your neutral foot angle to accommodate foot rotation during the pedal cycle. Mount the cleats so that you have as much float to the inside before hitting the cleat release point as you do to the outside when your foot has found its natural pedaling position.

iii-21 STANCE WIDTH

The width of a rider's stance (also known as the Q factor in cycling vernacular) can be changed by moving the cleats laterally on the shoe. Unfortunately, limitations in modern frame, crank, bottom bracket, pedal, and derailleur design typically do not allow much other change in Q factor, although a few pedals offer spindles of different lengths which permit a few millimeters of adjustment.

Women often need a narrower stance due to rotation and angulation in the bones of the upper and lower leg and also because their legs are generally shorter, meaning that they are more splayed out to reach the pedals.

Some people require a wider stance. Riders with total hip replacements, for instance, have reduced range of motion, and a wider stance helps them. If they cannot internally rotate their hips, then there is no way to pedal straight. To create a wider stance, you can move the cleats inboard, insert washers on the pedal axle threads, or use a wider crankset or bottom bracket.

iii-22 RELATIVE CLEAT HEIGHT

Shimming up one cleat can partially alleviate differences in leg length. This is a complicated subject and should not be done without a medical consultation, preferably with a sports medicine specialist.

iii-23 CLEAT WEAR

As your cleat wears, it can cause engagement problems with the pedals and your foot can yank out during hard efforts, leading to traumatic injury. You also lose efficiency if your foot is slopping around in the pedal due to worn cleats.

Cleat wear can also cause chronic injury. If the cleat is worn on the outside from walking, the foot may roll to the outside when riding, which can create iliotibial (IT) band, knee, and muscle problems. Even play between the foot and the pedal can cause knee pain.

So check your cleat wear frequently.

iii-24 FOOT TIP ON THE PEDAL

You may not know this, but the roll of your foot about its axis is an important issue during cycling. Studies have shown that 85–92 percent of humans have forefoot varus, also known as supination. That is, in the foot's neutral position, the big toe rises higher than the little toe because that configuration is part of a normal walking gait. If your knee swings inward as you push down, that indicates forefoot varus, since pushing down forces the foot to go from tipped up at the inside edge to flat, and the knee goes inward with it. Conversely, forefoot valgus is the opposite condition, also called pronation, in which the little toe is higher than the big toe.

If you know the correction you need (consultation with a foot specialist or qualified sports medicine doctor is required), you can tip the cleat inward or outward with varus or valgus wedges so your knees go up and down like pistons rather than waving around. Plastic cleat wedges are available at bike shops or via the Web. To correct for forefoot varus, wedge up the cleat on the medial (inboard) side. Some shoes, like Specialized Body Geometry models, have this correction built into the sole. Conversely, people with forefoot valgus are in the minority but need a wedge on the lateral (outboard) side of the shoe.

ROTATIONAL
CLEAT POSITION

STANCE WIDTH

RELATIVE CLEAT
HEIGHT

CLEAT WEAR

FOOT TIP ON
THE PEDAL

POSITIONING ON THE BIKE

3.15 **Custom cycling orthotics**

iii-25 ORTHOTICS

Your feet must be supported, cradled, and angled properly to apply the repeated forces pedaling requires. If you ride a lot and suffer from pain in the region of your lower back on down to your feet that persists after following all of the previous bike and cleat setup instructions, it is critical to address the support of your feet within your cycling shoes.

Custom orthotics (Fig. 3.15) can address pain in the feet as well as in the knee and hip. According to Russel Bollig, owner of Podium Footwear in Broomfield, Colorado, and builder of custom orthotics for many cycling stars, including Lance Armstrong and Tyler Hamilton, "People usually come to me because they have pain. Foot injuries, like ball of the foot pain [metatarsal pain], constitute the majority of cases. The second most common complaint I see is the foot collapsing on the medial arch, rolling inward [pronating] and causing knee pain. In about half of the cases, this results in medial [inboard] knee pain [associated with the knee coming in toward the top tube from the foot rolling in], but we also see it all over

the knee and in the back, depending on what their leg is doing."

Orthotics will help improve biomechanics, just as a good bike fit will. If there is less unwanted motion in the foot and ankle, then there is less unwanted motion in the knee.

If you have a difference in leg length of less than 3mm, a lift can be built directly into the orthotic rather than between the cleat and the shoe. Leg-length discrepancy can be indicated by hip pain and should be diagnosed by a medical professional.

The problem of numb feet can also be relieved by custom orthotics, but not just any orthotic in a cycling shoe will do. It should be made specifically for cycling; don't try to stuff a running shoe orthotic in a cycling shoe. The benefits of a cycling-specific orthotic include narrowness and low volume. These elements are especially important in the heel (in cases where a heel "post"—or angular support—is not needed), so that the heel can sit at the bottom of the shoe without lifting out. The best person to see for a cycling orthotic is someone who has experience making them and understands cycling biomechanics; it could be a pedorthist (also known as an orthotic maker), podiatrist, chiropractor, or physical therapist.

An orthotic can alleviate pain (neuroma) between metatarsals with pads placed under the metatarsals to support the metatarsal arch. It can also wedge the foot to get it to pedal more efficiently, and it can have hollowed-out areas to relieve pressure on inflamed areas.

Over-the-counter arch supports offer a great place to start and may work for you without the investment in custom orthotics. Think of an orthotic as a shoe gasket—a soft thing to fill spaces like a gasket in an engine. A custom orthotic fills in all of the void spaces to ensure a better fitting shoe, but if there is no injury, a prefabricated arch support may improve the fit of your shoe sufficiently.

iii-26 CRANK LENGTH

Most people stick with the crankset that came with their bike, but for some people, particularly short people and tall people, that will not be the ideal crank.

Obviously the longer the crank, the more leverage you have. If you want to pull a nail from a board, you will have to apply a lot less force with your hand to pull it out with a long crowbar than with a small claw hammer. On the other hand, pedaling is not a one-time action; you repeat it thousands of times every ride and must do it smoothly to be fast.

Your power to the rear wheel is determined by how much torque you apply around the bottom bracket times the rate at which your feet go around it. And torque about a pivot is the force applied perpendicular to the lever times the length of the lever from the pivot out to where the force is applied. So the equations indicate that you can put out just as much power with a 100mm crankset as with a 200mm one by applying the same force; you just have to turn the 100mm cranks around twice as fast. And for that matter, the same force on the end of a 10mm crank would give you the same power output if you turned it around 20 times as fast as you do the 200mm. Going the other way, if you were to apply the same force with a one-meter crank (1,000mm) but at only one-fifth the rate of the 200mm, you would put out the same power.

But clearly, at some point in either direction it gets ridiculous. Human legs cannot spin around like a sewing machine motor, so you can forget about using 10mm cranks. Similarly, you can forget about turning 1,000mm cranks smoothly enough to keep up with your buddies.

If everyone had cranks that were in the same proportion to their leg length, then their knees and hips would go through the same range of angles, and their muscles would extend and contract the same percentage. Instead, we go through vastly different ranges of motion depending on leg length. We are generally not aware of this range of motion variation among the cycling population because bike fitters only check the knee bend at the bottom of the stroke (see §iii-1d, Fig. 3.3) and not at the top of the stroke. Proportionality of crank length to leg length makes more intuitive sense than the status quo of everyone using essentially the same length cranks regardless of leg length. The 5mm variation over the standard range of lengths of 170mm–175mm (or even the 15mm from 165mm–180mm, available only in top-dollar cranks) is essentially no variation, when you consider that there are triathletes competing with leg lengths shorter than 65cm (26 inches) and longer than 100cm (39 inches).

Look at it this way: a 170mm crank is 26 percent of the 65cm-leg triathlete's inseam length (and a 165mm is 25 percent), while a 175mm crank is 17.5 percent of the 100cm-leg triathlete's inseam length (and a 180mm is 18 percent). The short rider will struggle to get her foot around the (for her) tall circle, her knees will hit her chest, her hips will be constricted, her hamstrings will be overstretched, and her quads will not be able to push the pedal down effectively with the knees so high (while provoking knee strain to boot). Conversely, the tall rider will have to spin his feet around the (for him) tiny circle, inefficiently moving his big, heavy legs through the air rapidly while not being able to use his muscles over their entire effective range.

PRO TIP

JOE FRIEL'S PEDALING TIP

Once you've had a bike fit, you need to learn to pedal the bike efficiently. Put your bike on a trainer, warm up, and then pedal with one leg only while the resting foot is on a chair next to the bike. You'll quickly discover "dead" spots in your pedal stroke. Repeating this drill is a great way to improve pedaling. Your goal should be to "unweight" the pedal on the recovery side and at the top and bottom of the stroke to learn to pedal "hor-

izontally." Your skills will improve faster if you work on them for short periods frequently. When it comes to skills training, a little bit every day is better than one long workout done occasionally.

— *Joe Friel*
Founder of Training Bible Coaching,
Ultrafit Associates, and
www.TrainingPeaks.com, and author
of the Training Bible *book series*

Over the past couple of decades, I have done lots of nonscientific crank-length testing with many riders, as well as attempts at rigorous, scientific testing of it. I also have anecdotal feedback from hundreds of customers of mine who have purchased custom-length cranks from me. And all of this input about crank length from a wide range of riders of various sizes on a wide range of crank lengths from 100mm–250mm leads me to believe that the cranks should be about 21.5 percent as long as the rider's inseam (measured as in §iii-1a). I think you would be surprised to see how many Tour de France and Ironman champions won their races on cranks near this proportion to their inseams. But even if you were to say that 21.5 percent sounds arbitrary and is too restrictive, and you were to expand the range to, say, 21–22 percent or even 20–23 percent, you would still find that the available range of crank lengths is too limited for the entire range of adults. Even with a 20–23 percent range, the 65cm-leg triathlete at 23 percent still needs 150mm cranks (and 140mm at 21.5 percent), and the 100cm-leg triathlete at 20 percent still would require 200mm cranks (and 215mm at 21.5 percent)!

The general unavailability of cranks proportional to rider size also leads to some weird conventions of bike frame dimensions at the small and large ends, which bike sellers and designers have generally accepted as "just the way it has to be." Bike frames, handlebar widths, aerobar lengths, and stem lengths are generally available proportional to the body size of at least the majority of cyclists. However, the unavailability of proportional cranks means that, in order for bike frames to allow all riders be positioned properly for applying power to the pedals, small frames and tall frames must have very different seat-tube angles than average-size frames.

Tall frames must have tipped-back (shallow) seat-tube angles to move the seat back relative to the bottom bracket. Otherwise, the long thigh of the tall rider would make the knee be too far forward of the pedal for proper force application on the 175mm crank that is such a small percentage of his leg length.

And small frames must have tipped-forward (steep) seat-tube angles to move the seat forward relative to the bottom bracket. Otherwise, the short thigh of the short rider would make the knee be too far behind the pedal for proper force application on the

170mm crank that is such a large percentage of her leg length. And unless the small rider with this proportionately long 170mm crank were using a bike with smaller wheels, she would also have problems with her toe hitting the front tire on tight turns. But the bottom bracket being moved back away from the front wheel by means of the steeper seat-tube angle (and the front wheel pushed away from the bottom bracket by means of a shallower head-tube angle) "fixes" that.

These conventions in frame design, while "solving" some problems, also result in strange distribution of the rider's weight over the wheels. The tall rider on the bike with the shallow seat-tube angle will be cantilevered over the rear wheel, resulting in high rear-tire wear rates and the feeling of pulling the front wheel up off of the road when climbing steep hills. And the short rider will have a very skittish bike when climbing out of the saddle and will struggle with sluggish steering at speed by virtue of the front wheel being so far out ahead.

Given that the crank lengths and wheel sizes of kids' bikes increase with the size of the bike, this concept of proportional cranks is not really so foreign. But the logical conclusion to draw is that most adult bikes have essentially the same crank length because of tradition and for business reasons like the expense of manufacturing and stocking many different crank lengths. In addition, almost all bikes for a given application have similar bottom-bracket heights, so low pedaling clearance for the tall rider with long cranks or a high center of gravity for the short rider with short cranks will be detriments. I have found no solution other than to make cranks myself in the sizes the big manufacturers do not and to build bike frames specifically for the appropriately sized cranks. You can find out more at www.zinncycles.com.

FITTING THE BIKE FRAME

A well-fitting bike frame is fundamental to an enjoyable cycling experience. If your frame does not fit properly, your bike cannot be made to fit your body without extreme adjustments of components that will compromise stability, weight distribution, or performance. But if your bike fits you well, you'll be more comfortable, not only increasing your riding enjoyment but also encouraging you to ride more, which improves your fitness and performance.

iii-27 MEASURING FRAME DIMENSIONS

It is important to understand how bike frames are measured before you take your own body measurements. The two most important measurements are top-tube length and seat-tube length. Since the vast majority of readers will be buying a stock frame (as opposed to a frame custom made to their measurements), I'll describe how to measure frames so those readers will know how to compare them. It is not generally enough to read manufacturer specification lists, since the measurement method varies from manufacturer to manufacturer, and you want to compare apples to apples.

Although most triathlon bikes have level top tubes, which are easy to measure (Fig. 3.16A), most road bikes now have sloping top tubes (a feature also known as compact geometry; Fig. 3.16B), which are more difficult to measure. You can get around this by extending a taut string in a horizontal line starting at the intersection of the top tube's upper edge and the head tube, and drawing the string back to the seatpost. The distance along this line (Fig. 3.16B), from the center of the head tube to the center of the seatpost, is the top-tube length. (You will notice that this length, the "effective top-tube length," is greater than the length

POSITIONING ON THE BIKE

3.16A Diagram of frame dimensions (on a horizontal top-tube frame)

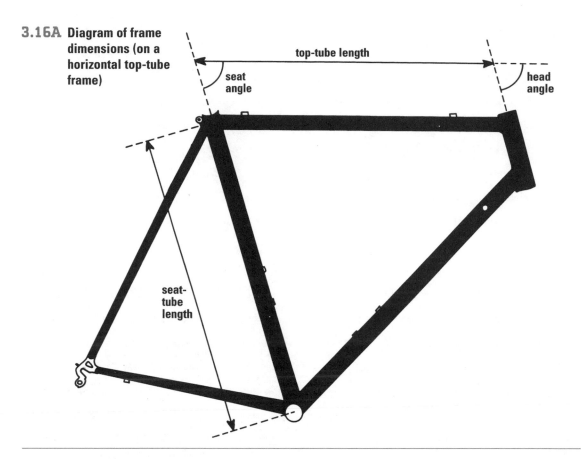

3.16B Bike dimensions on a sloping-top-tube (compact geometry) road bike

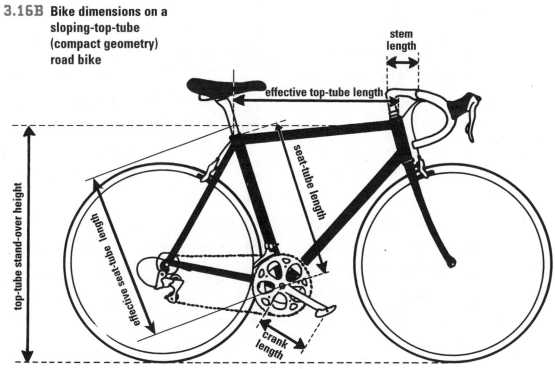

MEASURING
FRAME
DIMENSIONS

·

FINDING FRAME
DIMENSIONS TO
FIT YOUR BODY

measured center to center along the top tube itself. Elementary geometry explains this: Since the head tube and seat tube are approximately parallel, the shortest distance between two parallel lines is perpendicular to them both, and the sloping top tube is closer to perpendicular than is the effective top tube.)

The effective center-to-top seat-tube length in Figure 3.16B is measured along the seat tube from the center of the bottom bracket to the taut string horizontal line (representing the top of a hypothetical horizontal top tube). To convert this measurement to an effective center-to-center seat-tube length, subtract half the diameter of the top tube (around 2cm on many current frames) from the center-to-top seat-tube length.

Obviously on a frame with a horizontal top tube, measure the top tube's length from the center of the head tube to the center of the seat tube (Fig. 3.16A). The seat-tube length is simply measured from the bottom bracket center to the top tube's top edge or centerline where it intersects the seat-tube centerline, depending on whether you want a center-to-top or center-to-center measurement.

Once you have measured the frame properly, you can compare it to other frames measured in the same way.

But note that if you plan to install extra-long (or extra-short) cranks, you also want to be sure that the bottom bracket is high enough. You can measure bottom-bracket height yourself from the ground to the center of the bottom bracket when the wheels are in place and the tires pumped to the correct pressure.

Without that, you will need to refer to the manufacturer's specifications list.

The final measurements you may want to have are the angles of the head tube and seat tube. You will need to rely on the specification list for frame angles, unless you have an angle finder to measure them.

iii-28 FINDING FRAME DIMENSIONS TO FIT YOUR BODY

The next step is to calculate your ideal frame size from your body measurements and compare it with the frame's dimensions. I think the simplest thing to do is to use the free fit calculator page I have put up on my website, www.zinncycles.com. After you take three body measurements, you can click on one of three possible characterizations of your riding level and whether you want recommendations for a road or mountain frame. The calculator then spits out a recommended seat-tube length, top-tube length, and bottom bracket height, and if you are interested in a custom crank length, it suggests one, along with the accompanying bottom bracket height. It also suggests a seat height. Triathletes may wish to add one or two centimeters to the top-tube length recommendation to adjust for aerobars, especially if using a forward seat position.

In Appendix C of *Zinn and the Art of Road Bike Maintenance*, you'll find a manual frame fit method that will yield similar results to my online fit page.

Once you have a frame that fits you, you can choose and adjust the components so that you are riding in a comfortable and efficient position.

II

Maintenance & Repair

TOOLS

If the only tool you have is a hammer,
you tend to see every problem as a nail.
—Abraham Maslow

You can't do much useful work on a bike without a basic tool assortment. And bicycles—like other evolved machines such as automobiles and watches—have specific fasteners and threads that require specific tools to fit them. This chapter will clarify the tools you should consider owning based on your mechanical experience and interest.

As I mentioned in the introduction, the maintenance and repair procedures in this book are classified by degree of difficulty. Nearly all repairs are classified as level 1, because most bicycle repair jobs are easy once you understand the principles involved. The tools for levels 1, 2, and 3 are pictured in Figures 4.1, 4.2, and 4.3, respectively, and described on the following pages. In addition, the tools you may need for a specific repair are listed in the margin at the beginning of each chapter.

For the uninitiated, there is no need to rush out and buy a large number of bike-specific tools. With

LEVEL 1

LEVEL 2

LEVEL 3

few exceptions, the level 1 tool kit (Fig. 4.1) consists of standard metric tools, many of which you may already own. This is the same collection of tools, in compact form, that I recommend you carry on training rides (Figs. 4.4–5).

The level 2 tool kit (Fig. 4.2) contains several bike-specific tools that will allow you to do more complex work. Level 3 tools (Fig. 4.3) are extensive (and sometimes expensive) and ensure that your riding buddies will show up not only to ask your sage advice but to borrow your tools as well. If you do loan tools, by the way, you may want to mark your collection and keep a list of who borrowed what, to help recover items that may otherwise take a long time finding their way back to your workshop.

iv-1 LEVEL 1 TOOL KIT

LEVEL 1

Level 1 repairs are the simplest and do not require a workshop, although it is nice to have a comfortable, well-lit work space. For easy repairs, you will need the following tools (Fig. 4.1A):

- **Tire pump with a gauge** and a valve head to match your tubes (either Presta or Schrader valves; see Fig. 4.1B)

- **Standard slot-head screwdrivers**: small, medium, and large.

- **Phillips-head screwdrivers**: one small and one medium.

- Set of three **plastic tire levers**, if you have clincher tires.

- At least **two spare tubes**—or **tubulars**—of the same size and valve type as those on your bike.

- Container of regular **talcum powder** for coating tubes and the inner casings of tires.

N O T E : *Do not inhale this stuff; it is bad for your lungs.*

- **Patch kit**. Choose one that comes with sandpaper instead of a metal scratcher. Every year, check that the glue has not dried up.

- One 6-inch **adjustable wrench** ("Crescent wrench," which is a brand name).

- **Pliers**: regular and needle-nose.

- Set of **metric Allen wrenches** ("hex keys") that includes 2.5mm, 3mm, 4mm, 5mm, 6mm, and 8mm sizes. Folding sets are available and work nicely to keep wrenches organized. I also recommend buying extras of the 4mm, 5mm, and 6mm sizes and a long-handled 8mm hex key for removing and installing some pedals and crankarms.

- A **15mm pedal wrench**. The specific pedal wrench is thinner and longer than a standard 15mm

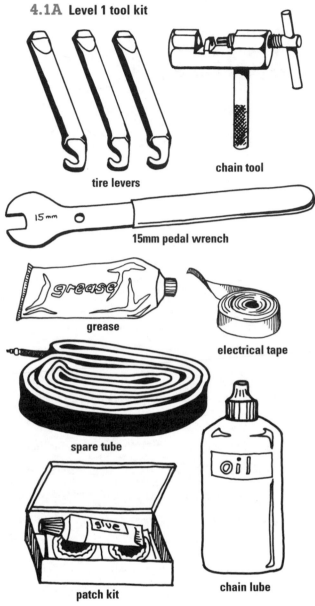

4.1A Level 1 tool kit

tire levers

chain tool

15mm pedal wrench

grease

electrical tape

spare tube

patch kit

glue

oil

chain lube

wrench to fit into the space between the pedal and crank (Fig. 12.2).

- **Chain tool** for breaking and reassembling chains. If you have a nine- or ten-speed system, you may need a narrower chain tool to avoid bending the center prongs of the tool. Shimano's TL-CN23 and TL-CN32 (Figs. 7.16, 7.17) work for seven-, eight-, nine-, and ten-speed chains. Many other chain tools work as well (Figs. 7.18–7.20); you can ask your bike shop for the brand of tool that

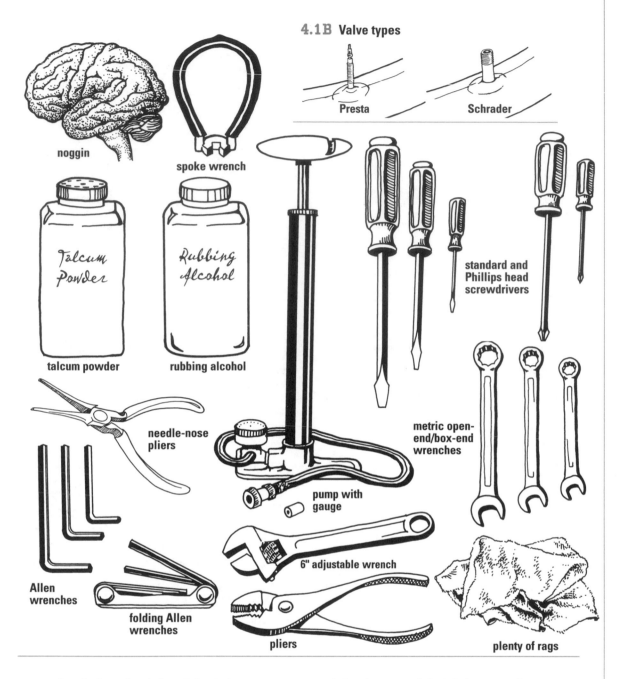

4.1B Valve types

Presta

Schrader

noggin

spoke wrench

talcum powder

rubbing alcohol

standard and Phillips head screwdrivers

needle-nose pliers

metric open-end/box-end wrenches

pump with gauge

Allen wrenches

folding Allen wrenches

6" adjustable wrench

pliers

plenty of rags

matches the brand and size of the chain on your bike.

- **Spoke wrench** to match the size and type of nipples used on the wheels.
- Set of **metric open-end wrenches** that includes 7mm, 8mm, 9mm, 10mm, 13mm, 14mm, 15mm, and 17mm sizes.
- Tube or jar of **grease**. I recommend using grease designed specifically for bicycles, but standard automotive grease is okay.

- Drip bottle or can of **chain lubricant**. Choose a non-aerosol; it is easier to control, uses less packaging, and wastes less in overspray.
- **Rubbing alcohol** for light cleaning.
- A roll of **electrical tape** for taping off the end of the handlebar and marking your seat height.
- A lot of **rags.** Old T-shirts work fine. Also get safety glasses and rubber gloves or a box of cheap latex gloves. A bucket, large brushes and sponges, and dish soap also will serve you well for cleaning a dirty machine.

iv-2 LEVEL 2 TOOL KIT

LEVEL 2

Level 2 repairs are a bit more complex, and I recommend that you attack them with specific tools and a well-organized workspace that includes a shop bench. Keeping your workspace organized is probably the best way to make maintenance and repair easy and quick. You will need the entire level 1 tool kit (Fig. 4.1) plus the following tools (Fig. 4.2):

· **Portable bike stand.** Be sure the stand is sturdy enough to remain stable when you're really cranking on the wrenches.

· **Shop apron** (to keep your nice duds nice).

· **Hacksaw** with a fine-toothed blade.

· Set of razor blades or a sharp **shop knife.**

· **Files:** one round and one flat, with medium-fine teeth.

· **Cable cutter** for cutting brake and shift cables without fraying the ends.

· **Cable-housing cutter** for cutting coaxial-indexed cable housing. If you purchase a Shimano, Park, Pedro's, or Wrench Force housing cutter, you won't need to buy a separate cable cutter, since they cleanly cut cables as well as housings.

· **TORX wrenches,** which look like hex keys with star-shaped tips; they fit some brake bolts and chainring bolts. TORX T25 and T30 are common sizes on bikes.

· **Chainring-nut tool** for holding the nut while you tighten or loosen a chainring bolt.

· Medium **ball-peen hammer.**

· Medium-size **bench vise** (bolted to a sturdy bench).

· **Cog lockring tool** for removing cogs from the rear hub (Fig. 9.33). Note that Campagnolo cogs require different tools than SRAM and Shimano.

· **Chain whip** for holding cogs while loosening the cogset lockring (Fig. 9.33).

4.2 Level 2 tool kit

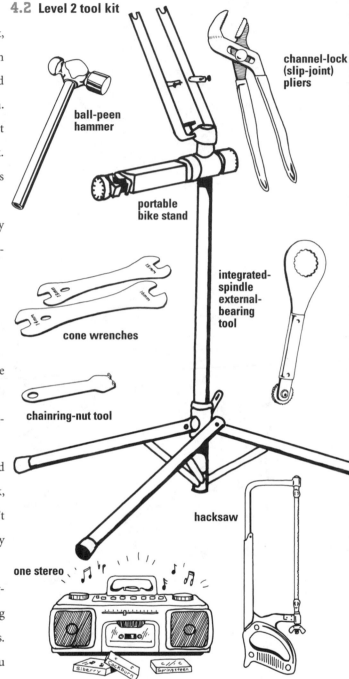

channel-lock (slip-joint) pliers

ball-peen hammer

portable bike stand

integrated-spindle external-bearing tool

cone wrenches

chainring-nut tool

hacksaw

one stereo

· **Bottom-bracket tools.** For cartridge-bearing bottom bracket cups (Figs. 11.10, 11.14) you'll need a splined cartridge bottom-bracket tool (Fig. 11.9). Note that if you have an ISIS or OctaLink splined-spindle bottom bracket, you need a tool with a bore large enough to swallow the fatter spindle (Fig.11.14). Also, Campagnolo square-taper bottom-bracket

Torx T25, T15 wrenches

splined pedal-spindle removal tool

rim cement

crank puller

chain whip

medium bench vise

shop apron

files: one flat, one round

cutter for cable and indexed cable housing

metric socket wrenches

bottom—bracket tools: toothed lockring spanner (t), pin spanner (b)

headset wrenches

cog lockring tool

cartridge bottom-bracket tool

woodworker's miter clamp

razor blades or sharp knife

cups employ a different spline, and hence require a different tool, than other manufacturers' cups. For external-bearing integrated-spindle cranks (Figs. 11.15–16), you'll need an oversize splined wrench to remove the cups, which are larger and sit outboard of the bottom-bracket shell (Fig. 11.20), and, in some cases, a little splined tool to tighten the left crank's adjustment cap. And for cup-and-cone bottom brackets (Fig. 11.11), you'll need a lockring spanner and a pin spanner (Fig. 11.19) to fit your bottom bracket. For Campagnolo Ultra-Torque integrated-spindle cranks (Fig. 11.16), you'll need a long, 10mm Allen wrench to tighten the bolt in the middle of the axle.

TOOLS

- **Crank puller** for removing crankarms (Fig. 11.3). The pushrod of this tool is sized for either square-taper spindles (Figs. 11.10–12) or ISIS/OctaLink spindles (Figs. 11.13–14), so get the right one for your crankset. This tool is not needed for most integrated-spindle cranks (Figs. 11.15–16), or for cranks with self-extracting crank bolts.

- **Cone wrenches,** if you have loose-bearing hubs (Fig. 9.31). The standard sizes are 13mm and 14mm, but check before buying (take the complete wheel to your bike shop).

- **Channel-lock** ("slip-joint") pliers.

- Splined **pedal-spindle removal tool.** Note that Shimano's plastic tool (Fig. 12.12) is different from Look's, although high-end Shimano and Look pedals no longer require either (they take standard 20mm and 19mm wrenches).

- Two **headset wrenches** (only needed for old bikes with threaded headsets; Fig. 14.21). Check the size of the headset on your bike before buying these.

- For older bikes, you'll want a set of **metric socket wrenches** that includes 7mm, 8mm, 9mm, 10mm, 13mm, 14mm, and 15mm sizes.

- **Rim cement** for gluing tubular tires (Fig. 9.15), if you have them. Use Continental clear glue or Vittoria Mastik'One for aluminum rims, but for carbon-fiber rims, stick to Mastik'One .

- Woodworker's **miter clamp** (optional) for gluing tubular tires to rims.

- Stereo, iPod, or other **sound system,** if you plan on spending a lot of time working on your bike.

iv-3 LEVEL 3 TOOL KIT

As an accomplished level 3 mechanic, you are completely independent of your local bike shop's service depart-

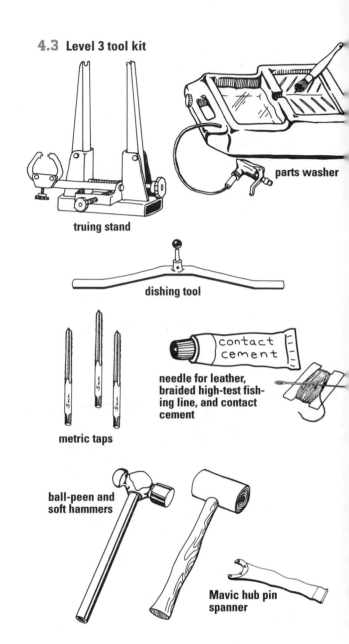

4.3 Level 3 tool kit

truing stand

parts washer

dishing tool

metric taps

contact cement

needle for leather, braided high-test fishing line, and contact cement

ball-peen and soft hammers

Mavic hub pin spanner

ment. You can even assemble a bike from scratch, starting with the bare frame. By now, you have a well-organized, separate space devoted to working on your bike. Some elements of the level 3 tool kit (Fig. 4.3) are heavier-duty replacements or substitutions for items in the level 2 tool kit (Fig. 4.2).

- **Parts washing tank.** Please use an environmentally safe degreaser. Dispose of used solvent responsibly; check with your local environmental safety office.

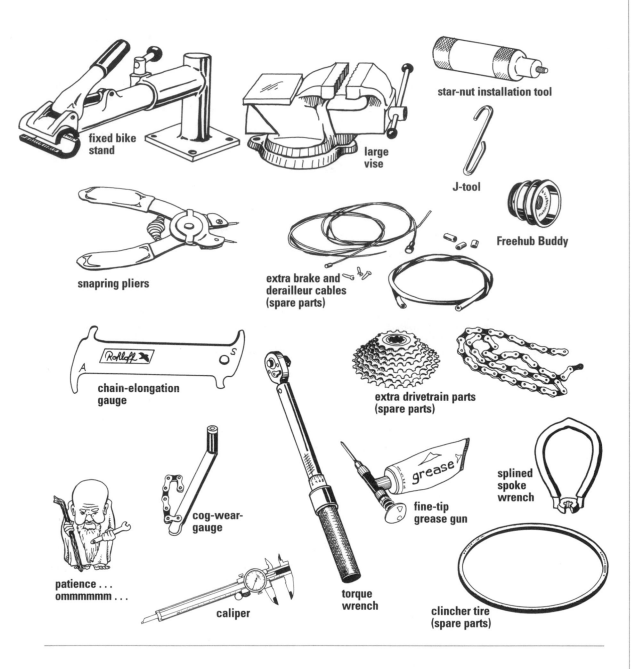

fixed bike stand

large vise

star-nut installation tool

J-tool

Freehub Buddy

snapring pliers

extra brake and derailleur cables (spare parts)

chain-elongation gauge

extra drivetrain parts (spare parts)

patience . . . ommmmmm . . .

cog-wear-gauge

caliper

torque wrench

fine-tip grease gun

splined spoke wrench

clincher tire (spare parts)

- Fixed **bike stand.** Be sure it comes with a clamp designed to fit any size of frame tube.
- Large **bench-mounted vise** so that you can free stuck parts.
- **Star-nut installation tool** for threadless headsets.
- Large **ball-peen hammer.**
- **Soft hammer.** Choose a rubber, plastic, or wooden mallet to prevent damage to parts.
- **Torque wrenches,** for checking proper bolt tightness. Most component manufacturers provide torque specs; observing them dissuades parts from stripping, breaking, or falling off while riding. There is a complete torque specification list in Appendix C.
- Set of **metric taps** that includes 5mm × 0.8, 6mm × 1, and 10mm × 1. These work for threading bottle bosses, seat binder clamps, and derailleur hangers.

TOOLS

- Pair of **snapring pliers** for removing snaprings ("circlips") from some pedals.
- **Fine-tip grease gun** for parts with grease fittings and for Campagnolo headsets with grease holes.
- Morningstar **Freehub Buddy** for lubricating Shimano freehubs (Figs. 9.35, 9.37).
- Morningstar **J-tool** for removing Shimano freehub dust covers (Fig. 9.36).
- **Chain-elongation gauge.** This handy little plastic item helps you quickly determine whether a chain needs to be replaced (Fig. 7.4). An accurate 12-inch ruler will substitute adequately.
- **Truing stand** for taking the wobble out of wheels.
- **Dishing tool** for checking whether a wheel is properly centered.
- A full range of **spoke wrenches** of various sizes, including splined ones.
- **Splined spoke wrench** for Mavic Zicral spokes.
- **Pin spanner** for adjusting Mavic hubs.
- **Cog-wear indicator gauge to determine whether cogs are worn out or not.**
- **Measuring caliper** with a Vernier, dial, or digital gauge for precisely measuring parts.
- **Needle** for leather, braided high-test **fishing line,** and contact **cement** for patching tubular tires.
- A healthy dose of **patience** and an equal willingness to work and rework jobs until they have been properly finished.

a. Other stuff

- **Spare parts** to save you from making a lot of runs to the bike shop for commonly used parts. Any well-equipped shop requires several sizes of ball bearings, bolts, spare cables, cable housing, and a lifetime supply of little housing ferrules (cylindrical caps) and

cable-end caps (Fig. 8.13). You should also have a good supply of spare tires, tubes, chains, and cogsets.

- **Various fluids.** Threadlock fluid, titanium anti-seize compound, outboard motor gear oil, or specialty freehub lubricants are required for some jobs.

iv-4 TOOLS TO CARRY WITH YOU WHILE RIDING

a. For racing

You can keep everything you need for light repairs (Fig. 4.4) in a small bag under your seat.

- **Spare inner tube or tubular.** Always carry one. Make sure the valve matches the ones on your bike, in length as well as type. If rarely needed, keep it in a plastic bag to prevent deterioration.
- **CO_2 cartridge inflator.** Make sure the chuck fits the valves on your bike (probably Presta), and get the correct size for your spare tube or tubular (probably 12 grams).
- At least two plastic **tire levers,** preferably three (for clincher tires only, although one is sometimes helpful for removing a well-glued tubular).

4.4 Tools and spares to take in races

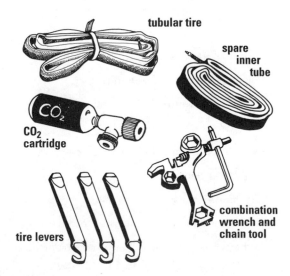

4.5 Additional tools to take on all training rides

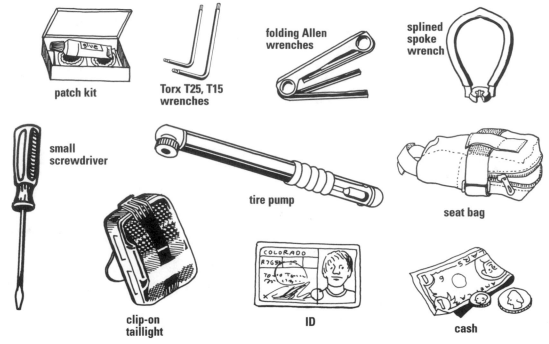

patch kit   Torx T25, T15 wrenches   folding Allen wrenches   splined spoke wrench

small screwdriver   tire pump   seat bag

clip-on taillight   ID   cash

- **Multitool** with a chain tool included, in case you need to tighten a loose brake cable, shift cable, aerobar, or elbow pad, fix a broken chain, and so on.

b. For most riding

This take-along kit includes everything you'd take in a race, shown in Figure 4.4, plus the following items, shown in Figure 4.5. As you stock your kit, look for tools that are light and serviceable. Many of the separate tools shown in Figure 4.5 are available in combination as "multitools." Make sure you try all tools at home before taking them on the road. Keep them in a bit bigger bag under your seat.

- **Patch kit.** You'll need something after you've used your spare tube. Check it at least once a year to make sure the glue has not dried up. You can also carry glueless patches.

- **Frame pump.** Road bike pumps need to be thin to attain high tire pressures (the longer the better for pumping, but heavier for carrying). Minipumps are okay, but they're slow. Make sure the pump has

the right head for the tire valves (probably Presta).

- Small **screwdriver** for adjusting derailleurs and other parts.

- Compact set of **Allen wrenches** (hex keys) that includes 2.5mm, 3mm, 4mm, 5mm, 6mm, and 8mm sizes, and even a Torx T25; a folding set with individual hex keys long enough for every bolt on your bike is a good investment.

- Properly sized **spoke wrench.**

- Small clip-on **taillight**.

- Carry-along **outerwear.** Arm warmers, knee warmers, nylon vest, and a cap for any ride in the mountains or on any day that is not just plain hot. In the mountains and in questionable weather, thin gloves and shoe covers are also a good idea.

- **Identification**.

- **Cash** for food, phone calls, and to plug sidewall cuts in tires.

- **Cell phone.** Like I need to remind anybody these days to carry their cell phone! It's a good idea to

4.6 Additional tools and spares for extended rides

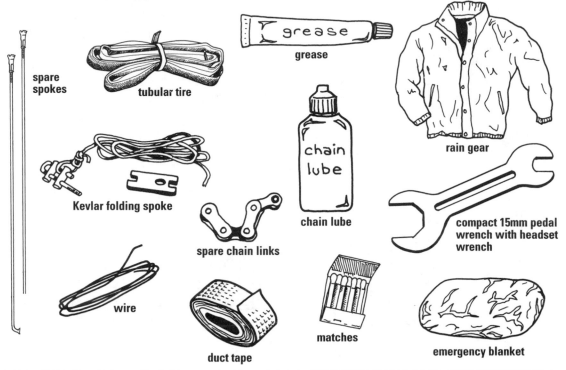

keep the phone in a plastic bag in your back pocket.

c. For extended or multiday rides

Carry the items in Figure 4.6, as well as all of the items in Figures 4.4 and 4.5.

- A **second spare tire.** Carry a spare folding clincher tire and a second spare inner tube or, if you ride tubulars, take two spare tubulars.
- **Rain gear.**
- **Spare chain links** from your chain or a master link. If you are using a Shimano eight- or nine-speed chain, carry at least two "subpin" rivets (Fig. 7.15); for ten-speed chains, either Shimano, SRAM, or Campagnolo. Unless you have installed a master link, you will have to replace the chain with a new one when you get home, so don't worry about the assembly pins. More on this subject comes up in Chapter 7.
- **Spare spokes.** Innovations in Cycling sells a really cool folding spoke made from Kevlar.

- Small blister pack of **chain lube.**
- Small blister pack of **grease.**
- Small amount of **duct tape.**
- Small amount of **wire.**
- **Compact 15mm pedal wrench,** if your pedals require it. You can get one with a headset wrench on the other end.
- **Headlight.** A lightweight unit that clips to the handlebar or a headlamp with a strap that will fit over your helmet is sufficient.
- **Matches.**
- A lightweight, aluminized folding **emergency blanket.**

N O T E : *Read Chapter 6 on emergency repairs before embarking on a lengthy trip. If you are planning a bike-centered vacation, be sure to take along a level 1 tool kit in your car, some headset wrenches (if your bike has a threaded headset; Fig. 14.21), and incidentals like duct tape and sandpaper.*

BASIC STUFF

Basic research is what I am doing
when I don't know what I am doing.
—Werner von Braun

TOOLS
chain lubricant
rags

Optional
solvent
  (citrus-based)
chain-cleaning tool
old water bottle

t is a good idea to get in the habit of checking your bike before heading out on a ride. Regular inspections can help you avoid getting stranded far from home due to parts failure. You should also know how to properly remove and reinstall a wheel to deal with minor annoyances like flat tires or jammed chains. And even if you do nothing else to your bike, keeping its chain clean and properly lubricated, as outlined in this chapter, will make every ride smoother and quieter.

v-1 PRERIDE INSPECTION

1. Make sure the quick-release levers securing the hub axle to the dropouts are tight.
2. Check the brake pads for excessive or unevenwear.
3. Grab and twist the brake pads and brake arms to make sure that the bolts are tight.
4. Squeeze the brake levers. A good squeeze should bring the brake pads flat against the wheel rims (or slightly toed in) without hitting the tires. Make certain you cannot squeeze the levers all of the way to the handlebar. For details, see Chapter 10 on brake adjustment.
5. Spin the wheels to check for wobbles (watch the rims, not the tires). Make sure the rims do not rub the brake pads.
6. Spin the wheels again, this time while eyeing the tires. If a tire wobbles excessively on a straight rim, it may not be fully seated in the rim. There is usually a mold line or an edge of a tape strip on the tire that should be parallel to the rim edge all the way around. Look for areas where the tire is bulging and/or the mold line or tape edge is higher above the rim or deeper into the rim than the rest of the way around the tire. To fix an improperly seated tire, you need to completely deflate the tire and carefully seat it uniformly all the way around before reinflating.
7. Check tire pressure; it should be between 80 and 120 pounds per square inch (psi), more on high-end tires (check the rating on the sidewall to make

PRERIDE
INSPECTION

·

REMOVING THE
FRONT WHEEL

·

RELEASING THE
BRAKE

sure you don't exceed it). Check that there are no foreign objects sticking in the tire. If there are, you may have to pull the tube out and repair or replace it. If you have an aversion to fixing flats, turn to section §ix-11 on tire sealants (i.e., the goop inside the tube that fills small holes) in Chapter 9.

8. Check the tires for excessive wear, cracks, or gashes.

9. Be certain the handlebar and stem are tight and the stem is aligned with the front tire.

10. Check that the gears shift smoothly and the chain does not skip or shift by itself. Ensure that each indexed ("click") shift moves the chain one cog, starting with the first click. Make sure the chain does not overshift the smallest or biggest rear cog or the inner or outer front chainring.

11. Check the chain for rust, dirt, stiff links, or notice-able signs of wear. It should be clean and lubri-cated (although overlubricated, gooey chains pick up lots of dirt). On a tri bike that only sees road use, the chain should be replaced about every 1,500–2,500 miles; see §vii-6 to accurately evalu-ate chain wear.

12. Apply the front brake and rock the bike forward and back. The headset should be tight and should not make clunking noises or allow the fork any fore-and-aft play.

13. Grasp one crankarm and push and pull it later-ally, toward and away from the frame, to ensure that the crank bearings are not loose.

14. Grasp each wheel and push and pull it laterally, perpendicular to the plane of the wheel, to ensure that the hub bearings are not loose.

15. If all this checks out, go ride your bike! If not, check the table of contents, go to the appropriate chapter, and fix the problems before you ride.

5.1 Releasing the brake

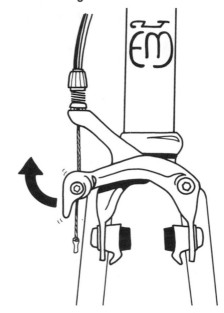

v-2 REMOVING THE FRONT WHEEL

You can't fix a flat if you can't remove the wheel. Front-wheel removal is also generally required for placing a bike on a roof rack or for putting it in a car. As out-lined in the following sections, wheel removal involves releasing the brake (in most cases) and opening the hub quick release or bolt-on skewer or the axle nuts on inexpensive bicycles.

v-3 RELEASING THE BRAKE

Most brakes have a quick-release (QR) mechanism to open the brake arms and move them away from the rim, allowing the tire to pass between the pads. Most road bike sidepull brakes have a lever on the brake caliper that is flipped up to open the brake (Fig. 5.1). Alternatively, Campagnolo Ergopower systems have a pin near the top of the brake lever that is pushed out-ward to allow the lever (and consequently the caliper) to open wider (Fig. 5.2). Cheap sidepull brakes on cheap bikes don't have a quick-release for the brake, and the same is often true with expensive triathlon

RELEASING THE
BRAKE
·
DETACHING A
FRONT WHEEL
WITH A
QUICK-RELEASE
SKEWER

5.2 Releasing a Campagnolo brake

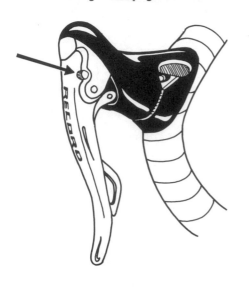

5.3 Opening quick-release skewer

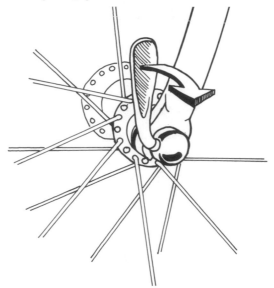

bikes equipped with Campagnolo brake calipers (with no QR) coupled with little aerodynamic brake levers on the ends of cowhorn bars (see Fig. 10.8).

If the brake has no quick-release and tire is too plump to fit between the brake pads, you will want to deflate the tire before removing the wheel to avoid damaging the tire and perhaps even dislodging the brake pads from their proper positions.

v-4 DETACHING A FRONT WHEEL WITH A QUICK-RELEASE SKEWER

You don't need a tool for this task.

1. Pull the lever outward to open it (Fig. 5.3).
2. After opening the hub quick-release lever, the wheel is ready to fall out on most bikes with forks older than 2003 or so. If it will not fall out, the fork most likely has wheel-retention tabs on its ends, which are designed to keep the wheel in place if the quick-release is left open by mistake (QR mechanisms rarely open by themselves). In this case, unscrew the nut on the opposite end of

5.4 Bolt-on skewer

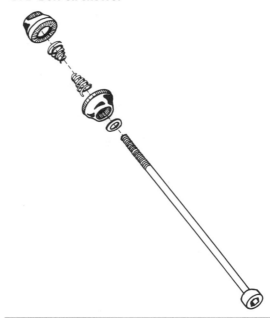

the quick-release skewer's shaft until it clears the fork's wheel-retention tabs.

3. Lift the bike so the wheel falls out.

N O T E : *Some bikes—usually only those of lightweight fanatics—have bolt-on skewers (Fig. 5.4), often made of titanium to save weight. The wheel is removed by unscrewing the skewer with a 5mm hex key.*

BASIC STUFF

v-5 INSTALLING THE FRONT WHEEL

Leaving the brake open (or the tire deflated, if you have no brake quick-release and the tire won't fit through the brake while inflated), lower the fork onto the wheel so that the bike's weight pushes the top of the dropout slots down onto the hub axle. This action will seat the axle fully into the fork and center the rim between the brake pads. If the fork or wheel is misaligned, you will need to hold the rim centered between the brake pads when securing the hub (and true the untrue wheel—see §ix-12—or get the bent fork fixed or replaced soon). To secure the wheel, continue with the steps given in the section that is appropriate for your bike's configuration (§v-6, §v-7, or §v-8).

v-6 TIGHTENING THE QUICK-RELEASE SKEWER

The quick-release skewer is not a glorified wing nut and should not be treated as such.

1. Hold the quick-release lever in the "open" position.
2. Tighten the opposite end nut until it snugs up against the face of the dropout. (If there are no wheel-retention tabs on the fork, and you did not unscrew the skewer nut, this step is unnecessary because the skewer will still be in adjustment.)
3. Push the lever over (Fig. 5.5) to the "closed" position (it should now be at a 90 degree angle to the axle). It should take a good amount of hand pressure to close the quick-release lever properly; the lever should leave its imprint on your palm for a few seconds.
4. If the quick-release lever does not close tightly, open the lever again, tighten the end nut a quarter turn, and close the lever again. Repeat until tight.
5. If the lever cannot be pushed down flat, the nut is too tight. Open the quick-release lever, unscrew

the end nut a quarter turn or so, and try closing the lever again. Repeat this procedure until the quick-release lever is fully closed and snug. The lever should leave an imprint on the palm of your hand for a few seconds. When you are done, have the lever pointing straight up or toward the back of the bike so that it cannot hook on obstacles and be accidentally opened.

6. Hit the top of the tire with your open palm to check that the wheel is not loose and you cannot bang it out.

v-7 TIGHTENING BOLT-ON SKEWERS

Hold the end nut with one hand and tighten the bolt-on skewer (Fig. 5.4) with a 5mm hex key. Control Tech recommends 65 inch-pounds (in-lbs) of tightening torque for steel bolt-on skewers and 85 in-lbs for titanium ones. You can approximate the accurate tightening torque by using a short hex key and tightening as much as you can with your fingers. Avoid over-tightening these skewers by being conscious of how much pressure a quick-release skewer applies and do not go higher than that, but make sure it is tight enough to securely hold the wheel.

v-8 CLOSING THE BRAKES

The steps required to close the brakes are always the reverse of what you did to release them.

1. With most road bikes, closing the brake caliper is simply a matter of flipping closed the quick-release lever on the sidepull brake caliper (Fig. 5.1 in reverse). With Campagnolo Ergopower, squeeze the brake lever and push the pin inward to its original position to engage the shallower notch in the lever body (Fig. 5.2).

5.5 Tightening quick-release

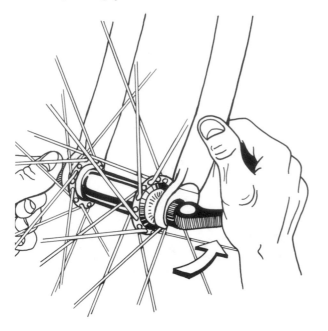

5.6 Removal and installation of rear wheel

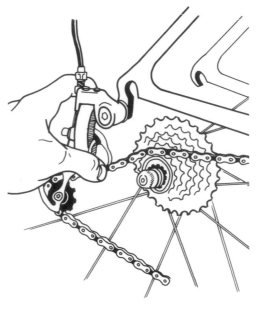

CLOSING THE
BRAKES

·

REMOVING THE
REAR WHEEL

·

REMOVING THE
REAR WHEEL
FROM REAR-
ENTRY DROPOUTS

2. Check that the brake cables are connected securely by squeezing the levers. Lift the front end of the bike and spin the front wheel, gently applying the brakes several times. Check that the pads are not dragging. If they are, recenter the wheel (or adjust the brakes as described in Chap. 10). If everything is reconnected and centered properly, you're all set.

v-9 REMOVING THE REAR WHEEL

Except on some bikes with aerodynamic configurations (see §v-10, below), removing the rear wheel is just like removing the front, with the slight added complication of the chain and cogs.

1. Open the brake as outlined in §v-3 (or deflate the tire).

2. Shift the chain onto the smallest rear cog by lifting the rear wheel off the ground, turning the cranks, and shifting.

3. To release the wheel from the rear dropouts and the brakes, follow the same procedure as for the

front wheel. When you push the wheel out, you will need to move the chain out of the way. This is usually a matter of grabbing the rear derailleur and pulling it back so that the jockey wheels (pulley wheels) move out of the way, while you push forward on the quick-release or axle nuts with your thumbs. The wheel should fall out as you hold the bike up (Fig. 5.6). If the bottom half of the chain catches the wheel as it falls, lift the wheel and jiggle it upward to free it.

v-10 REMOVING THE REAR WHEEL FROM REAR-ENTRY DROPOUTS

Some triathlon bikes have very tight clearance at the seat tube or even a cutout in the seat tube for the rear wheel to "hide" from the wind (Fig. I.1). These bikes use rear-entry dropouts for the back wheel. The dropouts work well but can be daunting if you've never dealt with them. Prepare to get your hands dirty.

REMOVING THE
REAR WHEEL
FROM REAR-
ENTRY DROPOUTS

·

INSTALLING THE
REAR WHEEL

5.7 **Removal and installation of rear wheel from rear-entry dropouts**

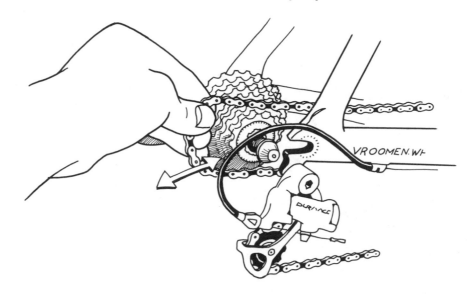

1. Open the brake (or deflate the tire), as outlined in §v-3.
2. Shift the chain onto the smallest cog by lifting the rear wheel off the ground, turning the cranks, and shifting. It's a good idea to shift onto the small chainring as well, to create more chain slack.
3. Open the rear quick-release skewer.
4. You must move the chain out of the way before you can release the wheel from the rear-facing dropouts. Grab the chain with your fingers and pull it back (off the rear cog) and to the right.
5. Open the rear quick-release skewer.
6. With the chain now out of the way, grab the rear wheel and pull it straight back and out of the bike (Fig. 5.7).

v-11 INSTALLING THE REAR WHEEL

1. Check to make sure the rear derailleur is shifted to its outermost position (over the smallest cog).
2. Slip the wheel between the seatstays and between the brake pads. Maneuver the upper section of chain onto the smallest cog (Fig. 5.6).

3. Set the bike down on the rear wheel.
4. As you let the bike drop down, pull the rear derailleur back with your right hand and pull the axle ends into the dropouts with your index fingers. Use your thumbs to push forward on the rear dropouts, which should now slide over the axle ends. (If the axle does not slip into the dropouts, you may need to spread the dropouts apart or squeeze them toward each other as you pull the wheel in.)
5. Check that the axle is fully seated in the dropouts, which should result in the wheel's being centered between the brake pads. If it is not, hold the rim in a centered position as you secure the axle. This procedure should not be necessary if the wheel and frame are straight and the brakes are centered.
6. Tighten the quick-release skewer, bolt-on skewer, or axle nuts as explained for the front wheel.
7. Reconnect the rear brake as explained above for the front wheel.

That's it. Go ride your bike.

v-12 **INSTALLING THE REAR WHEEL INTO REAR-ENTRY DROPOUTS**

Installing the wheel is the reverse of the removal procedure.

1. While still holding the chain off to the side as you did in §v-10, put the wheel straight into the rear-entry dropouts (Fig. 5.7). Slide it forward until it hits the front of the dropout.

2. Tighten the quick-release to lock the wheel in place.

3. Check to see if the wheel is centered in the chain-stays and rear brake. If the wheel is dished correctly and the frame is straight, the wheel should be centered in the frame. If it's not, loosen the quick-release and recenter the wheel.

    Many bikes with rear-entry dropouts have adjusters to set the depth for the axle. Use these to center the wheel.

    Cervélo aero bikes, for instance, have screws in the ends of the dropout slots. Remove the wheels and turn one or both of the screws as needed to center the wheel or to adjust its depth into the dropout to get the clearance you want between the tire and seat tube.

    BMC aero bikes have a little knurled dial in a hole in the dropout ahead of the end of the slot that works similarly to the barrel adjuster dial on the brake in Figure 10.2. With this system, you need not remove the wheel; just open the quick-release to release the wheel and turn one or both of the adjuster dials as desired to center or vary the depth of insertion of the wheel.

4. Grab the chain, pull it backward slightly, and put it back onto the small cog. Retighten the skewer.

5. Close the rear brake quick-release (as in §v-8), operate the rear brake several times to be sure the wheel is centered between the pads, and also pedal the bike in the stand and shift the rear derailleur to ensure that the shifting is normal.

v-13 **CLEANING YOUR BICYCLE**

Most cleaning can be done with soap, water, and a brush. Soap and water are easier on you and the earth than strong solvents, which are generally only needed to clean the drivetrain, if at all.

Avoid using high-pressure car washes to clean your bike. The soap is corrosive, and the high pressure forces it into bearings and frame tubes, causing extensive damage over time. If for some reason you do use a pressure washer, never point it toward the side of the bike, which can blow the bearing seals inward; instead, always point it in the plane of the bike.

The best way to set up your bike for cleaning is to put it in a bike stand. In the absence of a stand, you can hang the bike from a garage ceiling with rope. No good? Turn it upside down so it rests on the saddle and handlebar. Alternatively, you can remove the front wheel and stand the bike on the fork and handlebar, but you'll need to lean it against something, or it will pivot around its headset.

1. The wheels can be cleaned on the bike. Remove the wheels to clean the frame, fork, and components.

2. After you've removed the rear wheel, if the bike has a chain hanger (a little nub attached to the inner side of the right seatstay, a few centimeters above the dropout), hook the chain over it. If not, pull the chain back over a dowel rod (Fig. 5.8) or an old rear hub secured in the dropouts.

3. Fill a bucket with hot water and dish soap. With a stiff nylon bristle brush, scrub the entire bike and wheels. Wash the frame first, and leave the chain, cogs, chainrings, and derailleurs for last.

INSTALLING
THE REAR WHEEL
INTO REAR-ENTRY
DROPOUTS

CLEANING YOUR
BICYCLE

BASIC STUFF

5.8 **Loop the chain over a dowel rod for cleaning**

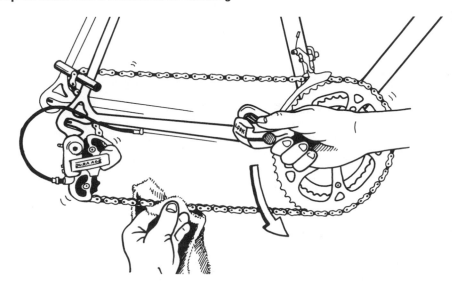

4. Rinse the bike with water from a hose (low pressure) or wipe it with a wet rag. Avoid getting water in the bearings of the bottom bracket, headset, pedals, or hubs. Note that most metal frames and forks have tiny vent holes in the tubes; these were drilled at the factory to allow hot air to escape during welding. The holes are often open to the outside on the seatstays, fork legs, chainstays, and seatstay and chainstay bridges. Avoid getting water in these holes. A piece of tape over the vent holes is a good idea, and leaving the holes permanently taped to keep water out is even better.

v-14 CLEANING THE DRIVETRAIN

The drivetrain consists of an oil-covered chain running over gears and through derailleurs. Sounds messy, doesn't it? Well, it is. In fact, because the whole affair is generally exposed to the elements, it inevitably picks up lots of dirt.

The drivetrain is what transfers your energy into the bike's forward motion, which means that you should clean and lubricate it frequently to keep it rolling well and to extend the life of your bike.

Fortunately, the drivetrain rarely needs to be completely disassembled for intensive cleaning. Regular maintenance can be confined to wiping down the chain, derailleur pulleys, and chainrings with a dry rag. I recommend wearing rubber dish gloves to keep your hands clean during this job.

1. To wipe the chain, turn the cranks while holding a rag in your hand and grabbing the chain (Fig. 5.8).

2. Holding a rag, squeeze the teeth of the jockey wheels between your index finger and thumb as you turn the cranks (Fig. 5.9). This procedure will remove grease and dirt that has built up on the jockey wheels.

3. Slip a rag between each pair of rear cogs and work it back and forth until each cog is clean (Fig. 5.10).

4. Wipe down the derailleurs and the front chainrings with the rag.

The chain will last much longer if you perform this sort of quick cleaning regularly, followed by lubricating it lightly and wiping it down again with a clean rag after that (to lubricate, drip one drop of chain oil onto each chain roller from a squeeze bottle). You will also be able

5.9 Cleaning jockey wheels

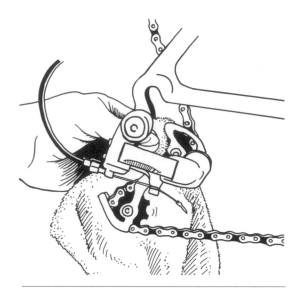

5.10 Cogset cleaning

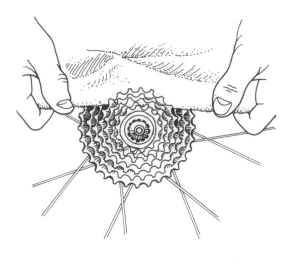

5.11 Solvent cleaning of the chain

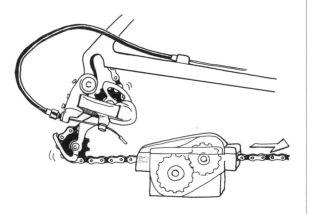

to skip the heavy-duty solvent cleanings that become necessary when the chain and cogs get really grungy.

You can also remove packed-up road grit from derailleurs and cogs with the soapy water and scrub brush. Note, however, that the soap will not dissolve the dirty lubricant that is all over the drivetrain; instead, the brush will smear it all over the bike if you're not careful. To avoid this, use a different brush than the one you use for cleaning the frame. Follow the drivetrain cleanup with a cloth wipe down.

v-15 CLEANING THE CHAIN WITH SOLVENT

When a chain gets really dirty, it must be immersed in solvent—a nasty task you can avoid by performing the regular maintenance just described. In fact, if you are sparing with the chain lube—if you only drip it on the chain rollers where it is needed rather than spraying it all over the chain—you can minimize, if not avoid, the need for solvent cleaning with its associated disposal and toxicity problems.

If you cannot avoid using a solvent, work in a well-ventilated area, use as little solvent as necessary, and

pick an environmentally friendly mixture. There are many citrus-based solvents on the market that will reduce the danger to your lungs and skin and pose less of a disposal problem. If you are using a lot of solvents, organic ones such as diesel fuel can be recycled, which may be preferable to using citrus solvents, as long as you protect yourself from the fumes with a respirator. All solvents suck the oils from your skin, so be sure to wear rubber gloves, even with green solvents.

A self-contained chain cleaner, which is a rectangular box with internal brushes and a solvent bath, is a convenient way to clean a chain (Fig. 5.11), but it may

CLEANING THE
CHAIN WITH
SOLVENT

•

GENERAL GUIDE
TO PERFORMING
MECHANICAL
WORK

not clean well deep inside the rollers. A nylon brush or a toothbrush dipped in solvent is good for cleaning cogs, pulleys, and chainrings, and it can be used for a quick cleanup of the chain as well. To clean a chain thoroughly, though, you must remove it and soak it in a solvent bath. Unfortunately modern ten-speed and even nine-speed chains don't allow this approach, because each chain rivet is so short that it can pop out of a hole enlarged by removal and reinstallation of the rivet. That said, chains with master links, which are available for all chains, can be removed for cleaning without being damaged.

1. Follow the directions in §vii-7 for removing the chain.

2. Put the chain in an old water bottle about one-quarter full of solvent.

3. Shake the bottle vigorously to clean the chain. Hold the bottle close to the ground and away from your eyes, in case it leaks.

4. Hang the chain to dry completely, especially inside the rollers.

5. Install the chain on the bike, following the directions in Chapter 7, §vii-8–§vii-12.

6. Drip chain lubricant into each of the chain's links and rollers as you turn the cranks to move the chain past the drip bottle. Drip lube on the moving chain by gently squeezing the bottle with the tip on each top edge of the chain (Fig. 5.12) for a couple of turns of the crank on each side.

7. Lightly wipe down the chain with a clean rag to remove excess lubricant on the outside, where it is not needed.

8. After this sorry episode is concluded, wipe the chain and lubricate it after every ride to avoid another visit to solvent city. Keep dish gloves by your bike so you can do it quickly on your return

5.12 Drip oil where it is needed

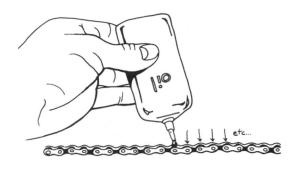

from a ride without having to scrub dirty oil off your hands later.

You can reuse much of the solvent by allowing it to stand in a container over a period of days or weeks. Decant and save the clear stuff and dispose of the settled sludge.

v-16 A GENERAL GUIDE TO PERFORMING MECHANICAL WORK

a. Threaded parts

All threads must be prepared (or, in mechanic's lingo, "prepped") before tightening. Depending on the bolt in question (see descriptions in the following list), prep with lubricant, threadlock compound, or anti-seize compound. Clean off excess thread-prepping compound to minimize dirt attraction.

1. Lubricated threads. Most threads should be lubricated with grease or oil. If a bolt is already installed, you can back it out, drip a little chain lube on it, and retighten. Bolts that appreciate lubrication include crank bolts, pedal axles, cleat bolts on shoes, derailleur- and brake-cable anchor bolts, and control-lever mounting bolts.

2. Locked threads. Some threads need to be locked to be kept from vibrating loose; these are bolts that need to stay in place but are not tightened down fully for some reason, usually to avoid seiz-

ing a moving part, throwing a part out of adjustment, or stripping threads in a soft material. Examples include derailleur limit screws, jockey-wheel center bolts, brake-mounting bolts, and spoke nipples. Use Loctite, Finish Line Threadlock, or the equivalent on bolts; use Wheelsmith Spoke-Prep or the equivalent on spokes.

3. Antiseize threads. Some threads have a tendency to bind up and gall, making full tightening as well as extraction problematic. They need antiseize compound to prevent galling. Any steel or aluminum bolt threaded into a titanium part (this statement includes any parts mounted to titanium frames, like bottom-bracket cups), and any titanium bolt threaded into a steel or aluminum part, must be coated with antiseize compound. Use Finish Line Ti-Prep or the equivalent.

CAUTIONARY NOTE: *Never thread a titanium bolt into a titanium part; even with the use of antiseize compound, these will almost certainly gall and rip apart when you try to remove them. If you must break this rule, use a liberal coating of antiseize compound on the threads, and every six months or so unscrew the bolt, clean it, and reapply the compound.*

Wrenches (see Fig. 5.13 for various types) must be fully engaged before tightening or loosening.

1. Hex keys and TORX wrenches must be fully inserted into the bolt head, or the wrench and/or bolt hole will round off. Shallow bolt heads, such as those used on shoe-cleat bolts, are especially susceptible, so be careful. And be sure to clean dirt and rocks out of bolt heads to get the hex key in all of the way.

2. Open-end, box-end, and socket wrenches must be properly seated around hex bolts, or they will round off. Triathlon bikes employ lots of

5.13 Types of wrenches

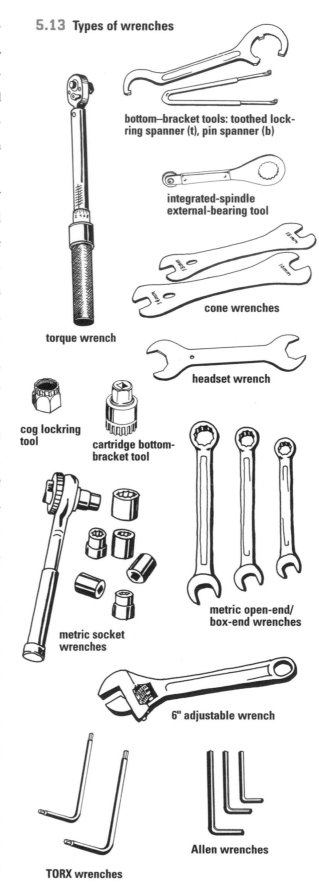

bottom–bracket tools: toothed lock-ring spanner (t), pin spanner (b)

integrated-spindle external-bearing tool

cone wrenches

torque wrench

headset wrench

cog lockring tool

cartridge bottom-bracket tool

metric open-end/box-end wrenches

metric socket wrenches

6" adjustable wrench

TORX wrenches

Allen wrenches

BASIC STUFF

wonderfully light but very soft aluminum nuts and bolts in the headset, brakes, and cranks that are easily damaged by a bad wrench fit.

3. Splined wrenches must be fully engaged; if they are not, the splines will be damaged or the tool will snap. Be especially careful when removing a cassette lockring; if you strip the splines, you've got a real problem on your hands.

4. Toothed-lockring spanners need to stay aligned on the lockring. If the teeth slide off, they will not only tear up the lockring but also damage the frame paint. Bottom-bracket adjustable cups are especially at risk here.

5. Pin spanners need to be fully seated in the holes to prevent their slipping out and damaging the holes in the part. You will find holes for a pin spanner in some bottom-bracket adjustable cups, hub-adjustment collars, and crank-bolt collars.

b. Tightening torque

The designation *M* in front of a bolt size number means millimeters and refers to the bolt shaft, not to the hex key that turns it. An M5 bolt, for example, is 5mm in diameter, an M6 is 6mm, and so on, but the M designation may not have any relationship to the wrench size. For instance, an M5 bolt usually takes a 4mm hex key (or in the case of a hex-head style, an 8mm box-end or socket wrench). However, M5 bolts on bicycles often accept different wrench sizes than are normally used on M5 bolts. Bolts that attach bottle cages to the frame are M5, and although some accept the normal 4mm hex key, many have a rounded "cap" head and take a 3mm hex key. The bolts that clamp a front derailleur around the seat tube or that anchor the cable on a front or rear derailleur are also M5, but they take a hex key size that is bigger than standard, namely 5mm. And when you get to the big single-

pinch bolts found on old stems, you find lots of different bolt sizes (M6, M7, and even M8), but usually only one wrench size (6mm hex key).

Generally, tightness can be classified in four levels:

1. Snug (10–30 in-lbs, or 1–3 N·m [Newton-meters in SI units]): Small setscrews (such as computer-magnet mounting screws), bearing preload bolts (such as on an Aheadset top cap), and screws going into plastic parts need to be snug.

2. Firmly tightened (30–80 in-lbs, or 3–9 N·m): Small bolts, often M5 size, such as shoe-cleat bolts, cable anchor bolts on brakes and derailleurs, small (M5) stem bolts, and brake-lever-clamp bolts need to be firmly tightened.

3. Tight (80–240 in-lbs, or 9–27 N·m): Wheel axles, old-style single-bolt stem bolts (M6, M7, or M8) and stem-quill wedge bolts, brake-caliper mounting bolts, seatpost binder bolts, and seatpost saddle-rail clamp bolts need to be tight.

4. Really tight (300–600 in-lbs, or 31–68 N·m): Crankarm bolts, cassette lockring bolts, and bottom-bracket cups need to be really tight.

A full list of tightening torques for bike components by brand and model can be found in Appendix C.

c. Cleanliness

1. Indiscriminately squirting or slathering lubricant on bike parts will not make them work better, no matter how good your intentions. The lube will pick up lots of dirt and get very gunky, and the grit in the gunk will chew up your expensive components.

2. Do not expect parts to work if you wash them without lubricating them. They will get dry and squeaky.

d. Test riding

Always ride the bike—slowly at first and then harder—after adjusting in the bike stand. Parts behave differently under load.

EMERGENCY REPAIRS

Eat a live toad first thing in the morning and nothing worse will happen to you the rest of the day.
—Anonymous

TOOLS

take-along tool kit shown in Figures 4.4 and 4.5—and Figure 4.6, too, for longer tours

If you ride your bike any distance from home, sooner or later you will encounter a situation that has the potential to turn into an emergency. The best way to avoid an unpleasant surprise is to plan ahead and be prepared before it happens. Proper planning involves carrying a few tools, spare tubes, food, and extra clothes. And acquiring a little knowledge.

This chapter will acquaint you with ways to deal with most emergencies, whether you have all the tools you need or not. A problem will usually involve only one component on the bike, for example, a flat tire or a broken derailleur cable, and in most cases an easy work-around will get you home. True, you always have the option of walking, but this chapter will help you avoid that miserable fate.

Incidentally, a cell phone (or at least some change for a pay phone) is worth carrying on long solo rides, in case you have a major breakdown. Bottle-shaped cases are available that allow you to keep your phone in one of your water bottle cages.

On the other hand, you may find yourself with a perfectly functioning bicycle and a fully charged phone—and be lost, cold, dehydrated, bonking (i.e., your body has run out of fuel), or injured. Read the final part of this chapter for pointers on how to avoid breakdowns and what to do if the worst does happen.

vi-1 RECOMMENDED TOOLS

The take-along tool kit for your seat bag is described in §iv-4. If you're going to be a long way from civilization, take along the extra tools recommended for longer trips.

vi-2 FLAT TIRE PREVENTION

The best way to avoid flats is to keep good tires on your bike. Check them regularly for wear, cracking, and tread cuts, and replace any questionable tires. Steer clear of potholes, broken glass, and nails (as if!), and you'll rarely have a problem.

Flat tires can be minimized with the use of tire sealants and thorn-proof inner tubes, but the extra rotating weight of either is unpopular with most triathletes.

vi-3 FIXING FLAT TIRES

a. If you have a spare or a patch kit

Simple flat tires are easy to deal with. If your bike has tubular tires, peel off the old tubular (§ix-7) and install your spare (§ix-9). For clincher tires, the first flat you get on a ride is most easily fixed by installing your spare tube (§ix-1–§ix-5). Make sure you remove whatever caused the flat (you'll probably see it sticking up from the tread), and feel around inside the tire for other sharp objects.

If you can't find a thorn, nail, piece of glass, or the like in the tire or tube, check the rim to see whether the flat was caused by a protruding spoke or nipple, a metal shard from the rim, or the edge of a spoke hole protruding through a worn rim strip. The rim strip is the piece of plastic or rubber that covers the spoke holes in the well of the rim. Many rim strips are too narrow or prone to cracking or tearing. Also, metal hunks left from the drilling of rims during manufacture can work their way out into the tube.

Flats from these sources are so common that I recommend removing the tires and tubes from a new bike and checking the rims before you ride it. Shake out any metal fragments that may be present. If the rim strips consist of limp, narrow strips of soft rubber or cloth, replace them with high-quality plastic or adhesive cotton rim strips, or apply a couple of layers of reinforced packing tape (the kind that has lengthwise fibers inside) to cover the spoke holes in place of the rim strips.

After you run out of spare tubes, you must patch additional flats, covered in §ix-2–§ix-4 for clinchers; for tubulars, see §ix-10.

6.1 Fixing torn tire casing (temporarily)

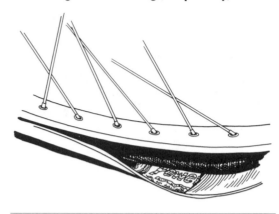

b. Torn sidewall

Rocks and glass can cut tire sidewalls. The likelihood of sidewall problems is reduced if you avoid riding on tires with rotten, weak cords. If the sidewall is torn or cut, the tube will stick out. Just patching or replacing the tube won't solve the problem. Without reinforcement, your tube will blow out again very soon.

First, you have to look for something to reinforce the tire sidewall (Fig. 6.1). Dollar bills work well as tire boots. The paper is strong and should hold for the rest of the ride if you are careful. (Credit cards are not acceptable for this purpose.) Business cards are small but work better than nothing. You might even try an energy bar wrapper or a piece of a plastic soda bottle. A small piece of lawn chair webbing cut in an oval shape might be a good addition to your patch kit for this purpose. You get the idea.

1. Lay the cash down inside the tire over the gash, or wrap it around the tube at that spot. Place several layers between the tire and tube to support the tube and prevent it from bulging out through the hole in the sidewall.

2. Put a little air in the tube to hold the makeshift reinforcement in place.

3. Mount the tire bead on the rim. You may need to let a little air out of the tube to do so.

4. After making sure that the tire is seated and the boot is still in place, inflate the tube to about 75psi, if you are good at estimating without a gauge. Pressures lower than this will allow the boot to move around and may also lead to a pinch flat if you cross a train track.

Check the boot periodically on the ride home to make certain that the tube is not bulging out again.

c. No more spare tubes or patches

Now comes the frustrating part: You have run out of spare tubes and have used up all of your patches (or your CO_2 cartridge is empty and you don't have a pump), and still you have a flat tire. The situation is obvious: You are going to have to ride home without air in the tire.

Riding a flat for a long way will destroy the tire and probably damage the rim. You can minimize that damage by filling the space in the tire with grass, leaves, or similar materials. Pack the stuff in tightly and then remount the tire on the rim. This "fix" should make the ride a little less dangerous by minimizing the flat tire's tendency to roll out from under the bike during a turn.

vi-4 JAMMED CHAIN

When the chain gets jammed between the chainrings and the chainstay, it can be difficult to extract. You tug and tug on the chain, and it won't come out. Chainrings are flexible, however, and if you apply some mechanical advantage, the chain will come free quite easily.

Insert a screwdriver or similar thin lever between the chainring and the chainstay, and pry the space open while pulling the chain out (Fig. 6.2). You will probably be amazed at how easy this operation is, especially when hard tugging would not free the chain.

6.2 Freeing jammed chain

6.3 Fixing broken chain

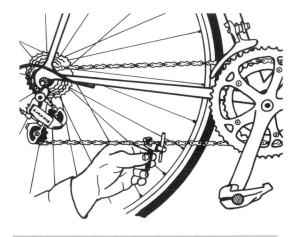

If you still cannot free the chain, however, disassemble the chain with a chain tool (Fig. 6.3, §vii-7), pull it out, and put it back together (§vii-9–§vii-11).

vi-5 BROKEN CHAIN

Although chains rarely used to break, this problem has become more common since the advent of supernarrow ten-speed chains. Any chain weakness is compounded by a bad cogset that causes the chain to skip. The chain "breaks" when a chain plate pops off the end of a rivet. As the chain rips apart, it can cause collateral damage as well. The open chain plate can snag the front-derailleur cage, bending it or tearing it off, or it can jam into the rear dropout.

EMERGENCY REPAIRS

When a chain breaks, the end link is shot, and some others in the area may be goners as well. A broken ten-speed chain is irreparable for further long-term use, but you can often repair it enough to ride home very carefully, pedaling gingerly.

1. Remove the damaged links with the chain tool (Fig. 6.3). (You or your riding partner did remember to bring a chain tool, right?) Again, the procedures for removing the damaged links and reinstalling the chain are covered in Chapter 7, §vii-7–§vii-11.

2. If you have brought along extra chain links, replace the same number you remove. If not, you'll need to use the chain in its shortened state; it will still work, but you probably won't be able to use the largest cogs when the chain is on the big chainring.

3. Join the ends and connect the chain (Fig. 6.3); the procedure is described in Chapter 7, §vii-9 and §vii-10. Some lightweight chain tools and multitools are more difficult to use than a shop chain tool. Some flex so badly that it is hard to keep the pushrod lined up with the rivet. Others pinch the plates so tightly that the chain link binds up. It's a good idea to try out the tool in the comfort of your shop before you need it on the road.

vi-6 BENT WHEEL

If the rim is banging against the brake pads—or worse yet, the frame or fork—pedaling becomes difficult. If you haven't hit a pothole or something similar that has bent the rim, the cause is probably a loose or broken spoke. Another culprit could be a broken rim, although that is fairly rare, even with ultra lightweight tubular wheels.

vi-7 LOOSE SPOKES

If a spoke loosens, the rim will wobble badly.

1. Find the loose spoke (or spokes) by feeling all of them. The really loose ones, which would cause a wobble of large magnitude, will be obvious. If you find a broken spoke, skip to the next section (§vi-8). If you find no loose or broken spokes, skip ahead to §vi-10.

2. Get out the spoke wrench that you carry for such an eventuality. If you don't have one, skip to §vi-9.

3. Mark the loose spokes, if necessary, by tying blades of grass, sandwich bag twist-ties, tape, or the like around them.

4. Tighten the loose spokes (Fig. 6.4) and true the wheel, following the procedures in §ix-12.

vi-8 BROKEN SPOKES

If a spoke breaks, the wheel will wobble wildly.

1. Locate the broken spoke.

2. Remove the remainders of the spoke, both the piece going through the hub and the piece threaded into the nipple. If the broken spoke is on the freewheel side of the rear wheel, you may not be able to remove it from the hub, because it will be behind the cogs. If so, skip to step 6 after wrapping the broken piece around neighboring spokes to prevent it from slapping around (Fig. 6.5).

3. Get out your spoke wrench. If you have no spoke wrench, skip to §vi-9.

4. If you brought along a spare spoke of the right length or the Kevlar replacement spoke mentioned in §iv-4c (Fig. 4.6), you're in business. If not, skip to step 6. Put the new spoke through the hub hole, weave it through the other spokes the same way the old one was, and thread it into the spoke nipple that is still sticking out of the rim. Mark it with

6.4 Spoke tightening and loosening

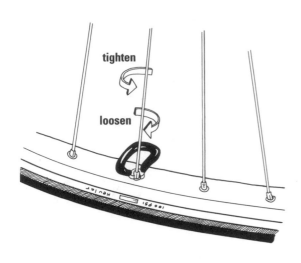

6.5 Wrapping a broken spoke

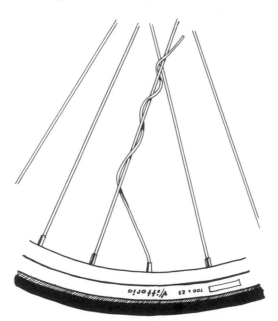

a pen or a blade of grass tied around it. With the Kevlar spoke, thread the Kevlar string through the hub hole, attach the ends to the enclosed stub of spoke, adjust the ends to length, tie them off, and tighten the spoke nipple.

5. Tighten the nipple on the new spoke with a spoke wrench (Fig. 6.4), checking the rim clearance with the brake pad as you go. Stop when the rim is reasonably straight, and finish your ride.

6. If you can't replace the spoke and you do have a spoke wrench, bring the wheel into rideable trueness by loosening the spoke on either side of the broken one. These two spokes come from the opposite side of the hub and will let the rim move toward the side with the broken spoke as they are loosened. A spoke nipple loosens counterclockwise when viewed from its top (see Fig. 6.4). Ride home conservatively, as this wheel will rapidly get worse.

7. Once at home, take the wheel to a bike shop for repair. If you break a spoke more than once on a wheel, have the wheel rebuilt with new spokes. The rim may need replacement as well.

vi-9 NO SPOKE WRENCH

If the rim is rubbing against the brake pads but the tire is not hitting the chainstays or fork blades, simply open the brake so that you can get home, as detailed here. If the tire is hitting the frame or fork, you may need more extreme measures to temporarily straighten it; see the next section.

1. Open the brake-caliper quick-release lever as far as necessary for the pads to clear the rim. The quick-release is mounted on the brake caliper at the cable, except on Campagnolo Ergopower, where it consists of a sliding pin mounted on the brake lever. If the pads still rub, loosen the brake-cable tension by screwing in (clockwise or

NO SPOKE
WRENCH

·

BENT RIM

·

DAMAGED FRONT
DERAILLEUR

counterclockwise, depending on type) the barrel adjuster on the caliper (Fig. 6.6). Remember that braking effectiveness on that wheel will be greatly reduced or nonexistent, so ride slowly and carefully.

2. If the rim is still rubbing the brakes and you have a wrench to loosen the brake cable (usually 5mm hex), do so, and then clamp it back down. You now have no brake on this wheel; ride carefully.

3. If this still does not cut it, you can disconnect the cable and remove the brake caliper from the fork or brake bridge, put it in your pocket, and pedal home slowly. You will usually need a 5mm hex key for this task.

vi-10 BENT RIM

If the rim is only mildly out of true and you brought a spoke wrench, you can fix it. Tighten the nipple of the spoke at the wobble (turn it clockwise as viewed from the top of the nipple).

If the wheel is really whacked out, spoke truing won't do much. To get the wheel to clear the brakes so that you can pedal home, follow the steps in §vi-9.

If the bent wheel won't turn even when the brake is removed, you can beat it straight as long as the rim is not broken.

1. Find the area that is bent outward the most and mark it.

2. Leaving the tire on and inflated, hold the wheel by its sides with the bent-outward part at the top facing away from you.

3. Smack the bent-outward section of the rim against flat ground (Fig. 6.7).

4. Put the wheel back in the frame or fork, and see if anything has changed.

6.6 Loosening the brake cable

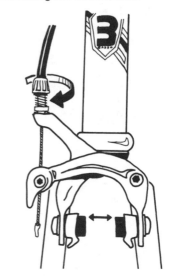

6.7 Fixing a bent rim

5. Repeat the process until the wheel can be ridden. You may be surprised how straight you can get a wheel in this way.

vi-11 DAMAGED FRONT DERAILLEUR

If the front derailleur is mildly bent, straighten it with your hands or leave it until you get home.

If the front derailleur has simply rotated around the seat tube or twisted in the tab it bolts to (see Fig. 6.8; the chain, your foot, or a pants leg can catch it and turn it), reposition it so that the cage is just above, and par-

6.8 Opening front-derailleur cage

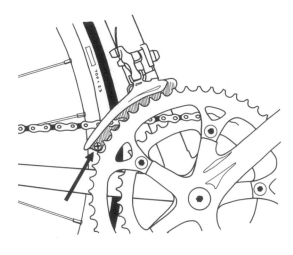

allel to, the chainrings. Tighten the derailleur in place (usually with a 5mm hex key).

If the derailleur is broken or is so bent that you can't ride, or if the mounting tab is bent, you will need to remove the derailleur or route the chain around it as described next. (If the tab is bent, trying to straighten it will either dent or crack the seat tube or cause a crack to form in the near future. You will need to have a frame builder remove the tab and put on a new one.)

a. If you have only a screwdriver

1. Get the chain out of the derailleur cage. To do this, open the cage by removing the screw at its tail (Fig. 6.8). If the cage can't be opened this way, you'll have to open the chain with a chain tool (see the next section).

2. Bypass the derailleur by putting the chain on a chainring that does not interfere with it (either shift the derailleur to the inside and put the chain on the big chainring, or vice versa).

b. If you have hex keys and a screwdriver (or a chain tool)

1. Remove the derailleur from the seat tube, usually with a 5mm hex key.

2. Remove the screw at the tail of the derailleur cage (Fig. 6.8) with a screwdriver, if it has one.

3. Pry the cage open and separate it from the chain. You can also disassemble the chain (Fig. 6.3), pull it out of the derailleur, and then reconnect it (§vii-7–§vii-12).

4. Put the chain on whichever chainring is most appropriate for the ride home. If in doubt, put it on the inner one (or middle one, if you have a triple).

5. Tie up the cable so that it won't catch in the front wheel.

6. Stuff the derailleur in your pocket and ride home.

vi-12 DAMAGED REAR DERAILLEUR

If the upper jockey wheel gets lost, put the lower one on top and thread a wire or zip-tie through three threaded Presta-valve collar nuts (off your inner tube valves) as a lower wheel. If one of the jockey-wheel bolts gets lost, and you found the jockey wheel, try replacing the bolt with one of the water-bottle-cage bolts. If the return spring on the rear-derailleur cage breaks, the chain will hang loosely. If you have a bungee cord, hook it to the lower cage, around the skewer (put the lever on the drive side), and up to the seat-tube bottle cage.

If the rear derailleur gets bent just a bit, you can probably straighten it enough to get home. If it is severely bent or broken or one of the jockey wheels falls off, you will need to bypass the derailleur, effectively turning your bike into a single-speed for the remainder of your ride (Fig. 6.9).

1. Separate the chain with a chain tool (§vii-7) and pull it out of the derailleur.

2. Pick a gear combination in which you think you can make it home and set the front derailleur over the chainring you have picked. Be aware that the

6.9 Bypassing a damaged rear derailleur

chain will tend to fall off the chainrings or move down to smaller cogs, unless it is really tight.

3. Wrap the chain over the chainring and the rear cog you have chosen, bypassing the rear derailleur entirely.

4. Remove any overlapping chain, making the chain as short as you can while still being able to connect the ends together.

5. Connect the chain with the chain tool as described in §vii-9–§vii-11.

6. Ride home.

vi-13 BROKEN FRONT-DERAILLEUR CABLE

The chain will be on the inner chainring, and you will still be able to use all of your rear cogs. Leave it on the inner ring and ride home.

vi-14 BROKEN REAR-DERAILLEUR CABLE

The chain will be on the smallest rear cog, and you will still be able to use both (or all three) front chainrings. You have three options:

1. Leave it on the small cog and ride home.

2. Move the chain to a larger cog, push inward on the derailleur with your hand, and tighten the high-end limit screw on the rear derailleur (usually the upper of the two screws) until it lines up with a larger cog (see Fig. 6.10). Move the chain to that cog and ride home. You may have to fine-tune the adjustment of the derailleur limit screw to get it to run quietly without skipping.

3. If you do not have a screwdriver, you can push inward on the rear derailleur while turning the crank with the rear wheel off the ground to shift

6.10 Tightening high-end limit screw

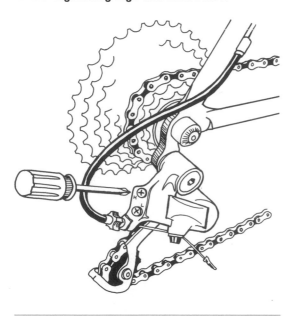

6.11 After breaking the cable, wedge the rear derailleur into an easier gear

to a larger cog. Jam a stick between the derailleur-cage plates to prevent the chain from moving back down to the small cog (Fig. 6.11).

vi-15 BROKEN BRAKE CABLE

Ride home slowly and carefully. Very slowly. Very carefully.

vi-16 BROKEN SEAT RAILS OR SEATPOST CLAMP

If you can't tape or tie the saddle back on, try wrapping your gloves or some clothing over the top of the seatpost to pad it. Otherwise, remove the seatpost and ride home standing up.

vi-17 BROKEN SEATPOST SHAFT

Ride home standing up.

vi-18 BROKEN HANDLEBAR

It's probably best to walk home (or phone home for a ride). You could splint it by jamming a stick inside, but the stick could easily break, leaving you with no way to control the bike. A sudden impact of your face with the road would follow.

If you decide to splint the handlebar, hold the pieces together with duct tape. If the break is adjacent the stem, slide the stem over the break so that both pieces are clamped.

vi-19 FROZEN PARTS

Riding in snow or freezing rain can freeze shift cables where they pass under the bottom bracket or can freeze the derailleurs themselves and fill the cogs you are not using with ice. You will just have to stay in the gear you are frozen in. But if the freehub mechanism freezes, you won't be able to coast at all. You may be able to free it by applying any hot liquid (even urine) and hitting the freehub with a stick until it rotates counterclockwise again.

vi-20 PREPARE FOR EVERY RIDE

1. Always take plenty of water.
2. Tell someone where you are going and when you expect to return. If someone goes missing, call the

police or sheriff, or see to it that someone gets an organized search under way.

3. Take extra food for any ride over an hour.

4. Take a road map if you don't know the area. Be willing to ask for directions.

5. Take a cell phone and/or change for a pay phone.

6. Take matches, extra clothing, and food, and perhaps a flashlight and an aluminized emergency blanket, in case you have to spend time huddled under a tree.

7. Ride carefully and attentively on wet roads, gravel-covered turns, and areas with lots of traffic, especially traffic turning into and out of side roads.

8. Wear a helmet. It's hard to ride home with a cracked skull.

9. Don't ride beyond your limits if you are a long way from home or civilization. Take a break. Get out of the hot sun. Avoid dehydration and bonking by drinking and eating enough.

10. Have your bike in good working order before you leave.

In short, make appropriate decisions when taking long rides. Prepare well. Even a $4,000 bike and safe, well-paved roads will not prevent mechanical problems or keep you from becoming exhausted, cold, bonked, injured, lost, or caught in the dark.

CHAINS

A chain is only as strong as its weakest link.
—Anonymous

A sausage is only as good as its last link.
—Bluto

TOOLS

chain lubricant
12-inch ruler
chain tool
lots of rags
rubber gloves

Optional

**solvent
(citrus-based)**
chain-cleaning tool
old water bottle
caliper
pliers
solvent tank
**chain-elongation
gauge**
**Rohloff cog-wear
indicator**

The bicycle chain is one of those wondrous technological breakthroughs that we take for granted, but without it a bike would be a clumsy and inefficient contraption. The chain is nothing more than a series of links connected by rivets (also called pins). Rollers surround each rivet between the link plates and engage the teeth of the cogs and chainrings. Nothing to it, and yet it is an efficient method of transmitting mechanical energy from the pedals to the rear wheel. In terms of weight, cost, and efficiency, the bicycle chain has no equal—and believe me, people have tried endlessly to improve upon it.

Perhaps because it is so simple and familiar, the chain is often ignored. To keep your bike running smoothly, though, you do have to pay attention to it. It needs to be kept clean and well lubricated in order to transfer your energy efficiently, shift smoothly, and operate noiselessly. Because its length increases as it wears, thus contacting gear teeth differently than intended, it needs to be replaced occasionally to pro-

long the working life of more expensive drivetrain components.

vii-1 LUBRICATION

For best results, use a lubricant intended for bicycle chains. Most lubes sold for this purpose work reasonably well for the basic task of keeping the chain protected and happy. However, I advise against wax-based lubricants as they don't lubricate under load. Chain life with them can be very short (1,000–1,500 miles).

If you want to get fancy, you can assess your riding conditions and choose specific lubricants. Dry lubricants are formulated to pick up less dirt in dry conditions. Sticky lubes are less prone to wash off in wet conditions. "Metal conditioners" penetrate and alter the surface of the metal. Pro Gold's Pro Link, a metal conditioner, gives me longer chain life in all riding conditions, with daily use, than anything else I have tried.

Lubricant companies usually advise against switching among types, and there is probably something to this from the standpoint of maintaining particular properties. Once you start using a "dry" lube, for example, it's best to stick with it if most of your riding calls for that type of stuff (remember—don't use wax-based lubes!). But the main thing is to take care of the chain regularly. If that means using a different brand of oil from time to time, due to travel or changing weather, so be it.

Chain lubes are generally sold in spray cans and bottles. Avoid sprays for regular maintenance chores because they tend to spew oil over everything. The chain only needs a reservoir of oil inside each link; on the outside, a thin film is sufficient to keep corrosion at bay. More oil on the outside will only attract dirt and gunk; it does nothing to improve the function of the chain.

1. Drip a small amount of lubricant across each roller from the inside out (Fig. 7.1), periodically moving the chain to give easy access to the links you are working on. One drop on each roller is usually sufficient. If you're in a hurry, you can turn the crank slowly while dripping lubricant onto the chain as it goes by, but this method will cause you to apply too much lubricant, which picks up more dirt. Most of us don't have the time or patience to lubricate each roller on a daily basis, so don't sweat it. Overlubricating is preferable to not lubricating.

2. Wipe the chain off lightly with a clean rag to remove excess oil.

3. If you want to do a champion job, perform this task at night, before putting the bike to bed, and then wipe the chain clean again the next morning or before the next ride. That way, you'll remove additional oil that has seeped onto the outside of the links, where it isn't needed.

7.1 Dripping oil only where it is needed

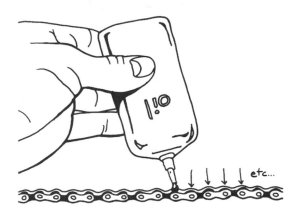

If you're riding in wet conditions, you'll need to apply lubricant frequently (after every ride or several times during a long, rainy ride). The lubricant for wet conditions is thick and sticky, since it needs to adhere well to the chain and not be easily washed off. For dry conditions, a smaller amount of a lubricant that does not pick up dirt is preferable.

vii-2 CLEANING BY FREQUENT WIPING AND LUBRICATION

The simplest way to maintain a chain is to wipe it down frequently and then lubricate it. If you follow this scheme prior to every ride, you will never need to clean your chain with a solvent. The lubricant softens the old sludge buildup, which is driven out of the chain when you ride.

The problem, you're undoubtedly eager to point out, is that the fresh lubricant also picks up new dirt and grime. But if this gunk is wiped off before it is driven deep into the chain and the chain is relubricated frequently, it will stay relatively clean as well as sup-

7.2 Wiping chain

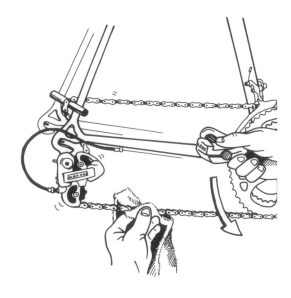

CLEANING BY
FREQUENT
WIPING AND
LUBRICATION

·

USING CHAIN-
CLEANING UNITS

GALE BERNHARDT'S DRIVETRAIN MAINTENANCE TIP

I give my bike chain a quick wipe and light lube before each ride. This method keeps the chain well lubricated and much cleaner than waiting to clean the chain once every month or so.

—*Gale Bernhardt*

USA Olympic Triathlon and

World Championship coach, and author of

Training Plans for Multisport Athletes,

Triathlon Training Basics, and

The Female Cyclist: Gearing Up a Level

ple. Chain cleaning can be performed with the bike standing on the ground or in a bike stand.

1. With a rag in your hand, grasp the lower length of the chain (between the bottom of the chainring and the lower jockey wheel of the rear derailleur).

2. Turn the crank backward a number of revolutions, pulling the chain through the rag (Fig. 7.2). Periodically rotate the rag to present a clean section of it to the chain.

3. Lubricate each chain roller carefully as in Figure 7.1, or take the faster method of running the chain past the dripping bottle tip.

To simplify this procedure, I recommend storing a pair of rubber gloves, a rag, and some chain lube next to your bike. Whenever you return from a ride, put on the gloves, wipe and lube the chain, and put your bike away. It takes maybe a minute, your hands stay clean, and your bike is ready for the next ride. Wipe the chainrings, cogs, front derailleur, and jockey wheels while you're at it, and the entire drivetrain will always work ideally.

vii-3 USING CHAIN-CLEANING UNITS

Several companies make chain-cleaning gizmos that scrub the chain with solvent while the chain is in place on the bike. These chain cleaners are generally made of clear plastic and have two or three rotating brushes that scrub the chain as it moves through the solvent bath (Fig. 7.3). They offer the advantage of cleaning the chain without removing it from the bike; regularly removing the chain is a pain and shortens its life.

Most chain cleaners come with a nontoxic, citrus-based solvent. For your safety and other environmental reasons, I strongly recommend that you purchase nontoxic citrus solvents for your chain cleaner if the unit came with a petroleum-based solvent. If you recycle used diesel fuel, you can use it instead. In either case, wear gloves and glasses when using any sort of solvent, citrus- or petroleum-based. Citrus-based chain solvents often contain some lubricants to avoid drying the chain excessively. The lubricant carried with the solvent is one reason diesel fuel used to have such

7.3 Chain cleaning on the bike

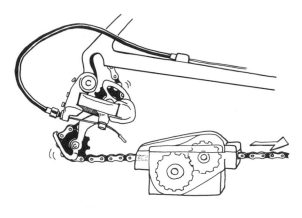

a following as a chain cleaner. A really strong solvent without lubricant (acetone, for example) will displace the oil from inside the rollers. It will then evaporate, leaving a dry, squeaking chain that is hard to rehabilitate. The same thing can happen with a citrus-based solvent without an included lubricant, especially if the chain is not allowed to dry sufficiently before it is relubricated.

To clean a chain with a chain-cleaning unit:

1. Remove the top of the chain cleaner case and pour in solvent to the fill line.

2. Place the unit against the bottom of the chain and reinstall the top of the unit so that the chain runs through it (Fig. 7.3).

3. Turn the bike's crank backward.

4. Remove the unit, wipe off the chain with a clean cloth, and let it dry.

5. Lubricate the chain as described in §vii-1.

6. Pour the solvent into a jar and let it settle for a few days. Decant the solvent, reserving it for future use, and discard the dregs in the jar.

vii-4 REMOVAL AND CLEANING

You can also clean the chain by removing it from the bicycle and cleaning it in a solvent. I do not recommend this approach unless your chain has a master link, since repeated disassembly by pushing rivets in and out weakens the chain.

Chain disassembly and reassembly also expands the size of the rivet hole where you put it together, allowing the rivet to pop out more easily. Shimano supplies two special "subpins" for reassembly of its chains that are meant to prevent this problem. Campagnolo supplies only one, making removal and reinstallation impossible.

A hand-opened "master link" allows you to avoid weakening the chain. Master links are standard on Wippermann and Taya chains, many KMC chains, and on Sachs and SRAM chains of 1998 and beyond. The aftermarket "Super Link" or any of the brand-name master links can be installed into any chain, as long as the master link is of the right width.

If you disassemble the chain to clean it (see §vii-7 for instructions), just drop it into an old jar or water bottle half filled with solvent and then agitate. Using an old water bottle or jar allows you to clean the chain without touching or breathing the solvent—something to be avoided even with citrus solvents.

Here's the procedure for cleaning the chain if you don't want to use a chain-cleaning unit:

1. Remove the chain from the bike (§vii-7).

2. Drop it in a water bottle or jar.

3. Pour in enough solvent to cover the chain.

4. Shake the bottle vigorously (low to the ground and away from your eyes, in case the top pops off).

5. Hang the chain to air dry.

6. Reassemble it on the bike (see §vii-8–§vii-11).

7. Lubricate it as described in §vii-1.

7.4 Checking chain wear

REMOVAL AND

CLEANING

○

CHAIN

REPLACEMENT

○

CHECKING

FOR CHAIN

ELONGATION

Allow the solvent in the bottle to stand for a few days so that you can decant the clear stuff and use it again. I'll say it again: it is important to use a citrus-based solvent. It is not only safer for the environment, it is gentler on your skin and less harmful to breathe. Wear rubber gloves when working with any solvent, and use a respirator meant for volatile organic compounds if you are not using a citrus-based solvent. There is no sense in fixing your bike so that it goes faster if you end up becoming a sickly rider.

vii-5 CHAIN REPLACEMENT

As the rollers, pins, and plates wear out, the chain lengthens. That in turn will hasten wear and tear on the other parts of the drivetrain. An elongated chain (see §vii-6) will concentrate the load on each individual gear tooth rather than distributing it over all of the teeth that the chain contacts. The concentrated load will cause the gear teeth to become hook-shaped and the tooth valleys to become wider.

If such wear has already occurred, a new chain will not solve the problem. A new chain will not mesh with deformed teeth, and it is likely to skip whenever you pedal hard. The only cure is to replace the chain, the chainrings, and the rear cogset. Before extra wear and tear takes place, get in the habit of checking the chain on a regular basis (§vii-6) and replacing it as needed.

Chain life varies, depending on chain type, maintenance, riding conditions, and strength and weight of the rider. As a ballpark number, figure on replacing the chain every 1,000–1,500 miles if the bike is ridden in dirty conditions or with infrequent lubrication (or with wax-based lubricants) by a heavy rider. Lighter riders on clean, dry roads can extend the replacement time to 2,000–3,000 miles with poor maintenance and up to 5,000 miles with daily lubrication with a good lube.

vii-6 CHECKING FOR CHAIN ELONGATION

The most reliable way to see whether the chain is worn out is to employ a chain-elongation gauge, such as the model made by Rohloff (Fig. 7.4). If the chain is shot, the indicator's curved tooth falls completely into the chain. If it is still in good shape, the tooth will not go all of the way in. Use the tooth marked "S" for steel cogs and the tooth marked "A" for aluminum and titanium cogs. Park, Wippermann, Pro Gold, Bicicletta, and other companies offer similar chain-elongation gauges.

Another way to measure for elongation is with an accurate ruler. Bicycle chains are on an inch standard, and they measure a half inch between adjacent rivets. There should be exactly 12 links in one foot, where each complete link consists of an inner and outer pair of plates (Fig. 7.5).

CHAINS

7.5 One complete chain link

1. Set one end of the ruler on a rivet edge and measure to the rivet edge at the other end of the ruler.

2. The distance between these rivets should be 12 inches exactly. If it is 12⅛ inches or greater, replace the chain; if it is 12¹⁄₁₆ inches or more, it is a good idea to replace it (and a necessity to do so if you have any titanium or aluminum cogs or an 11-tooth small cog).

Chain manufacturer SRAM recommends replacement if elongation is 1 percent, or ½ inch in 100 links (50 inches). If the chain is off the bike, you can hang it next to a new chain; if it is more than a half link longer for the same number of links, replace it.

If you always replace the chain as soon as it becomes elongated beyond spec, as indicated by a chain-elongation gauge, you will replace three to four chains before needing to change the cogs, a big cost savings in the long run.

vii-7 CHAIN OPENING

The following procedure applies to all new derailleur chains and to shortening them to the correct length for your bike's specific drivetrain. It also applies to removing a chain from a bike, except for those chains with a "master link" that can be opened by hand, without a chain tool (see Figs. 7.21–23). Chains equipped with master links include all Wippermann, Taya, SRAM, KMC, and late "Power Link"–equipped Sachs chains, and chains with the "Super Link"; all

7.6 Pushing out the pin (link rivet)

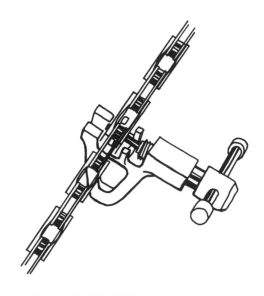

of these chains snap open by hand at the master link (see §vii-12), although they can also be opened at any other link with a chain tool, as described next. Current SRAM ten-speed chains and old Campagnolo ten-speed chains have a master link that cannot be opened, so while you separate those chains at a different link like any other chain, they can't be used again (see §vii-11).

1. Place any link over the back teeth on a chain tool (Fig. 7.6).

2. For most chains, tighten the chain-tool handle clockwise to push the pin almost all the way out. Be careful to leave a millimeter or so of pin protruding inward from the chain plate to hook the chain back together when reassembling. However, if you have a chain with a master link or a Shimano or Campagnolo chain and a new connecting pin for it, drive the pin all the way out.

3. Separate the chain by flexing it away from the pushed-out pin if you left the stub in. If you pushed the pin all of the way out, the two ends will just pull apart.

Incidentally, removing the chain from the bike creates an ideal opportunity to check the rear-derailleur limit-screw adjustment. The derailleur limit screws are the marshals that keep the derailleur from moving too far at the travel extremes—keep it, in other words, from shifting into the spokes or throwing the chain into the dropout; see Chapter 8, §viii-2, and Figs. 8.2, 8.4, and 8.5.

To check the limit adjustments with the chain out of the way, shift the derailleur to high gear (Fig. 8.4) and, while looking at the derailleur from the rear, see whether the jockey wheel in the cage is aligned with the smallest cog. Then push the derailleur inward by hand until it contacts the inner adjustment screw (Fig. 8.5) and look to see whether the jockey wheel is aligned below the largest cog. If either adjustment is off, adjust the limit screw by using the procedure in §viii-2.

vii-8 DETERMINING CHAIN LENGTH AND ROUTING

a. Methods for determining the chain length

If you are putting on a new chain for a double crank (including a compact-drive double), determine how many links you will need in one of the following four ways. Methods 2 and 3 are approximately equivalent, and both work for standard double-chainring setups as well as for compact-drive (smaller) double chainrings.

1. Under the assumption that your old chain was the correct length, compare the new with the old chain and use the same number of links.

2. With a standard double-chainring setup, route the chain through the derailleurs and over the large chainring and smallest cog. The jockey wheels in the rear derailleur should then align vertically (Fig. 7.7).

7.7 Determining chain length, method one

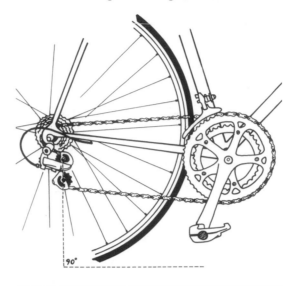

7.8 Determining chain length, method two

3. Wrap the chain around the big chainring and the biggest cog without going through either derailleur. Bring the two ends together until the ends overlap; one full link (Fig. 7.5) should be the amount of overlap (Fig. 7.8).

4. Campagnolo suggests a different method with a double crank—routing the chain over the inner chainring and the smallest cog, as shown in Figure 7.9. You need to make sure that the lower jockey wheel does not lift the chain to the point that the chain going around the bottom of the

DETERMINING
CHAIN LENGTH
AND ROUTING

°

CONNECTING A
STANDARD CHAIN
(WITHOUT A
MASTER LINK OR
A SPECIAL
CONNECTING PIN)

upper jockey wheel hits the section of chain coming from the bottom of the chainring. Campagnolo further suggests checking for about 10–15mm of clearance between the upper jockey wheel and the chain (see Fig. 7.9).

5. Remove the remaining links (§vii-7, Fig. 7.6) and save them in your spare tire bag in case the chain breaks on the road.

b. Route the chain properly

Shift the derailleurs so that the chain will rest on the smallest cog in the rear and on the smallest chainring up front. Starting with the rear-derailleur pulley that is farthest from the derailleur body (this will be the bottom pulley once the chain is taut), guide the chain up through the rear derailleur, going around the two jockey pulleys. Make sure the chain passes inside of the prongs on the rear-derailleur cage. Guide the chain over the smallest rear cog and through the front-derailleur cage. Wrap the chain around the smallest front chainring and bring the chain ends together so that they meet (Fig. 7.9).

7.9 Determining chain length, method three

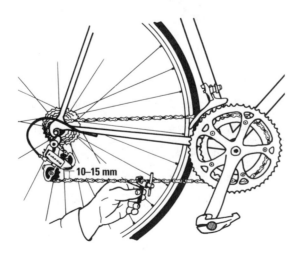

10–15 mm

vii-9 CONNECTING A STANDARD CHAIN (WITHOUT A MASTER LINK OR A SPECIAL CONNECTING PIN)

N O T E : *If you have a Shimano or Campagnolo chain, or a chain with a master link, go to the appropriate section below; however, DO NOT connect it as described in this section by using the original rivet. Ignoring this warning could result in injury if the chain breaks.*

F U R T H E R N O T E : *This section only applies to wide chains, such as five-, six-, seven-, and most eight-speed chains. Never use the same pin (except in an emergency on a ride) on a nine- or ten-speed chain or on any Shimano or Campagnolo chain.*

Connecting a chain that has no special connecting pin or link is much easier if the link rivet (pin) that was partially removed when the chain was taken apart is facing outward (toward you). Positioning the link rivet this way allows you to use the chain tool (Fig. 7.9) in a more comfortable manner (driving the rivet toward the bike, instead of back at you). Be sure that the chain length allows about 10–15mm of clearance between the upper jockey wheel and the lower length of chain.

1. Push the ends together, snapping the end link over the stub of pin you left sticking out to the inside between the opposite end plates. You will need to flex the plates open as you push the link in to get the pin to snap into the hole.

2. Push the pin through with the chain tool (Fig. 7.10) until the same amount protrudes on either end. If you have a nine-speed system, you shouldn't be using the original rivet. But if you are, and your chain tool prongs seem to be getting bent as you push the rivet, see the note in §vii-10, after step 7.

3. If there is a stiff link (Fig. 7.11), free it by either flexing it back and forth with your fingers (Fig.

7.10 Pushing in the pin (link rivet)

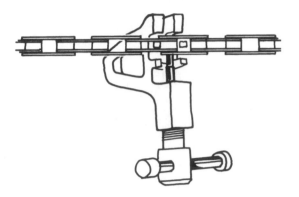

7.11 A stiff link

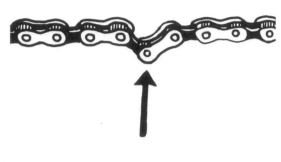

7.12) or, better, by using the chain tool's second set of teeth, as illustrated in Figure 7.13. Push the pin a fraction of a turn to spread the plates apart.

7.12 Freeing a stiff link

vii-10 CONNECTING A SHIMANO CHAIN (NON-TEN-SPEED)

1. Make sure you have the appropriate Shimano "sub-pin" connecting pin, which looks like a segmented rivet with one segment ending in a pointed tip. The two segments are created by a breakage groove at the middle of its length. Two subpins come with each new Shimano chain. If you are reinstalling an old Shimano chain, use a new subpin and make sure it is the right length for the chain (ten-speed subpins are shorter than nine-speed subpins, which are shorter than seven- or eight-speed subpins; see §vii-11). If you don't have a subpin and are going to connect a seven- or eight-speed chain anyway, follow the procedure in §vii-9, but be aware that the chain is now more likely to break than if it had been assembled with the proper subpin. With a nine-speed chain, this is an extremely dangerous approach; don't do it. With a ten-speed chain, it is a complete no-no to connect the chain without a new connector pin; the chain will likely break

7.13 Loosening a stiff link

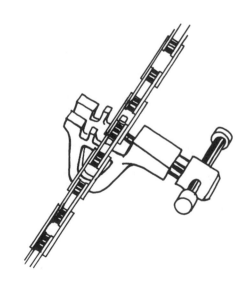

CHAINS

CONNECTING A
SHIMANO CHAIN
(NON-TEN SPEED)

·

CONNECTING
TEN-SPEED
CHAINS

immediately. A broken chain can wreck other parts, and you can get injured. Before assembling a ten-speed chain, read §vii-11.

2. Remove any extra links, pushing the appropriate rivet completely out (§vii-7, Fig. 7.6).

3. Line up the chain ends.

4. Drip some oil on the subpin and push it in with your fingers, pointed end first. It will go in about halfway.

5. With the chain tool (Fig. 7.14), push the subpin through until there is only as much left protruding at the tail end as the other rivets in the chain. It will feel hard, then easy, and then very hard to tighten the tool as you move the pin past its various high points and valleys. Stop when it gets very hard and check for binding. Go by feel more than by sight to determine when the pin is seated correctly.

6. Break off the leading half of the subpin with the hole in the end of a Shimano chain tool or with a pair of pliers (Fig. 7.15).

7. The individual links should move freely when the pin is correctly seated. If not, push the link rivet in a little deeper (Fig. 7.10), or push it back a hair from the other side with the chain on the teeth closer to the screw (Fig. 7.13). As a (poor) last resort (and never with ten-speed chains), flex the chain back and forth with your thumbs at the stiff rivet (Fig. 7.12).

NOTE: *If you have a nine-speed chain and an older chain tool, you may find that the prongs in the tool to hold the chain are too far from the backing plate of the tool and will get bent. Shimano tools TL-CN23 (Fig. 7.16) and TL-CN32 (Fig. 7.17) work on all Shimano chains. Many other brands also work.*

7.14 **Pushing a connector pin into a Campagnolo (or Shimano) chain with a tool**

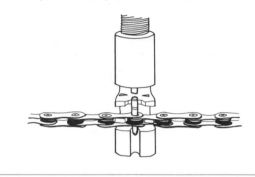

7.15 **Breaking off a Shimano subpin**

7.16 **Shimano TL-CN23, TL-CN22, or TL-CN21 chain tool (for ten-, nine-, eight-, or seven-speed chains respectively)**

vii-11 CONNECTING TEN-SPEED CHAINS

Campagnolo introduced ten-speed rear drivetrains and the more complex chain-assembly methods that come with them. Due to the tighter spacing between the ten cogs required to fit them onto a hub the same width as an eight- or a nine-speed hub, ten-speed chains are narrow. However, the cog and chainring teeth are not significantly narrower, so the inner spacing of the chains is about the same. On the other hand, the outer chain width has come down substantially, from 7.3mm for five-speed chains of many years ago to 5.9mm for Campagnolo's latest ten-speed chains. New problems come with a chain whose outer width is narrower; because the spacing between the inner plates has remained fixed, there is very little protrusion of the chain rivets and hence less security of the chain against breakage under high side loads. It is critically important to install the connecting pin on a ten-speed chain properly; you must use a good chain tool that is intended for use on ten-speed chains (see Figs. 7.16–20). The only exception is that some ten-speed chains (Wippermann) have master links that can be opened by hand (Figs. 7.21–23), which means the chain can be opened without a chain tool. If yours has a master link, skip to §vii-12.

Campagnolo original ten-speed chain rivets protrude very little (only 0.1mm), and Shimano (as well as 2006 and later Campagnolo) ten-speed chain rivets protrude not at all. Less rivet protrusion means that the safety margin of a rivet popping out of a chain plate is reduced, and steps must be taken to prevent chain plates from peeling off the end of rivets.

7.17 Shimano TL-CN32, TL-CN31, or TL-CN30 professional chain tool (for ten-, nine-, eight-, or seven-speed chains respectively). Has an extra pair of chain-retaining teeth extending out to either side of the tool.

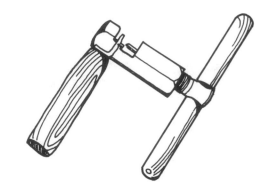

7.18 Pedro's chain tool. Note the flange with an extra chain-retaining tooth extending out to either side of the tool.

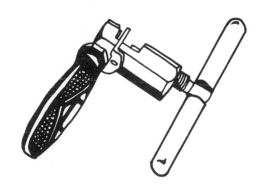

7.19 Rohloff Revolver chain tool. The large-diameter knurled knob can be turned to select different backing-plate shapes. The smaller-diameter knurled knob tightens the backing plate against the chain.

7.20 Park CT-3 chain tool has front and back pairs of teeth.

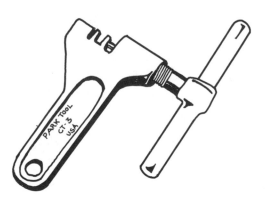

CHAINS

When a chain breaks, it usually does so under high load while shifting. Lateral stress is created because, when the rear derailleur shifts with a modern cogset, the chain is simultaneously engaged on two cogs. And when the front derailleur pushes the chain from one chainring to another, it flexes the links sideways. Easing off on the pedals when you shift will greatly decrease the possibility of a broken chain. However, a chain can break under any high load if a cage plate is just barely hanging onto the end of a rivet. Breaking a chain is dangerous; when the tension on the chain is suddenly removed, your

PRO TIP

PROPER CHAIN TOOLS

If you ride a lot, you will change your chain frequently, and it then becomes worthwhile to have a good chain tool (i.e., chain-breaker tool). If you currently just have a cheap little chain tool, you will be glad you made the investment to upgrade.

If you're strictly a Campagnolo ten-speed rider and don't ride mountain bikes, you might as well get the Campy C10 HD-L ten-speed tool. Campagnolo is pretty proud of that tool—it retails for $150 or so. It looks similar to the tool in Figure 7.17, except that it has no wing with extra teeth extending out to either side and it has a wire loop that you push in once the chain is in place to hold the links down.

According to Shimano, you should only use its $35 TL-CN23 or its $120 TL-CN32 tool on its ten-speed chains; in addition, both of these tools work on all seven-, eight-, nine-speed Shimano chains. The Shimano TL-CN23 is a small tool (Fig. 7.16), and the TL-CN32 (as well as its predecessors, the TL-CN31 and TL-CN30) is a professional tool with wooden handles (Fig. 7.17) that even has spare driver pins hidden in the base. The most important feature of the TL-CN32 (and the TL-CN31 and TL-CN30) is that it has four locating teeth in a row to hold the chain, rather than just two, as most chain tools have. These extra two teeth, one extending out on either side of the tool, really hold the chain well and do much of what Campagnolo's tool accomplishes with its wires to hold the chain down. Pedro's $45 Pro Chain Tool (Fig. 7.18) also has these extra two locating teeth extending out on either side.

Holding the chain in place is nothing new. Before the invention of special connecting pins, we really needed to hold the chain lined up properly, because we did not have a leading tip on a connecting pin that we could slip in by hand and hold the chain together (§vii-9). The $200 Rohloff Revolver tool (Fig. 7.19), which has been around for well over a decade, has a thumbscrew that tightens down against the chain and really holds it in place. The tool also has a revolving plate with different patterns on it to repeen the end of the rivet in whatever style you choose. Park's $35 CT-3 (Fig. 7.20) is a standard shop chain tool, with both a front set of teeth and a back set of teeth, for prying a link apart a bit to free a stiff link, as shown in Figure 7.13.

I have used a Shimano TL-CN31 (nine-speed tool) for years on every kind of chain from Shimano, Campagnolo, Wippermann, and SRAM, for seven, eight, nine, and ten speeds. As the chains became narrower on the outside, the supporting center sec-

weight drops straight down because there is no longer anything supporting your pushing foot. You can easily fall hard. Very hard.

So pay attention to the extra steps required with a ten-speed chain to ensure its security. To reuse a Campagnolo ten-speed chain, you must have a new sec-

tion on newer Shimano chain tools was moved closer to the chain-locating teeth, to fully support the rear outer link plate while driving the pin in. If you use an older-generation chain tool (for wider chains) with a one-generation newer (narrower) chain, eventually you will damage the tool as it puts too much lateral load on the chain-locating teeth. A two-generation-older chain tool will not seat the chain connector pins, so don't use it. Ideally, to do the best job with the latest chains, get the latest tool, and it will also be compatible with all of the older (wider) chains.

If you are careful, I think that you only need one good tool that is at most one generation back (i.e., it is meant for at least nine-speed chains) and that can be used on any chain. By "careful," I mean that you must make sure that the connecting pin and the holes are all lined up perfectly (which the Campy, Rohloff, Shimano, and Pedro's pro tools definitely help guarantee). Furthermore, by "careful," I mean that you must make sure that you stop at the right point and do not go too far or not far enough. You must have a feel for the loose-tight-loose-tight pressure changes as you push a Shimano or Campagnolo connecting pin into place, as well as an eye for when the pin is protruding (or recessed) the same amount on both faces of the chain.

tion of chain with a "virgin" outer link at either end and two new connector pins. Shimano's new ten-speed connector pin (on the 7801, 6600, and 5600 chains) can be installed in an old chain. This new connector pin is not compatible with CN-7800 first-generation Dura-Ace ten-speed chains.

a. Connecting a Campagnolo ten-speed chain

Campagnolo's first chain, introduced in 1999, came with a separate closing link with two pins called a PermaLink, and it required a special installation tool. Fortunately, Campagnolo abandoned that closing method and replaced it with a system similar to Shimano's.

Now Campagnolo has a connecting pin—a two-piece unit that slides together rather than a one-piece pin with a break-off end like Shimano's. Remember, you get only one connecting pin with each Campagnolo chain (as opposed to the two you get with a Shimano chain), so don't lose it! Replacing one ain't cheap.

Campagnolo, like Shimano, has a special chain tool and highly recommends that you use it. Its distinguishing feature is a wire retainer that slides into the tool to hold the chain down. The Campy tool also has a locator stop for the drive pin specific for its chains. I recommend that you use this tool if you have a Campy ten-speed bike. Campagnolo will not guarantee the results with any other tool. However, I find that a Shimano tool also works, as long as you are careful to hold the chain down well and make sure that you push the pin in so that exactly the same amount protrudes at either end.

1. Cut excess length from the chain (§vii-8) only from the end that terminates in an inner link. That way, the holes in the plates of the outer link you will be connecting will never have had a rivet through them and consequently will not have been

enlarged and distorted by the insertion and removal of a rivet. Campagnolo calls these the "virgin holes," and ships its chains with a zip-tie through this pair of holes at the end of the final outer link so that you will be sure to close the chain by using them.

2. Remove the zip-tie from the virgin holes and install the connecting pin as in §vii-10, being careful to insert the connecting pin from the bike side of the chain outward. If you don't have the Campagnolo chain tool, hold the chain down in the chain tool so that the tool's drive pin lines up exactly with the connecting pin. Note that the Campy connecting pin is in two pieces, and you can insert the leading "guide pin" segment by hand, with or without the other half of the pin on it. The segment that you press into the chain has two hole sizes in it, so that only one end will fit on the guide pin, thus ensuring proper orientation. Make sure the same amount of pin is sticking out of both ends (it will only be about 0.1mm) and that you have no stiff link.

b. Connecting a Shimano ten-speed chain

The assembly is nearly the same as in §vii-10, with a couple of important differences.

1. Cut excess length from the chain (§vii-8) only from the end that terminates in an inner link. That way, the holes in the plates of the outer link you will be connecting will have never had a rivet through them and consequently will not have been enlarged and distorted by the insertion and removal of a rivet.

2. You want the connecting pin you insert to be the leading pin, as the outer link it is on comes over the top of the chainring and—critically—leads

when shifting onto the next larger rear cog. Accomplish this link orientation by making sure that, if you are connecting the chain at the bottom as in Figure 7.9, the inner link on one end is to the left (toward the rear derailleur) of the outer link on the other end you are connecting it to. (This approach will ensure that, at the top of the chainring or cog, the inner link is to the right of the outer link, and thus the connecting pin will be to the right of the other rivet in the same outer plate, i.e., leading it.)

3. Make sure that you are using a Shimano ten-speed connecting pin. Two connecting pins come with the chain.

4. Follow the instructions in §vii-10, except that, rather than having both ends of the connecting pins protruding a bit from their plates (as they are for seven-, eight-, and nine-speed chains), you want the ten-speed connector pin to be slightly recessed, below flush. Go by feel rather than by how much pin you see exposed. It will feel easy and then very hard while you continue to push. At this point, stop to check for binding. The chain will be connected perfectly when there is no binding at the connector pin link, without the need for you to flex it sideways to free it. Back off on the chain-tool screw, check the link for freedom of movement, and retighten the tool if you feel any binding. According to Shimano, if the link is still binding, there is a 99 percent chance that the pin isn't pushed in far enough to be fully seated. As usual, finish by breaking off the tip of the connecting pin, as shown in Figure 7.15, or by slipping the hole at the end of the Shimano chain tool over the end of the pin and using that to snap it off.

vii-12 CONNECTING AND DISCONNECTING A MASTER LINK

a. SRAM (Sachs) Power Link, KMC Missing Link-9 and Missing Link-10, and Super Link

These links all work in the same way; SRAM (which purchased Sachs) licensed Lickton's Super Link design (Fig. 7.21), and the KMC design is the same. The master link is made up of two symmetrical link halves, each of which has a single pin sticking out of it. There is a round hole in the center of each plate that tapers into a slot on the end opposite the pin.

Connecting

1. Put the pin of each half of the link through the hole in each end of the chain; one pin will go down and one up (Fig. 7.21).

2. Pull the links close together so that each pin goes through the keyhole in the opposite plate.

3. Pull the chain ends apart so that the groove at the top of each pin slides to the end of the slot in each plate.

Disconnecting

1. While squeezing the master-link plates together to free the pins, push the chain ends toward each other so that the pins come to the center hole in each plate.

2. Pull the two halves of the master link apart.

N O T E : *In practice, this is often hard to do with an old chain. Try squeezing the link plates toward each other with a clothespin or a pair of Visegrip pliers set on very low pressure to disengage the link plates from the pin grooves while you push the ends toward each other. In desperation, you may have to open the chain somewhere else, reassembling it as in §vii-9 or using a second master link.*

A N O T H E R N O T E : *The master link in the SRAM ten-speed chain is not to be opened; it's a permanent link.*

7.21 SRAM/Sachs Power Link, KMC Missing Link-9 and -10, and Lickton's Super Link

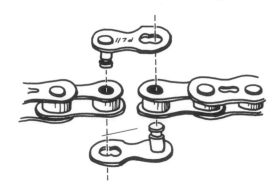

7.22 Wippermann ConneX link—note its orientation with the link's high bump away from the chainring

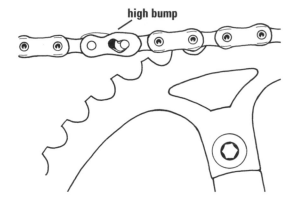

high bump

7.23 Taya Master Link

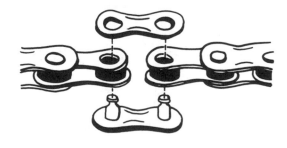

b. Wippermann ConneX link

The Wippermann ConneX link works in much the same way as the SRAM Power Link, but the edges of the link plates are not symmetrical. This asymmetry means that there is a definite orientation for the link; make sure you don't install it upside down.

CHAINS

Orient the chain so that the convex edge is away from the chainring or cog (Fig. 7.22). The link plate is bowl-shaped, and if you install it incorrectly, the convex edge will ride up on the spacer between the 11-, 12- and perhaps 13-tooth cogs, lifting the rollers out of the tooth valleys and causing the chain to skip under load.

Remove and install the ConneX link the same way as the SRAM Power Link in §vii-12a, but make sure the convex link edge is facing outward from the chain loop (Fig. 7.22), so that the concave edge can run over the cog spacers on the smallest cogs without lifting the chain.

c. Taya Master Link connecting

Connecting

1. Connect the two ends of the chain with the master link that has two rivets sticking out of it (Fig. 7.23).

2. Snap the outer master-link plate over the rivets and into their grooves. To facilitate hooking each keyhole-shaped hole over its corresponding rivet, flex the plate with the protruding rivets so that the ends of the rivets are closer together.

Disconnecting

1. Flex the master link so that the pins come closer together.

2. Pull the plate with the oval holes off the rivets.

TROUBLESHOOTING CHAIN PROBLEMS

vii-13 CHAIN SUCK

"Chain suck" is the horribly appropriate name for a condition that occurs when the chain does not release from the bottom of the chainring. Instead, it sticks to the ring and gets "sucked" up until it hits the chainstay. Sometimes the chain becomes wedged between the chainstay and the chainring.

Chain suck is rare on a double-chainring setup on a triathlon bike, but it does happen.

A number of things can cause chain suck. To eliminate it, try the simplest methods first.

1. Clean and lubricate the chain and see whether it improves; a dry, rusty chain will hold the curved shape of the chainring too long.

2. Check for tight links by watching the chain move through the derailleur jockey wheels as you slowly turn the crank backward. Loosen tight links by flexing them side to side with your thumbs (Fig. 7.12).

3. If chain suck persists, check that there are no bent or torn teeth on the chainring. Straighten any broken or torn teeth with pliers.

4. If the chain still sucks, try another chain with wider spacing between link plates (a chain that is too narrow will pinch the chainring). You can use a measuring caliper (Fig. 4.3) to compare spacing between inner link plates of various chains.

5. Another approach is to replace the inner chainring. The new, unworn rings will release the chain more easily, and some chainrings are thinner than others.

vii-14 SQUEAKING CHAIN

Squeaking is caused by dry or rusted surfaces inside the chain rubbing on each other.

1. Lubricate and wipe down the chain (Figs. 7.1–2), and then lubricate it again. Do not use a wax-based lubricant. If you have already used one, it may have brought on the chain chirp in the first place.

2. If the squeak does not go away after a single ride with fresh lubricant, replace the chain. (If the initial remedy does not work, the chain is too dry inside and probably rusted as well. Chains seldom heal from this condition. Bike riding is too joyful to put up with the sound of a squeaking chain.)

vii-15 SKIPPING CHAIN

There can be a number of causes for a chain to skip and jump as you pedal.

a. Stiff links

1. Turn the crank backward slowly to see whether a stiff chain link exists (Fig. 7.11); a stiff link will be visible because it will be unable to bend properly as it goes through the rear-derailleur jockey wheels. It will jump and move the jockey wheels as it passes through.

2. Loosen stiff links by flexing them side-to-side between the index finger and thumb of both hands (Fig. 7.12) or by using the second set of teeth on a chain tool (Fig. 7.13). Set the stiff link over the teeth closest to the screw handle, and push the pin a fraction of a turn to spread the link.

3. Wipe down and lubricate the chain (Figs. 7.1–2).

b. Rusted chain

A rusted chain will squeak. If you watch it move through the rear derailleur, it will look like many links are tight; the links will not bend easily and will cause the jockey wheels to jump back and forth.

1. Lubricate the chain (Fig. 7.1).

2. If this does not fix the problem after a few miles of riding, replace the chain.

c. Worn-out chain

A worn-out chain will be elongated and will skip because it does not mesh properly with the cogs. A new chain will fix the problem if the condition has not persisted long enough to ruin the cogs.

1. Check for chain elongation as described in §vii-6.

2. If the chain is stretched beyond the specifications in §vii-6, replace it.

3. If replacing the chain does not help—or actually makes matters worse—see the next section.

d. Worn cogs

If you just replaced the chain and it is now skipping, it is likely that at least one of the cogs is worn out. The chain will probably skip on the cogs you use most frequently and not on others. However, if it only skips on the smallest cog or two and you have a Wippermann chain, check that you have not installed the ConneX Link upside down; see §vii-12b.

1. Check each cog visually for wear. If any teeth are hook-shaped, the cog is shot and should be replaced. Rohloff makes a simple tool (see Fig. 4.3) that checks for cog wear by putting tension on a length of chain wrapped around the cog. If the last chain link on the tool can be flipped in and out of the tooth pocket while the tool is under tension, the cog is worn out.

2. Replace the offending cogs or the entire cassette or freewheel. See cog installation in §ix-19.

3. Replace the chain as well, if you have not just done so. An old chain will wear out new cogs rapidly.

e. Maladjusted rear derailleur

If the rear derailleur is poorly adjusted or bent, it can cause the chain to skip by lining up the chain between gears.

1. Check that the rear derailleur shifts equally well in both directions and that the chain can be pedaled backward without catching.

2. Adjust the rear derailleur by following the procedure described in §viii-2.

f. Sticky shift cable

If the shift cable does not move freely enough to let the derailleur spring over to be lined up under the cog, the chain will jump off under load. Frayed, rough, dirty, rusted, or worn cables or housings will cause the problem, as will kinked or sharply bent housings.

CHAINS

Replacing the shift cables and housings (see Chap. 8, §viii-6–§viii-14) should eliminate the problem.

g. Loose rear-derailleur jockey wheel(s)

A loose jockey wheel on the rear derailleur can cause the chain to skip by letting it move too far laterally.

1. Check that the bolts holding the jockey wheel to the cage are tight, by using an appropriately sized wrench (usually 3mm hex).

2. Tighten the jockey-wheel bolts if necessary; choke up on the wrench and hold it close to its bend so that you don't have enough leverage to overtighten the bolts. If the jockey-wheel bolts loosen regularly, put Loctite or a similar threadlock compound on them.

h. Bent rear derailleur or rear-derailleur hanger

If the derailleur or derailleur hanger is bent, adjustments won't work. You will probably know when the damage occurred, too. It was either when you shifted your derailleur into your spokes, when you crashed onto the derailleur, or when you pedaled a plastic bag, stick, or tumbleweed through the derailleur.

1. Unless you have a derailleur-hanger-alignment tool and know how to use it, take the bike to a shop and have it checked for correct dropout-hanger alignment. Some bikes, especially those made of aluminum or carbon, have a replaceable (bolt-on) right-rear dropout and derailleur hanger, which you can purchase and install yourself.

2. If a straight derailleur hanger does not correct the misalignment, the rear derailleur is bent. This is generally cause for replacement of the entire derailleur. With some derailleurs, you can replace the jockey-wheel cage, which is usually what is bent (see §viii-30). If you know what you are doing and are careful, you can sometimes bend a bent derailleur cage back with your hands. This

cure seldom works well, but it's worth a try if your only alternative is to replace the entire rear derailleur. Just make sure you don't bend the derailleur hanger in the process.

i. Worn derailleur pivots

If the derailleur pivots are worn, the derailleur will be loose and will move around under the cogs, causing the chain to skip. Replacing the derailleur is the solution.

j. Bent rear-derailleur mounting bolt

If the mounting bolt is bent, the derailleur will not line up straight. To fix it, get a new bolt and install it following the "upper-pivot overhaul" in §viii-23. Observe how the spring-loaded assembly goes together during disassembly to ease reassembly.

k. Missing chain rollers

A chain that passes the elongation tests mentioned in §vii-6 can yet skip because every here and there, one of the cylindrical rollers has broken and fallen off its rivet or is so worn that it is spool-shaped. If you don't happen to check that particular link with the chain-elongation gauge, you'll likely miss broken rollers. The width of the gauge is the same as between the inner plates, so that it won't catch spool-shaped rollers either, because it will ride up on the edges of the rollers and not fall down into the center of the narrower waist of the worn roller. The only way to get to the bottom of the problem is to inspect every link.

l. Inverted ConneX link

If you have a Wippermann chain and have the ConneX master link upside down (described in §vii-12b), the taller link edge will ride up on the spacers between the smallest cogs, lift the rollers off the cog, and cause the chain to skip. Remove, invert, and reinstall the ConneX master link as described in §vii-12b.

SHIFTING SYSTEM

Never mistake motion for action.
—Ernest Hemingway

TOOLS

2mm, 3mm, 4mm, 5mm, and 6mm hex keys

flat-blade and Phillips screwdrivers, small and medium

pliers

indexed-housing cutter

cable cutter

grease

chain lubricant

rubbing alcohol

Optional

Vernier caliper

Riding a bike is much more enjoyable when the derailleurs are working well. It is so sweet to feel the chain respond quickly and positively to shifting commands. On the other hand, having the chain shift unexpectedly or skip when you pedal hard can really ruin your ride.

Fortunately derailleurs are simple beasts. When they act up, a few turns of some screws or a cable-tension adjustment will usually get them working again.

THE REAR DERAILLEUR

The rear derailleur (Figs. 8.1–2) moves the chain from one rear cog to another, and it also takes up chain slack (such as when shifting the front derailleur or bouncing over a bump). The rear derailleur bolts to a hanger on the frame's rear dropout (Fig. 8.3).

Two jockey wheels (pulley wheels) that live in a guide assembly called a chain cage hold the chain tight and help guide the chain as the derailleur shifts. Depending on the model, a rear derailleur has either one or two springs that pull the jockey wheels tight against the chain, creating a desirable amount of chain tension.

Increasing the tension on the rear shift cable (as when you shift to a lower gear) moves the derailleur inward toward the larger cogs. When cable tension is released (that is, when you shift to a higher gear), a spring between the derailleur's two parallelogram plates pulls the chain back toward the smallest cogs. The two limit screws on the rear derailleur (Fig. 8.2) prevent the derailleur from moving the chain too far to the inside (into the spokes) or to the outside (into the dropout).

In addition to limit screws, most rear derailleurs have a barrel adjuster at the point where the cable enters the derailleur (Fig. 8.2). The barrel adjuster increases cable tension when it is unscrewed (and reduces cable tension when it is screwed in). The barrel adjuster is thus used to fine-tune the shifting mechanism to land the chain precisely on each cog with each corresponding click of the shifter.

8.1 **Rear derailleur exploded**

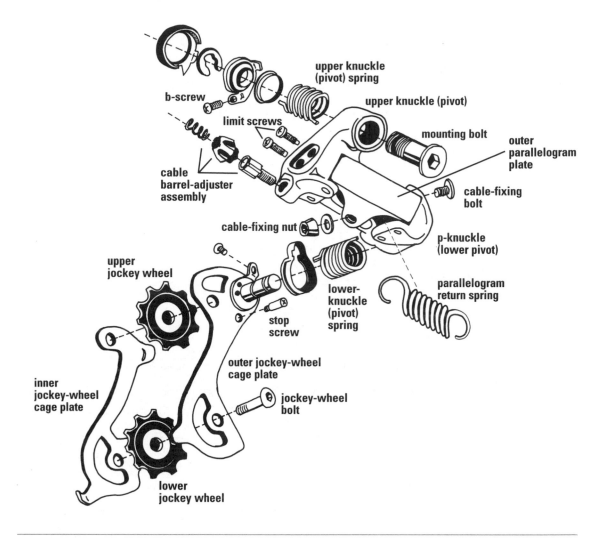

Rear derailleurs also often have a screw underneath and to the rear (visible in Fig. 8.3). This screw, conventionally called the "b-tension" screw, presses against the dropout or a tab attached to the dropout and is largely responsible for controlling the space between the bottom of the cogs and the upper jockey wheel (Figs. 8.4–5). The other factor affecting the size of this space is chain length.

The chain length, the balance between the springs in the upper and lower pivots, and the b-screw (Fig. 8.3) adjustment determine how closely the derailleur tracks the cogs during its lateral movement and keeps the chain from bouncing off the front chainrings when the bike hits bumps.

viii-1 REAR-DERAILLEUR INSTALLATION

1. Apply a small amount of grease to the derailleur's mounting bolt and then thread the bolt a few turns into the large hole on the right-rear dropout.

2. Pull the derailleur back so that the b-screw or tab on the derailleur ends up behind the tab on the dropout (Fig. 8.3).

REAR-
DERAILLEUR
INSTALLATION

.

ADJUSTMENT OF
REAR DERAILLEUR
AND RIGHT-HAND
SHIFTER

8.2 **Limit screws and barrel adjuster**

8.3 **Right rear dropout**

3. Tighten the mounting bolt until the derailleur fits snugly against the hanger.

4. Install the rear wheel with the gear cassette in place. Adjust the rear derailleur limit screws (see next section). Since the chain is not in place, you can adjust the high-gear limit screw by turning it in or out until the upper jockey wheel is centered below the smallest cog. Then push the derailleur inwards all the way and adjust the low-gear limit screw so that the upper jockey wheel is aligned with the largest cog.

5. Route the chain through the jockey wheels and connect it (see Chap. 7, §vii-8–§vii-12).

6. Install the cables and housings (see §viii-6–§viii-12).

7. Pull the cable tight with a pair of pliers, and tighten the cable-fixing bolt (Fig. 8.20).

8. Follow the adjustment procedure described in the next section.

viii-2 ADJUSTMENT OF REAR DERAILLEUR AND RIGHT-HAND SHIFTER

Perform the following derailleur adjustments with the bike in a bike stand or hung from the ceiling. That way, you can turn the crank and shift gears while you put the derailleur through its paces. After adjusting it, test the shifting while riding. Derailleurs often perform differently under load than in a bike stand.

Before starting, lubricate or replace the chain (Chap. 7) so that the whole drivetrain runs smoothly.

a. Limit-screw adjustments

The first and most important rear-derailleur adjustment is of the limit screws. Properly set, these screws (Fig. 8.2) should make certain that you will not ruin your frame, wheel, or derailleur by shifting into the spokes or by jamming the chain between the dropout and the smallest cog. It is never pleasant to see your expensive equipment turned into shredded metal. Adjustment requires nothing more than a small

SHIFTING SYSTEM

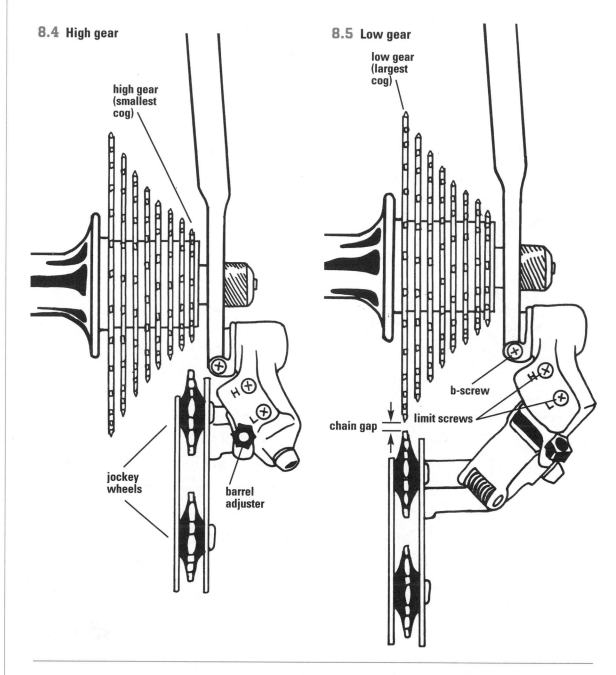

8.4 High gear

high gear
(smallest
cog)

jockey
wheels

barrel
adjuster

H

L

8.5 Low gear

low gear
(largest
cog)

b-screw

limit screws

chain gap

H

L

screwdriver; remember, it's "lefty loosey, righty tighty" for the limit screws.

b. High-gear limit-screw adjustment

This screw limits the outward movement of the rear derailleur. You tighten or loosen this screw until the derailleur shifts the chain to the smallest cog quickly but does not overshift.

How do you determine which limit screw works on the high gear? Often it will be labeled with an *H*,

and it is usually the upper of the two screws (Fig. 8.2). If you're not certain, try each screw. Whichever one moves the derailleur when the cable tension is released (and the chain is on the smallest cog) is the one you're looking for. On most derailleurs, you can also see which screw to adjust by looking between the derailleur's parallelogram side plates. You will see one tab on the back end of each plate. Each is designed to hit a limit screw at one end of the movement. Shift to the smallest cog, and notice which screw is touching one of the tabs; that is the high-gear limit screw.

1. Shift the chain to the large front chainring.

2. While slowly turning the crank, shift the rear derailleur to the smallest rear cog (highest gear; Fig. 8.4).

3. If there is hesitation in the chain's shifting movement, loosen the cable a little to see if it is stopping the derailleur from moving out far enough. You loosen the cable either (a) with a clockwise turn of the barrel adjuster on the derailleur (Fig. 8.2) or the barrel adjuster at the cable stop on the down tube (Fig. 8.6) or head-tube, or (b) by loosening the cable-fixing bolt (Fig. 8.20).

4. If the chain still won't drop smoothly and without hesitation to the smallest cog, loosen (counterclockwise) the high-gear limit screw one-quarter turn at a time, continuously repeating the shift, until the chain repeatedly drops quickly and easily.

5. If the derailleur throws the chain into the dropout, or it tries to go past the smallest cog, tighten (clockwise) the high-gear limit screw one-quarter turn and redo the shift. Repeat until the derailleur shifts the chain quickly and easily into the highest gear without throwing the chain into the dropout.

N O T E : *Make sure that the washer under the cable-fixing bolt on the rear derailleur is rotated into the right position, or it may hit the derailleur cage and stop the rear derailleur from getting to the smallest cog. Some derailleurs have a tooth or two on the washer to dovetail into a corresponding notch or notches in the derailleur, and a number of positions may seem to fit. Look at the cable groove scored in the underside of the washer for a locating hint.*

c. Low-gear limit-screw adjustment

This screw stops the inward movement of the rear derailleur, preventing it from going into the spokes. This screw is often labeled L, and it is usually the bottom screw (Fig. 8.2). You can check which one it is by shifting to the largest cog, and while maintaining pressure on the shifter, turn the screw to see if it changes the position of the derailleur. You can also look between the derailleur's parallelogram plates when it is in the low-gear (largest cog) position and see which screw's tip is contacting, or almost contacting, a tab that moves toward the screw as it shifts to ever-lower gears.

1. Shift the chain to the inner chainring on the front. Shift the rear derailleur to the lowest gear (largest cog, Fig. 8.5). Do it gently, in case the limit screw does not stop the derailleur from moving into the spokes.

2. If the derailleur touches the spokes or pushes the chain over the largest cog, tighten (clockwise) the low-gear limit screw until the derailleur does not.

3. If the derailleur cannot bring the chain onto the largest cog, loosen (counterclockwise) the screw one-quarter turn. Repeat this step until the chain shifts easily up to the largest cog but does not touch the spokes or push the chain over the top of the cog.

d. Cable-tension adjustment on indexed rear shifters

With an indexed shifting system (one that "clicks" into each gear), it is the cable tension that determines whether the derailleur moves to the proper gear with each click.

1. With the chain on the large chainring in the front, shift the rear derailleur to the smallest cog (obviously, you must be turning the crank). Keep clicking the shifter until you are sure it will not let out any more cable.

2. Shift back one click; this should move the chain smoothly to the second cog.

3. If the chain does not climb to the second cog, or if it does so slowly, increase the tension in the cable by unscrewing (counterclockwise) either the cable-tensioning barrel adjuster on the derailleur (Fig. 8.2) or the barrel adjuster on the frame-mounted cable stop (Fig. 8.6), or, on Campagnolo (Fig. 8.23B), the oval adjuster knob on the bar-end shift lever that the head of the cable sits in. If you run out of barrel-adjustment range, retighten (clockwise) the adjusters, loosen the cable-fixing bolt on the derailleur, and pull the slack out of the cable. Tighten the cable-fixing bolt and repeat the adjustment.

4. If the chain over-shifts the second cog or comes close to over-shifting, decrease the cable tension by turning one of the barrel adjusters clockwise (that is, screw it in). If the barrel adjusters are already screwed in, you will need to loosen the cable at the cable-fixing bolt.

5. Keep adjusting the cable tension in small increments while shifting back and forth between the two smallest cogs until the chain moves easily in both directions.

6. Shift the rear derailleur back and forth among the smallest five cogs, again checking for precise and quick movement of the chain from cog to cog. Fine-tune the shifting by making small cable tension corrections with the barrel adjusters.

7. Shift to the inner chainring in the front and to the largest cog in the rear. Shift up and down one click in the rear, again checking for symmetry and precision of chain movement in either direction between the two largest cogs. Fine-tune the barrel adjusters until you get the shifting just right.

8. Go back through the gears. With the chain on the big chainring, the rear derailleur should shift easily on all but perhaps the largest one or two cogs in the rear. With the chain on the inner chainring, the rear derailleur should shift easily on all but perhaps the two smallest cogs. Fine-tune while riding.

N O T E : *If you can't get the tension to work properly on all cogs, there is likely something incompatible between the cogs and shifter or something wrong with the cogset. See §viii-32a, §viii-32c, and §viii-32d regarding compatibility between shifters and cogsets. If the cogs and shifters are supposed to work with each other, then the spacing between cogs may be incorrect. If, for instance, shifting is fine in mid-size cogs but acts like the cable tension is too high in the large cogs and too low in the small cogs (and your shift cables and housings are new or in good working order—see the next Pro Tip), you need some more spacing somewhere within the cogset. Try cutting a circular shim from a beer can that just fits over the freehub body, and slip the shim between a spacer and a cog somewhere in the middle of the cogset. If it improves things, you can play with the number and position of the shims to perfect the shifting.*

e. Cable-tension adjustment on frictional rear shifters

If you do not have indexed shifting, adjustment is complete after you remove the slack in the cable. With proper cable tension, when the chain is on the smallest cog, the derailleur should move as soon as the shift lever does. If there is free play in the lever, tighten the cable by turning the barrel adjuster on the derailleur counterclockwise. If your rear derailleur has no barrel adjuster, loosen the cable-fixing bolt, pull tension on the cable with pliers, and retighten the bolt.

f. Final details of rear-derailleur adjustment: b-screw adjustment

You can obtain a bit more precision by adjusting the small screw (b-screw) that changes the derailleur's position against the derailleur hanger tab on the right-rear dropout (Fig. 8.3).

NOTE: *This does not apply to Campagnolo ten-speed rear derailleurs, since they do not have a b-screw. You adjust the jockey wheel to cog spacing by changing the spring tension in the lower pivot. See §viii-24.*

View the bike from the rear with the chain on the inner chainring and largest cog (Fig. 8.5), and adjust the screw so that the upper jockey wheel is close to the cog, but not pinching the chain against the cog. Repeat on the smallest cog (Fig. 8.4). You'll know that you've moved the jockey wheel in too closely when it starts making noise when you turn the crank.

NOTE: *If, despite your best efforts, you cannot get the rear derailleur to shift well and not make noise, refer to the chainline discussion, §viii-34.*

THE FRONT DERAILLEUR

The front derailleur moves the chain between the chainrings. The working parts consist of a cage, a linkage mechanism, and an arm attached to the shift cable. The front derailleur is attached to the frame, often by a bolt through a boss attached to the frame's seat tube (Fig. 8.7). (This boss, or tab, is often called a "braze-on," hearkening back to the days of steel frames when the attaching bits were brazed to the steel tubes, and a derailleur that uses this mounting system is often called a "braze-on front derailleur," even though it is clearly not brazed to anything.) In an alternative arrangement, a braze-on type front derailleur may bolt to a separate wraparound clamp that has an integral front-derailleur boss shaped like that in Fig. 8.7.

8.6 **Barrel adjuster on down-tube shifter boss**

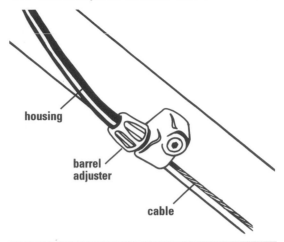

housing

barrel adjuster

cable

8.7 **Front-derailleur boss on seat tube with front derailleur and mounting bolt**

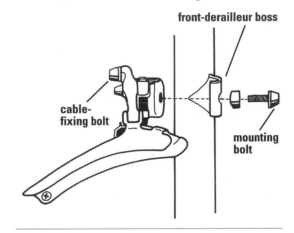

front-derailleur boss

cable-fixing bolt

mounting bolt

8.8 **Band-clamp front derailleur**

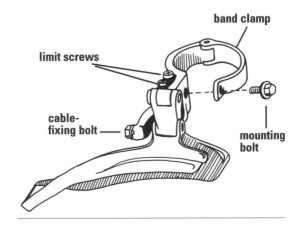

band clamp

limit screws

cable-fixing bolt

mounting bolt

A derailleur may also be a clamp type (also called "band type"), which has an integral clamp surrounding the seat tube (Fig. 8.8).

FRONT-
DERAILLEUR
INSTALLATION

○

ADJUSTMENT
OF FRONT
DERAILLEUR AND
LEFT-HAND
SHIFTER

8.9 **Proper front-derailleur vertical clearance**

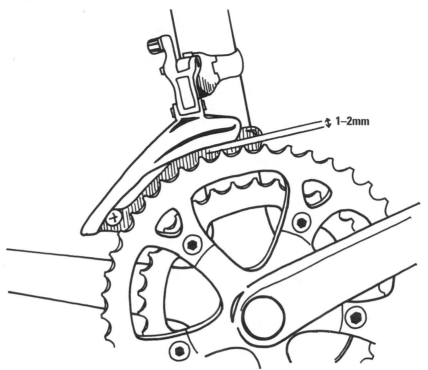

1–2mm

---

viii-3 FRONT-DERAILLEUR INSTALLATION

1. Bolt the front derailleur to the frame boss or clamp it around the seat tube.

2. Adjust the height and rotation as described in §viii-4a.

3. Tighten the clamp or mounting bolt (Fig. 8.7 or 8.8).

viii-4 ADJUSTMENT OF FRONT DERAILLEUR AND LEFT-HAND SHIFTER

a. Position adjustments

A 5mm hex key (Allen wrench) is all you need to adjust the position of a front derailleur attached to a front-derailleur boss (Fig. 8.7). With a band-type front derailleur (Fig. 8.8), the position is adjusted with a 5mm hex key or 8mm box wrench on the band-clamp bolt.

1. Position the height of the front derailleur so that the outer cage passes 1–2mm (¹⁄₁₆–¹⁄₈ inch) above the highest point of the outer chainring (Fig. 8.9).

2. Position the outer plate of the derailleur cage parallel to the chainrings or to the chain in the lowest and highest gears when viewed from above. When on the inner (smallest) chainring and largest cog, the inner cage plate should be parallel to the chainring or the chain (Fig. 8.10). Check this by shifting to the big chainring and smallest cog and sighting from the top (Fig. 8.11).

b. Limit-screw adjustments

The front derailleur has two limit screws that stop the derailleur from throwing the chain to the inside or outside of the chainrings. These are sometimes labeled L for low gear (small chainring) and H for high gear (large chainring) (Fig. 8.12). On most derailleurs, the low-gear screw is closer to the frame.

If in doubt, you can determine which limit screw controls which function by the same trial-and-error method outlined in §viii-2b for the rear derailleur. Shift the chain to the inner ring, and then tighten

8.10 Proper rotational alignment of front derailleur on smallest chainring

8.11 Proper rotational alignment of front derailleur on largest chainring

8.12 Front-derailleur limit screws

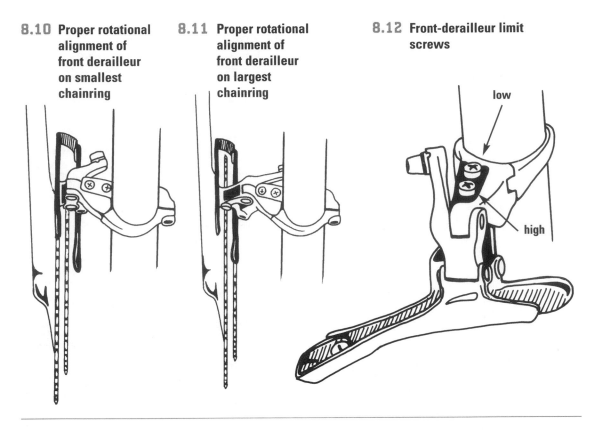

low

high

one of the limit screws. If turning that screw moves the front derailleur outward, then it is the low-gear limit screw. If turning that screw does not move the front derailleur, then the other screw is the low-gear limit screw.

c. Low-gear limit-screw adjustment

1. Shift back and forth between chainrings.

2. If the chain drops off the inner ring to the inside, tighten the low-gear limit screw (clockwise) one-quarter turn, and try shifting again.

3. If the chain does not shift easily onto the inner chainring, loosen (counterclockwise) the low-gear limit screw one-quarter turn and repeat the shift.

d. High-gear limit-screw adjustment

1. Shift the chain back and forth between chain-rings.

2. If the chain jumps over the big chainring, tighten the high-gear limit screw one-quarter turn and repeat the shift.

3. If the chain is sluggish going up to the big chain-ring or does not go up at all, loosen the high-gear limit screw one-quarter turn and try the shift again.

e. Cable-tension adjustment

1. With the chain on the inner chainring, remove any excess cable slack by turning the barrel adjuster on the cable stop on the left side of the bike (Fig. 8.6) counterclockwise (or loosen the cable-fixing bolt, pull the cable tight with pliers, and tighten the bolt).

2. Check that the cable is loose enough to allow the chain to shift smoothly and repeatedly from the outer (or middle on a triple) to the inner chainring.

3. When the cable tension is correct, the derailleur will start to move as soon as you move the shifter. Fine-tune while riding.

N O T E : *This method of tension adjustment should work for indexed as well as friction shifters. With indexed*

ADJUSTMENT
OF FRONT
DERAILLEUR AND
LEFT-HAND
SHIFTER

°

FRONT-
DERAILLEUR
FEATHERING
ADJUSTMENT

front shifting, you may want to fine-tune the cable tension to avoid noise from the chain dragging on the derailleur in some cross gears or to get more precise shifting.

ANOTHER NOTE: *Some front derailleurs have a cam screw at the end of the return spring to adjust the spring tension. For quicker shifting to the smaller rings, increase the spring tension by turning the screw clockwise one-quarter or one-half turn.*

NOTE ON SHIFTING TROUBLE: *If you cannot get the front derailleur to shift well, not rub in cross gears, or not throw the chain off, refer to the chainline discussion under "Troubleshooting" at the end of this chapter.*

CHAIN WATCHER: *If you can't stop the chain from falling off to the inside, install a Third Eye Chain Watcher (see Fig. 8.31), Deda Dog Fang, or N'Gear Jump Stop; these are inner-stop gizmos clamped to the seat tube that nudge the chain back up onto the inner ring whenever it tries to drop off.*

viii-5 FRONT-DERAILLEUR FEATHERING ADJUSTMENT

"Feathering" is adjusting the front derailleur slightly to not rub the chain in cross-gears.

a. Bar-end shifters

The left bar-end shifter is frictional (Figs. 8.22A, 8.23A), so you can move it as needed to avoid chain rub.

b. Shimano STI shifters

To stop the chain from rubbing the front-derailleur cage while on a small rear cog and the inner chainring of a double crank, you push the brake lever blade inward about half as far as you would to shift to the big chainring and let go. You will feel a soft click, and the front derailleur will stay a few millimeters out from its farthest-in position.

If the chain is rubbing in a cross-gear while on the big chainring, move the derailleur inward a couple of millimeters by pushing the chain-dump lever (the small lever behind the brake lever) inward lightly a few degrees. When you feel a soft click, let go.

If the derailleurs are adjusted properly, the frame is in alignment, and the chain and chainline are to Shimano specification, these feathering positions will eliminate chain rub in all of the cross-gears except perhaps a small-small or big-big combination.

NOTE: *You lose the feathering adjustment of an STI lever if you are using it with a triple crank.*

c. Campagnolo Ergopower shifters

The Campagnolo Ergopower front shift lever has a number of closely spaced click stops; it does not have two definitive "indexed" positions. This setup means that you can move the derailleur in small increments by a single click in either direction. Feathering is simple and obvious, and you can generally avoid chain rub in any gear. The front shifter's incremental movements are small enough to find a rub-free position as long as the outer chainring is not bent and the frame is aligned properly. As you ride, you may want to play with the barrel adjuster on the front derailleur cable a bit to get the chain tension just right for noise-free operation in cross-gears.

d. SRAM DoubleTap shifters

SRAM's design has only a single shift lever (behind the brake lever), and there is only a feather adjustment when on the inner chainring. Since a light tap on the lever when the chain is on the big chainring simply drops the chain down to the inner chainring, there is no feather adjustment when the chain is on the big chainring. When the chain is on the inner chainring, however, a lighter push on the lever moves the derailleur outward slightly to feather the derailleur to prevent chain rub in cross gears.

Replace your cables and housings before you think they need it. Increased drag on shift cables caused by contamination will prevent accurate and consistent shifts.

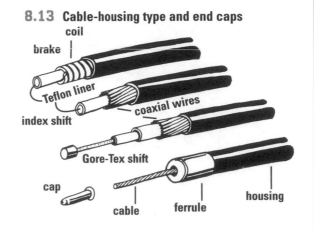

8.13 Cable-housing type and end caps

REPLACING AND LUBRICATING SHIFT CABLES AND HOUSINGS

To function properly, derailleurs need to have clean, smooth-running cables (also called "inner wires"). As with replacing a chain, replacing cables is a maintenance operation, not a repair operation. Do not wait until cables break to replace them. Replace any cables that have broken strands, kinks, or fraying between the shifter and the derailleur. You should also replace housings (also called "outer wires") if they are bent, mashed, or gritty, or if their color clashes with your bike (this is really important!).

viii-6 BUYING CABLES

1. Buy new cables and housing that are at least as long as the ones you are replacing.

2. Make sure that the cables and housing are for indexed systems. These cables will stretch minimally, and the housings will not compress in length. Under its external plastic sheath, indexed housing is not made of steel coil like brake housings; it is made of parallel (coaxial) steel strands of thin wire. If you look at the end (Fig. 8.13), you will see numerous wire ends sticking out surrounding a central plastic tube (make sure the housing you buy has this liner!).

3. Buy two cable-end crimp caps (Fig. 8.13) to prevent the cable end from fraying after it is cut to

length, and a ferrule (tubular cable-housing end) for each end of every housing section. These ferrules will prevent kinking at the cable-entry points, cable stops, shifters, and derailleurs.

4. If your cables run inside the frame or handlebars, buy some thin, plastic cable-liner tubes at the bike shop to route through the frame and bars and simplify cable installation as well as reduce friction.

5. It is a good idea to buy extra cables, cable caps, and ferrules (Fig. 8.13) to keep on hand in your work area. They're inexpensive, and if you have a small supply, you will be able to change cables when you need to without making a special trip to the bike shop for these little parts.

viii-7 CUTTING HOUSING TO LENGTH AND ROUTING IT

1. Use a special cutter made for the purpose; Pedro's, Park, Shimano (Fig. 8.16), and Wrench Force make good ones (see Chap. 4, Fig. 4.2). Standard wire cutters (i.e., side cutters) will not cleanly cut index-style shift housing.

2. Cut the housing to the same lengths as the pieces you are replacing. If you have no old housings for comparison, cut the new pieces so that they

CUTTING HOUSING
TO LENGTH AND
ROUTING IT

○

REPLACING CABLE
IN A BAR-END
SHIFT LEVER OR
DOWN-TUBE
SHIFT LEVER

8.14 Rear derailleur swinging back to check housing length

8.15 Rear derailleur swinging forward to check housing length

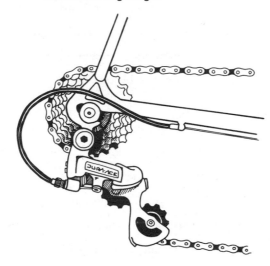

8.16 Crimping the cable-end cap

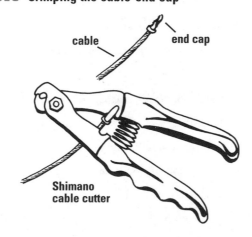

cable   end cap

**Shimano
cable cutter**

curve smoothly. When you turn the handlebar, the housing should not pull or kink. Allow enough length for the rear derailleur to swing backward (Fig. 8.14) and forward (Fig. 8.15) freely.

3. With a nail or toothpick, open each plastic sleeve-end that has been smashed shut by the cutter.

4. Place a ferrule over each housing end (Fig. 8.13) and insert the pieces into the cable stops on the frame and shifters.

5. If the housing runs through the inside of the handlebar or frame, leave the old cable in and pull the old housing off of it. Then slide the new housing onto the old cable to simplify and speed routing it through the bar or frame. Then pull the old cable out in anticipation of the new cable.

viii-8 REPLACING CABLE IN A BAR-END SHIFT LEVER OR DOWN-TUBE SHIFT LEVER

1. Disconnect the cable at the derailleur and snip off the cable-end cap.

2. Flip the lever forward (i.e., down) to the gear setting that lets the most cable out. This setting will be the highest gear position for the rear shift lever (small cog) and the lowest for the front (small chainring).

3. Push the cable until the cable head pops out of the hole in the shift lever. Pull out the old cable and recycle it.

4. Thread the new cable through the shift lever hole and out through the other side of the lever (Fig. 8.17).

5. Guide the cable through each housing segment (making sure each housing segment has a ferrule on the end; see Fig. 8.13) and cable guide and cable stop to the derailleur. If the cables run

through the frame or handlebars, make sure that there is either cable housing or a plastic liner inside for them to run in. Before pulling the old cable from inside the frame or bars, slide a new piece of housing or liner tubing onto the old cable, depending on which the frame or bar accepts, and pull it through. Then you can easily slip the new cable in through the frame or bar through the new plastic tube without any fishing around.

viii-9 REPLACING SHIFT CABLE IN SHIMANO STI SHIFT/BRAKE LEVER

1. Disconnect the cable at the derailleur and snip off the cable-end cap (if installed).

2. Shift the inner chain-dump lever to the gear setting that lets the most cable out. This setting will be the highest-gear position for the rear shift lever (small cog) and the lowest for the front (small chainring).

3. Pull the brake lever to reveal the access hole for the shift cable; the hole is on the outboard side of the lever. On Dura-Ace levers, you must first remove a thin, black plastic cover with a small Phillips screwdriver to get at the access hole. Push the cable until the cable head emerges from the hole far enough to grab it. Pull out the old cable and recycle it.

4. The recessed hole into which the cable head seats should be visible through the access hole. Thread the new cable through the hole and out through the inboard side of the lever (Fig. 8.18).

5. Guide the cable through each housing segment (making sure each segment has a ferrule on the end; see Fig. 8.13) and cable guide and cable stop to the derailleur.

8.17 Replacing cable in bar-end shifters

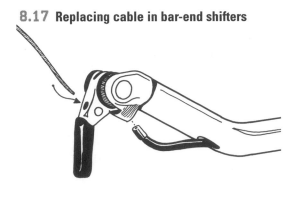

8.18 Threading in a new Shimano STI shift cable

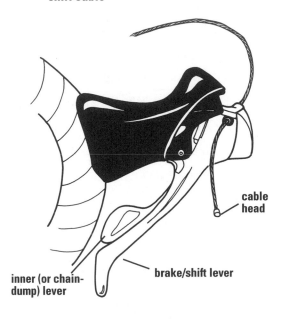

cable head

inner (or chain-dump) lever

brake/shift lever

8.19 Threading in a new Campagnolo Ergopower shift cable

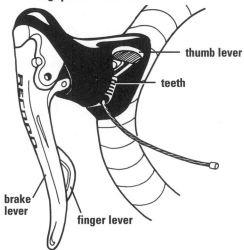

thumb lever

teeth

brake lever

finger lever

viii-10 REPLACING SHIFT CABLE IN CAMPAGNOLO ERGOPOWER OR SRAM DOUBLETAP LEVER

1. Disconnect the cable at the derailleur and snip off the cable-end cap (if installed).

2. Release the maximum amount of shift cable from the lever. On Ergopower, click the thumb lever until it will click no more. On SRAM, click the shift lever with light taps (not with the second click) until it will let out no more cable.

3. Push the cable until the cable head emerges from the cable hole. On Ergopower, it will be in the slot near the bottom of the lever toward the outboard side—just outboard of the little gear teeth (Fig. 8.19). On SRAM, it will be out of an oval hole near the base of the lever body on the inboard side. Push the cable head out far enough to grab it. Pull out the old cable and recycle it.

4. Push the new cable in through the hole and up through the lever body until the cable emerges from the housing-entry hole at the upper base of the lever body.

5. Guide the cable through each housing segment (making sure each segment has a ferrule on the end; see Fig. 8.13) and cable guide and cable stop to the derailleur.

NOTE: *The Ergopower cable hook (i.e., the enlarged, countersunk hole into which the cable head seats; see Fig. 8.19) is too small to fit a Shimano cable head—just another of those maddening parts incompatibilities. You can file down a Shimano cable head enough to fit in, but expect to need to push hard with pliers to get the cable back out next time. It's simplest to just buy a new Campagnolo shift cable.*

viii-11 ATTACH CABLE TO REAR DERAILLEUR

1. Put the chain on the smallest cog so that the rear derailleur moves to the outside.

2. Run the cable through the barrel adjuster, and route it through each of the housing segments (see §viii-8 for internal cable routing) until you reach the cable-fixing bolt on the derailleur. Make sure that the rear shifter is on the highest-gear setting so that the maximum amount of cable is available to the derailleur.

3. Pull the cable taut and into its groove under the cable-fixing bolt (Fig. 8.20).

4. Tighten the bolt. On most derailleurs this step takes a 5mm hex key.

5. Clip the cable 1–2cm past the bolt and crimp on a cap to prevent fraying (Fig. 8.16).

viii-12 ATTACH CABLE TO FRONT DERAILLEUR

1. Shift the chain to the inner chainring so that the derailleur moves farthest to the inside. This ensures that the maximum amount of cable is available to the derailleur.

2. Run the cable to the front derailleur (see §viii-8).

3. Be sure that the cable lies in the groove beneath the cable-fixing bolt (Fig. 8.21). Pull the cable taut with pliers. With a 5mm hex key, tighten the cable to the cable anchor on the derailleur.

4. Clip the cable 1–2cm past the bolt and crimp on a cap to prevent fraying (Fig. 8.16).

viii-13 CABLE LUBRICATION

New cables and housings with plastic liners do not need to be lubricated. Old cables can be lubricated with chain lubricant. Standard bike grease can slow

8.20 Attaching rear-derailleur cable

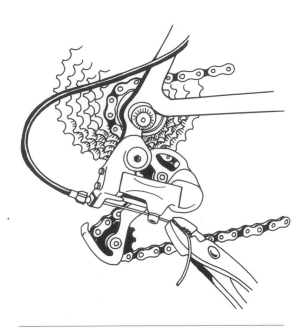

8.21 Attaching front-derailleur cable

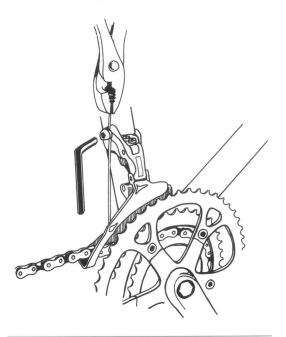

their movement, but some manufacturers recommend (and supply) molybdenum disulfide grease for cables.

1. Disconnect the cable at the derailleur, and clip off the cable-crimp end. Be aware that if the cable frays at all when clipped, you may not be able to slide it back in through the housings and may have to replace both the cable and its housings. This is why you need a good cable cutter (see §viii-7, step 1).

2. With chain lubricant, coat the areas of the cable that will be inside of the cable-housing segments. Squirt lubricant into each housing section.

NOTE: *If you have any trouble reinstalling the cable because of fraying, or if the housings are dirty or rusty, replace both the cable and the housings*

ANOTHER NOTE: *On bikes with a slotted chainstay cable stop, pull the housing out of the stop, slide it up the cable, and lubricate that section of cable without disconnecting it from the derailleur.*

viii-14 REDUCE CABLE FRICTION

In addition to replacing the cables and housings with good-quality cables and lined housings, the following specific steps can improve shifting efficiency:

1. The most important friction-reducing step is to route each cable so that it makes smooth bends. You don't want excessively long loops, though; instead, make sure the housing is just long enough so that the tension on the shift cables does not increase when you turn the handlebar.

2. Choose cables that offer especially low friction. "Die-drawn" cables, which have been mechanically pulled through a die (a small hole in a piece of hard steel), move with lower friction than standard cables. Die drawing flattens the outer strands, smoothing the cable surface. Thinner cables and Teflon-lined housings with a large inside diameter also reduce friction.

3. If the cables run through the frame or handlebars, make sure that there is some sort of a plastic liner inside for them to run in. With some brands, you

8.22A–B Exploded left (A) and right (B) Shimano bar-end shifters

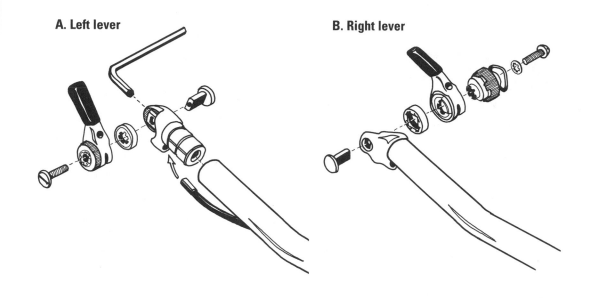

A. Left lever   B. Right lever

can run standard cable housing right through the frame and bars, which of course already has a plastic liner inside. But many frames and handlebars do not allow the housing to run through, and it is these that require this thin, plastic, friction-removing tubing, which is similar to the liner used in cable housing. Before pulling the old cable from inside the frame or bars, slide a new piece of this tubing onto the old cable and pull it through. Then you can slip a new cable in through the frame or bar easily without any fishing around.

THE SHIFTERS

viii-15 REMOVE AND INSTALL BAR-END SHIFTERS

1. Release the cable at the derailleur so the lever will be free to pull away from the lever base.

2. Remove the screw holding the shift lever to its mount, and pull the shifter off. On Campagnolo and Shimano, this is the bolt on the lever side (Figs. 8.22A–B, 8.23A–B). On SRAM, the lever-side bolt does not allow you to remove the lever; it only adjusts the lever tension. On SRAM, unscrew the bolt passing through the mount housing into the lever from the opposite side with a 4mm hex key, and now the lever will come off.

3. Loosen the expander bolt in the lever base's throat with a hex key to contract the expander prongs, and tap the hex key with a hammer to free the expander plug. If there is a tall nut that the lever bolt went into sticking out of the mount housing and in the way of getting at the expander bolt, move it out of the way first. If you are removing the lever, you can pull it out now, and if you are installing it, you can insert it into the end of the bar now and tighten it up. Make sure the cable hole in the mount housing is on the bottom, and insert the end of the cable housing into it.

8.23A–B Exploded left (A) and right (B) Campagnolo bar-end shifters

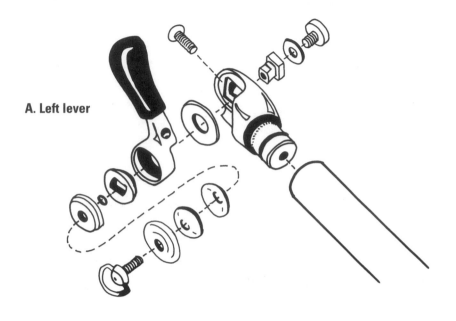

A. Left lever

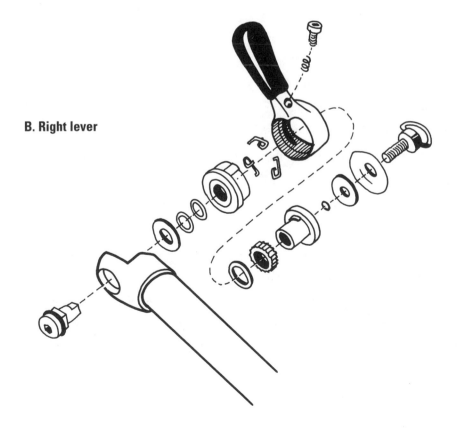

B. Right lever

REMOVE AND
INSTALL BAR-END
SHIFTERS

·

REMOVE AND
INSTALL
DUAL-CONTROL
LEVERS

·

OVERHAUL
BAR-END
SHIFTERS

4. Lining the lever up in its cable-release position (i.e., flipped down), fit the lever mechanism back in place as it was on the shifter mount.

5. Tighten the mounting screw into the backing nut snugly. It must be tight enough that the lever does not wobble, but not so tight that it binds.

6. Install the cable and tighten it at the derailleur (see §viii-8).

viii-16 REMOVE AND INSTALL DUAL-CONTROL LEVERS

Dual-control (brake/shift) levers are generally labeled right and left, but if you're in doubt, you can tell which is which because the shift lever should swing toward the centerline of the bike. Here are the steps for you to replace the entire dual-control lever unit:

1. Remove the handlebar tape and bar plugs.

2. Remove the old lever by loosening its mounting bolt with a 5mm hex key and sliding the lever assembly off. The position of the bolt varies. On current dual-control levers, it is on the outside of the lever body under the lever hood. It is often easier to slip the hex wrench down from the top between the lever body and the hood rather than trying to roll back the hood far enough to get at it from outside of the hood (Chap. 10, Fig. 10.7). On Campagnolo Ergopower, the bolt is on the outboard side toward the top; on Shimano STI the bolt is on the middle of the outboard side; on SRAM DoubleTap, the bolt is on the back of the lever body—on top, where the web of your thumb would rest.

3. Slide the new lever on the bar to where you like it. A good rule of thumb is to put a straightedge against the bottom of the bar and slide the lever down until its end touches the straightedge. The

lever can sit a little higher than this, but generally not any lower. Put a long straightedge across the top of both levers to make sure that they are level with each other.

4. Tighten the mounting bolt.

5. Install the cables (see §viii-6–§viii-14 and Chap. 10, §x-4).

6. Wrap the handlebar with tape (see Chap. 14, §xiv-11).

viii-17 OVERHAUL BAR-END SHIFTERS

Bar-end shifters sticking out in front of the bike will eventually get dirty and perform less well after a lot of riding in the rain, especially when riding behind other riders whose rear tires shoot up dirty water. You cannot overhaul Shimano or SRAM bar-end shifter mechanisms.

1. Release the cable at the derailleur so the lever will be free to pull away from its mount housing.

2. Remove the screw holding the shifter to its mount, and pull the shifter off. At this point, it is possible to remove the lever mount housing (by loosening the expander bolt in its throat with a hex wrench and releasing the expander plugs and pulling the whole thing out), but there is no need to do so.

3. Left lever: The Shimano (Fig. 8.22A) and SRAM lever mechanisms cannot be disassembled, but you can rinse or blow grit out of them. To get the Campagnolo frictional shifter (Fig. 8.23A) working smoothly, simply clean the parts and put them back together. You generally do not want to grease the mechanism, since that will only demand higher bolt tightening torque to get the lever to hold its position.

4. Right lever: If you have a Shimano indexed shifter (Fig. 8.22B), the mechanism cannot be serviced;

buy a new lever if the mechanism has failed. On SRAM, you can blow out the area around the index gear with compressed air and grease the teeth and the three G-springs, which might rehabilitate it fully. With Campy (Fig 8.23B), pull the T-shaped (or pedestal-shaped) bushing out of the center of the outboard side of the lever. Now you can see the index gear and the three G-springs that click into the teeth. To get the plastic housing holding the G-springs out of the hollow in the base of the lever, push on the index gear and, with a screwdriver, pry on the edge of the plastic housing protruding from the lever as well. You can blow out the area and grease the springs and gear teeth, but you can also push the index gear out if you want to clean or replace the springs or the index gear (you can change the number of speeds this way). Pull or pry the index gear up out from the springs. Clean the springs and gear, and grease them. Line up the arrow on the index gear with the G-spring prong on the side of the plastic housing that has a nub on it to engage a notch under the cable hole on the lever. Tip the index gear down to engage two springs, fit a screwdriver in between the third spring and the other side of the gear and pry with it, while pushing the gear down into place. Push the plastic spring housing back into the lever, lining up the nub with the notch in the hollow of the lever. Make sure you replace any washers that may have fallen out. Push the T-shaped (or pedestal-shaped) bushing pack into place, lining up its two teeth on the underside of its flange with the two notches in the index gear.

5. Lining the lever up in its cable-release position (i.e., flipped down), fit the notches inside the bushing's bore over the ledges on the backing nut, once you have pushed it back through the shifter mount housing.

6. Tighten the mounting screw into the backing nut snugly. It must be tight enough that the lever does not wobble, but not so tight that it binds.

7. Install the cable and tighten it at the derailleur.

DERAILLEUR MAINTENANCE

viii-18 JOCKEY-WHEEL MAINTENANCE

With proper attention, the jockey wheels on the rear derailleur will last a long time. They should be wiped off every time you wipe down and lubricate the chain (after every ride is a good idea). The only other maintenance involved is a light overhaul every 1,000–2,000 miles in dirty conditions; otherwise an overhaul every time you replace the chain should be frequent enough.

The mounting bolts on jockey wheels also should be checked regularly. If a loose jockey-wheel bolt falls off while you are riding, you'll need to follow the procedure for a broken rear derailleur on the road in Chapter 6, §vi-12.

Standard jockey wheels turn on a bushing made of steel or ceramic. Some high-end models have cartridge bearings. A washer with an inwardly bent rim is usually installed on each side of a standard jockey wheel. Some jockey wheels also have rubber seals around the edges of these washers.

viii-19 OVERHAULING STANDARD JOCKEY WHEELS

1. Remove the jockey wheels by undoing the bolts that hold them to the derailleur (Fig. 8.24A). The bolts usually take a 3mm hex key.

OVERHAUL
BAR-END
SHIFTERS

·

JOCKEY-WHEEL
MAINTENANCE

·

OVERHAULING
STANDARD JOCKEY
WHEELS

2. Wipe all parts clean with a rag. Solvent is usually not necessary but can be used.

3. If the teeth on the jockey wheels are broken or badly worn, replace the wheels.

4. Smear grease over each bolt and bushing and inside each jockey wheel.

5. Reassemble the jockey wheels onto the derailleur. Be sure to orient the inner cage plate properly (the larger part of the inner cage plate should be at the bottom jockey wheel).

viii-20 OVERHAULING CARTRIDGE-BEARING JOCKEY WHEELS

If the cartridge bearings in high-end jockey wheels (Fig. 8.24B) do not turn freely, they can usually be overhauled.

1. With a single-edge razor blade, pry the plastic cover (bearing seal) off one side or—preferably—both sides of the bearing (Fig. 9.29). (Steel covers on bearings cannot be removed. If such a bearing is not turning freely, the bearing must be replaced.)

2. With a toothbrush and solvent, clean the bearings. Use citrus-based solvent, and wear gloves and glasses to protect skin and eyes.

3. Blow the solvent out with compressed air or your tire pump, and allow the parts to dry.

4. Squeeze new grease into the bearings and replace the covers.

viii-21 REAR-DERAILLEUR OVERHAUL

Except for the jockey wheels and pivots, most rear derailleurs are not designed to be disassembled. If the pivot springs seem to be operating effectively, all you need to do is maintain the jockey wheels (see previ-

8.24A Exploded derailleur

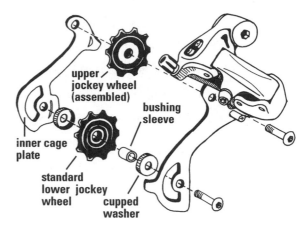

8.24B Exploded jockey wheels with cartridge bearing

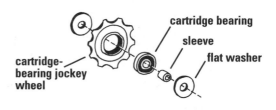

ous section), and clean and lubricate the parallelogram and spring as described next.

viii-22 REAR-DERAILLEUR WIPE AND LUBE

1. Clean the derailleur as well as you can with a rag, including between the parallelogram plates.

2. Drip chain lube on both ends of every pivot pin.

3. If there is a clothespin-type spring between the plates of the parallelogram (as opposed to the full coil spring running diagonally from one corner of the parallelogram to the other), put a dab of grease where the spring end slides along the underside of the outer parallelogram plate.

8.25 Rear-derailleur pivots

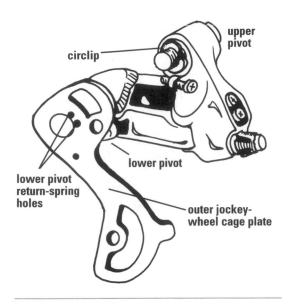

circlip / upper pivot / lower pivot / lower pivot return-spring holes / outer jockey-wheel cage plate

viii-23 REAR-DERAILLEUR UPPER-PIVOT OVERHAUL

LEVEL 3

These steps apply to Shimano derailleurs. CAUTION: *Do not undertake this job unless absolutely necessary to rehabilitate a poorly functioning rear derailleur. The strong spring resists your best intentions at reassembly, and you may not be able to get the derailleur back together properly, even with a second set of hands.*

1. Remove the rear derailleur; the mounting bolt and cable bolt usually require a 5mm hex key.

2. With a screwdriver, pry the circlip (Fig. 8.25) off the threaded end of the mounting bolt. Don't lose it; it will tend to fly when it comes off.

3. Pull the mounting bolt and the upper pivot spring out of the derailleur (Fig. 8.1).

4. Clean and dry the parts with or without the use of a solvent.

5. Grease liberally, and replace the parts.

6. Each end of the spring fits a hole in the derailleur. If there are several holes, and you don't know which was used before, try the middle one. (If the derailleur does not keep tension on the chain well enough, you can later try another hole that increases the spring tension.)

7. Push it all together and replace the circlip with pliers.

viii-24 REAR-DERAILLEUR LOWER-PIVOT OVERHAUL AND SPRING TENSION ADJUSTMENT

LEVEL 3

On its ten-speed rear derailleurs, Campagnolo has eliminated the b-screw, the traditional means of adjusting the space between the upper jockey wheel and the cogs (see §viii-2f). Instead, an external screw engaging a number of external teeth around the base of the rear derailleur's lower pivot performs the adjustment.

If shifting is sluggish with a Campagnolo rear derailleur, tighten the lower-pivot spring by turning the adjusting screw clockwise until the upper jockey wheel is close to the cog but not pinching the chain against it. Perform this adjustment when the chain is on the inner chainring and on the largest cog.

Similarly, if the drivetrain is making noise or running roughly in low gears (because the chain is bumping along or being pinched between the cog and the upper jockey wheel), turn the adjusting screw counterclockwise to loosen the lower-pivot spring. This drops the upper jockey wheel down away from the cogs.

On a Shimano rear derailleur, fine-tuning the lower-pivot spring tension is a secondary adjustment to turning the b-screw, and the derailleur must first be disassembled to perform the lower-pivot spring tension adjustment.

REAR-
DERAILLEUR
LOWER-PIVOT
OVERHAUL AND
SPRING TENSION
ADJUSTMENT

8.26 **Removing and installing the lower-pivot setscrew from a modern Shimano rear derailleur**

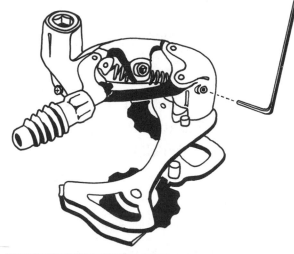

8.27 **Removing and replacing the cage-stop screw from an older Shimano rear derailleur**

1. Remove the derailleur from the bike.

2. Shimano derailleurs can be divided into two types: those that have a setscrew on the side of the lower pivot, and older ones that do not.

   (a) If it has a setscrew (Fig. 8.26), remove it using a 2mm hex key and pull the jockey cage away from the derailleur.

   (b) If the derailleur has no setscrew, find and unscrew the tall cage-stop screw on the de- railleur cage (Fig. 8.27); it is located near the upper jockey wheel. It is designed to main- tain tension on the lower pivot spring and prevent the cage from springing all the way around. Once the stop screw is removed, slowly guide the cage around until the spring tension is relieved. Remove the upper jockey pulley and unscrew the pivot bolt from the back with a 5mm (sometimes 6mm) hex key (Fig. 8.28). Be sure to hold the jockey-wheel cage to keep it from twisting.

3. Determine in which hole the spring end has been placed, and then remove the spring.

4. Clean and dry the bolt and the spring with a rag. A solvent may be used if necessary.

5. Grease all parts liberally.

6. Replace the spring ends in their holes in the derailleur body and jockey-wheel cage (Fig. 8.29). Put the spring in the adjacent hole in the jockey- wheel cage plate if you want to increase its ten- sion. Increasing the lower-pivot spring tension pulls the chain tighter; if you have problems with the chain drooping or falling off, increasing the spring tension is worth a try.

7. Reassemble the derailleur lower pivot.

   (a) If the derailleur has a setscrew, push the assembly together, wind the spring, and replace the setscrew (Fig. 8.26).

   (b) If the derailleur does not take a setscrew, wind the jockey-wheel cage back around, screw it all back together with the pivot bolt (Fig. 8.28), and replace the stop screw (Fig. 8.27).

8.28 **Removing and replacing lower-pivot center bolt from an older Shimano rear derailleur**

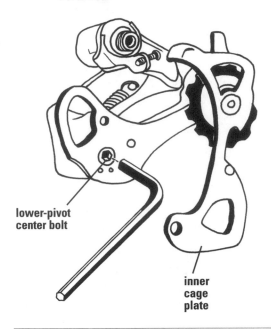

lower-pivot center bolt

inner cage plate

8.29 **Removing and replacing the lower-pivot return spring in one of the two holes in the jockey-wheel inner cage plate**

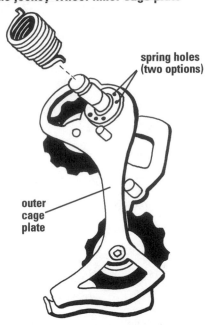

spring holes (two options)

outer cage plate

REAR-
DERAILLEUR
PARALLELOGRAM
OVERHAUL

·

REPLACING STOCK
REAR-
DERAILLEUR
BOLTS WITH
LIGHTWEIGHT
VERSIONS

viii-25 REAR-DERAILLEUR PARALLELOGRAM OVERHAUL

LEVEL 3

Very few derailleurs can be completely disassembled. Those that can (Mavic cable-actuated derailleurs) have removable pins holding them together. The pins have circlips on the ends that can be popped off with a screwdriver to remove the pins. If you have such a derailleur, disassemble it in a box so that the circlips do not fly away, and make note of where each part belongs so that you can get it back together again. Clean all parts, grease them, and reassemble.

viii-26 REPLACING STOCK REAR-DERAILLEUR BOLTS WITH LIGHTWEIGHT VERSIONS

LEVEL 3

Lightweight aluminum and titanium derailleur bolts are available as replacement items for many derailleurs. Removing and replacing

jockey-wheel bolts is simple, as long as you keep all of the jockey-wheel parts together (Fig. 8.24) and put the inner cage plate back on the way it was. Upper and lower pivot bolts (Fig. 8.1) are replaced following the instructions outlined above for overhauling the pivots (§viii-23 and §viii-24).

TROUBLESHOOTING DERAILLEUR AND SHIFTER PROBLEMS

Once you have made the adjustments outlined previously in this chapter, the drivetrain should operate quietly and shift smoothly. The drivetrain should stay in gear, even if you turn the crank backward. If you cannot fine-tune the adjustment so that each click with the right shifter results in a clean, quick shift, you need to check some of the following possibilities. For skipping- and jumping-chain problems, see also the Troubleshooting section at the end of Chapter 7.

viii-27 SHIFTER COMPATIBILITY

Make certain that the shifter and derailleur are made by the same company, are compatible models, and are made for the cogset you have (brand, model, and number of cogs). If the brands are different, make sure that they are designed to work together. For instance, Modolo makes an integral brake/shift lever that can be set up to work with either Campagnolo or Shimano derailleurs. If the shifter and derailleur are incompatible, you will need to change one of them (probably whichever item is less costly). For more on compatibility, see §viii-32.

viii-28 STICKY CABLES

Check to see whether the derailleur cables run smoothly through the housing. Sticky cable movement will cause sluggish shifting. Lubricate the cable by smearing it with chain lube or a specific lubricant that came with your shifters (§viii-13) and check the cables and cable routing for smoothness (§viii-14). If lubricating the cable does not help, replace the cable and housing (see §viii-6–§viii-12).

viii-29 BENT REAR-DERAILLEUR HANGER

A bent hanger will misalign the derailleur and bedevil shifting. On modern bikes, the derailleur hanger is replaceable. If the hanger cannot be replaced, take your bike to a shop and have them align the hanger with the proper tool.

viii-30 BENT REAR-DERAILLEUR CAGE

A bent derailleur cage will hold the jockey wheels away from the vertical. Mild misalignment can be straightened by hand; eyeball the crankset for a vertical reference.

viii-31 LOOSE OR WORN-OUT REAR DERAILLEUR

Grab the derailleur and twist it with your fingers to feel for excessive play. Loose pivots, a symptom of a worn-out rear derailleur, will cause the rear derailleur to be loose and floppy. Replace it if it has this problem.

A loose mounting bolt will also mess up shifting by allowing the derailleur to flop around. Tighten the bolt.

viii-32 COMPATIBILITY ISSUES BETWEEN BRANDS, MODELS, AND SIX-, SEVEN-, EIGHT-, NINE-, AND TEN-SPEEDS

The number of rear cogs keeps going up. But does any of the old stuff work with any of the new stuff? And can you mix Shimano, Campagnolo, and SRAM parts?

Well, if you have resolutely stuck with your old frictional down-tube or bar-end shifters, you can let Shimano, Campagnolo, and SRAM throw however many cogs they want at you, and you will still be able to shift. That old Campagnolo Nuovo Record shifter and derailleur worked on five cogs, six cogs, seven cogs, eight cogs, nine cogs, and it will probably work on ten cogs! Modern indexed systems shift faster and more precisely, but they don't offer that kind of flexibility.

Compatibility problems occur as more and more cogs are squeezed into the same amount of space. The chain required gets narrower as the number of cogs goes up, and the spacing narrows between chainrings, between rear-derailleur jockey-wheel plates, between front-derailleur cage plates, and between the right-rear hub flange and the largest cog. Also, the rear hub axles have gotten longer. The spacing between rear dropouts (and hence the rear-axle "overlock" dimen-

COMPATIBILITY
ISSUES BETWEEN
BRANDS, MODELS,
AND SIX-, SEVEN-,
EIGHT-, NINE-,
AND TEN-SPEEDS

sion) was at 120mm during five-speed days, 126mm during the six- and seven-speed era, and it is now 130mm for eight-, nine-, and ten-speeds.

a. Cassette freehubs

Shimano's spacing between cogs has narrowed from 3.70mm for five- and six-speeds, to 3.10mm for seven-speed, 3.00mm for eight-speed, 2.56mm for nine-speed, and 2.35mm for ten-speed. Shimano freehubs appeared around 1980 and accepted six speeds widely spaced (at 3.70mm apart) on a 126mm hub. The first five cogs were splined to fit on the splined freehub body, and the last cog threaded on. Shimano Uniglide chains were wide and had the bent-plate configuration of present-day Shimano chains. Shimano began making its first indexed shifting systems in the mid-1980s as well.

When SunTour introduced narrow Ultra-7 freewheels in the early 1980s, Shimano countered with wider freehub bodies that fit seven widely spaced cogs (at 3.70mm apart) and the wide Shimano chain.

In the second half of the 1980s, Shimano succumbed to the rising popularity of narrow chains and made narrow bent-plate (Uniglide) chains. Its new freehub body was the old six-speed length, and it fit seven narrowly spaced cogs (at 3.10mm apart). But the new cogs would not fit on the old freehub bodies because a lockring now secured the cogs instead of a threaded small cog, and one spline groove was wider than the others.

The 1990s began with Shimano's introduction of eight-speed cogsets with 3.0mm cog spacing. Shimano had dictated that frames now had to have 130mm rear ends to accommodate new hubs with wider freehub bodies. Its one-wide-spline arrangement and threaded lockrings continued, but eight cogs would not fit a seven-speed body.

This set the stage for nine-speed Shimano cogsets, which had narrower (2.56mm) spacing, a narrower chain, and fit on eight-speed freehubs at first. But the desire for an 11-tooth cog forced the reduction of the freehub diameter by removing the outboard 2–3mm of spline ridges, which required new hubs (although enterprising do-it-yourselfers managed to salvage old hubs by grinding down the last couple of millimeters of the spline ridges flush with the freehub outer diameter).

With the advent of ten-speed cogs, Shimano's freehub body changed again, utilizing deeper spline valleys so that soft aluminum freehub bodies would not get torn up by the cogs. The outer diameter of the bottom of the spline valleys in the freehub body remains unchanged, so ten-speed cogs will fit on nine-speed freehub bodies. But nine-speed Shimano cogs will not fit Shimano ten-speed freehub bodies.

What of SunTour, Mavic, and Campagnolo? Well, all of them began making freehub bodies and cogs with their own spline configurations, and only Campagnolo's systems survived the shakeout. SunTour disappeared completely from the road market, while Mavic went with the flow, making Shimano- and Campagnolo-compatible hubs, wheels, and cogs. Campagnolo, the great, reliable, and unchanging bastion of compatibility and small parts availability in the 1970s and early 1980s, changed its eight-speed freehub body when it came out with nine speeds. Campagnolo nine-speed freehub bodies have deeper splines that do not fit Campy eight-speed cogs, but its ten-speed cogsets, fortunately, fit on the same Campy nine-speed freehub bodies. The ultra-narrow, 5.9mm- to 6.1mm-wide ten-speed chain allows ten cogs to fit in the same space that used to only accept nine with the wider nine-speed chain and cogset. The tooth-to-tooth distance on

COMPATIBILITY
ISSUES BETWEEN
BRANDS, MODELS,
AND SIX-, SEVEN-,
EIGHT-, NINE-,
AND TEN-SPEEDS

Campagnolo nine-speed is 4.55mm, and 4.15mm on Campagnolo ten-speed.

SRAM ten-speed cogs fit on Shimano nine-speed freehub bodies (Shimano ten-speed cogs do as well).

b. Chainrings

The spacing between chainrings keeps getting narrower with more speeds, as does the width and index spacing of the front derailleur. If you have upgraded piecemeal, you may find your nine- or ten-speed chain falling between the two chainrings held over from an earlier seven- or eight-speed system. The narrow chain will generally slip uselessly as you pedal, but it can jam between the rings as well, causing all sorts of expensive havoc.

Chainring teeth are made to fit closer together either by reducing the thickness of the chainring-mounting flats on the crank spider arms or by offsetting the teeth to one side of the chainring. Shimano seven-, eight-, nine-, and ten-speed spider arm mounting tabs are all the same thickness, but the teeth on Shimano nine- and ten-speed chainrings are offset toward each other.

Campagnolo's spider arms got thinner when going from seven- and eight-speed to nine-speed, but the chainring teeth got offset going to ten-speed, and the spider arms stayed the same as nine-speed. You can upgrade a Campagnolo nine-speed crank to ten-speed by changing the rings.

In general, I have encountered no problems using nine-speed cranks and chainrings of any brand with ten-speed drivetrains from Campagnolo, Shimano, or SRAM.

Compact-drive double cranks have smaller chainrings, with tooth counts like 34-48, 34-50, or 36-50. These cranks have a 110mm bolt circle diameter, rather than the 130mm of Shimano or the 135mm or (old)

144mm bolt circle diameters of Campagnolo. With the smaller curvature to the chainrings, standard front derailleurs do not work great, although they do work. Campagnolo's CT system has a dedicated compact crank with a dedicated compact front derailleur and works well. An IRD or FSA compact front derailleur often improves shifting with many brands of compact cranks. Shimano's and SRAM's compact chainrings are designed to work with their standard double front derailleurs.

c. Shifting compatibility of models within brands

All Campagnolo shifting system components can be interchanged within models. In other words, you can use Athena nine-speed Ergopower shifters with a Veloce rear derailleur, Mirage front derailleur, Record cogs, Chorus crank, and Centaur hub. The same holds true if all components are eight-speed or ten-speed.

Shimano components have more interchangeability exceptions. Until nine-speed came out, the stroke length for Dura-Ace derailleurs was different from all other Shimano derailleurs, mountain or road. Put another way, you could use any Shimano shifter you wanted with any Shimano derailleur except that Dura-Ace was only compatible with Dura-Ace.

With the advent of nine speeds, all Shimano rear derailleurs and shifters work together. But the same is not true with front derailleurs. If you try to use a road STI shift/brake lever with a top-swing (low-mount) top-pull mountain bike front derailleur (you might do this for a triple chainring setup, for instance), it won't work. However, you can use any Shimano top-mount, top-pull front derailleur with road STI. You can also use a nine-speed Shimano front or rear derailleur with Shimano ten-speed shifters, chain, and cogs.

All SRAM Force and Rival components are interchangeable. SRAM mountain bike derailleurs do not work with SRAM road shifters.

d. Shifting compatibility between brands

Until the advent of nine-speeds, a Campagnolo cogset did not shift acceptably on a Shimano indexed drivetrain, and vice versa. But the limited amount of space available for nine-speeds brought Shimano's and Campagnolo's cog spacing close enough that rear wheels could be switched back and forth between the two with decent shifting performance—not as good as you would pay big bucks for, but acceptable for normal riding and for wheel changes during races. Neutral support vehicles only had to stock one variety of nine-speed wheels to cover every rider in a race.

Of course, ten-speed systems have changed all of that again. For instance, in a Shimano ten-speed drivetrain, a Campy ten-speed cogset shifts acceptably in perhaps eight of the ten gears, the ninth cog just barely, and the tenth cog not at all. Shimano ten-speed cogsets work flawlessly in SRAM road drivetrains.

Mavic Zap was designed for Shimano eight-speed systems, and Mavic Mektronic is built for Shimano nine-speed systems but works decently on Campagnolo nine-speed cassettes as well.

As for front derailleurs and cranksets, mixing parts seems to cause few problems as long as you use parts designed for the same number of speeds. Campagnolo, Shimano, and SRAM road front derailleurs and cranksets work fine with each other's road shifters. Mavic Mektronic left levers work with any front derailleur.

All nine-speed chains work with all nine-speed systems. And any eight-speed chain works on any seven- or eight-speed system. For ten-speeds, it's best to stick with a ten-speed chain meant for that system. The seven- and eight-speed chains are 7.0–7.2mm wide;

nine-speed chains are 6.5–6.7mm wide; and Shimano's, Campagnolo's, and SRAM's ten-speed chains are 6.1mm wide. In theory, ten-speed chains should interchange, but the manufacturers discourage the practice.

viii-33 CHAIN SUCK

Though rare on triathlon bikes, chain suck (where the chain sticks to the chainring and is dragged around until it jams between the chainring and the chainstay) can still occur. See Troubleshooting Chain Problems at the end of Chapter 7, §vii-13.

viii-34 CHAINLINE

Chainline is the relative alignment of the front chainrings with the rear cogs; it is the imaginary line connecting the center of the middle chainring with the middle of the cogset (Fig. 8.30). This line should in theory be straight and parallel with the vertical plane of the bicycle. However, even owners of new bikes may discover poor chainlines on their bikes, due to mismatched cranks and bottom brackets.

Assuming that the frame is aligned properly, chainline can be adjusted by moving or replacing the bottom bracket to move the cranks left or right. You can roughly check the chainline by placing a long straightedge between the two chainrings and back to the rear cogs; it should come out in the center of the rear cogs. (If that's not good enough for your purposes, a more precise method is outlined below.)

If the chain falls off to the inside no matter how much you adjust the derailleur's low-gear limit screw, cable tension, and derailleur position, or you have chain rub, noise, or auto-shift problems in mild cross-gears that are not corrected with derailleur adjustments, a likely culprit is poor chainline.

8.30 **Measuring chainline**

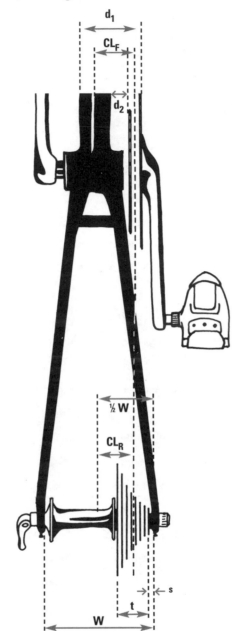

1. Find the position of the plane centered between the chainrings, or front point of the chainline (CL_F in Fig. 8.30).

   (a) Measure from the left side of the down tube to the outside of the large chainring (d1 in Fig. 8.30). (Do not measure from the seat tube; this tube is often ovalized at the bottom).

   (b) Measure the distance from the right side of the down tube to the inside of the inner chainring (d_2 in Fig. 8.30).

   (c) To find CL_F (the front chainline), add these two measurements, and divide the sum by two:

$$CL_F = (d_1 + d_2) \div 2$$

2. Find the rear end point of the chainline (CL_R in Fig. 8.30), which is the distance from the center of the plane of the bicycle to the center of the cogset.

   (a) Measure the thickness of the cog stack, end to end (t in Fig. 8.30).

   (b) Measure the space between the face of the smallest cog and the inside face of the dropout (s in Fig. 8.30).

   (c) Measure the length of the axle from dropout to dropout (W in Fig. 8.30); this length is also called the "axle overlock dimension," referring to the distance from locknut face to locknut face on either end. Generally, on any road bike built since the late 1980s, this will be 130mm.

   (d) To find CL_R, subtract half of the thickness of the cog stack and the distance from the inside face of the right rear dropout from half of the rear axle length:

$$CL_R = w \div 2 - t \div 2 - s$$

viii-35 PRECISE CHAINLINE MEASUREMENT

You will need a caliper with a Vernier (or digital) scale (Fig. 4.3).

The position of the plane centered between the two chainrings, as measured from the center of the seat tube to the center between the chainrings, is often called the chainline, although this is only the front point of the line.

3. If $CL_F = CL_R$ (the rear chainline), the chainline is perfect. This may not be possible to attain, however, due to considerations of chainstay clearance and prevention of chain rub on large chainrings in cross gears. Shimano specifies a "chainline" (i.e., CL_F, the front point of the chainline) of 43.5mm for a double and 45.0mm for a triple on road bikes. CL_F, the rear end point of the chainline, on the other hand, usually comes out around 42.6mm for Shimano nine-speed, 41.8mm for Campagnolo nine-speed, and 41.7mm for Campagnolo eight-speed.

Your bike will shift best and run quietest if the chainline (CL_F) measures around 42mm. However, this ideal may cause problems on your particular bike because (1) the inner chainring might rub the chainstay, (2) the front derailleur may bottom out on the seat tube before moving inward enough to shift to the inner chainring (this is particularly a problem with bikes with triple cranksets and oversized seat tubes), or (3) when crossing to the smallest cog from the inner chainring, the chain may rub on the next larger ring (this is not a problem if you simply avoid those cross gears).

My general recommendation is to have the chainrings in toward the frame as far as possible without rubbing the frame or bottoming out the front derailleur before it shifts cleanly to the inner chainring.

4. To improve the chainline, move the chainrings. The chainrings are moved by using a different bottom bracket, by exchanging bottom bracket spindles, or by moving the bottom bracket right or left (bottom bracket installation is covered in Chap. 11).

NOTE: *It's rare now with integrated-spindle cranksets (Figs. 11.15–16), but some bikes came new with terrible chainlines (chainrings out too far) that can only be corrected by buying a new bottom bracket. You will end up having to replace the long bottom bracket with a shorter one if you want the bike to shift properly. Good shops will replace the bottom bracket before selling the bike to you.*

ANOTHER NOTE: *The chainline can also be incorrect if the frame is misaligned. Alignment on metal frames generally can be corrected; your bike shop may offer this service. Carbon fiber frames usually cannot be altered; consult the manufacturer for advice on a misaligned carbon frame.*

5. If improving the chainline does not fix the shifting problem or if you don't want to mess with the chainline, buy and install an anti-chain-drop device like a Third Eye Chain Watcher (Fig. 8.31), Deda Dog Fang, or N'Gear Jump Stop. These are inexpensive gizmos that clamp around the seat tube next to the inner chainring. Adjust its position so that it nudges the chain back on when the chain tries to fall off to the inside.

8.31 Third Eye Chain Watcher

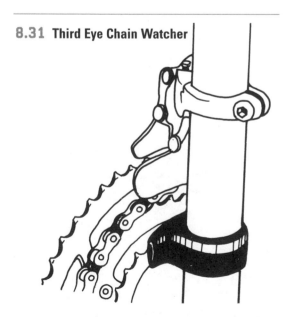

SHIFTING SYSTEM

WHEELS AND TIRES

All you need in this life is ignorance and confidence,
and then success is sure.
—Mark Twain

TOOLS

tire levers

pump

patch kit

spoke wrench

grease

5mm hex keys

13mm, 14mm, and
   15mm cone
   wrenches

metric open-end
   wrenches or
   adjustable
   wrenches

freehub cassette-
   lockring remover

Optional

tubular rim cement

Teflon tape

pliers

miter clamp

sewing needle for
   leather

braided high-test
   fishing line

thimble

barge cement (or
   other strong
   contact cement)

truing stand

tire sealant

freewheel remover

citrus solvent

soft hammer

Rohloff cog-wear
   indicator

Freehub Buddy

J-tool

fine-tip grease gun

Most road bike wheels are strung together with spokes connecting the hub to the rim. The rim, which both supports the tire and serves as the surface on which the brakes are applied, is supported and aligned by the tension on the spokes. Bearings in the hub, when clean and properly adjusted, allow the wheel to turn freely around the axle.

Composite wheels, be they disc wheels or three-, four-, or five-spoke wheels, generally use rigid members to hold the wheel up. An exception is the Spinergy Rev-X, which relies on tension on eight flat carbon spokes to support the wheel. Composite wheels generally cannot be trued, although the rim is replaceable on some models.

Wheels intended for aerodynamic efficiency have either solid sides (disc wheels) or aerodynamically shaped rims and few spokes, which are often themselves aerodynamic in shape. The spokes can be steel, titanium, or composite (often carbon fiber).

A cassette freehub or freewheel with cogs attached allows the rear wheel to spin while you are coasting, and it engages when force is applied to the pedals (Fig. 9.1).

The tires provide suspension as well as grip and traction for propulsion and steering. The air pressure in the tire is the primary suspension system on a road bike.

Two types of road bike tires are available. "Clinchers" (Fig. 9.2), which are C-shaped in cross section, are held into a C-shaped rim by a steel or Kevlar bead on each edge of the tire. A separate inner tube inside of the clincher holds the air. Tubulars (Fig. 9.3), which are circular in cross-section, have a casing that is wrapped around an inner tube and stitched or glued together. The tire is glued onto a box-section rim that has no vertical rim walls like a clincher rim.

This chapter addresses how to fix a flat or replace a tire or tube, true a wheel, fix a broken spoke or bent rim, overhaul hubs, change rear cogs, and lubricate cassettes and freewheels. Have at it!

9.1 The whole thing

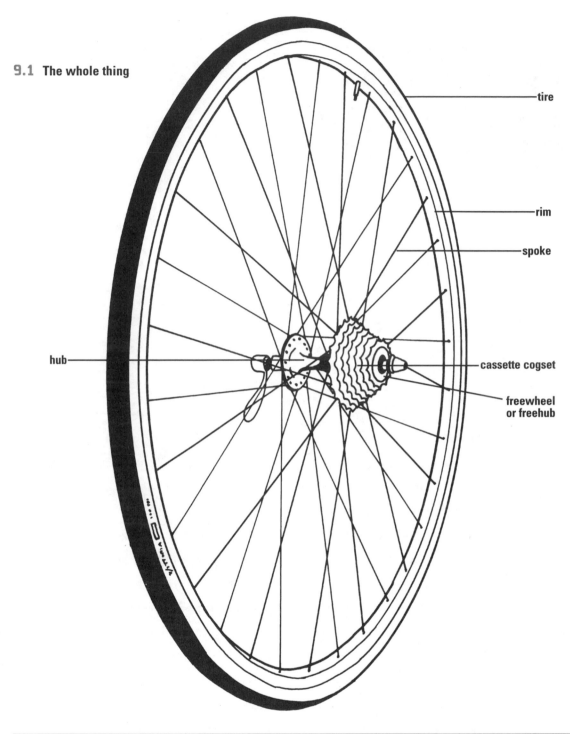

tire

rim

spoke

hub

cassette cogset

freewheel
or freehub

9.2 Clincher tire

9.3 Tubular tire

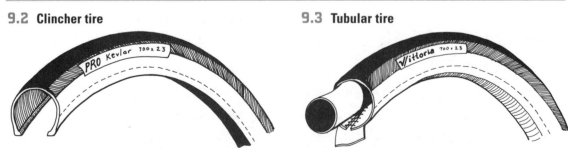

9.4 Presta valve

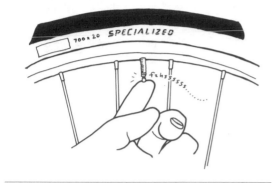

9.5 Schrader valve

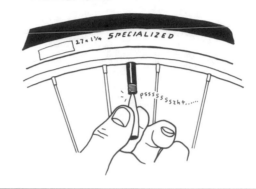

CLINCHER TIRES

ix-1 REMOVING THE TIRE

1. Remove the wheel (see Chap. 5, §v-2 and §v-9–10).

2. If your tire is not already flat, deflate it. First remove the valve cap (if installed) to get to the valve. Most road bike tires have Presta, or French, valves. These valves are thinner than Schrader valves (the kind found on cars) and have a small threaded rod with a tiny nut on the end. To let air out, unscrew the little nut a few turns, and push down on the thin rod (Fig. 9.4). To seal, tighten the little nut down again (with your fingers only!); leave it tightened down for riding. To deflate a Schrader valve, push down on the valve pin with something thin enough to fit in that won't break off, like a pen cap or a paper clip (Fig. 9.5).

NOTE: *If you have deep-section rims (i.e., Mavic Cosmic, Campagnolo Shamal, Vento, or Bora, Hed, Rolf, Spinergy, Zipp, or any of a myriad of others), inflating the tires will likely require valve extenders—thin threaded tubes that screw onto the Presta valve stems. To deflate tires that have valve extenders installed, you need to insert a thin rod (a spoke is perfect) down into the valve extender to release the air.*

To install valve extenders so that they seal properly and allow easy inflation, you need to unscrew the little nut on the Presta valve until it is against the mashed threads at the top of the valve shaft (they are mashed to keep the nut from unscrewing completely). Back the nut firmly into these mashed threads with a pair of pliers so that it stays unscrewed and does not tighten back down against the valve stem from the vibration of riding and prevent air from going in when you pump it. Some valve extenders (like Spinergy) also extend the valve nut and thus do not require this procedure; they actually allow you to tighten or loosen the valve nut with the extender in place.

You also should wrap a turn or two of Teflon pipe thread tape (made for household plumbing) around the top threads on the valve stem to seal it when the valve extender is installed; if you do not, air will leak out when pumping, and the pressure gauge on your pump will not give an accurate reading of the pressure in the tire. Tighten the valve extender onto the valve stem with a pair of pliers.

Some inner tubes now come with extra long Presta valves for deep-section wheels. These are operated just like standard Presta valves.

3. If you can push the tire bead off the rim with your thumbs without using tire levers, do so because there is less chance of damaging the tube and tire

9.6 Removing clincher tire with levers

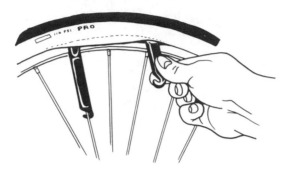

9.7 Prying out bead with third lever

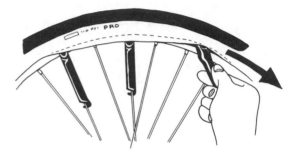

if you avoid the use of levers or other tools. It's easiest if you start just to one side or the other of the valve, after squeezing the tire beads into the center of the rim all of the way around (see the Pro Tip on tire removal).

4. If you can't get the tire off with your hands alone, insert a tire lever (with its scoop toward you) between the rim sidewall and the tire until you catch the edge of the tire bead. Make sure you do not pinch the tube between the lever and the tire. Again, start near the valve. This approach allows

---

PRO TIP

TIRE REMOVAL

Removal of the tire is most easily accomplished by starting near the valve stem. That way, the beads of the deflated tire can fall into the dropped center of the rim on the opposite side of the wheel, making it effectively a smaller-circumference rim off of which you are pushing the tire bead. If you instead try to push the tire bead off of (or onto) the rim on the side opposite the valve stem, the circumference on which the bead is resting is larger, because the valve stem is forcing the beads to stay up on their seating ledges opposite where you are working.

---

the beads on the side opposite the valve to drop into the center of the rim, effectively reducing the diameter about which the tire is stretched.

5. Pry down on the lever until the tire bead is pulled out over the rim (Fig. 9.6). If the lever has a hook on the other end, hook it onto the nearest spoke. Otherwise, keep holding it down.

6. Place the next lever a few inches away, and do the same thing with it (Fig. 9.6).

7. If needed, place a third lever a few inches farther on, pry it out, and continue sliding this lever around the tire, pulling the bead out as you go (Fig. 9.7). Some people slide their fingers around under the tire bead, but beware of cutting your fingers on a sharp bead.

N O T E : *There are a few quick-change tire levers on the market that work differently and more quickly than separate tire levers. If the tire bead is very tight on the rim, though, using separate tire levers may be the only method that works effectively.*

8. Once the bead is off the rim on one side, pull the tube out (Fig. 9.8).

9. If you are patching or replacing the tube, you do not need to remove the other side of the tire from the rim. If you are replacing the tire, the other bead should come off easily with your fingers. If it does not, use the tire levers as just outlined.

CHAPTER 9

159

PATCHING AN
INNER TUBE
·
STANDARD
PATCHES

9.8 Removing the inner tube

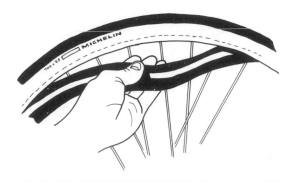

9.9 Checking for puncture

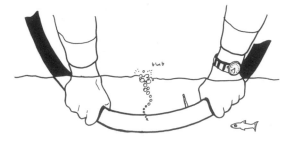

ix-2 PATCHING AN INNER TUBE

If the leak location is not obvious, put some air in the tube to inflate it until it is two to three times larger than its deflated size. Be careful. It will explode if you put too much air in, especially with lightweight latex or urethane tubes.

1. Listen and feel for air coming out, and mark the leak(s).

2. If you cannot find the leak by listening, submerge the tube in water. Look for air bubbling out (Fig. 9.9), and mark the spot(s).

N O T E : *Keep in mind that you can only patch small holes. If the hole is bigger than the eraser end of a pencil, a round patch is not likely to work. A slit as much as an inch long can be repaired with an oval patch.*

ix-3 STANDARD PATCHES

Use a patch designed for bicycle tires; it will generally have a thin, usually orange, gummy edge surrounding a slightly thicker patch of black rubber. Rema and Delta are common brands.

1. Dry the tube thoroughly near the puncture and mark the location of the hole with a pen.

2. To provide a suitable surface for the patch, clean and then rough up the tube surface within about a 1-inch radius around the hole with a small piece of sandpaper (usually supplied with the patch kit).

Do not touch the sanded area. If the patch kit you are using came with a little metal "cheese grater" for the purpose, discard it and replace it with sandpaper. The grater-style rougheners tend to do to your tube what they do to cheese.

3. Apply glue (patch cement) in a thin, smooth layer all over an area centered on the hole (Fig. 9.10). Use the end of the glue container or a brush, rather than your finger, to spread the glue around. Cover an area that is bigger than the size of the patch. The glue is similar to rubber cement, so if the tube in your patch kit has dried out, you can use any rubber cement sold in office supply and hardware stores for the purpose. If you do this, and use the brush attached to the top of the bottle cap, wipe the brush almost dry before spreading the cement on the tube. You only need a thin layer for the patch.

4. Let the glue dry 10 minutes or so until there are no more shiny, wet spots.

5. Peel the patch from its foil backing (but do not remove the cellophane top cover yet).

6. Stick the patch over the hole, and push it down in place, making sure that all of the gummy edges are stuck down. With the tube sitting on a hard surface, burnish the patch with the plastic handle of a screwdriver to stick the edges down securely.

STANDARD

PATCHES

·

GLUELESS

PATCHES

·

INSTALLING

PATCHED OR

NEW TUBE

9.10 Applying glue

9.11 Removing cellophane

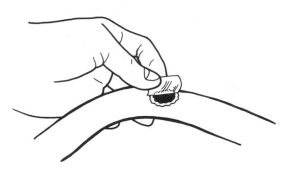

7. (Optional) Remove the cellophane top covering, being careful not to peel up the edges of the patch (Fig. 9.11). Often the cellophane top patch is scored. If you fold the patch, the cellophane will split at the scored cuts, allowing you to peel outward and avoid pulling the newly adhered patch up off the tube. If you can't get the cellophane off without peeling up the patch, just leave it alone. It won't do any harm in the tire.

ix-4 GLUELESS PATCHES

There are a number of adhesive-backed patches on the market that do not require additional cement. Most often you simply need to clean the area around the hole with the little alcohol pad supplied with the patch. Let the alcohol dry, peel the backing, and stick on the patch.

The advantages of glueless patches are that they are very fast to use and take little room in a seat bag; also, you never open your patch kit to discover that your glue tube is dried up. On the downside, I have not found any glueless patches that stick nearly as well as the standard type. With a standard patch installed, you can inflate the tube to look for more leaks without having it in the tire. If you do that with a glueless patch, the patch usually lifts enough to start leaking.

You must install the tube in the tire and on the rim before putting air in it after glueless patching. And unlike a standard patch, a glueless patch is not a permanent fix.

ix-5 INSTALLING PATCHED OR NEW TUBE

If you've just fixed a flat, feel around the inside of the tire to see whether there is still anything sticking through that can puncture the tube again. Sliding a rag all the way around the inside of the tire works well. The rag will catch on anything sharp and will save your fingers from being cut by whatever is stuck in the tire.

1. Replace any tire that has damaged areas (inside or out) where the casing fibers appear to be cut or frayed.

2. Examine the rim to be certain that the rim tape is in place and that there are no spokes or anything else sticking up that can puncture the tube. Replace the rim tape if necessary. Two layers of fiberglass strapping tape work fine for this purpose.

3. By hand, push one bead of the tire onto the rim.

4. (Optional) Spread talcum powder around the inside of the tire and on the outside of the tube, so the two do not adhere to each other. Don't inhale this stuff, by the way.

9.12 Installing tire by hand

9.13 Finishing at the valve

5. Put just enough air in the tube to give it shape. Close the valve, if Presta.

N O T E : *If you have a deep-section rim and a standard-length Presta valve, you will need to install a valve extender so that you can get air into the tire once it is on the rim. To install valve extenders so that they seal properly and allow easy inflation, unscrew the little nut on the Presta valve against the mashed threads at the top of the valve shaft (they are mashed to keep the nut from unscrewing completely). Back the nut firmly into these mashed threads with a pair of pliers so that the nut stays unscrewed and does not tighten back down against the valve stem and prevent air from going in when you pump it. You also should wrap a turn or two of Teflon pipe thread tape, made for household plumbing, around the top threads on the valve stem to create a seal when the valve extender is screwed on. If you do not, air will leak out when pumping, and the pressure gauge on the pump will not give an accurate reading of the pressure in the tire. Tighten the valve extender onto the valve stem with pliers.*

6. Push the valve through the valve hole in the rim.

7. Push the tube up inside the tire all of the way around.

8. Starting at the side opposite the valve stem, push the tire bead onto the rim with your thumbs. Be sure that the tube doesn't get pinched between the tire bead and the rim.

9. Work around the rim in both directions with your thumbs, pushing the tire onto the rim (Fig. 9.12). Finish from both sides at the valve (Fig. 9.13), deflating the tube when it gets hard to push more of the tire onto the rim. (See Pro Tip on tire removal.) You can often install a tire without tools. If you cannot, use tire levers, but make sure you don't catch any of the tube under the edge of the bead. Finish the same way, at the valve.

10. Reseat the valve stem by pushing up on the valve after you have pushed the last bit of bead onto the rim (Fig. 9.14). You may have to manipulate the tire so that all the tube is tucked under the tire bead.

11. Go around the rim and inspect for any part of the tube that may be protruding from under the edge of the tire bead. If you have a fold of the tube under the edge of the bead, it can blow the tire off the rim when you inflate it or while you are riding. It will sound like a gun went off next to you and will leave you with an un-patchable tube.

12. Pump the tire up. Generally, 85–120psi is correct for a good-quality road bike tire. Much less, and you run the risk of a pinch flat or "snake bite." And more pressure buys you nothing; see Pro Tip on tire pressure.

WHEELS AND TIRES

9.14 Seating the tube

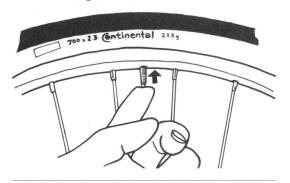

ix-6 PATCHING TIRE CASING (SIDEWALL)

Unless it is an emergency, don't do it! If the tire casing is cut, get a new tire. Patching the tire casing is dangerous. No matter what you use as a patch, the tube will find a way to bulge out of the patched hole, and when it does, your tire will go flat immediately. Imagine coming down a steep hill and suddenly your front tire goes completely flat . . . you get the picture.

In an emergency, you can put layers of non-stretchable material between the tube and tire (see Chap. 6, §vi-3b, Fig. 6.1). Candidates for this duty include a dollar bill, an empty energy bar wrapper (or two), or even a short section of the exploded tube (double thickness is better).

TUBULAR TIRES

Tubular tires, or sew-ups, are expensive, hard to install (they must be glued to the rim), hard to repair, and these days can even be hard to find. So why bother with them?

Many triathletes like tubulars because they are faster to change when they go flat than clinchers. This can be a decisive difference in a race.

For another thing, tubular wheelsets (front/rear wheel pairs) are generally lighter than clincher wheelsets, because tubular rims do not require flanges for the tire bead. Tubular tires by themselves are usually lighter than clinchers, too, although the difference these days is often quite small. Tubulars are enjoying a renaissance with the advent of superlight carbon-fiber tubular rims for racing.

PRO TIP

TIRE PRESSURE AND ROLLING RESISTANCE

Using overly high pressure is a common mistake triathletes are prone to. The danger of blowing the tire off of the rim and really hurting yourself is high. Beyond that, high inflation does not accomplish what its devotees believe, which is to reduce rolling resistance. If the tire cannot absorb small bumps into its surface because it is pumped up too high, the bike will roll slower, even though it may feel very fast because it is so stiff and bouncy and lively. Every little bump lifts the bike and rider, also providing a backward force on impact. This costs energy compared to absorbing the bump into the tire while the bike and rider continue to roll along smoothly without up-down motion.

Pressures of 140psi and higher are only fast on a very smooth surface, which you find nowhere other than a polished velodrome (banked track). On any road surface, anything higher than 120psi is costing you speed.

A handmade tire with tightly packed threads forming the casing will always roll faster than one with a casing made of a few, thick, stiff threads. If you want to roll fast, choose a tire with a high thread count that feels supple when you fold it in your hand, and forget the bomber tire pressures that also endanger your life! And, never put more in than the max pressure rating on the tire sidewall.

Yet another reason for the continuing popularity of these quirky throwbacks is that a lot of people say that they ride and corner better than clinchers. And being sewn together, they can be made to hold extremely high pressures.

But perhaps the main reason to consider tubulars is their inherent safety. In the event of a blowout, they stay on the rim. Clincher tires, when flat, fall into the rim well, and you may find yourself trying to ride on the slippery metal rim, rather than on a piece of rubber.

Tubulars usually deflate more slowly when punctured than clinchers too, because the air can only escape through the puncture hole. Clinchers can let air escape all the way around the rim.

If these advantages appeal to you—and the disadvantages listed here don't put you off—tubulars are a worthwhile alternative to the standard clincher setup.

ix-7 REMOVING A TUBULAR

1. Remove the wheel (see Chap. 5, §v-2 and §v-9–10).
2. If the tire is not already flat, deflate it. Tubular tires have Presta, or French, valves. To let air out, unscrew the little nut atop the valve stem a few turns, and push down on the thin rod (Fig. 9.4). To seal, tighten the little nut down again (with your fingers only); leave it tightened for riding.

N O T E : *If you have deep-section rims (i.e., Mavic Cosmic, Campagnolo Shamal, Vento, Bora, Hed, Rolf, Spinergy, Zipp, or any of a myriad of others), the wheels will likely have valve extenders—thin threaded tubes that screw onto the valve stems. To deflate the tire, you may need to insert a thin rod (a spoke is perfect) into the valve extender to release the air.*

Some tubulars now come with extra long Presta valves for deep-section wheels. These are operated just like standard Presta valves.

3. Push the tire off the rim in one section with your thumbs pushing up against one side. Avoid using tools. If you use a tool to pry the tire away from the glue, you will tear the base tape at the least and more likely tear casing cords as well. The tire will always be lumpy in that area after such damage.
4. Peel the tire off the rim by hand.

ix-8 GLUING TUBULAR TIRES

LEVEL 2

Gluing tubular tires to the rims properly is critical to continuing the attachment you have with your epidermis. I can say from experience and from watching many riders roll improperly glued tires off rims that you do not want it to happen to you. Follow these steps and your tire will really be secure! Pay particular attention to the second step, since all the rim cement in the world will not keep your tire on if the cement is not adhered to the tire.

N O T E : *For tires without a latex coating on the base tape (or after scraping; see step 2), Tufo sells easy-to-use, single-hand double-sided tape to attach a tubular to a rim without using rim cement. Tufo standard, or cyclocross tape, has backing on one side only. To use, peel the backing off, stick it on the rim, and cut open the valve hole to then install, center, and inflate the tire. Tufo Extreme tape has backing on both sides. Remove the rim-side backing (it will be labeled) first, and stick the tape onto the rim. Peel back the corners of the top-side backing at each end so that the corners stick out from the sides of the rim. Cut open the valve hole and then install, inflate, and center the tire. Centering is easy with the help of the slick backing. Pull the backing out from under the entire tire before inflating it to 130psi. Ride on the tire for five minutes. Tufo tapes are ready to ride immediately after completing the inflation and five minutes of riding on the tire.*

1. Before gluing a new tubular, first stretch it over the rim (Fig. 9.15). To do this, install the tire without any glue by using the method described in step 9.

2. Once the tire is stretched, remove it and scrape the base tape of the tubular with a serrated knife edge or metal file edge to produce a good gluing surface. The base tape on most tires is cotton and has a coating of latex, to which the rim cement will not bond well. The tire can roll off even a thick layer of cement on the rim if the base tape has not been properly prepared. This step does not apply to most Continental tubulars, which usually have no latex over the base tape.

3. Start by pumping the tire (not on the rim) until it turns inside out and the base tape faces outward. By using the serrations of a table knife or the rough side of a metal file, scrape the base tape back and forth (Fig. 9.16) until the latex coating on the tape balls up into little sticky hunks. I have also heard of people brushing rubbing alcohol on the base tape to make the surface tacky. I generally discourage the use of solvents on the base tape for fear of solvent penetrating the tape and dissolving the glue holding the tape onto the tire. I have seen many a tire roll right off the base tape, even though the tape is well-adhered to the rim.

4. Prepare the rim for glue. With a new rim, clean off any oil with alcohol or acetone (while wearing rubber gloves and a respirator) and sandpaper. Roughing up the gluing surface with sandpaper does not help the tire stick to the rim better, but solvent will not remove everything (Teflon, for instance), and sandpaper can remove some invisible contaminants that would prevent the glue from sticking to the rim.

9.15 Stretching the tubular tire over the rim

5. With a rim that has been glued before, you can just apply a uniform layer of glue, unless there is a really thick, lumpy layer of old glue on the rim. In this case, scrape the big lumps off, and get the surface as uniform as you can, or strip the entire rim with acetone.

6. Put a thin layer of glue on the rim, edge-to-edge, and edge-to-edge on the base tape of the tire, as well. I recommend squeezing a bead of glue from the tube and then putting a plastic bag over your finger and spreading the glue on the tire and rim thinly and uniformly, or, better yet, brushing it on with a small, stiff brush. Let it dry overnight. Repeat.

N O T E : *Except for carbon rims (see Pro Tip on gluing a tubular onto a carbon rim), I recommend using clear tubular rim cement, ideally either Continental rim cement or Vittoria Mastik'One, rather than red glues.*

9.16 Scrape the base tape before gluing

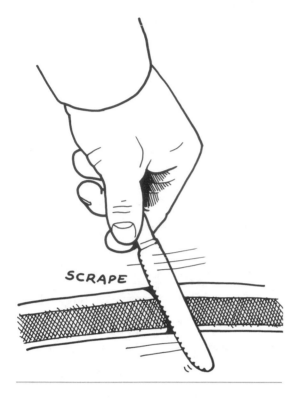

SCRAPE

Red glues harden up; if you leave them on for years, they get so dried out that the tire is not held well and will need to be reglued. Red glues also do not act as contact cement, whereas the recommended glues stay sticky and continually reglue the tire wherever it may peel up a bit.

7. After the second layer of glue on the rim and tire has dried overnight as well, smear another thin layer of glue on the rim. Let this layer set overnight again.

8. After the glue on the rim and tire has dried overnight again, smear or brush another thin layer of glue on the rim. Let this layer set for 15 minutes.

9. Deflate and mount the tire as follows:

   (a) Stand the wheel up with the valve hole facing up.

   (b) Put the valve stem through the hole, and, leaning over the wheel, grab the tire and stretch outward as you push the base tape into the top of the rim. Keep stretching down on the tire with both hands, using your body weight, as you push the tire down around the rim (Fig. 9.15). I like to lean hard enough on the tire that my feet lift repeatedly off the ground. The farther you can stretch the tire at this point, the easier it will be to get the last bit of tire onto the rim.

   (c) Lifting the rim up to horizontal with the valve side against your belly, roll the last bit of the tire onto the opposite side of the rim. If you can't get the tire to pop over the rim, peel the tire back and start over, pushing down again from the valve stem. Avoid the temptation of prying a stubborn tire onto the rim with screwdrivers or other tools, as you will likely tear cords in the base tape and tire casing, leading to a bulge in the tire in this area.

10. By pulling the tire this way and that, get the edge of the base tape aligned with the rim. You want to see the same amount sticking out from the rim all the way around on both sides around the wheel.

11. Pump the tire to 100psi and spin the wheel, looking for wobbles in the tire. If you find that the tread snakes back and forth as you spin the wheel, deflate the tire and push it over where required. Reinflate and check again, repeating the process until the tire is as straight as you are willing to get it. The final process will depend somewhat on how accurately the tubular was made; you'll find that some brands and models glue on straighter than others.

12. Pump the tire up to 120–130psi and leave it overnight to bond firmly.

13. You can get an even better bond by using a woodworker's band (miter) clamp around the entire inflated tire. The miter clamp (see Fig. 4.2

in Chap. 4) is a piece of nylon webbing with a cam-lock buckle on it. Depress the tab on the buckle to let out enough strap to surround the inflated tire and wheel. Pull the end of the strap to tighten the loop around the tire. Use a wrench to tighten the clamp and put extra pressure on the tire to conform its bottom surface to the rim and bond it tightly. Tomorrow you can release the miter clamp (by using the release [thumb] tab) and go ride or race on this wheel.

PRO TIP

GLUING A TUBULAR ONTO A CARBON RIM

Carbon rims are notoriously hard to glue to. In this case, the thick, gloppy red glue of yesteryear, namely Clément rim cement, seems to adhere to the rim best, but it is no longer available unless you know somebody with a stash. Otherwise, Vittoria Mastik'One seems to be the best available glue choice, according to research done at the University of Kansas; see www.engr.ku.edu/~ktl. Tires tend to snap off of carbon rims, rather than peel off, meaning that the same amount of force that would only slightly dislodge a tubular on an aluminum rim can push the tire entirely off a carbon rim. The best way to prevent this is to follow the above multiple-layer gluing procedure with clean rims and scraped base tape. The first time you glue a tubular to a carbon rim, it is worth pulling the tire off to check your work. If the adhesion is good, reglue it using the same method. If not, you should increase the number of layers of glue and make sure that you allow the glue to set up after installing the tire.

ix-9 CHANGING A TUBULAR TIRE ON THE ROAD

When you get a puncture with a tubular tire, you will find that it is easier to deal with than a clincher. You want to make sure that you are carrying a spare tubular that already has glue on the base tape. For your spare, carry an old tubular that has been glued to a rim in the past, or, with a new tire as a spare, follow steps 1–3 and 6 in §ix-8.

Remove the wheel and pull the flat tire off the rim. If you did a good gluing job, this may take some doing. (On the other hand, if the tubular is easy to peel off, you need to improve your gluing technique.) Stretch the spare tire onto the rim as in steps 9 and 10 in §ix-8. Pump it up hard (over 100psi) to get it to stay on the rim for the rest of the ride. Corner carefully going home, as the glue bond is marginal. When you get home, glue a tire securely on the rim before riding on that wheel again.

ix-10 PATCHING TUBULAR TIRES

LEVEL 2

In the early 1980s, my racing buddies and I spent countless hours patching tubular tires, often while sitting in the car on the way to distant races. Now that everyone trains on clinchers, nobody seems to patch tubulars any more. Tubulars are arguably still the best tires for racing, being lighter, requiring lighter rims, and having a more supple casing which in turn offers greater traction and a better ride at high inflation pressures. However, even though tubulars are expensive, it makes no sense to patch a racing tire, because you invest too much time, energy, and money competing in races to run the risk of getting a puncture because of a weakened tire.

If you still wish to patch a tubular, here are the steps involved:

1. Remove the tire from the rim.

2. Pump up the tire to at least 70psi and submerge it in a bucket of water to find the leak. If you're lucky, air will come out through a hole in the tread. In the case of a pinched tube, though, the air may seep out through the casing randomly at the stitches, and be hard to localize. See the next step for help.

3. For 2 inches on either side of the puncture, peel away the base tape covering the stitching. If you were unable to precisely locate the hole, try submerging the inflated tire now to watch the bubbles coming out through the stitching. Peel more base tape back if necessary until you are sure that you have exposed the stitching at the hole.

4. Deflate the tire and carefully cut the outer layer of stitching threads for about an inch or so on either side of the hole. Pull the casing open in that spot, and pull enough of the tube out through the hole to find and access the hole(s) in it.

5. Patch the tube in the same manner as outlined in §ix-2. Use the same type of recommended patches.

6. Push the tube back in place, and sew up the opening in the stitching. I recommend using a needle for leather with a triangular cross-section tip and braided high-test fishing line. Stitch one way across the opening, turn the tire around, and double back over the stitches again. For obvious reasons, be careful not to poke the tube. You may need a thimble to push the needle in and a pair of pliers to pull it out on each stitch.

7. Inflate the tire to 70psi or so to make sure all of the leaks have been patched.

8. Deflate the tire and coat the peeled-back section of base tape and the exposed stitching area with contact cement. Barge glue for shoes works great.

Wait 15 minutes or so for the glue to set, and carefully stick the base tape back down over the stitching. (If the tape stretched when you pulled it loose, it's okay to cut it and overlap the ends.)

9. Coat the rim and the tire base tape with a thin layer of rim cement. Let it sit 15 minutes to an hour. Because this is an old tire, there should already be a good layer of rim cement on the tire and the rim.

10. Glue the tire onto the rim (see §ix-8).

ix-11 TIRE SEALANTS

Tire sealants can virtually eliminate flat tires caused by tread punctures; they do not fix sidewall cuts, pinch flats, or rim-side punctures. The most popular tire sealant, Slime, is a green goo full of chopped fibers; when poured into an inner tube, it flows to punctures and seals them. There are other brands and colors of tire sealants as well; these instructions generally apply to them all.

Only use sealant in a clincher tube without cuts in it. The tube must also have a Schrader valve in good condition (Figs. 4.1B and 9.5); you cannot insert sealant into a Presta valve because it will block the valve. By the way, you can put sealant in a tube that already has a slow leak; simply inject it as detailed in the next section, pump it up, and spin the wheel for about five minutes.

N O T E : *If you have Presta valves (Figs. 4.1B and 9.4) and you want to use tire sealant, you can purchase tubes with sealant already inside. If you have a slow leak in a tubular or you want to have some puncture resistance in a Presta tube, you can pour a can of evaporated milk into a pump you don't care about and pump it into the tire via the Presta valve. It works quite well for tiny leaks, but if you get a blowout, boy, does it ever stink!*

a. Sealant installation into a tube that's already installed in a tire

1. Shake the bottle.

2. Remove the Schrader valve core by using the valve-cap core remover; it is packaged with most sealants, or you can get one at an auto tire store.

3. Rotate the wheel so that the valve stem is at the four o'clock position.

4. Cut off the bottle spout and connect the bottle spout and valve stem with the supplied tubing.

5. Squeeze the bottle slowly to inject the sealant.

6. Stop squeezing after injecting four ounces; wait several minutes to clear the stem.

7. Remove the tube.

8. Screw the valve core firmly back into the valve stem in a clockwise direction.

9. Inflate the tube.

10. If the tube has a leak, spin the wheel for five minutes to spread the sealant in the tube.

b. Maintaining tire sealant–filled tubes

Inflating

Always have the stem at four o'clock and wait a minute for the sealant to drain away; if you don't, sealant will leak out, eventually clogging the valve.

Sealing punctures

1. If you find the tire has gone flat, pump it up and ride it a bit to see if it seals.

2. If you get numerous punctures, you may need to pump repeatedly and ride before the tube seals up.

3. Pinch flats, caused by pinching the tube between the tire and rim, are hard to seal because the two "snake-bite" holes are on the side. Try laying the bike on the same side as the holes.

4. Imbedded nails and other foreign objects can be removed; spin the wheel to seal the hole.

5. Punctures on the rim side of the tube will not seal because the sealant is thrown to the outside by centrifugal force.

6. Sidewall gashes will require new tubes and tires.

RIMS AND SPOKES

ix-12 TRUING A WHEEL

LEVEL 3

If a spoked wheel has a mild wobble, you can fix it by adjusting the tension on the spokes. An extreme bend in the rim cannot be fixed by spoke truing alone because the spoke tension on the two sides of the wheel will be so uneven that the wheel will rapidly fall apart.

1. Check that there are no broken spokes in the wheel or any spokes that are so loose that they flop around. If there is a broken spoke, follow the replacement procedure in §ix-13. If there is a single loose spoke, check to see that the rim is not dented or cracked in that area. Replace the rim if it is. If the rim looks okay, mark the loose spoke with a piece of tape and tighten it with the spoke wrench until it has the same tension as adjacent spokes on the same side of the wheel (pluck the spoke and listen to the tone). Then follow the truing procedure in step 2.

2. Grab the rim while the wheel is on the bike and flex it side to side to check the hub-bearing adjustment. If the bearings are loose, the wheel will clunk from side to side. The play in the bearings will have to be eliminated before you true the wheel or the rim will wobble erratically because of the loose hub. Follow the hub-adjustment procedure, §ix-16d, steps 28–34.

3. Put the wheel in a truing stand, if you have one. Otherwise, leave it on the bike and suspend the

9.17 Lateral truing if rim scrapes on left

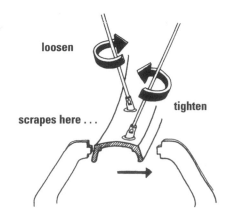

loosen

scrapes here . . .

tighten

9.18 Lateral truing if rim scrapes on right

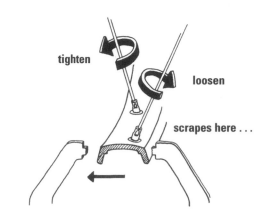

tighten

loosen

scrapes here . . .

bike in a bike stand or from the ceiling, or turn it upside down on the handlebar and saddle.

4. Adjust the truing stand feeler, or hold one of your brake pads so that it scrapes the rim at the biggest wobble.

5. Where the rim scrapes, tighten the spoke (or spokes) that comes to the rim from the opposite side of the hub, and loosen the spoke that comes from the same side of the hub (Figs. 9.17–18). This process will pull the rim away from the feeler or brake pad.

NOTE: *When correcting a wheel that is laterally out of true (wobbles side-to-side), always adjust spokes in pairs: one spoke coming from one side of the wheel, the other coming from the opposite side. Tightening spokes is like opening a jar upside down. With the jar right side up, turning the lid to the left (counterclockwise) opens the jar, but this direction apparently reverses when you turn the jar upside down (try it and see). Spoke nipples are just like the lid on that upside-down jar: When the nipples are at the bottom of the rim, counterclockwise tightens, and clockwise loosens (Fig. 9.19). The opposite is true when the nipples to be turned are at the top. It may take you a few attempts before*

you catch on, but you will eventually get it. If you temporarily make the wheel worse, simply undo what you have done and start over.

It is best to tighten and loosen by small amounts (about a quarter-turn at a time), decreasing the amount you turn the spoke nipples as you move away from the spot where the rim scrapes the hardest. If the wobble gets worse, then you are turning the spokes in the wrong direction.

ANOTHER NOTE: *Some wheels have their spoke nipples at the hub, not at the rim. Before you turn them, think carefully about which way tightens and which way loosens.*

6. As the rim moves into proper alignment, readjust the truing-stand feeler or the brake pad so that it again finds the most out-of-true spot on the wheel.

7. Check the wobble first on one side of the wheel and then the other, adjusting spokes accordingly, so that you don't end up pulling the whole wheel off center by chasing wobbles only on one side. As the wheel gets closer to true, you will need to decrease the amount you turn the spokes; otherwise, you will overcorrect.

WHEELS AND TIRES

9.19 **Tightening and loosening spokes**

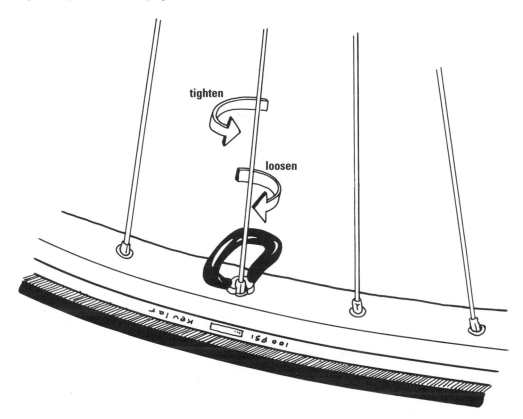

tighten

loosen

8. Accept a certain amount of wobble, especially if you are truing the wheel in a bike; the method is not very accurate and is not at all suited for making a wheel absolutely true. If you have access to a wheel-dishing tool, check to make sure that the wheel is centered.

ix-13 REPLACING A BROKEN SPOKE

LEVEL 2

Go to the bike store and get a new spoke of the same length. Remember: the spokes on the front wheel are usually not the same length as the spokes on the rear wheel. Also, the spokes on the drive (right) side of the rear wheel are almost always shorter than those on the nondrive (left) side.

1. Make sure you are using a replacement spoke of the proper thickness and length.

9.20 **Weaving a new spoke**

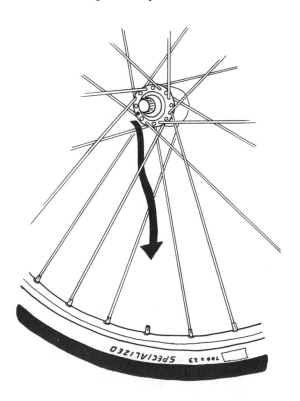

2. Thread the spoke through the spoke hole in the hub flange. If the broken spoke is on the drive side of the rear wheel, you will need to remove the cassette cogs to get at the hub flange (§ix-19).

3. Weave the new spoke in with the other spokes just as it was before (Fig. 9.20). It may take some bending to get it in place.

4. Thread it into the same nipple, if the nipple is in good shape. Otherwise, use a new nipple; you'll need to remove the tire, tube, and rim strip (or the tubular tire) to install the nipple.

5. Mark the new spoke with a piece of tape, and tighten it up about as snugly as the neighboring spokes on that side of the wheel.

6. Follow the steps for truing a wheel as outlined in §ix-12.

HUBS

ix-14 OVERHAULING HUBS

LEVEL 2

Hubs should turn smoothly and noiselessly. If you maintain them regularly, you can expect them to still be running smoothly when you are ready to give up on the rest of your bike.

All hubs have a hub shell that contains the axle and bearings and is connected to the rim with spokes or, in the case of disc wheels, by sheets of composite material. Beyond that, they diverge into two types: the standard cup-and-cone type (Fig. 9.21) and the sealed-bearing (or cartridge-bearing) type (Fig. 9.22).

Standard cup-and-cone hubs have loose ball bearings that roll along very smooth bearing surfaces called "races" or "cups"; an axle runs through the center of the hub. Conical nuts, called "cones" (Fig. 9.21), thread onto the axle. The cones create an inner race for the bearings. In high-quality hubs, the cup-and-cone surfaces that contact the bearings are precisely machined to minimize friction. The operation of the hub depends on the smoothness and lubrication of the cones, ball bearings, and bearing cups. The cones are held in place on the axle by one or more spacers (washers) followed by threaded locknuts that tighten down against the cones and spacers to keep the hub in proper adjustment. The rear hub will have more spacers on both sides, especially on the drive side (Fig. 9.31).

The term "sealed-bearing" hub is a bit of a misnomer, because many cup-and-cone hubs offer better protection against dirt and water than some sealed-bearing hubs. The phrase "cartridge-bearing hub" is more accurate because the distinguishing feature of these hubs is that the bearings, races, and cones are assembled at the bearing factory as a complete unit—the cartridge—that is then plugged into a hub shell machined to accept the pre-made cartridge. Cartridge-bearing front hubs have two bearings, one on each end of the hub shell (Fig. 9.22). Rear hubs (Fig. 9.30) may have a cartridge bearing on the left side only and may employ a stock Shimano freehub with loose hub bearings as well as loose freehub bearings on the drive side. Some manufacturers make their own freehubs and have cartridge bearings on both sides of the hub as well as internal to the freehub.

Cartridge-bearing hubs can have any number of axle-assembly types. Some have a threaded axle with locknuts similar to a cup-and-cone hub. Common in the more expensive setups are aluminum axles, often very fat with correspondingly large bearings. Their end caps usually snap on or are held on with setscrews or circlips. The end caps may also thread into the axle and accept a 5mm hex key in the end of each cap.

ALL HUBS,

PRELIMINARY

•

OVERHAUL

STANDARD CUP-

AND-CONE HUB

(FRONT OR REAR)

9.21 **Cup-and-cone front hub with standard ball bearings**

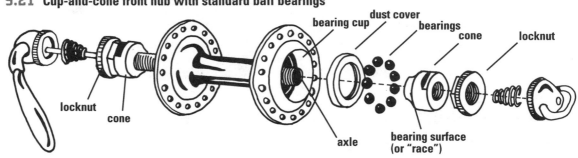

9.22 **Front hub with cartridge bearing**

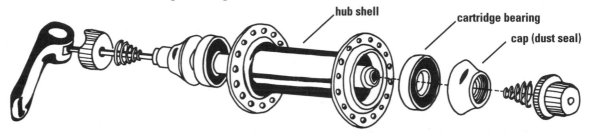

ix-15 ALL HUBS, PRELIMINARY

1. Remove the wheel from the bike (Chap. 5, §v-2 and §v-11–12).

2. Remove the quick-release skewer or the nuts and washers holding the wheel onto the bike. (This step is unnecessary for hubs that have solid axles held on with nuts or wing nuts, rather than having skewers that pass through hollow axles.)

ix-16 OVERHAUL STANDARD CUP-AND-CONE HUB (FRONT OR REAR)

To isolate problems, take some time to evaluate the hub's condition before disassembling it. Spin the hub while holding the axle and turn the axle while holding the hub. Does it turn roughly? Is the axle bent or broken? Wobble the axle side to side. Is the bearing adjustment loose?

a. Disassembly

1. Set the wheel flat on a table or workbench. Slip a cone wrench of the appropriate size (usually 13mm, 14mm, or 15mm) onto the wrench flats on one of the cones. On a rear wheel, work on the left (noncog) side.

N O T E : *On current Campagnolo and Fulcrum high-end hubs, you unscrew the axle into two pieces with 5mm hex keys inserted into either end of the axle. Loosen the setscrew on the large aluminum split locknut with a 2.5mm hex key (loosen the setscrew three turns). Unscrew and remove the locknut with your fingers or with a 22mm (or adjustable) wrench. Push the axle end toward the hub to free the slide-on cone. Follow steps 7–26, and then assemble in the reverse order. For a rear hub, see §ix-20e for hints on reinstalling the freehub pawls into the hub shell. Adjust the hub by turning the lock-nut by hand or with a 22mm (or adjustable) wrench until the bearing end play is removed, and tighten the setscrew with a 2.5mm hex key. This adjustment can even be performed while the wheel is installed in the frame or fork to get it extremely precise—free running with no end play.*

9.23 Loosening and tightening locknut

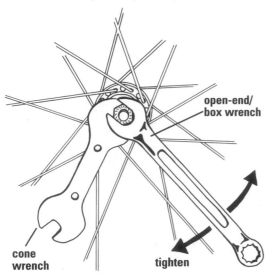

6. Unscrew the cone from the axle. Again, you may need to hold the opposite cone with a wrench. An easy way to keep track of the various nuts, spacers, and cones is to lay them on your workbench in the order they were removed. If that seems too casual, you can slide a twist-tie through all the parts in the correct order and orientation. Either method serves as an easy guide when reassembling the hub.

7. To catch any bearings that might fall out, put your hand over the end of the hub from which you removed the nuts and spacers and flip the wheel over. Have a rag underneath the wheel to catch stray bearings.

8. Pull the axle up and out, being careful not to lose any bearings that might fall out of the hub or might stick briefly to the axle. Leave the cone, spacers, and locknut all tightened together on the opposite end of the axle from the one you disassembled. If you are replacing a bent or broken axle, measure the amount of axle sticking out beyond the locknut. Put the cone, spacers, and locknut on the new axle identically.

9. Remove all of the ball bearings from both sides of the hub. They may stick to a screwdriver with a coating of grease on the tip, or you can push them down through the center of the hub and out the other side with the screwdriver. Tweezers or a magnetic screwdriver might also be useful for removing bearings. Put the bearings in a cup, a jar lid, or the like. Count the bearings and make sure you have the same number from each side.

2. Put an appropriately sized wrench or adjustable wrench on the locknut on the same side.

3. While holding the cone with the cone wrench, loosen the locknut (Fig. 9.23). This may take considerable force because the parts are usually tightened against each other very securely to maintain the hub's adjustment. Make sure that you are unscrewing the locknut counterclockwise ("lefty loosey, righty tighty").

4. As soon as the locknut loosens, move the cone wrench from the cone on top to the cone on the opposite end of the axle, in order to hold the axle in place as you unscrew the locknut. On a rear hub, put another open-end wrench on the opposite locknut. Unscrew the loose locknut with your fingers; use a wrench if necessary.

5. Slide any spacers off, keeping track of where they came from. If they will not slide off, the cone will push them off when you unscrew it. Note that some spacers have a small tooth or "key" that corresponds to a lengthwise groove along the axle. Keep these lined up to facilitate removal.

10. With a screwdriver, gently pop off the seals (i.e., the dust caps) that press into either end of the hub shell (Fig. 9.24). Be careful not to deform them; leave them in if you can't pop them out without

damage. If they are not removed, it is tedious, but not impossible, to clean the dirty grease out of their concave interior with a rag and a thin screwdriver.

b. Cleaning

11. Wipe out the hub shell with a rag. Remove all dirt and grease from the bearing surfaces. With a screwdriver, push a rag through the hub shell and spin it to clean out the hub-shell axle hole. Wipe off the outer faces of the shell. Finish with a very clean rag on the bearing surfaces, which should be shiny and completely free of dirt or grease. If the hub has been neglected, the grease may have solidified and glazed over so completely that you will need a solvent to remove it. Use gloves with the solvent. If you are working on a rear cassette hub, take this opportunity to lubricate the cassette. (See §ix-20 on lubricating cassettes and freewheels.)

12. Wipe down the axle, nuts, and cones with a rag. Clean the cones well with a clean rag; strive for spotless. Again, solvent may be required to remove the grease if it has solidified. Get any dirt out of the threads on the disassembled axle end to prevent the cone from pushing the dirt into the hub upon reassembly.

13. Wipe the grease and dirt off the seals. A rag over the end of a screwdriver is sometimes useful to get inside. Again, glaze-hard grease may have to be removed with a solvent. Keep solvent out of the freehub body.

14. Wipe off the bearings by rubbing all of them together between two rags. This may be sufficient to clean them completely, but small specks of dirt can still adhere to them, so I advise the next step as well.

9.24 **Removing dust cap**

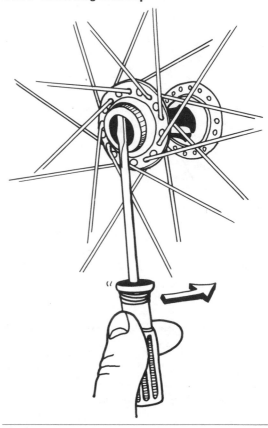

15. If you are overhauling low-quality hubs, skip to step 16. Otherwise, polish the bearings. I prefer to wash them in a plugged sink with an abrasive soap like Lava, rubbing them between my hands as if I were washing my palms. This really gets them shining, unless they are caked with glaze-hard grease. Make sure you have plugged the sink drain! This method has the added advantage of getting my hands clean for the assembly step. It is silly to contaminate your superclean parts with dirty hands. If there is hardened glaze on the bearings, soak them in solvent. If that does not remove it, buy new bearings at the bike shop. Take a few of the old bearings along so that you get the right size.

16. Dry all bearings and any other wet parts. Inspect the bearings and bearing surfaces carefully. If any

of the bearings have pits or gouges in them, replace all of them. Same goes for the cones. A patina or lack of sheen on balls and cones indicates wear and is cause for replacement. Most bike shops stock replacement cones. If the bearing races (or cups) in the hub shell are pitted, the only thing you can do is buy new hubs. Regular maintenance and proper adjustment can prevent pitted bearing races.

N O T E : *Using new ball bearings when overhauling standard cup-and-cone hubs assures round, smooth bearings; however, do not avoid performing an overhaul just because you don't have any new ball bearings. Inspect the bearings carefully. If there is even the slightest hint of uneven wear or pitting on the balls, cups, or cones, throw the bearings out and complete the overhaul with new bearings. Err on the side of caution.*

c. Assembly and lubrication

17. Press the seals or dust covers in on both ends of the hub shell.

18. Smear grease with your clean finger into the bearing race on one end of the hub shell. I prefer light-colored or clear grease so that I can see if it gets dirty, but any bike grease will do. Grease not only lubricates the bearings, it also forms a barrier to dirt and water, so use enough grease to cover the balls halfway. Too much grease will slow the hub by packing around the axle.

19. Stick half of the ball bearings into the grease, making sure you put in the same number of bearings that came out. Distribute them uniformly around in the bearing race.

20. Smear grease on the cone that is still attached to the axle, and slide the axle into the hub shell. Lift the wheel up a bit (30 degree angle), so that you can push the axle in until the cone slides into

9.25 Push inward on the axle and flip the wheel over

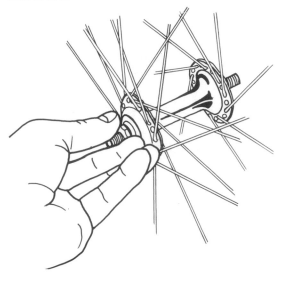

position, keeping all the bearings in place. On rear hubs, it is important to replace the axle and cone assembly into the same side of the hub from which it was removed to preserve drive-side cog spacing.

21. Holding the axle pushed inward with one hand to secure the bearings, turn the wheel over (Fig. 9.25).

22. Smear grease into the bearing race that is now facing up. Lift the wheel and allow the axle to slide down just enough that it is not sticking up past the bearing race. Make sure no bearings fall out of the bottom. If the race and bearings are properly greased and the axle remains in the hub shell, they are not likely to fall out.

23. While the top end of the axle is still below the bearing race, place the remaining bearings uniformly around in the grease. Make sure you have inserted the correct number of bearings.

24. Slide the axle back up into place by setting the wheel down on the table, so that the wheel rests on the lower axle end, seating the cone into the bearings (Fig. 9.26).

9.26 Seat the bottom cone in the bearings

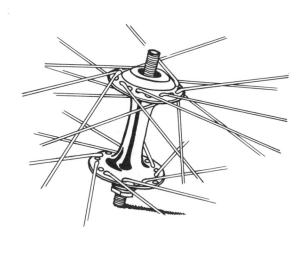

9.27 Loosening and tightening locknut

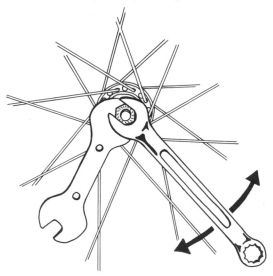

25. Cover the top cone with a film of grease and then, with your fingers, screw it into place, seating it snugly onto the bearings.

26. In correct order, slide on the washer and any spacers. Properly align any washers that have a little tooth or "key" that fits into a lengthwise groove in the axle.

27. Use your finger to screw on the locknut. Note that the two sides of the locknut are not the same. If you are unsure about which way the locknut goes back on, check the orientation of the locknut that is on the opposite end of the axle (this locknut was not removed during this overhaul and is assumed to be in the correct orientation). As a general rule, the rough surface of the locknut faces out so that it can get a better purchase on the dropout.

d. Hub adjustment

28. Thread the cone onto the axle until it lightly contacts the bearings. The axle should turn smoothly without any roughness or grinding, and there should be a small amount of lateral play. Thread the locknut down until it is snug against the cone.

29. Place the cone wrench into the flats of the hub cone. While holding the cone steady, tighten the locknut with another wrench (Fig. 9.27). Tighten it about as snugly as you can against the cone and spacers, in order to hold the adjustment. Be sure that you are tightening the locknut and not the cone; you can ruin the hub if you tighten the cone hard against the bearings.

30. If there is too much play in the axle when you are done, or if the bearings are tight, loosen the locknut while holding the cone with the cone wrench. If the hub is too tight, unscrew the cone a bit. If the hub is too loose, screw the cone in a bit. You may need to put a wrench on the opposite-side cone to effectively tighten or loosen the cone you are adjusting.

31. Repeat steps 28–30 until the hub adjustment feels right. There should be a slight amount of axle-end play so that the pressure of the quick-release skewer will compress it to perfect adjustment. (A hub held on with a nut—no quick-release—should be adjusted with no bearing play.) Tighten the locknut firmly against the cone to hold the adjustment.

OVERHAUL
STANDARD CUP-
AND-CONE HUB
(FRONT OR REAR)

OVERHAUL
CARTRIDGE-
BEARING HUB

NOTE: *You may find that tightening the locknut against the cone suddenly turns your "Mona Lisa" perfect hub adjustment into something slightly less beautiful. If it is too tight, back off both cones (with a cone wrench on either side of the hub, each on one cone) a fraction of a turn. If too loose, tighten both locknuts a bit. If still off, you might have to loosen one side and go back to step 29. It's rare that I get a hub adjustment perfectly dialed-in on the first try, so don't be dismayed if you have to tinker with the adjustment a bit before it's right. You have to have the wheel tightened into the bike to assess the hub adjustment.*

32. Put the skewer back into the hub. Make sure that the conical springs have their narrow ends toward the inside (Fig. 9.21).

33. Install the wheel in the bike and tighten the skewer. Check that the wheel spins well without any side play at the rim. If it needs readjustment, go back to step 31.

34. Congratulate yourself on a job well done! Hub overhaul is a delicate job that makes a difference in the longevity and performance of your bike.

ix-17 OVERHAUL CARTRIDGE-BEARING HUB

LEVEL 2

Cartridge-bearing hubs generally do not need much maintenance. If you ride through water above the hubs, however, you can expect water and dirt to get through any kind of seal. If the ball bearings inside the cartridges get wet, they should be overhauled or replaced.

There are many types of cartridge-bearing hubs, and it is outside the scope of this book to explain how to disassemble every one of them, but it is usually not too hard to figure out how to take apart any hub by looking at it. Some types have externally threaded axles with locknuts that you simply unscrew. After that, they may still require insertion of hex keys in the ends to unscrew parts from internal axle threads. On those devoid of external locknuts, though, there will generally be end caps that can be removed by one of the following approaches (overhauling Mavic hubs is explained in §ix-20d):

- Pulling or prying them off
- Sliding them off after loosening a setscrew on each cap
- Unscrewing the caps with a 5mm hex key inserted into the 5mm hex flats in the through-hole in either axle end
- On Mavic, unscrewing the axle with a 5mm hex wrench while holding the other end with either a pin tool in the adjuster ring or a 5mm hex key or a 10mm Allen wrench in the bore of the axle, often after pulling off the end cap on the adjuster end
- Yanking the rear freehub straight off the hub by hand

Once the end cap is removed, you can often smack the end of the axle with a soft hammer or on a table to remove the axle and perhaps even to dislodge the opposite bearing (Fig. 9.28). Pop the other bearing out the same way. The axle sometimes has a shoulder on each side, internal to the bearings, which can force the bearings out when tapping on the end of the axle.

If the axle has no shoulder to push out the bearing (i.e., Mavic), you need to tap the bearings out with another tool. There are bearing pullers made for this job. Otherwise, you can often place a large screwdriver through the bore of the hub against the bearing and tap on it. Move the tip of the screwdriver around against different points along the inner bearing ring.

9.28 **Tapping out cartridge bearing**

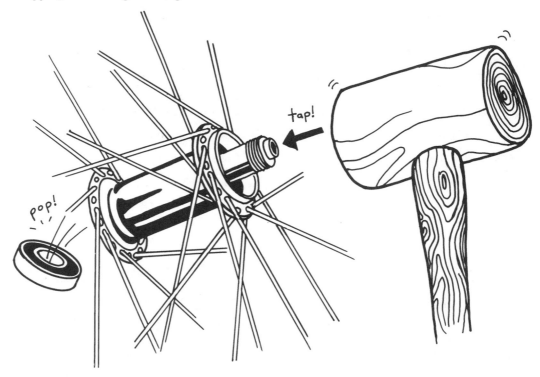

Cartridge bearings are vulnerable to lateral stress; if you have damaged them by pounding them out, they will need to be replaced. Be careful when tapping them back in; hold one of the old bearings against each new bearing, and tap the old bearing with the hammer to drive the new one into place.

Once the cartridge bearings are out, you can sometimes overhaul them (otherwise you'll need to buy new ones):

1. Gently pop the bearing covers (i.e., bearing seals) off with a single-edge razor blade (Fig. 9.29). If the bearing seals are steel, you cannot remove them; buy new bearings.

2. Squirt citrus-based solvent into the bearing under pressure (wear rubber gloves and protective glasses) to wash out the grease, water, and dirt. Scrub with a clean toothbrush.

3. Dry the bearing with compressed air.

9.29 **Removing bearing seal**

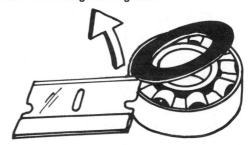

4. Pack the bearing with grease and snap the bearing covers back on. Replace the bearing if it doesn't turn smoothly.

5. Reassemble the hub the opposite way it came apart. Sometimes the bearings will be out of alignment slightly after installation, making the hub noticeably hard to turn. A light tap on either end of the axle with a soft hammer will often free them.

On Mavic, adjust the bearing with a pin tool on the adjuster ring, once the hub is tightened into the frame or fork with the quick-release

9.30 Rear freehub with cartridge bearings and cassette cogs

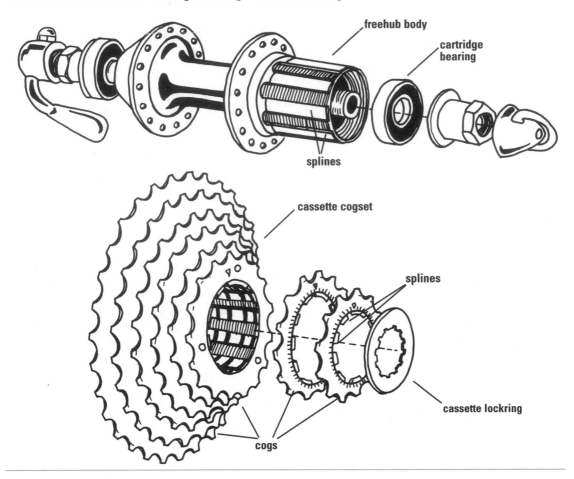

FREEHUBS AND COGS

skewer. A little threadlock on the adjuster's threads is a good idea.

N O T E : *Reinstalling the bearings in most of today's car-tridge-bearing hubs is relatively easy: simply press the bearings with your hand, or use the shoulder on the axle as a punch to press the bearings into place. In most cases, even a soft hammer is not necessary. However, with some cartridge-bearing hubs (SunTour, Sanshin, Specialized, Mavic, and others), it isn't so easy. The tolerance between the hub cups and the outer surface of the bearing is so tight that these bearings must be pressed in or pounded in with a hammer. A direct blow from a hammer would ruin the bearing, so with these types of hubs, it is best to place the old cartridge bearing you just removed against the new bearing and tap against the old bearing with a hammer.*

Freehubs allow the rear wheel to freewheel, turning independent of the chain. Most rely on a series of spring-loaded pawls that engage when pressure is applied to the pedals and disengage when the rider is coasting.

A freehub is an integral part of the rear hub. The cogs slide onto the longitudinal splines of the freehub body (Fig. 9.30). Changing gear combinations is accomplished by removing the cogs from the freehub body and putting on different ones. A freehub can usually be lubricated without removing it from the hub. A freewheel (Fig. 9.31) has the freewheeling mechanism inside it and threads onto the rear hub (Fig. 9.31). This system is found only on very old bikes.

9.31 Threaded rear hub with standard ball bearings and freewheel

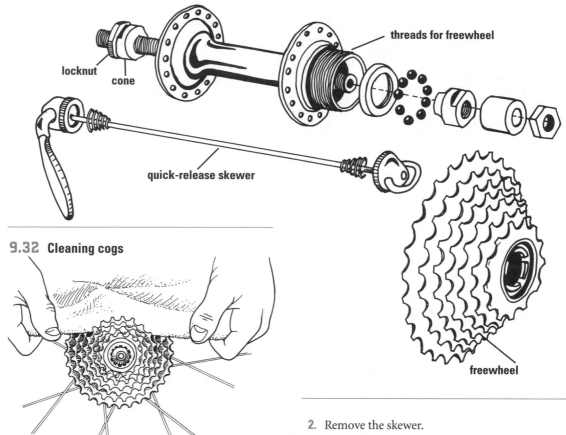

threads for freewheel

locknut

cone

quick-release skewer

freewheel

9.32 Cleaning cogs

ix-18 CLEANING REAR COGS

The quickest, albeit perfunctory, way to clean the rear cogs is to slide a rag back and forth between each pair while they are on the hub (Fig. 9.32). The other way—usually unnecessary unless the bike has been neglected—is to remove them (see §ix-19) and wipe them off with a rag or immerse them in solvent.

ix-19 CHANGING CASSETTE COGS

1. You need a chain whip, a cassette-lockring remover, a wrench (adjustable or open) to fit the remover, and the cog(s) you want to install. (Some very old freehubs have a threaded smallest cog instead of a lockring. These require two chain whips and no lockring remover.)

2. Remove the skewer.

3. Wrap the chain whip around a cog at least two up from the smallest cog. Wrap in the drive direction (clockwise) so that the cassette is held in place.

4. Insert the splined lockring remover into the lockring; it's the internally splined ring that holds the smallest cog in place. Unscrew it in a counterclockwise direction while using the chain whip to keep the cassette from turning (Fig. 9.33). If the lockring is so tight that the tool pops out without loosening it, install and tighten the skewer, sans springs, through the hub and lockring tool. Loosen the lockring a fraction of a turn, remove the skewer, and unscrew the lockring the rest of the way.

5. Pull the cogs straight off. Some cassette cogsets are composed of single cogs separated by loose

9.33 Removing a cassette lockring

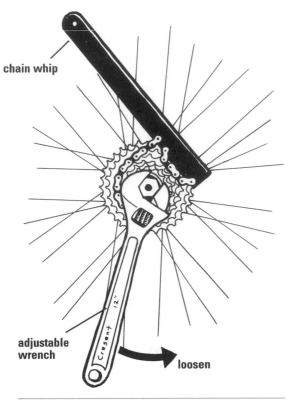

chain whip

adjustable
wrench

loosen

9.34 Spline vs. spleen

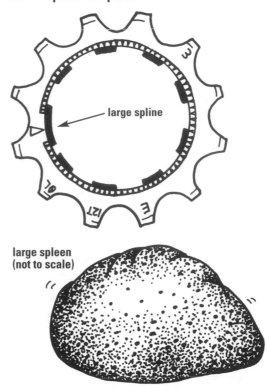

large spline

large spleen
(not to scale)

spacers, some cogsets are bolted together, and some cogsets are a combination of both.

6. Clean the cogs with a rag or a toothbrush; use solvent if necessary, observing the usual precautions.

7. Inspect the cogs for wear. If the teeth are hooked, they may be ripe for replacement. Rohloff makes a cog-wear indicator tool; if you have access to one, use it according to its supplied instructions.

8. Replace the cogs.

    (a) If you are replacing the entire cogset, just slide the new set on. Usually you'll find that one spline is wider than the others (Fig. 9.34), so line them up accordingly.

    (b) If you are installing a ten- or nine-speed cassette, see the note under step 9.

    (c) If you are replacing some individual cogs within your cogset, be certain that they are of the same type and model. For example,

not all 16-tooth Shimano cogs are alike. Most cogs have shifting ramps, differentially shaped teeth, and other asymmetries. They differ with model as well as with sizes of the adjacent cogs, so you'll need to buy one for the exact location and model. Install cogs in decreasing numerical sequence with the numbers facing out.

N O T E : *Some bolt-together cogsets can be disassembled for cleaning and then reinstalled onto the freehub as separate cogs to facilitate future cog changes and cleaning (the bolts are there for the manufacturer's convenience, not yours). Note that there are two kinds of bolt-together cogsets: (1) those with three long, thin bolts holding the stack of cogs and spacers together and (2) those with cogs bolted or riveted to an aluminum spider that has internal splines to fit on the cassette body. For the type with the three bolts, just unscrew the bolts, take it apart, and put in the replacement cogs. The other type is not to be disassembled from the aluminum spider, and the individual cogs are not to be replaced; you must replace each carrier with its attached cogs as a complete assembly.*

9. First, ensure that the lockring you are using is the right one for both the freehub and the particular cogset. The diameter of the lockring depends on the size of the first cog. With everything back in place, tighten the lockring with the lockring remover and wrench. (If you have the old-type six- or seven-speed freehub with the thread-on first cog, tighten that with a chain whip instead.) Make sure that all of the cogs are seated and can't wobble from side to side, which would indicate that the first or second cog is sitting against the ends of the splines. If the cogs are loose after tightening the lockring, loosen the lockring, line up the first and second cogs to make sure they are in place, and tighten the lockring again.

NOTE ON COMPATIBILITY: *These instructions for removing and replacing cogs apply for ten-, nine-, eight-, seven-, and six-speed cogsets. But the freehub body is usually different for each, so make sure you only use a seven-speed cogset on a seven-speed freehub body.*

NOTE ON 11-TOOTH COGS: *Although all Shimano eight-speed freehubs are wide enough for a ten- or nine-speed cogset, some eight- or nine-speed freehub bodies will not accept 11-tooth cogs (for instance, 1992– 1994 Shimano eight-speed freehub bodies will not accept 11-tooth cogs). To accept the small, 11-tooth cog, the splines of current freehub bodies stop about 2mm before the outer end of the freehub body. You can file the last 2mm of splines off an old-style eight-speed freehub so that it will accept an 11-tooth cog. The steel is very hard on high-end freehubs, so a grinder may be needed for this job.*

ix-20 LUBRICATING FREEHUBS

a. Minor freehub lubrication

LEVEL 2

Freehubs and freewheels can usually be lubricated for the short term simply by dripping chain lube into them. Some high-end freehubs have grease-injection holes on the freehub body; remove the cogs to get at the hole, and meticulously clean any dirt out of the hole. To be thorough, inject diesel fuel or biodegradable chain cleaner into the hole from a squeeze bottle with a thin tip pressed into the hole. Keep adding solvent until it spins without any crunching noises. With a fine-tip grease gun (Fig. 4.3), add lightweight grease (frequently) to avoid grease thickening up inside.

If the freehub has teeth on the faces of the hub shell and freehub (DT-Hügi and old Mavic freehubs have these radial teeth), just drip oil into the crease between the freehub and the hub shell as you turn the freehub counterclockwise.

For most freehubs, here is the general procedure; details for lubricating major types of freehubs follow.

1. Disassemble the hub axle assembly; see §ix-14– §ix-17.

2. Wipe clean the inside of the drive-side bearing surface.

3. With the wheel lying flat and the freehub pointed up toward you, flow chain lube between the bearing surface and the freehub body as you spin the freehub counterclockwise. You will hear the clicking noise of the freehub pawls smooth out as lubricant reaches them. Keep it flowing until old black oil finishes flowing out of the other end of the freehub.

4. Wipe off the excess lube, and continue with the hub overhaul (§ix-16, §ix-17).

9.35 Morningstar Freehub Buddy tool

9.36 Prying out freehub dust cover with a J-tool

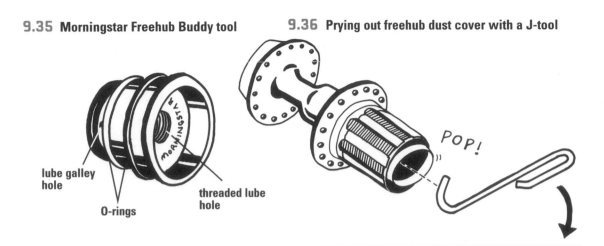

lube galley
hole

O-rings

threaded lube
hole

POP!

b. Thorough Shimano freehub lubrication

LEVEL 3

By far the best way to lubricate a Shimano freehub is to inject lubricant under pressure into it using a Morningstar Freehub Buddy tool (Fig. 9.35). Once the hub is apart, most of the work is done. This tool is easy to use, but first you may want to order a reusable dust cap from Morningstar (see the note after step 4).

1. To use this tool, you must first disassemble the hub-axle assembly as described in §ix-16 or §ix-17.

2. Pry out the freehub dust cover—ideally with the Morningstar J-tool (Fig. 9.36)—to expose the hub bearing race. On newer, deeper freehubs for ten- or nine-speeds, start removing the dust cap by prying against the freehub-fixing bolt. Then drop a 6mm bolt down into the 10mm-hex-key hole of the freehub-fixing bolt deep down inside and use its head as a fulcrum for the J-tool to pry against to remove the dust cover the rest of the way.

3. Once the dust cover is removed, push the Freehub Buddy into the bearing race (Fig. 9.37).

4. If the freehub has a crunchy feel to it when you spin it, first inject diesel fuel or bio-degreaser (as a cleaning solvent) followed by a lubricant into

9.37 Freehub Buddy installed in the end of a Shimano freehub

the threaded hole (or the smaller tapered section below the threads) in the center of the Freehub Buddy; it will exit through the lube galley hole in the side of the tool between the two rubber O-rings (Fig. 9.35). The smaller O-ring at the closed end of the Freehub Buddy seals off the center of the hub to prevent lubricant from going in there, and the larger O-ring prevents lube from squirting back out the front of the freehub.

I recommend force-threading the tip of a turkey baster filled with bio-degreaser or diesel fuel into the threaded hole in the center of the Freehub Buddy and squirting it in as you slowly turn the freehub. Tilt the wheel with a bucket below to catch the dirty solvent. Then force-thread the tip of a tube of outboard-motor gear oil or

Morningstar's Freehub Soup syringe into the Free-hub Buddy's threaded hole and squeeze the gear oil in. Outboard-motor gear oil works great—it's the perfect weight for a freehub, and it comes in a huge toothpaste-type tube whose end fits nicely into the center hole of the tool. Morningstar also sells a "Freehub Soup" lubricant mixture that comes in a syringe that fits in the Freehub Buddy. You can also force-thread a tube of grease, or, better yet, the tip of a glue syringe or turkey baster filled with oil or your own custom mixture of compatible (i.e., synthetic with synthetic or petro-leum with petroleum) oil and grease into the Freehub Buddy. Aerosol chain lube can also be squirted into the Freehub Buddy via an included plastic adapter that screws into the threaded hole and accepts the long, thin tube that comes with the spray lube.

Whatever lubricant you use, squeeze it into the Freehub Buddy until all the solvent of old, dirty lubricant squeezes through the freehub and out the back end of it. Keep going until clean lube oozes out.

Other than by disassembling the entire free-hub, the Freehub Buddy is the only way you can get a lubricant thicker than thin chain lube into the freehub, and a thicker lubricant protects bet-ter. Be certain that it's not too thick, however. Fill-ing a freehub with thick grease in cold weather may cause the pawls to stick and not spring back into the freehub teeth to lock it up when you want to pedal forward. You could end up freewheeling in both directions! Always spin the freehub by hand, and, if it does not engage well, purge again with lighter oil that is compatible with the grease you put inside.

N O T E : *Many freehub dust caps will be ruined upon removal; they are usually made of stamped sheet metal. Shimano does not sell them separately, which compli-cates freehub service considerably. Morningstar sells machined, removable dust caps with an O-ring seal as well as freehub tools and lubricants. Contact Morningstar Tooling at P.O. Box 213, Bodfish, CA 93205-0213; e-mail: sales@morningstartools.com.*

Once the freehub is done, overhaul the hub and replace the axle assembly.

c. Alternative method of thorough Shimano freehub lubrication

LEVEL 3

Another way to clean and lubricate a Shimano freehub without completely disassembling it is to:

1. Disassemble the hub-axle assembly as described in §ix-16 or §ix-17. Remove the freehub body with a 10mm Allen wrench inserted into the freehub-fixing bolt.

2. Completely flush it out. With a rubber stopper from a hardware store, close off the bottom of the freehub body. Pour solvent into the outer open-ing, spinning the mechanism, letting contami-nants run out. If there is a rubber seal, remove it. Repeat until clean.

3. Squirt in a quantity of outboard gear lube, then park the body on paper towel and let the excess drain off. With this method, you do not need to remove the freehub body dust seal.

N O T E : *You can also disassemble a Shimano free-hub by unscrewing (clockwise—it's left-hand threaded) the hub's bearing cup (that the hub bearings roll in). Morningstar sells a tool that fits into the bearing cup's two notches. I won't go into the details here, but I do illustrate it photographically in my* Mountain Bike Per-formance Handbook.

9.38 Removing a Mavic Ksyrium axle and freehub in order to lubricate the freehub and pawls

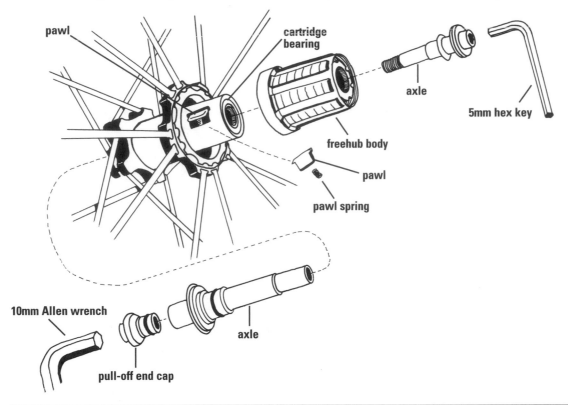

d. Mavic freehub lubrication

LEVEL 2

1. Remove the axle. Depending on model, this involves usually first pulling the non-drive-side dust cap straight off, or unscrewing external locknuts from external threads on a steel axle.

2. Depending on model, using two hex keys, one in either end, either both 5mm, or one 10mm (aka, an Allen wrench) and one 5mm, loosen the axle counterclockwise, unscrew, and remove.

3. Turn the wheel on its side, freehub up, on a clear surface where you can catch, or at least see, any pawls or pawl springs that might fly away.

   Rotate the freehub body slowly counterclockwise as you pull up on it, and remove it (Fig. 9.38).

4. Clean the pawls, springs, and hub shell.

5. Replace the springs and pawls and put 10–20 drops of light oil (Mavic has a mineral oil, M40122 for this) into the freehub (on the plastic bushing and the ratchet teeth).

6. Reinstall the freehub body, turning it counterclockwise while holding the pawls down with your fingers.

7. Replace the axle.

N O T E : *Use this same method to switch Mavic freehub bodies between Shimano- and Campagnolo-compatible types.*

e. Campagnolo freehub lubrication

LEVEL 3

On recent high-end Campagnolo or Fulcrum rear hubs:

1. Remove the skewer.

2. Insert a 5mm hex key into the drive-side axle end, and put a 17mm open-end or box wrench on the drive-side locknut. While holding the 5mm hex key, unscrew the locknut clockwise (in other words, it's left-hand threaded, and

you need to unscrew it the OPPOSITE direction from what you would expect). Older Campagnolo models instead have a little setscrew on the 17mm locknut that is loosened with a 2mm hex key to unscrew the locknut.

3. Now pull the freehub straight off. Older Campagnolo models have individual coil springs under each of the three pawls. These can go flying, and they are hard to clean and to insert back into the hub shell. Newer Campagnolo and Fulcrum models have a single, circular, wire spring wrapped around all three pawls (it fits in a groove in the freehub body as well as one cut across the flanks of each pawl). With the new style, you can pull the freehub off with abandon, and nothing will go flying. When removing the freehub body, older models require wrapping a twist-tie around the three pawls as they expose themselves from the hub shell as you pull; if you don't do this, the three pawls and the three springs will fly away.

4. Clean and grease the three pawls and the radial teeth inside of the hub shell.

5. Slide the freehub back in while slowly turning it backwards. Push inward on each pawl with a pen-

cil tip as you do this, until all three are engaged and the freehub body drops into place. Again, older Campagnolo models require using a twist-tie to hold the pawls in place as you push it in. Pull the twist-tie off after the pawls are inside the hub shell and before the freehub is pushed all the way in.

6. While holding the drive-side end of the axle with a 5mm hex key inside its bore, tighten the locknut, counterclockwise—remember, it's left-hand threaded!—with a 17mm Allen wrench. Elegant, eh?

N O T E : *Use this same method to switch Campagnolo or Fulcrum freehub bodies between Shimano- and Campagnolo-compatible types.*

f. Lubrication of recent high-end DT Swiss and DT-Hügi freehubs

LEVEL 2

1. Lay the wheel on its side, cogs up.
2. Grasp the cogset and pull straight up; it will pull the hub end cap off and the freehub will come off.
3. Clean and grease the spring, both star-shaped ratchets, and the teeth they engage.
4. Push the freehub and dust cap back on.

BRAKES

What do I say to complaints that my brakes are no good?
I'll tell you this: Anyone can stop. But it takes a genius to go fast.
—Enzo Ferrari

TOOLS

2mm, 3mm, 4mm,
5mm, and 6mm
hex keys

cable cutter

wet chain lube

grease

pliers

Optional

8mm socket wrench

8mm and 10mm
open-end
wrenches

13mm and 14mm
cone wrenches

adjustable wrench

By far the most common brake for road bikes is the dual-pivot sidepull brake (Fig. 10.1). Its predecessor is the center-pivot sidepull brake (Fig. 10.2), which is nearly as powerful. Campagnolo has returned to it for the rear brake to save weight and reduce braking power, thus making the rear wheel less likely to skid under heavy braking.

x-1 RELEASING BRAKES TO REMOVE A WHEEL

Triathlon bike tires are often narrow enough to slip past the brake pads without opening the brakes. With a wide tire or with a brake adjusted for very little clearance between the rim and the pads, the brake will need to be opened a bit. The following instructions describe how to open the vast majority of road bike brakes, both old and new. When you put your wheel back in, remember to follow these instructions in reverse so that your brakes will work when you need them.

1. Opening dual-pivot sidepull brakes: For Shimano (Fig. 10.1) and other dual-pivot sidepull brakes besides Campagnolo and Mavic, flip open the quick-release lever on the brake arm. Campagnolo and recent Mavic dual-pivot sidepull brakes and Campagnolo dual-pivot center-pull brakes do not have a quick-release mechanism on the brake caliper. Instead, there is a cable-release button on the brake/shift lever. On a Campagnolo Ergopower lever (Fig. 10.3), push the button inward so that it clears the edge of the lever housing and allows the lever to flip open wider.

2. Opening center-pivot sidepull brakes: Flip open the lever on the brake arm (Fig. 10.2), the same as on a Shimano dual-pivot sidepull brake. Although older Campagnolo brakes open this way (after the mid-1980s), modern Campagnolo center-pivot sidepull brakes have the quick-release on the brake/shift lever (as in Fig. 10.3) and not on the caliper.

10.1 Shimano dual-pivot sidepull brake caliper

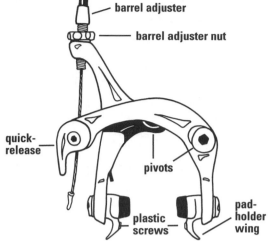

- barrel adjuster
- barrel adjuster nut
- quick-release
- pivots
- plastic screws
- pad-holder wing

10.2 Center-pivot sidepull brake caliper

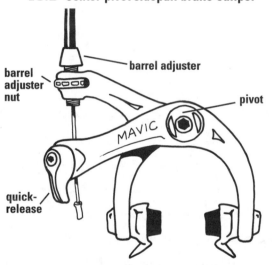

- barrel adjuster
- barrel adjuster nut
- pivot
- quick-release

10.3 Cable-release button on a Campagnolo Ergopower lever

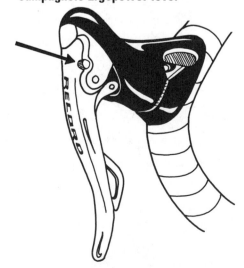

CABLES AND HOUSINGS

Given that cables transfer braking force from the levers to the brakes, their proper installation and maintenance are critical to good brake performance. If there is excess friction in the cable system, the brakes will not work properly, no matter how well the brakes, calipers, and levers are adjusted. Cables with broken strands should be replaced immediately.

x-2 CABLE TENSIONING

As brake pads wear and cables stretch, the cable needs to be tightened. The barrel adjuster on the brake arm of any road bike sidepull brake (Fig. 10.4) serves exactly this purpose.

The cable should be tight enough that the lever cannot be pulled to the bar, yet loose enough that the brakes—assuming they are centered and the wheels are true—are not dragging on the rims.

a. Increasing cable tension

1. For brakes with the barrel adjuster on the caliper, back out the barrel adjuster by turning its collar nut clockwise when viewed from above (Figs. 10.1–2). For lower-end brakes with a threaded hole in the brake arm (Fig. 10.4), turn the barrel adjuster counterclockwise. On higher-end brakes, the underside of the adjuster nut usually has bumps that drop in and out of notches in the top of the brake arm (Fig. 10.1) to hold its adjustment, so you may wish to hold the pads against the rim with your thumb and fingers to make turning the nut easier.

2. Increase the tension sufficiently that the brake lever (or brake/shift lever) does not hit the handlebar when the brake is applied fully, yet do not make the tension so tight that the brake rubs or comes on with very little movement of

10.4 Turning the barrel adjuster on the brake arm of sidepull brake caliper

10.5 Pull the brake cable taut and tighten the cable-fixing bolt

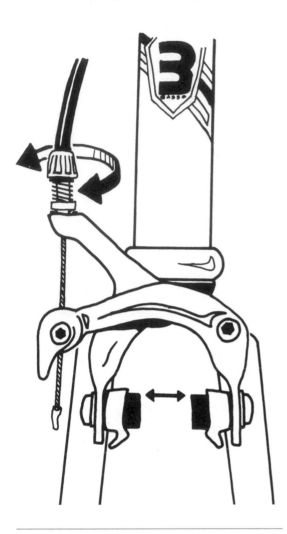

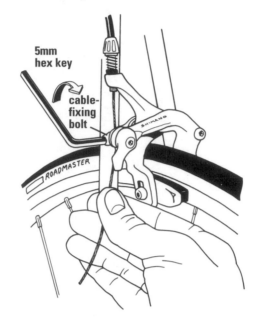

5mm
hex key

cable-
fixing
bolt

ROADMASTER

the lever. Lock in the adjustment with the notches in the top of the caliper arm engaging the adjuster nut.

3. You may find that the barrel adjuster cannot take up enough cable slack alone to get the brakes as tight as you want. If so, you need to tighten the cable at the brake. First, screw the barrel adjuster back in most of the way; this step leaves some adjustment in the system for brake setup and cable stretch over time. Loosen the cable-fixing bolt clamping the cable at the brake (Fig. 10.5). Check the cable for wear. If it's badly frayed, replace it.

(See Cable Replacement and Installation, §x-4.) Otherwise, pull the cable tight, and retighten the clamping bolt. Tension the cable as needed with the barrel adjuster.

b. Reducing cable tension

1. Turn the barrel adjuster nut (Figs. 10.1–2) counterclockwise (when viewed from the top) until the brake pads are properly spaced from the rim. With threaded brake arms, turn the barrel adjuster clockwise (Fig. 10.4). You want some movement of the lever before the pads contact the rim, but not so much that the lever comes back to the handlebar under hard braking. Within that range it is up to your personal preference.

2. Let the notches and bumps in the barrel adjuster and brake arm engage to lock in the adjustment.

3. Double-check that the cable is tight enough that the lever cannot be squeezed all the way to the handlebar.

BRAKES

CABLE
MAINTENANCE

∘

CABLE
REPLACEMENT
AND
INSTALLATION

x-3 CABLE MAINTENANCE

1. If the cable is frayed or kinked or has any broken strands, replace it (see §x-4).

2. If the cable is not sliding well, lubricate it. Use an oil-based chain lubricant (not a chain wax or other dry lube) or molybdenum disulfide grease, if possible. Lithium-based greases and chain waxes can eventually gum up cables and restrict movement.

3. To lubricate, open the brake (via the cable quick-release as when you remove a wheel; see §x-1).

4. If you have slotted cable stops, pull the ends of the rear brake-cable-housing segments out of each stop. On the front brake—and on the rear brake if your bike does not have slotted cable stops—you will have to disconnect the cable at the brake, clip off the cable end, and pull out the entire cable.

5. Slide the housing up the cable, wipe the cable clean with a rag, rub chain lubricant on the cable section that was inside the housing, and slide the housing back into place. If you pulled the housing completely off the cable, squirt chain lube through the housing as well.

6. If the cable still sticks, replace the cable and housing.

x-4 CABLE REPLACEMENT AND INSTALLATION

1. Disconnect the cable at the brake caliper, clip off the cable-end cap, and pull out the old cable from the lever (Fig. 10.6). You will need to pull the lever and then let it back a bit to free the head of the cable from the cable hook in the lever.

NOTE: *When installing a new cable, it is a good idea to replace the housings as well, even if they seem okay. Daily riding in particularly dirty conditions may require cables and housings to be replaced every few months.*

10.6 **Insert the cable into the lever, through the cable hook, and out the exit hole**

As with chains and derailleur cables, brake-cable replacement is a maintenance operation, not a repair operation; don't wait until a cable breaks or seizes up to replace it.

2. Purchase good-quality cables and lined housings. For cables, look for "die-drawn" cables; the exterior strands have been flattened by being pulled through a constricting die. They will move with less friction. For housing, you'll find that most brake-cable housing is spiral-wrapped to prevent splitting under braking pressure (see Fig. 8.13). Plastic-lined housing (Teflon is a popular material) reduces friction and is a must.

3. Cut the housing sections long enough to reach the brakes, and route them so that they do not make any sharp bends. If you are replacing existing housing, look at the bends before removing the old housings (after unwrapping the handlebar tape to get at them). If the housing bends are smooth and do not bind when the front wheel is swung through its arc, cut the new housings to the same lengths. Otherwise, cut each new segment longer than you

10.7 Tightening a Shimano STI brake-shift lever to the bar with a 5mm hex key

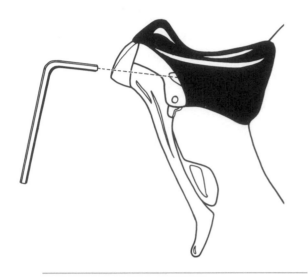

10.8 Installing a third brake lever on the aero extension and routing cable through it

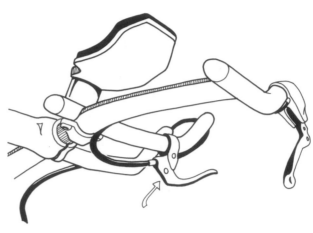

think necessary and keep trimming it back until it gives the smoothest path possible for the cable, without the cable tension being affected by steering. Use a cutter specifically designed for cutting housings, or a sharp side-cutter.

4. After cutting, make sure the end faces are flat. If not, square them off with a file or a clipper.

5. If the end of the plastic liner is mashed shut after cutting, open it up with a sharp object like a nail or a toothpick.

6. Slip a ferrule (cylindrical cap) over each housing end for support (see Chap. 8, Fig. 8.13). Some brake-arm barrel adjusters function as a ferrule and are too narrow for a ferrule to fit in; they are designed to accept only bare cable housing.

7. Decide which hand you want to control which brake (the standard is that the right hand controls the rear brake, but if you're the only one riding the bike, you can switch it around to match the setup on your motorcycle, for example). Install the housings into each housing stop, brake lever (or brake/shift lever), and brake caliper.

8. Tighten the adjusting barrel on the brake caliper to within one turn of being screwed all of the way in (Fig. 10.1, 10.2, or 10.4).

9. Insert the cable into the lever, through the cable hook, and out the cable exit hole (Fig. 10.6).

On dual-control (Figs. 10.3 and 10.7) or standard (Fig. 10.6)-brake levers, the cable exits the inboard side of the lever under the edge of the lever hood so that it can be wrapped under the handlebar tape.

On bar-end brake levers (Fig. 10.8), the cable pops out right below the lever blade, and on integrated bar-end levers (look on the book cover), the cable goes straight down inside of the handlebar. Some bar-end levers have a simple enlarged hole as a cable hook (Fig. 10.8), so sliding a standard road brake cable in is simple, as is pulling it back out.

Unfortunately, many plug-in bar-end brake levers use a complicated cable hook accepting mountain-bike style brake cables with the big, disc-shaped head on the end (although some plug-in

CABLE
REPLACEMENT
AND
INSTALLATION
·
LUBRICATION
AND SERVICE

levers accept this type of cable but have the hook off to the side of the lever so the cable can go straight in). You'll see what I mean if you hook one up. The complicated cable hook on the end of the lever makes directing the cable straight into the housing difficult, requiring sharply bending the cable near the lever to get it to go in. And simply pulling the cable back out to allow cutting the housings shorter is an incredible pain. You either have to throw out a new cable and start over, or you have to unscrew the lever pivot and take the lever blade out. This wouldn't be so bad if there weren't a return spring inside you have to futz with when replacing the lever blade.

10. Slide the cable through the housings and to the brake, making sure there is a ferrule (Fig. 8.13) on the end of the housing, if one will fit into the barrel adjuster. If the cables run through the frame or handlebars, make sure that there is either cable housing or a plastic liner inside for them to run in. Before pulling the old cable from inside the frame or bars, slide a new piece of housing or liner tubing onto the old cable, depending on which the frame or bar accepts, and pull it through. Then you can slip the new cable in through the frame or bar easily without any fishing around—and, as a bonus, you reduce cable friction and have better braking.

N O T E : *With new cables and lined housing, it is usually best not to use a lubricant on the cable. It is not necessary, so why run the risk of it gumming up inside the housing and attracting dirt? (Down the road, when the cable starts to stick, you may need to lubricate it; see §x-3.)*

11. Attach the cable to the brake caliper. Pull it taut and tighten the cable-fixing bolt (Fig. 10.5). Pull the lever as hard as you can and hold it for 60 seconds to stretch the new cable.

12. Adjust cable tension with the caliper barrel adjuster (as in §x-2).

13. Cut off the cable about an inch past the cable-fixing bolt. Crimp an end cap on the exposed cable end to prevent fraying (Fig. 8.16). Wrap the handlebar tape (see §xiv-11 in Chap. 14).

N O T E : *Once the cable has been properly installed, the lever should snap back quickly when released. If it does not, recheck the cable and housing for free movement and sharp bends. Release the cable quick-release and hold the pads to the rim with your hand while checking the lever for free movement. With the cable still loose, check that the brake pads do not drag on the tire as they return to the neutral position; make sure the brake arms rotate freely on their pivots, and check that the brake-arm return springs snap the pads away from the rims. If the lever and caliper move freely and spring back strongly, and if there are no obvious binds in the system, check for frayed strands within the housing sections, and then try lubricating the cable as in §x-5.*

BRAKE LEVERS (OR BRAKE/SHIFT LEVERS)

The levers must operate smoothly and be set up so that you can reach them easily while riding.

x-5 LUBRICATION AND SERVICE

1. Lubricate all pivot points in the lever with grease or oil.

2. Check return-spring function on the lever (note that not all levers have springs in them).

3. Make sure that the lever or lever body is not bent in a way that hinders movement.

4. Check for stress cracks. If you find any, replace the lever.

5. Replace torn or cracked lever hoods.

x-6 REMOVAL, INSTALLATION, AND POSITIONING

Most current brake levers integrate the brake lever and the shifter in a single "dual control" unit (Figs. 10.3 and 10.7). On the base bar of an aerobar (which has shifters on the aero extensions), the brake lever may also be a standard brake lever (Fig. 10.6), a small lever that clamps around the end of the bar (Fig. 10.8) or inserts into it, or, in the case of some high-end aerobars, a small lever integrated into the end of the bar (as on the book cover).

Small, bar-end levers can either have a band clamp (Fig. 10.8), in which case you loosen its pinch bolt, or an expander plug, in which case you loosen the bolt in the throat of the lever and push inward on it to free the wedges inside. Remove integrated lever blades by unscrewing and removing the pivot bolt.

To remove and install standard brake levers or dual control levers, follow these steps:

1. Remove the handlebar tape.
2. Loosen the brake/shift lever's (or the brake lever's) mounting bolt with a 5mm hex key and slide the lever off. The position of the bolt varies. On current dual-control levers, it is on the outboard side of the lever under the lever hood. Slip the hex key down from the top between the lever body and the hood rather than trying to roll back the hood far enough to get at it from outside (Fig. 10.7). On Campagnolo Ergopower (Fig. 10.3) and SRAM DoubleTap, the bolt is on the outside toward the top; on Shimano STI (Fig. 10.7), it is on the middle of the outer side.

    Standard brake levers have the mounting bolt inside the throat of the lever body; reach it by squeezing the lever and sticking the hex wrench straight in. Campagnolo and other European levers from the early 1980s and before instead employed a hex nut accessed down the lever throat with an 8mm socket wrench.

3. Slide the new lever on the bar—at the end of the base bar, or to where you like it on a drop bar. A good rule of thumb for a drop bar is to put a straightedge against the bottom of the bar and slide the lever down until its end touches the straightedge; the lever can also sit a little higher than this if you like, but generally not any lower. Put a straightedge across the top of both levers to make sure they are level.
4. Tighten the mounting bolt.
5. Install the cables (see §viii-6–§viii-12 and §x-4).
6. Wrap the handlebar tape (see §xiv-11 in Chap. 14).

x-7 REACH

There is no reach-adjustment screw on a road bike brake lever or brake/shift lever. If you have small hands and have difficulty reaching the levers, there are a few things you can try.

First, you can try different positions on the bar for the lever. This may bring the lever closer to the bar.

Another option is to buy a bar with a different bend that puts the palm of the hand closer to the lever. There are bars specifically made for this.

Finally, you can try to buy a smaller lever. This used to be relatively simple when brake levers were just brake levers. But now, with dual-control levers that incorporate the shifters, you cannot swap a shorter lever from another manufacturer, and the levers made by derailleur manufacturers do not come in different reaches, with one mid-range exception from Shimano. You can buy a whole new brake and derailleur system to get one with a reach you prefer, if necessary, but I recommend investigating a different handlebar first.

INSTALLING A
THIRD BRAKE
LEVER ON AERO
EXTENSION BAR

·

DUAL-PIVOT
SIDEPULL BRAKES

x-8 INSTALLING A THIRD BRAKE LEVER ON AERO EXTENSION BAR

When you're riding on your aero extensions, your hands are a long way from your brake levers, which are out at the ends of the base bar. This can be a bit hair-raising at high speeds when riding close to other people. Wouldn't it be nice if you could ride in the full aero position while still having a brake at your fingertips? Adding a third brake lever on the aero extensions offers you that alternative, without compromising your braking when you are riding on the base bar.

The simplest and least expensive method is to run the rear brake cable from the rear lever on the base bar through the third lever (Fig. 10.8) so that either lever pulls the same cable. Another option, available from HED Cycling Products, is to merge in a second cable section pulling the rear brake from a small lever that bolts onto the side of the right bar-end shifter. A machined junction piece splices the cable from this lever into the standard brake cable. With this elegant little lever, there is no need for the extra loop of housing or the superlong cable described here.

To set up the simpler, cheaper third lever, use an aero lever like the one pictured in Figure 10.8 or a cyclocross bar-top lever. The lever has to slide down over the extension tube, and the cable housing is cut into two lengths, stopping from one side at the lever body and from the other side atop the lever blade.

1. Clamp the third lever onto the handlebar, with the lever tip facing forward.

2. Assuming your rear brake lever is your right-hand lever, cut a section of brake-cable housing so that it runs from its insertion point on the base bar's right brake lever, inside or under the bar, looping around under the right extension bar to the cable hook atop the third lever blade (Fig. 10.8).

3. Start another section of housing at its insertion hole at the base of the third lever's clamp. Continue the housing forward to loop from the end of the right extension bar back under the left extension bar (Fig. 10.8). Continue it under or inside the left extension and into or along the frame to the rear brake.

4. Reinforce each end of the housing with a ferrule (see Fig. 8.13).

5. Install the rear brake cable, running it right through the third lever to pass from one housing section into the next, and continue it to the rear brake caliper. This will be a long cable run and may require a tandem-bike brake cable.

8. Hook up the brake cable as normal (as shown in §x-4, steps 11–13). Turn the barrel adjuster (see Figs. 10.1, 10.2, or 10.4) to get the right cable tension so that the brake applies well from either lever. You now have another position from which to brake!

BRAKE CALIPERS

The caliper of a brake is the mechanism that pinches the pads inward against the wheel rim. In most cases, a road bike caliper is a sidepull device that bolts on through a hole in the brake bridge or fork crown (Figs. 10.1, 10.2, 10.9, and 10.10).

x-9 DUAL-PIVOT SIDEPULL BRAKES

Dual-pivot sidepull brakes (Figs. 10.1 and 10.10) have become the industry standard. They are powerful and easy to keep in adjustment.

Campagnolo and Mavic dual-pivot brakes have some features distinct from Shimano brakes in this category. Other brands of calipers generally copy the features of Shimano brakes.

10.9 Tightening (or affixing) a caliper to the brake bridge with a 5mm hex key

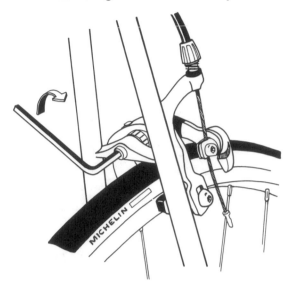

10.10 Turning setscrew with a 3mm hex key to center a Shimano dual-pivot brake caliper

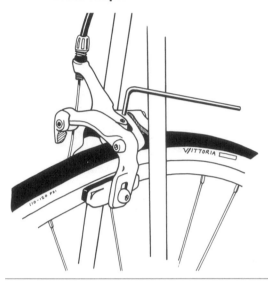

a. Installation

Stick the center bolt through the hole in the brake bridge or fork crown and tighten it in place with a 5mm hex key inserted into the recessed nut (Fig. 10.9). Hold it roughly centered over the wheel as you tighten the nut.

b. Cable hookup

Open the quick-release on the caliper (or on the lever on Campagnolo) before you do the cable hookup. Route the cable housing into the barrel adjuster on the upper brake arm. On the end of the housing, install a ferrule if one will fit into the barrel adjuster (see §x-4). Push the cable through the housing and the barrel adjuster and under the cable-fixing-bolt washer on the lower brake arm. Pull the cable taut, and tighten the bolt (Fig. 10.5). Close the quick-release after the cable is connected.

c. Centering

You are trying to achieve an equal amount of space between the pad and the rim on each side. The simplest and quickest way to center these brakes requires no tools. Just grab the brake and twist the entire thing

into position (don't mess with the mounting bolt; leave it tight). Or just pull outward on the pad that is closer to the rim. But before riding, do make sure that the recessed nut on the back of the brake bridge or fork is tight (Fig. 10.9).

Campagnolo and Shimano brakes can also be centered with a setscrew, while SRAM and Mavic dual-pivot brakes have no setscrew but are easy to center by simply twisting the entire caliper by hand.

Campagnolo has a 2mm hex setscrew on the side opposite the cable on single-pivot rear calipers and on both sides on current dual-pivot front calipers (one adjusts the relative positions of the arms, and the other tightens and loosens the return spring), just above the pad on the arm. As you tighten the screw, the pad on that side moves away from the rim. Loosen the screw, and the other pad (the one on the cable side) will move away from the rim.

Shimano's setscrew is on the upper end of the opposite brake arm. It takes a 3mm hex key or Phillips screwdriver (Fig. 10.10), and tightening it moves the pad on that side away from the rim. Loosen it, and

10.11 Line the pad up with the rim

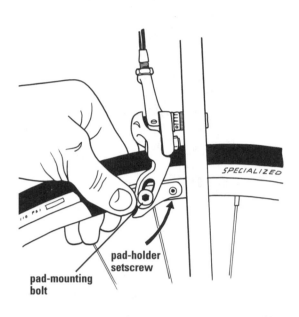

pad-holder
setscrew

pad-mounting
bolt

10.12 Centering a center-pivot sidepull brake with a cone wrench

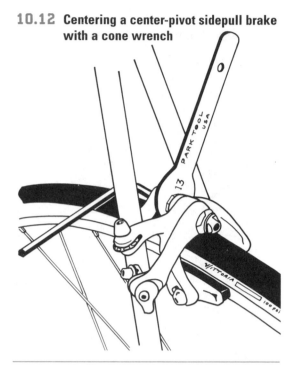

the other pad (the one on the cable side) will move away from the rim.

Mavic dual-pivot sidepull brakes require working a 5mm hex key in the recessed mounting nut along with a 14mm cone wrench on the nut behind the brake caliper (similar to center-pivot centering; see Fig. 10.12). SRAM brakes can be adjusted the same way, if you can find a 12mm cone wrench.

d. Pad adjustment

Loosen the pad-mounting bolt (generally with a 4mm or 5mm hex key; in some cases with a TORX T25 key). Slide the pad up and down along the groove in the arm to get the pad even with the height of the rim's braking surface. Twist the pad in the vertical plane to have the top edge of the pad follow the curve of the top edge of the rim (Fig. 10.11). While squeezing the brake lever to hold the pad against the rim, tighten the pad-mounting bolt. Make sure the pad does not twist as you tighten (if it does, you will have to hold it with your fingers as you cinch the bolt).

Some brakes (Campagnolo, recent high-end Shimano, and SRAM) also have an orbital adjustment of the pads to align the face of the pad flat against the rim and to allow a toe-in adjustment of the pad by means of a concave washer that nests against the convex face of the pad holder. If you have brake squeal or want to reduce grabbiness, toe the pads in a bit so that the forward end of the pad is a little closer to the rim than the rearward end. A 1mm toe-in is sufficient to eliminate squeal and grabbiness.

NOTE: *Users of Shimano brakes and early Shimano prebuilt wheels that have the spoke head inside the rim and the spoke elbow emanating from it will want to remove the little plastic screw in the pad-holder wing (below the pad; see Fig. 10.1). Otherwise, as soon as the pad gets a bit worn, that screw will thump-thump-thump against the bend in the spoke where it exits the side of the rim.*

e. Spring-tension adjustment

Campagnolo dual-pivot brakes have a setscrew that pushes on the end of the return spring. It is located on the side of the arm above the cable-side pad. If you tighten this screw (with a 2mm hex key), you tighten the spring, thus making the brake both harder to pull and quicker to snap back. There is no tension adjustment on Shimano brake springs or on the leaf spring in new Mavic brakes. Some springs can be bent with pliers to increase tension.

f. Cable-tension adjustment

Follow the instructions in §x-2.

g. Pad replacement

When the pads get so worn that the grooves cut into the pads are almost gone, you ought to replace them. Most pads these days are molded in one piece with the mounting nut insert or stud, so you just unscrew the old pad and bolt the new one in place.

High-end Shimano, Campagnolo, SRAM, and Mavic dual-pivot brakes surround the pad with an aluminum holder that is bolted to the brake arm. The pad can be replaced separately by sliding it from the holder. Some Shimano, SRAM, and Mavic pad holders have a setscrew (Fig. 10.11) that must first be backed out to free the pad. Buy the correct pad for the year and model of your brake.

It is not easy to slide any pad in or out of the holder. You may have to yank out the old pad with pliers and slide in the new pad with the aid of a vise, or hold the post in a vise while you push on the pad grooves with a screwdriver.

Make sure that you put the proper pad in the proper holder; look at the old one for guidance. Campagnolo pads say DX (right) or SX (left) on the back side. Shimano pads often say R or L on the back side and indicate the forward direction. Be prepared for some work pushing the new pads into the holders, at least with Campagnolo; use a vise and keep cutting off the burrs of pad material that may get peeled back by the edges of the pad holder.

When you reinstall the pad to the brake arm, make sure that the closed end of the pad holder faces forward. Otherwise, the first time you brake hard, you may see two pieces of rubber fly ahead of you and feel two more hit the backs of your legs. You may not remember anything after that.

x-10 CENTER-PIVOT SIDEPULL BRAKES

Center-pivot sidepull brakes (Fig. 10.2) are found on lots of bikes, since they were the standard from the late 1970s to the early 1990s. Current high-end Campagnolo brakesets use them on the rear to save weight. They too work great and are easy to set up and adjust. Many adjustments are the same as those on dual-pivot brakes.

a. Installation

Stick the center bolt through the hole in the brake bridge or fork crown and tighten it in place with a 5mm hex key inserted into the recessed nut (Fig. 10.9). Hold it roughly centered over the wheel as you tighten the nut.

Some older bikes do not have a countersunk hole in the back of the brake bridge and fork crown. With these, you need a brake with a longer center bolt and a standard nut, which you tighten with a 10mm box wrench.

b. Cable hookup

Open the quick release on the caliper (or on the lever on some current Campagnolo levers) before you make this hookup. Route the cable housing into the barrel adjuster on the upper brake arm. If a ferrule will fit into the barrel adjuster, install one on the end of the housing (see §x-4). Push the cable through the housing and the barrel adjuster and under the cable-fixing bolt washer on the lower brake arm. Pull the cable tight and tighten the bolt with a 5mm hex key (same as with a dual-pivot brake, Fig. 10.5) or an 8mm box wrench.

BRAKES

c. Centering

You want an equal amount of space between the pad and the rim on each side. Turn the brake the direction you need with a cone wrench (usually 13mm or 14mm) slipped onto the flats of the center bolt between the brake and the frame (Fig. 10.12). Hold the brake-mounting nut at the same time, making sure it is tight when you are finished.

Current Campagnolo rear calipers have a centering setscrew on the side opposite the cable, just above the pad on the arm. As you tighten the screw (with a 2mm hex key), the pad on that side moves away from the rim. Loosen the screw, and the other pad (the one on the cable side) moves away from the rim.

d. Pad adjustment

Loosen the pad-mounting bolt. Slide the pad up and down along the groove in the arm to get the pad even with the height of the rim's braking surface. Twist the pad in the vertical plane to make the top edge of the pad follow the curve of the top edge of the rim (the same as with a dual-pivot brake, Fig. 10.11). While squeezing the brake lever to hold the pad against the rim, tighten the bolt. Make sure the pad does not twist as you tighten (if it does, you will have to hold it with your fingers as you cinch down on the bolt).

e. Spring-tension adjustment

Some center-pivot sidepull brakes have a spring-tension adjusting screw. And on some Shimano center-pivot brakes, the piece of plastic at each end of the spring can be reversed to tighten or loosen the spring. The hole through which the end of the spring slides is offset in the wafer-shaped plastic piece. Push inward on the end of the spring to free the plastic wafer from the brake-arm tab, flip the wafer over, and push it back in place under the tab. If the hole is to the outside, the spring is looser; if the wafer is flipped so that the hole is toward the inside, the spring is as tight as it is going to get.

f. Cable-tension adjustment

Follow the instructions in §x-2.

g. Pad replacement

When the pads are worn down to the point that the grooves cut into the pads are almost gone, you ought to replace them.

Most pads are molded in one piece with the mounting nut insert or mounting stud, so you just unscrew the pad and bolt the new one in place.

High-end Shimano, Campagnolo, SRAM, Mavic, and Modolo brake pads are held inside a holder that is bolted to the brake arm. You slide the rubber pad to remove it from the holder, but often it is not easy. You may have to yank out the old pad with pliers and slide in the new pad with the aid of a vise; see §x-9g for more on this.

When you reinstall the pad to the brake arm, make sure that the closed end of the pad holder faces forward. Otherwise, the first time you brake hard, the pads will likely exit the holders, leaving you with no brakes.

x-11 TROUBLESHOOTING

1. Possible causes for squealing brakes include the following:
   - Grease or oil on the rim and/or pad
   - Toe-out of the pads under hard braking so that the heel of the pad does the work
   - Brake arms that are too flimsy for the rider (and chatter or toe-out when the brakes are applied)
   - Ceramic-coated rims paired with pads not intended for ceramic braking surfaces

   Solutions include the following:

(a) If the rims are dirty or oily, clean them with solvent (rubbing alcohol may be sufficient) and wipe them clean. If the pads are dirty, reveal a clean layer of the pad with sandpaper.

(b) If your pads toe-out while braking, you should toe them in. Some pads (Campagnolo, recent high-end Shimano, and SRAM) have an orbital adjustment on the pads that allows toe-in. Otherwise, the only way to toe road bike pads is to remove the pad, put an adjustable wrench on the end of the brake arm, and twist it. This will help eliminate squeal on a brake with flimsy arms too. If the arms flex too much for you, get new brakes.

(c) High-end rims with ceramic braking surfaces can squeal if the pads are not specifically made for ceramic rims. Easy enough— get new pads.

2. Insufficient braking power is available. Possible causes include the following:

   • Flexing of brake arms or lever

   • Stretching of cable

   • Compression of brake housing

   • Squishing of pads

   • Insufficient coefficient of friction between the pads and rim

   • Oil and grime on the rims and pads (or water, but that will dry off soon)

   • The pads may not work with your particular rim

   Try the following solutions:

   (a) If the brake arms or levers are too flexible, you need new brakes, but you can try eliminating the other factors first to see whether braking power increases enough for you.

(b) If the cables and housings are old, frayed, thin, or cheap, chances are the cable is stretching more than a new one would, and the cable housing is compressing more than new housing would. Replace both.

(c) If the pads are too soft, they will squish rather than applying full pressure against the rim. Replace them with higher-quality ones.

(d) Insufficient friction is common with chromed steel rims (found only on cheap bikes). The only cure is to fit especially aggressive pads (or replace the rims—not a bad idea, because chromed steel rims do not provide much braking power when wet).

(e) Another cause of weak braking power can be oil and grime on the rims and pads. The pads might also be overly worn and need replacement.

(f) Finally, try different pads.

3. The levers come back all the way to the bar before the bike slows down enough:

   (a) Check that the brake quick-release is closed. If so, the cable needs to be tightened. See §x-2.

   (b) The causes and solutions in item 2 (insufficient braking power) may also apply.

4. Brake rubs on wheel because of off-center caliper, the brakes are too tight, or a wheel is untrue. Solutions:

   (a) If one pad rubs all the way around the rim, see the sections regarding centering the caliper for your type of brakes.

   (b) If both pads rub all the way around, loosen the cable as in §x-2.

   (c) If the wheel wobbles back and forth against the pad(s), true the wheel; see Chapter 9, §ix-12.

BRAKES

5. Pads do not meet flat to the rim:

   (a) Other than on late-model high-end Shimano and Campagnolo brakes, if the pad will not mount so that it meets the rim flat or slightly toed-in, the only way to adjust it is to remove the pad and twist the end of the arm with an adjustable wrench. (Late-model high-end Shimano, SRAM, and Campy brakes have an orbital pad mount that allows freedom of adjustment in all planes, once the pad bolt is loosened.)

   (b) If one pad toes in and one toes out, either the brake center-bolt may be bent or the brake hole in the frame or fork may be drilled crooked.

6. Brake caliper returns slowly or not at all. Possible causes include the following:

   • The caliper's center bolt or secondary pivot bolt is bent or the nuts on it are too tight where it passes through the brake arm.

   • The end of the spring is not riding in its plastic friction piece or it needs lubrication.

   • The cable is sticking.

Solutions include the following:

   (a) You can adjust the tightness of the pivot-bolt nuts and replace bent bolts.

   (b) Replacing the end of the spring in its plastic friction-reducing piece is easy enough, and you can put a dab of grease between the spring and the spring tab on the arm for those springs without the friction-reducing piece.

   (c) If the cable is sticking, replace or lubricate it (see §x-3 and §x-4).

7. Brake arms are loose or the front nut is missing from a center-pivot sidepull brake:

   (a) The nut(s) holding the caliper together are missing. Replace any missing nuts.

   (b) Tighten the nuts until there is no play in the caliper, yet it still moves freely. If the brake has two nuts, make sure they are both there (the end of the bolt should be covered by the front cap-nut). Hold the back one with one wrench while you tighten the front one against it with another wrench.

CRANKSETS

When someone tells you something defies description,
you can be pretty sure he's going to have a go at it anyway.
—Clyde B. Aster

TOOLS

5mm and 6mm
   hex keys

7mm, 8mm, and
   10mm Allen
   wrenches

14mm socket
   wrench

crank puller

chainring-nut tool

pin spanner (or
   adjustable pin
   tool)

splined bottom-
   bracket wrench

adjustable wrench

toothed lockring
   spanner

15mm and 16mm
   socket wrenches

dust-cap pin tool

⅜-inch drive torque-
   wrench handle

ISIS bottom-bracket
   installation tool

integrated-spindle
   bottom-bracket
   installation tool

left arm-cap instal-
   lation tool for
   Shimano inte-
   grated bottom
   brackets

grease

The crankset consists of the crankarms, bottom bracket, chainrings, chainring bolts, and crank bolt (Fig. 11.1). The forces applied through this system are large, so all parts need to be quite tight. If you use them when they're loose you'll ruin expensive components. In addition, bottom-bracket bearings need to run smoothly under high loads to conserve your energy.

CRANKARMS AND CHAINRINGS

xi-1 CRANK REMOVAL AND INSTALLATION

To take off traditional crankarms, you will need—depending on the crankset—either a large hex key (a 7mm or 8mm Allen wrench) alone, or a socket wrench (Fig. 11.2) and a large hex key along with a crank puller (Fig. 11.3).

Until 2003, most Shimano cranks and their clones were secured with a crank bolt accepting either an 8mm Allen wrench (large "hex key") or a 14mm socket wrench. Current Campagnolo cranks accept an 8mm Allen wrench; older Campagnolo cranks take either a 7mm Allen wrench or a 15mm socket.

Integrated-spindle cranks (Figs. 11.15–16), which first appeared on road bikes in 2003, only require removing one of the crankarms because the other arm is permanently fixed to the oversize bottom-bracket spindle, except in the case of the Campagnolo Ultra-Torque crank (Fig. 11.16), which has half of the spindle permanently fixed to each crankarm. The spindle just slides in and out of the bearings, which are external to the bottom bracket (Fig. 11.20), and to remove the arm, you may only need a 5mm hex key or a 8mm Allen wrench. For Shimano, you also need a special splined tool for the left arm cap.

N O T E : *"Right" in this chapter and generally through-out this book refers to the drive side of the bike, and "left" refers to the nondrive side.*

11.1 **An exploded traditional crankset**

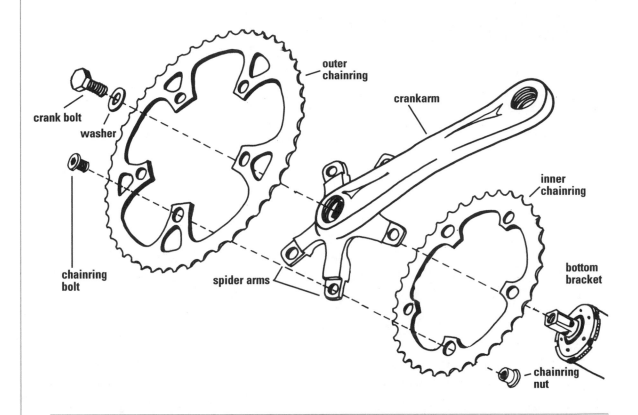

crank bolt

washer

chainring
bolt

spider arms

outer
chainring

crankarm

inner
chainring

bottom
bracket

chainring
nut

---

a. Removal

***Traditional cranks (square-taper, Shimano
OctaLink, and ISIS)***

1. Older cranksets (and some newer inexpensive
   ones) have a dust cap covering the crank bolt. If
   it's there, remove it. Depending on the type, it may
   take a 5mm hex key, a two-pin dust-cap tool, or
   a screwdriver.

2. Unscrew the crank bolt by using the appropriate
   wrench (Fig. 11.2). If the crank does not pull off
   as the bolt unscrews (see the next Note), make
   sure you remove the washer under the bolt after
   you remove the bolt (Fig. 11.1). A washer that is
   left in will prevent the crank puller from pushing
   on the end of the axle. If the crank comes right
   off, read the note following this step, and skip steps
   that follow the note.

N O T E : *Many recent traditional road bike cranks are
self-extracting—they require no crank puller. A ring
threaded into the crank holds down the crank bolt; as the
bolt is unscrewed, its outer lip pushes on the ring and
pushes the crank off. Sometimes the ring is not properly
secured, and it unscrews. In this case, you need to hold
the ring by its two holes with a pin tool while you unscrew
the bolt with a hex wrench. If this approach fails, you can
unscrew and remove the ring, remove the crank bolt, and
use a crank puller to remove the crankarm (see step 3).*

3. Holding the crank puller (Fig. 11.3) in your hand,
   unscrew its center push bolt so that the inner
   and outer threaded ends of the tool are flush.
   Crank pullers vary in size of the pushrod. The
   standard type, pictured in Figure 11.3, has a
   1.15cm-diameter pushrod just small enough to
   pass through the square hole in the crankarm

11.2 Removing and installing crank bolt

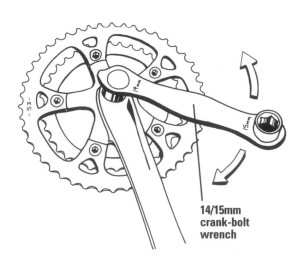

**14/15mm
crank-bolt
wrench**

11.3 Using crank puller

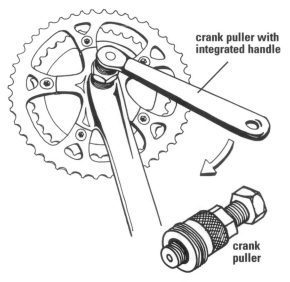

**crank puller with
integrated handle**

**crank
puller**

to push it off a square-taper bottom bracket (Figs. 11.10–12). However, if you need to use a puller to get a crank off a Shimano OctaLink or splined ISIS pipe-spindle bottom bracket (Figs. 11.13–14), you need a crank puller with a larger (1.7cm-diameter) pushrod.

4. Thread the outer part of the crank puller into the hole in the crankarm. Thread it in as far as it can go (preferably by hand; clean the threads if it won't thread in easily); otherwise, you will not engage sufficient crank threads when you tighten the push bolt, and the threads will be damaged. Future crank removal depends on those threads being in good condition.

5. Tighten the push bolt clockwise (Fig. 11.3), using a wrench or a socket-wrench handle or a handle built into the tool, until the crankarm pulls off of the axle. Unscrew the puller from the crankarm.

Integrated-spindle cranks

1. On first-generation Shimano (Fig. 11.15) and FSA aluminum integrated-spindle cranks, unscrew and remove the cap on the end of the left arm (with the special splined tool for Shimano; with

a hex key for FSA). With a 5mm hex key, loosen the two pinch bolts holding the arm onto the spindle, and pull off the left arm. On many other integrated-spindle cranks, unscrew the left arm with an 8mm Allen wrench, in the same way as for a nonintegrated self-extracting crank; the arm will come right off. On Campagnolo Ultra-Torque (Fig. 11.16), unscrew the bolt from deep inside the drive-side bottom bracket spindle with a long 10mm Allen wrench with a cheater bar on the short end, or with Campagnolo's UT-BB110 tool on a socket-wrench handle; pull the left arm and wave washer off.

2. Pull the right arm straight outward by hand, which brings the spindle out of the cups with it. On some FSA cranks, you will have a rubber O-ring to pull off each end of the spindle. On Campagnolo Ultra-Torque (Fig. 11.16), pop the retaining spring off of the drive-side cup with the tip of a screwdriver. Pull the right crank straight out.

N O T E : *Race Face integrated-spindle cranks are the opposite; the left arm is fixed to the spindle, and the right, drive-side crank is removable.*

b. Installation

Traditional cranks (square taper, ISIS, and OctaLink)

1. Slide the crankarm onto the bottom-bracket axle. With square-taper spindles, clean off all grease from both parts. Greasing the axle may allow the soft aluminum crank to slide too far onto the hard steel or titanium axle and could deform the square hole in the crank. Apply grease to an ISIS or Shimano OctaLink splined spindle. With ISIS and OctaLink cranks, you must be careful to line up the crank splines with those on the spindle before tightening the crank bolt. You can wreck a crank if you do not align the parts; no warranty covers improper installation.

2. Install the crank bolt. Apply grease or threadlock compound on the threads, and tighten (Fig. 11.2). Apply titanium-specific antiseize compound for titanium spindles or crank bolts. If you have aluminum or titanium crank bolts, tighten the cranks on to the specified torque with a greased steel bolt first, then replace the steel bolt with the lightweight bolt and tighten that to spec.

NOTE: *If you have a torque wrench, here is an excellent place to break it out and tighten the bolt to about 32–49 N·m (300–435 in-lbs) and as high as 59 N·m for steel oversize bolts for splined spindle. If you're not using a torque wrench, make sure that the bolt is quite snug, but don't muscle it until your veins pop.*

3. Replace the dust cover, if the crank has one.

4. Removing and reinstalling the right crankarm could position the crank farther inboard than it was previously, which will affect shifting, so check the front-derailleur adjustment. (See Chapter 8, §viii-4.)

5. Recheck the bolt torque after the first few hours of riding. Retighten it to the proper torque spec if it has loosened up. Check it again after a few more hours of riding until you are assured that it is snug.

Integrated-spindle cranks

1. Push the bottom-bracket spindle (which is attached to the right crankarm—Fig. 11.15, or, in the case of Race Face, to the left arm) in through the cups, whose oversize bearings are external to the bottom-bracket shell (Fig. 11.20).

   On Campagnolo Ultra-Torque (Fig. 11.16), position the retaining spring around the drive-side bearing cup so that its two ends are near the holes in the cup. Insert the right crank fully, and press on the retaining spring to slide its two ends into the holes in the drive-side bearing cup. Gently pull outward on the crank to check that the spring is in place and is retaining the crankarm.

2. Slide the left arm onto the spindle protruding on that side from the cups; check that the crank is at 180 degrees from the right arm (Shimano IS spindles have two wider splines to ensure this). On Campagnolo Ultra-Torque (Fig. 11.16), place the wave washer into the bearing seat of the left-hand cup and push the left crank in so that the right and left spindle stubs meet in the center. Ensure that the two arms are at 180 degrees from each other.

3. Finish the installation according to the type of crank you have:

   (a) On Truvativ and SRAM Giga X Pipe cranks, FSA Mega Exo carbon-fiber cranks, and many others, tighten the left arm with an 8mm Allen wrench, the same as for a normal crank. Put on your pedals and go riding.

   (b) On Shimano and FSA aluminum arms, tighten the left-side dust cap (not very tightly

[0.4–0.7 N·m], just enough to pull the right and left cranks over against the bottom-bracket cups) with the special splined cap tool for Shimano and a hex wrench for FSA. Shimano's tool is just a round disc meant to be turned by hand to prevent overtightening it; be cautious with any tool for this task that has a long handle.

(c) On Shimano and FSA aluminum arms, with a 5mm hex key, tighten the two opposing (greased) pinch bolts (to 10–15 N·m) by alternately tightening each one a quarter turn at a time.

(d) On Campagnolo Ultra-Torque (Fig. 11.16), drop the short fixing bolt deep inside the drive-side bottom bracket spindle, and tighten it to 42 N·m with a long 10mm Allen wrench with a cheater bar on the stubby end, or with Campagnolo's UT-BB110 tool on a torque-wrench handle.

4. Recheck the torque after one ride, as the crank may settle in and the bolts will need retightening. Periodically check the torque from then on.

xi-2 CHAINRINGS

Get into the habit of checking the chainrings regularly. They do wear out and need to be replaced. It's hard to say how often, so include chainrings as part of your regular maintenance checklist. Always check them for wear when you replace the chain.

Check the chainring teeth periodically for wear and periodically examine the chainring bolts for tightness. Check the chainrings themselves for trueness by watching them as they spin past the front derailleur.

1. Wipe the chainring down and inspect each tooth. The teeth should be straight and uniform in size

11.4 Chainring shifting ramps and asymmetrical teeth

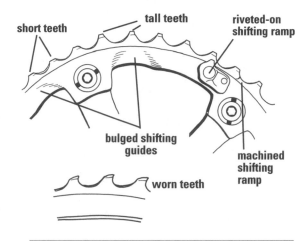

and shape. If the teeth are worn into a hook shape, the chainring needs to be replaced. The chain should be replaced as well (see §vii-5 in Chap. 7), because this tooth shape effectively changes the spacing between teeth and accelerates wear on the chain, and it indicates that the chain was already worn in order to cause the hook shape in the first place.

CAUTION: *Don't be deceived by the erratic tooth shapes (some tall, some short) on modern chainrings designed to facilitate shifting (Fig. 11.4); that's probably what they are supposed to look like if the odd shapes repeat regularly. Shifting ramps on the inboard side, meant to speed chain movement between the rings, often look like cracks on cheaper chainrings, where they are pressed into the ring rather than consisting of a separate piece riveted on.*

NOTE: *Another wear evaluation method is to lift the chain from the top of the chainring; the greater the wear of either part, the farther the chain separates. If it lifts more than one tooth, the chain, and perhaps the chainring, should be replaced.*

2. Remove minor gouges in the chainrings with a file.

3. If an individual tooth is bent, try bending it back carefully with a pair of pliers or an adjustable

11.5 Straightening warped chainrings

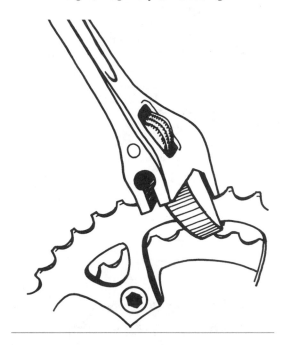

11.6 Removing and installing chainring bolts

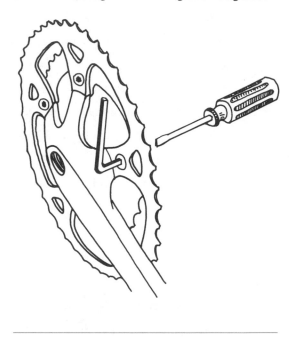

wrench (Fig. 11.5). If it breaks off, take the message and buy a new chainring.

4. While turning the crank slowly, watch where the chain exits the bottom of the chainring. See if any of the teeth are reluctant to let go of the chain. If the chain gets pulled up a bit as it leaves the bottom of the chainring, it can get sucked up between the chainring and the chainstay. Locate any offending teeth and see if you can correct the problem. If the teeth are really chewed up or cannot be improved with pliers and a file, you need to replace the chainring.

N O T E : *Never rotate the chainring position relative to the spider arms of the crank, because the shifting ramps will not be in the proper places to function correctly in picking up the chain as you shift. The outer chainring will generally have a protruding pin to locate it behind the crankarm, and the inner ring or rings will have a radially inward-pointed tooth, also to line up behind the crankarm.*

xi-3 CHAINRING BOLTS

Check that the bolts are tight by turning them clockwise (usually with a 5mm hex key, Fig. 11.6). As you try to tighten the bolt, its nut may turn; if so, hold the nut with a two-pronged chainring-nut tool (left side of Fig. 4.2) designed especially for this purpose or with a screwdriver. Use a screwdriver (Fig. 11.6) with caution because it can slip off the chainring nut.

Some chainring bolts take a star-shaped TORX T30 tool instead of a 5mm hex key. Yet others take a 6mm hex wrench on the nut on the backside, rather than the pronged chainring-nut tool.

xi-4 WARPED CHAINRINGS

Looking down from above, turn the crank slowly to see whether the chainrings wobble back and forth relative to the plane of the front derailleur.

If they do, make sure there is no play in the bottom bracket by grabbing the crankarms and attempting to rock the bottom-bracket axle back and forth.

If there is play, adjust the bottom bracket (step 15, §xi-8). A small amount of chainring wobble and flex is normal when you pedal hard, but excessive wobbling will compromise shifting. Small, localized bends can be straightened with an adjustable wrench (Fig. 11.5). If a ring is really bent, replace it.

xi-5 BENT CRANKARM SPIDERS

If you installed a new chainring and are still seeing serious back-and-forth wobble, chances are good that the spider arms on the crank are bent. If the crank is new, this is a warranty item, so return it to your bike shop.

xi-6 CHAINRING REPLACEMENT

Either of the chainrings on a double crank (Fig. 11.7) can be replaced with the crank on the bike.

1. Unscrew the chainring bolts with a 5mm hex key (Fig. 11.6), or on some bolts, a TORX T30 wrench. You may need to hold the nut on the backside with either a chainring-nut tool (Fig. 4.2), a thin screwdriver (Fig. 11.6) or, with some nuts, a 6mm hex key).

2. Install the new chainrings, lubricate the bolts and the little recesses that accept them in the chainring faces, and tighten them (Fig. 11.6) in a star pattern, as you would a car tire. The outer chainring has a protruding pin meant to keep the chain from falling down between it and the crankarm. Make sure this pin lines up under the crankarm and faces away from the bicycle. The inner ring has a little bump protruding radially inward that is also to line up under the crankarm. Both chainrings have recesses for the heads of the chainring bolts and nuts, so make sure that these recesses receive those parts and are not facing inward toward the spider. If the chainrings are rotated relative to the crank or inverted, the shift ramps will not work.

11.7 **Outer and inner chainrings on a double crank**

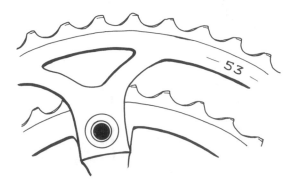

N O T E : *Whenever you change the size of the outer chainring, you must reposition the front derailleur for proper chainring clearance, as described in Chapter 8, §viii-4.*

BOTTOM BRACKETS

Most bottom brackets simply thread into the frame's bottom-bracket shell and accept the crankarms (Fig. 11.8). Simple enough, but it's important to remember that not all bottom-bracket shells are the same.

Almost all current triathlon bikes use English standard threads for the bottom bracket. That translates into a 1.370 inch diameter and a thread pitch of 24 threads per inch. These numbers are usually engraved on the bottom-bracket cups. If you are replacing a bottom bracket, make sure that the new cups have the same threads. It is important to remember that the drive side (right side) of an English standard bottom bracket has left-hand threads. In other words, turning counterclockwise tightens the drive-side cup (Fig. 11.18). Meanwhile, the left cup has right-hand threads that are, therefore, tightened clockwise (Fig. 11.9).

Other threads you may run across are Italian (with a 36mm diameter, and note that both cups

WARPED
CHAINRINGS

·

BENT CRANKARM
SPIDERS

·

CHAINRING
REPLACEMENT

11.8 Traditional bottom-bracket assembly

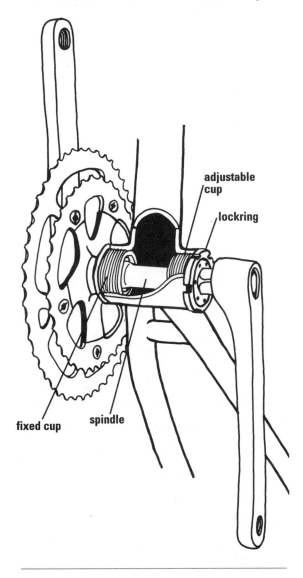

adjustable
cup

lockring

fixed cup   spindle

Pinarello. The most common type of bottom bracket in the 1990s was the Shimano-style cartridge-bearing bottom bracket with splined cups (Fig. 11.10). The most common bottom bracket in the 1980s and before was the cup-and-cone style with loose ball bearings (Figs. 11.8 and 11.11). Another bottom-bracket type has a sealed cartridge bearing on either end secured by an adjustable cup and lockring at either end (Fig. 11.12).

From 1996 to 2003, Shimano's high-end bottom brackets, called OctaLink, had a large "pipe" spindle with splined ends (Fig. 11.13), rather than square-taper ends, as in Figs. 11.10–12. Most OctaLink BBS are the cartridge type shown in Figure 11.10 but with a large splined axle. The first generation of Shimano Dura-Ace OctaLink bottom brackets, though, had four sets of loose, adjustable, and serviceable bearings: two sets of tiny balls and two sets of needle bearings (Fig. 11.13).

To counter Shimano's patented OctaLink designs, which offer increased stiffness and lower weight than square-taper designs, a number of manufacturers banded together in the late 1990s to create the ISIS standard (Fig. 11.14). Like OctaLink, ISIS has a larger-diameter splined spindle, but it features longer and deeper splines.

In 2003, Shimano upped the high-end ante again with the integrated-spindle design (Fig. 11.15), in which the right arm is permanently joined to the spindle, and the bearing cups place the bearings external to the bottom-bracket shell, making a larger spindle and larger bearings possible. Other manufacturers have followed suit but offer different attachment systems for the left arm and different spindle diameters (like Campagnolo Ultra-Torque; Fig. 11.16) so their bearings are not usually interchangeable with Shimano's.

have right-hand threads), French, and Swiss (both of these come in 35mm diameter but use different thread directions). The latter two thread patterns are rare, although French threading was common until the early 1980s.

Currently, integrated-spindle bottom brackets with the bearings external to the bottom-bracket shell (Figs. 11.15–16) are all the rage. Additionally, there are a few bike brands with oversize, internally mounted bearings and oversize bottom-bracket shells to accept them, most notably Cannondale, Specialized, and

BOTTOM-BRACKET INSTALLATION

The most important item in bottom-bracket installation is to make sure that the axle length in the bottom bracket is correct. If it's incorrect, the chainrings will not line up well with the rear cogs (i.e., the chainline will be off; see §viii-34 and §viii-35 in Chap. 8). Some bikes come from the factory with the wrong length bottom bracket. No amount of fiddling with the derailleurs will get such a bike to shift properly. Get a bottom bracket specifically recommended for your crankset, and double-check that it has the proper threading for your frame. Before installing a new bottom bracket of a brand and model different from your crank, see Figure 8.30 and read the chainline sections (§viii-34 and §viii-35) at the end of Chapter 8.

For one-piece cartridge-style bottom brackets (Figs. 11.10 and 11.14) with cups that thread into the bottom-bracket shell, the axle length is not as critical.

But for loose-bearing and integrated-spindle bottom brackets (Figs. 11.11, 11.13, 11.15, and 11.16) to work properly, the threads on both sides of the frame's bottom-bracket shell must be lined up with each other, and the end faces of the shell must be parallel. If you have any doubts about your frame and are installing an expensive bottom bracket, it is a good idea to have the bottom-bracket shell tapped (threaded) and faced (ends cut parallel) by a qualified shop possessing the proper tools. Doing so will improve adjustment and freedom of movement with loose-bearing bottom brackets and will reduce binding and the likelihood of creaking with integrated-spindle cranksets.

Always grease the threads when installing bottom brackets (or use an antiseize compound on them).

xi-7 SHIMANO OR CAMPAGNOLO SEALED CARTRIDGE-BEARING BOTTOM BRACKETS (AND CLONES)

Shimano- and Campagnolo-style sealed cartridge units (Fig. 11.10) are installed with a splined tool (Fig. 4.2, bottom). The tool is different for the two manufacturers, although lots of other bottom bracket brands accept the Shimano tool. A Shimano-style cartridge-bearing bottom bracket can have either a square-taper axle (Fig. 11.10) or a large tubular axle with splined ends like the OctaLink spindle in Figure 11.13 or the ISIS spindle in Figure 11.14. These instructions apply to cartridge-bearing bottom brackets like those shown in Figures 11.10 and 11.14, as well as to ones with this type of cartridge body and a Shimano OctaLink splined spindle.

1. Thread the left cup (clockwise) in three to four turns by hand.

2. Slide the cartridge into the bottom-bracket shell, paying particular attention to the "right" and "left"

11.9 **Tightening and loosening nondrive-side bottom-bracket cup**

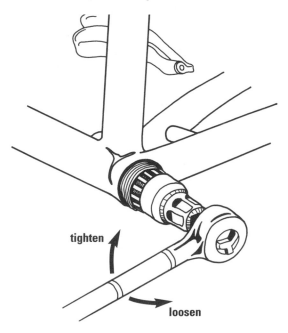

tighten

loosen

11.10–16 Types of bottom brackets

11.10 Shimano-style cartridge with square taper spindle

11.11 Loose-bearing square taper

11.12 Adjustable cartridge-bearing square taper

11.13 Shimano Dura-Ace Octalink loose-bearing splined-splindle

11.14 ISIS cartridge

11.15 Shimano integrated spindle

11.16 Campagnolo Ultra-Torque integrated spindle

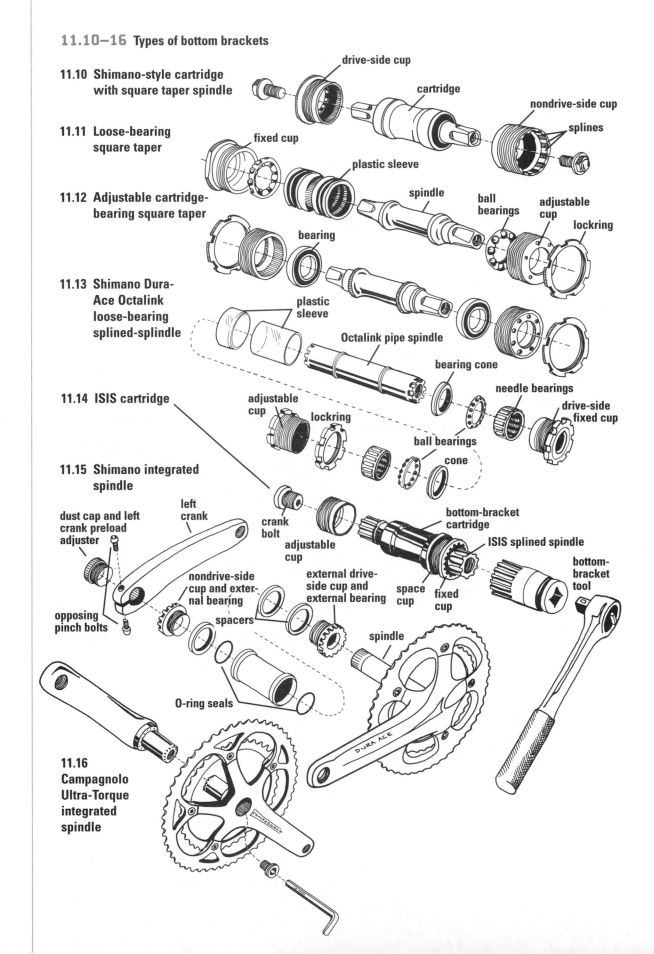

drive-side cup

cartridge

nondrive-side cup

splines

fixed cup

plastic sleeve

spindle

ball bearings

adjustable cup

lockring

bearing

plastic sleeve

Octalink pipe spindle

bearing cone

needle bearings

drive-side fixed cup

adjustable cup

lockring

ball bearings

cone

dust cap and left crank preload adjuster

left crank

crank bolt

adjustable cup

bottom-bracket cartridge

ISIS splined spindle

bottom-bracket tool

opposing pinch bolts

nondrive-side cup and external bearing

spacers

external drive-side cup and external bearing

space cup

fixed cup

spindle

O-ring seals

markings on the cartridge. The cup with the raised lip is the drive-side cup (the cup shown in Figs. 11.10 and 11.14). The drive-side cup is left-hand threaded on an English-thread bottom bracket and right-hand threaded on an Italian-threaded one.

3. By using the splined cup tool (for Shimano or Campagnolo) with either an open-end wrench or a ⅜-inch drive socket wrench, tighten the drive-side cup into the drive side of the bottom-bracket shell until the lip seats against the face of the shell (as in Fig. 11.9, except on the drive side instead of the nondrive side as illustrated).

NOTE: *Again, on most bikes, this drive-side cup will tighten counterclockwise. On Italian bikes, though, it will tighten clockwise.*

4. With the same tool, turn the left (nondrive) cup clockwise until it tightens against the cartridge (see Fig. 11.9). The torque required is the same as for the right cup. There is no adjustment of the bearings to be done; you can put on the crank now (§xi-1b).

xi-8 CUP-AND-CONE BOTTOM BRACKETS

Cup-and-cone (or "loose-ball") bottom brackets (Figs. 11.11 and 11.13) use ball bearings that ride between cone-shaped bearing surfaces on the axle and cup-shaped races in the threaded cups. One cup, called the fixed cup (the cup on the left in Fig. 11.11), has a lip on it and fits on the drive side (right side) of the bike. The other, called the adjustable cup (the right cup in Fig. 11.11), has a lockring that threads onto the cup and against the face of the bottom-bracket shell. The individual ball bearings are usually held together by a retaining cage, which varies in shape depending on bottom bracket. Some folks prefer to do without the retainer; it works fine either way.

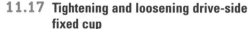

11.17 Tightening and loosening drive-side fixed cup

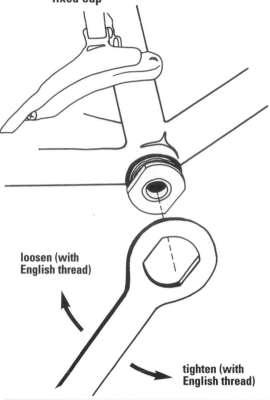

loosen (with English thread)

tighten (with English thread)

In order for cup-and-cone bottom brackets to turn smoothly, the bearing surfaces of the cups must be parallel. Because the cups thread into the bottom-bracket shell, the threads on both sides of the shell must be lined up with each other, and the end faces of the shell must be parallel. If you have any doubts about your frame, it is a good idea to have the bottom-bracket shell tapped (threaded) and faced (ends cut parallel) by a qualified shop possessing the proper tools.

1. Unless you own a fixed-cup tool, have a shop install the fixed cup for you. The shop tool ensures that the cup goes in straight and tight. The tool pictured in Figure 11.17 can be used in a pinch, but it can let the cup go in crooked and will slip off before you get it really tight. The fixed cup must be very tight so that it does not vibrate loose. Remember that English-threaded fixed cups are tightened counterclockwise.

11.18 Placing axle and drive-side bearings in bottom-bracket shell

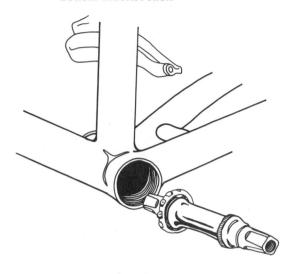

2. Wipe the inside surface of both cups with a clean rag and put a thin layer of clean grease on the bearing surfaces. Apply enough to half cover the balls; more than that will be wasted and will attract dirt.

3. Wipe the axle (also called a spindle) with a clean rag.

4. Figure out which end of the bottom-bracket axle is the drive side. The drive side may be marked with an R; if not, you can tell by choosing the side with the longer end (when measured from the bearing surface). If there is writing on the axle, it will usually read right side up for a rider sitting on the bike. If there is no marking and no length difference, the axle orientation is irrelevant.

5. Slide one set of bearings onto the drive-side end of the axle (Fig. 11.18). If you're using a retainer cage, make sure you put it on correctly. The balls, rather than the retainer cage, should rest against the axle bearing surfaces. Because there are two types of retainers with opposite designs, you need to be careful to avoid binding, as well as smashing of the retainers. If you're still confused, there is

one easy test: If it's in right, it'll turn smoothly; if it's in wrong, it won't. If you have loose ball bearings with no retainer cage, stick them into the greased cup. Most setups rely on nine balls; you can confirm that you are using the correct number by inserting and removing the axle and checking to make sure that they are evenly distributed in the grease with no extra gap for more balls.

6. Slide the axle into the bottom bracket so that it pushes the bearings into the fixed cup (Fig. 11.18). You can use your pinkie stuck through from the other side to stabilize the end of the axle as you slide it in.

7. Insert the protective plastic sleeve (shown in Figs. 11.11 and 11.13) into the shell against the inside edge of the fixed cup. The sleeve keeps dirt and rust from falling from the frame tubes into the bearings, so if you don't have one, get one.

8. Now turn your attention to the other cup. Place the bearing set into the greased adjustable cup. If you are using a bearing retainer, make sure it is properly oriented. If you are using loose balls, press them lightly into the grease so that they stay in place.

9. Without the lockring, slide the adjustable cup over the axle and tighten it clockwise by hand into the shell, being certain that it is going in straight. Screw the cup in as far as you can by hand—ideally all the way until the bearings seat between axle and cup.

10. Locate the appropriate tool for tightening the adjustable cup. Most cups have two holes that accept the ends, or pins, of an adjustable cup wrench called a "pin spanner" (Fig. 4.2). Another common type of adjustable cup has two flats for a wrench; on this type, you may use an adjustable wrench.

11.19 Tightening lockring; hold adjustable cup in place with pin spanner

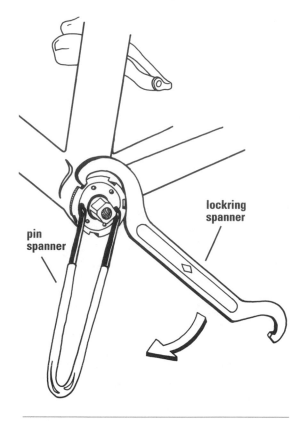

pin spanner

lockring spanner

11. Carefully tighten the adjustable cup against the bearings, taking great care not to overtighten. Turn the axle periodically with your fingers to ensure that it moves freely. If it binds up, you have gone too far; back off a bit. The danger of overtightening is that the bearings can force dents into the bearing surfaces of the cups, and the bearings will never turn smoothly again.

12. Screw the lockring onto the adjustable cup and select the proper tool for it. Lockrings come in different shapes, as do lockring spanners; make sure yours mate properly with each other.

13. Tighten the lockring against the face of the bottom-bracket shell with the lockring spanner while holding the adjustable cup in place with a pin spanner (Fig. 11.19). If you turn the bicycle upside down, you can pull down harder on the wrenches.

14. As you snug the lockring against the bottom-bracket shell, check the axle periodically. The lockring can pull the cup out of the shell minutely and loosen the adjustment. The axle should turn smoothly without free play in the bearings. I recommend installing and tightening the drive-side crankarm onto the drive end of the axle (Fig. 11.2) at this time so that you can check for free play by wiggling the end of the crank; it will give you a better feel for any looseness in the system.

15. Adjust the cup so that the axle play is just barely eliminated. While holding the cup in place, tighten the lockring as much as you can (Fig. 11.19) so that the bottom bracket does not come out of adjustment while riding. You may have to repeat this step a time or two until you get the ideal adjustment.

xi-9 INTEGRATED-SPINDLE BOTTOM BRACKETS

1. There will be a plastic sleeve attached to the right cup to keep contamination from falling onto the spindle inside of the frame. Leave this sleeve on when installing the cup.

2. After greasing their threads and starting them by hand first, tighten the right (drive-side) cup counterclockwise and the left cup clockwise by using the splined tool for the purpose (Fig. 11.20), leaving the cup spacers in place. Torque is high (35–50 N·m), so tighten the cups pretty hard; you are not likely to have a splined tool for this task that works with a torque wrench to measure it to spec.

3. Grease the face and internal bore of each bearing, as well as the left end and areas of the spindle that will contact the bearings. From the right side, push the spindle through the cups as far as you can (the

INTEGRATED-
SPINDLE
BOTTOM
BRACKETS

○

OTHER TYPES
OF BOTTOM
BRACKETS

11.20 **Installing external-bearing cups**

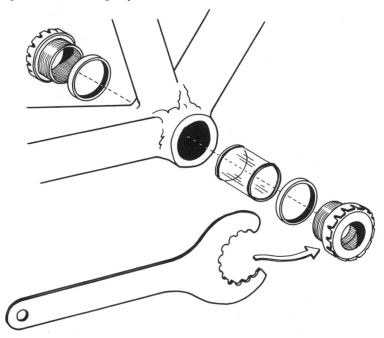

spindle splines will protrude from the left bearing, and the right arm will be close to or contacting the right bearing).

4. Slip the left crank on the splines, ensuring that it is at 180 degrees from the right arm (Shimano IS spindles have two wider splines to ensure this).

5. Finish the installation according to the type of crank you have:

   (a) On Truvativ and SRAM Giga X Pipe cranks and on FSA Mega Exo and carbon-fiber cranks, install the greased crank bolt and tighten the left arm with an 8mm Allen wrench, the same as for a normal crank (torque varies but is relatively high; use 41–47 N·m for Truvativ/SRAM). You're done, if you have one of these and you feel no end play in the bottom bracket.

   (b) On Shimano (Fig. 11.15) and FSA aluminum arms, tighten the left-side dust cap (not very tightly [0.4–0.7 N·m], just enough

to pull the right and left cranks over against the bottom-bracket cups) with the special splined cap tool for Shimano and an Allen wrench for FSA. Shimano's tool is just a round disc meant to be turned by hand to prevent overtightening it.

   (c) On Shimano and FSA aluminum arms, with a 5mm hex key, tighten the two opposing (greased) pinch bolts (to 10–15 N·m), by alternately tightening each one a quarter turn at a time. Check for play in the spindle.

   (d) On Campagnolo Ultra-Torque (Fig. 11.16), position the retaining spring around the drive-side bearing cup so that its two ends are near the holes in the cup. Insert the right crank fully, and press on the retaining spring to slide its two ends into the holes in the drive-side bearing cup. Gently pull outward on the crank to check that the spring is in place and is retaining the crankarm.

Place the wave washer into the bearing seat of the left-hand cup and push the left crank in so that the right and left spindle stubs meet in the center. Ensure that the two arms are at 180 degrees from each other. Drop the short fixing bolt deep inside the drive-side bottom bracket spindle, and tighten it to 42 N·m with a long 10mm Allen wrench with a cheater bar on the stubby end, or with Campagnolo's UT-BB110 tool on a torque-wrench handle.

6. Recheck the torque after one ride, as the crank may settle in and the bolts may need retightening. Periodically check the torque from then on.

xi-10 OTHER TYPES OF BOTTOM BRACKETS

The three bottom-bracket types just described probably represent about 95 percent of the road bikes in circulation. However, there is one variation worth mentioning.

Cartridge-bearing bottom brackets with adjustable cups (Fig. 11.12) are reasonably easy to install. These come with an adjustable cup at each end. With this type, you simply install the drive-side cup and lockring, slide the cartridge bearing in (if it is not already pressed into the cup), slip the axle in, and then install the other bearing, cup, and lockring. Tighten each lockring while holding the adjustable cup in place with a pin spanner (Fig. 11.19). Adjust for free play as in §xi-8, steps 11–15.

The advantage of having two adjustable cups is that you can center the cartridge by moving it side to side in the bottom-bracket shell. If the chainrings end up too close or too far away from the frame (see chainline discussion in §viii-34 and §viii-35 in Chap. 8),

you can move one cup in and one out to shift the position of the spindle.

Sometimes cartridge-bearing bottom brackets bind up a bit during adjustment and installation. A light tap on each end of the axle usually seats them.

OVERHAULING THE BOTTOM BRACKET

A bottom-bracket overhaul consists of cleaning or replacing the bearings, cleaning the axle and bearing surfaces, and regreasing them. With any type, both crankarms must be removed (§xi-1).

xi-11 CARTRIDGE-BEARING BOTTOM BRACKETS

Cartridge bottom brackets (Figs. 11.10 and 11.14) are sealed units and cannot be overhauled. They must be replaced when they stop performing properly. Remove the cranks as in §xi-1. Remove the bottom bracket by unscrewing the cups with the splined cup tool (Fig. 11.9), and install a new bottom bracket as directed in §xi-7.

xi-12 CUP-AND-CONE BOTTOM BRACKETS

Cup-and-cone bottom brackets (Figs. 11.11 and 11.13) can be overhauled entirely from the nondrive side, after you have removed the crankarms as described in §xi-1.

1. Remove the lockring with the lockring spanner (as in Fig. 11.19, except the lockring spanner and the rotation direction will be reversed).

2. Remove the adjustable cup with the tool that fits yours (usually a pin spanner [Fig. 4.2], installed into the cup as in Fig. 11.19).

3. Leave the fixed cup in place, and check that it is tight in the frame by putting a fixed-cup wrench

on it and trying to tighten it (counterclockwise for English thread, clockwise for Italian) (Fig. 11.17).

4. Clean the cups and axle with a rag. There should be no need for a solvent unless the parts are glazed.

5. Clean the bearings with a citrus-based solvent, without removing them from their retainer cages. A simple way to do this is to drop the bearings in a plastic bottle, fill it with solvent, cap it, and shake it. A toothbrush may be required afterward, and a solvent tank is certainly handy if you have access to one. If the bearings are not shiny and in perfect shape, replace them. Balls with dull luster and/or rough spots or rust on them should be replaced.

6. Wash the bearings in soap and water to remove the solvent and any remaining grit. Towel them off thoroughly and then let dry completely. An air compressor is handy here.

7. Follow the installation procedure described in §xi-8.

8. Install the crankarms as in §xi-1, Figure 11.2

xi-13 INTEGRATED-SPINDLE BOTTOM BRACKETS

LEVEL 2

Following the method of §xi-9, replace the cups and you are done! The bearings are not designed to be removed from the cups, so you probably cannot replace the bearings separately. If you're determined to avoid replacing the cups and bearings, you can try to pry off the bearing cover and clean the bearing (Fig. 9.29); be prepared to replace everything if you screw it up.

xi-14 OTHER TYPES OF BOTTOM BRACKETS

If any cartridge-bearing bottom bracket becomes difficult to turn, the bearings must be replaced. If they are pressed into cups, then you may also have to buy new cups. Be sure to get the correct size.

1. Reverse the installation procedure outlined in §xi-10 to remove the bottom bracket.

2. Replace the bearings.

3. Reinstall the bottom bracket (§xi-10) and crankarms (§xi-1).

TROUBLESHOOTING CRANK AND BOTTOM-BRACKET NOISE

xi-15 CREAKING NOISES

Mysterious creaking noises can drive you nuts. Just when you think you have your bike tuned to perfection, a little noise comes along to ruin your ride. What's worse, these annoying little creaks, pops, and groans can be difficult to locate.

Pedaling-induced noises can originate from almost anything connected to the crankset, including movement of the cleats on your shoes, loose crankarms on the bottom-bracket axle, loose chainrings, or poorly adjusted pedal or bottom-bracket bearings. Of course, noise could also originate from seemingly unrelated components like the seat, seatpost, wheel skewer frame, wheels, headset, or handlebar.

Before spending hours overhauling the drivetrain, spend some time trying to isolate the source of the noise. Try different pedals and shoes and wheels. Pedal out of the saddle, and pedal without flexing the handlebar. If the source of the creak turns out to be the saddle, seatpost, wheel quick-release skewer, headset, pedals, wheels, or handlebar, turn to the appropriate chapter for directions on how to correct the problem.

If the creaking is definitely in the crank area, here are some steps to resolve it.

1. Check to make sure the chainring bolts are tight, and tighten them if they are not (Fig. 11.6). Greasing them can also help.

2. If that does not solve the problem, make certain that the crankarm bolts are tight (Fig. 11.2). If they are not, the resulting movement between the crankarm and the bottom-bracket axle is a likely source of noise. If the crank is of a different brand than the bottom bracket, check with the manufacturers or your local shop to make sure that they are recommended for use together. Incompatible cranks and axles will never properly join and are a potential problem area.

3. Rusting can break the glue bond between a Shimano-style cartridge-bearing bottom bracket and one or both of its cups (Figs. 11.10 and 11.14), allowing movement between cartridge and cup. This movement can make creaking noises when pedaling. To quiet the noises, remove the cartridge, grease the inside of the cup(s) as well as the threads, and reinstall the bottom bracket.

4. The bottom bracket itself can creak owing to improper adjustment, lack of grease, cracked bearings, worn parts, or loose cups. All of these things require adjustment or overhaul procedures, outlined in the sections under the heading Bottom-Bracket Installation in this chapter. Many integrated-spindle designs are very sensitive to being out of parallel, and creaking can occur if the bottom-bracket shell is not perfectly tapped and faced to meet the external bearings (Fig. 11.20). Tapping and facing the bottom bracket shell is a job for a good bike shop.

5. If you have an unpainted titanium or aluminum frame, check to make sure that the front-derailleur clamp is tight. The noise from a loose clamp while pedaling, especially under heavy load, can seem to emanate from the crankset.

6. Now for the bad news. If creaking persists, the problem can be rooted in the frame. Creaks can originate from cracks in and around the bottom-bracket shell. Or the threads in the bottom-bracket shell can be so worn that they allow the cups to move slightly. Neither of these is a good sign—unless, of course, you were hoping for an excuse to buy a new frame.

xi-16 CLUNKING NOISES

1. Crankarm play: Grab the crankarm and push on it side to side.

   (a) If there is play in the crankarm, tighten the crankarm bolt (Fig. 11.2; torque spec is in Appendix C).

   (b) If there is still crankarm play, and you have a cup-and-cone bottom bracket (Figs. 11.11 and 11.13) or a cartridge-bearing bottom bracket with a lockring on each side (Fig. 11.12), adjust the bottom-bracket axle-end play (steps 11–15, §xi-8).

   (c) If bottom-bracket adjustment does not eliminate crankarm play or you have a non-adjustable cartridge-bearing bottom bracket (Fig. 11.10 or 11.13), the bottom bracket is loose in the frame threads. With a cup-and-cone bottom bracket, you can go back to §xi-8 and start over, making sure that the fixed cup is very tight. You may need to use a cheater bar (extension tube) on the fixed-cup wrench to tighten the fixed cup to sufficient torque. Adjustable-cup lockrings need to be equally tight (Fig. 11.19), once the axle-end play is adjusted properly.

(d)　The lockrings and fixed-cup flanges must be flush against the bottom-bracket shell all the way around; if they are not, the bottom bracket must be removed, and the bottom-bracket shell must be tapped (threaded) and faced (cut parallel) by a shop equipped with the proper tools.

(e)　If the crankarm play persists or the bottom-bracket fixed cup or lockring will not tighten completely, then either the bottom-bracket cups are stripped or undersized, or the frame's bottom-bracket-shell threads are stripped or oversized. Either way, it's an expensive fix, especially the frame-replacement option! Get a second opinion if you reach this point.

2.　Pedal end play: Grab each pedal and wobble it to check for play. See the sections on Overhauling Pedals in Chapter 12 if you find axle-end play.

xi-17 HARD-TO-TURN CRANKS

If the cranks are hard to turn, you need to overhaul the bottom bracket (see §xi-11–§xi-14), unless you want to continue intensifying your workout or boost the egos of your cycling companions. The bottom bracket may be shot and need replacement.

xi-18 INNER CHAINRING DRAGS ON CHAINSTAY

If the inner chainring drags on the chainstay, possibly the bottom-bracket axle is too short or the square hole in the crankarm is so deformed that the crank slides on too far. If you have switched to a larger inner chainring and the chainring is too large, get a smaller one. A misaligned frame, with either bent chainstays or a twisted bottom-bracket shell, can cause chainring rub as well. A badly misaligned frame needs to be replaced.

With an adjustable cartridge-bearing bottom bracket (Fig. 11.12) with a lockring on each end, it is possible to fix the problem by offsetting the entire bottom bracket to the left (Fig. 11.19). If the bottom-bracket axle is too short, replace it with one of the correct length. If the square hole in the crank is badly deformed, replace the crankarm. There's no other cure; it will continue to loosen up and cause problems otherwise.

N O T E : *See §viii-35 and Figure 8.30 in Chapter 8 concerning chainline to establish proper crank-to-frame spacing.*

PEDALS

*Experience is that marvelous thing that enables
you to recognize a mistake when you make it again.*

—F. P. Jones

Pedals come in all shapes, types, and sizes, but triathletes use only the most efficient clip-in pedals (Fig. 12.1). They retain the foot with spring-loaded clips (like a ski binding) and are all but universal on today's mid- to high-end triathlon bikes.

Clip-in pedals are sometimes called "clipless" because they have no toeclip, an old technology consisting of a cage and a strap—the cage captures the front of the foot and the strap helps hold the foot in place. For added security, most racing shoes for toeclips are equipped with cleats to grip the pedal — or were so equipped, because it is almost impossible to find road racing shoes made for toeclips these days (although inexpensive mountain bike shoes are still designed to be compatible with toeclips, which continue to be found on some entry-level mountain bikes).

Clip-in models (Figs. 12.1–3) offer the secure grip of a toeclip, strap, and cleat, yet they allow easier entry and exit from the pedal. They require special shoes and may require accurate mounting of the cleats. Your choice of shoes is limited to stiff-sole models that accept cleats for your particular pedal. If you have never used clip-in pedals, you will find, once you have them properly mounted and adjusted, that they waste less energy through flex and slippage and allow you to transfer more power directly to the pedals.

This chapter explains how to remove and replace pedals, how to mount the cleats and adjust the release tension with clip-in pedals, how to troubleshoot pedal problems, and how to overhaul and replace the axles, or spindles, on almost all road bike pedals. I use the terms "axle" and "spindle" interchangeably because you'll hear both terms used at your bike shop when you're looking for replacement parts.

12.1 Clip-in pedal

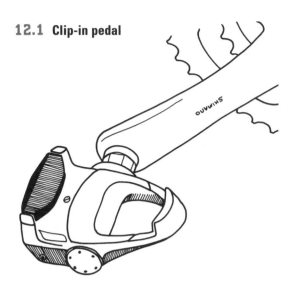

12.2 Removing or installing pedal with 15mm pedal wrench

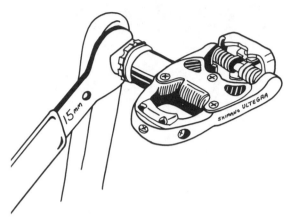

xii-1 PEDAL REMOVAL AND INSTALLATION

Note that the right pedal axle is right-hand threaded and the left is left-hand (reverse) threaded. Both unscrew from the crank in the pedaling direction. There's an interesting bit of history behind the threading of pedal axles this way. In the early days of cycling, fixed-gear bikes were the norm, and it was decided that if the pedal bearings were to seize up, the pedal should unscrew from the crank rather than tear up the rider's strapped-in feet. This isn't a concern on a modern bike because the freewheel (on the rear hub) eliminates the bodily danger of a seized pedal, and the bearing quality makes seizing highly unlikely.

a. Removal

1. Slide a 15mm pedal wrench onto the wrench flats of the pedal axle (Fig. 12.2). Or if the pedal axle is designed to accept it, you can use a 6mm hex key or a 8mm Allen wrench from the back side of the crankarm (Fig. 12.3). Either is particularly handy on the road because you probably won't be carrying a 15mm pedal wrench. But if you are at home and the pedal is really tight, it will be eas-

ier to use the standard pedal wrench. Note that some new models have no wrench flats and only accept a hex key. In this case, if you have difficulty unscrewing the pedal, use a longer hex key or slip a section of pipe over a short one for more mechanical advantage.

2. Unscrew the pedal in the appropriate direction. The right, or drive-side, pedal unscrews counterclockwise when viewed from that side. The left-side pedal is reverse threaded, so it unscrews in a clockwise direction when viewed from the left side of the bike. Once you have loosened it, you can quickly unscrew either pedal by lifting the rear wheel of the bike off the ground and turning the crank forward with a 15mm pedal wrench engaged on the pedal spindle.

b. Installation

1. Use a rag to wipe the threads clean on the pedal axle and inside the crankarm.

2. Apply a light coat of grease to the pedal threads.

3. Start screwing the pedal in with your fingers, clockwise for the right pedal, counterclockwise for the left.

12.3 Removing or installing pedal with a 6mm hex key

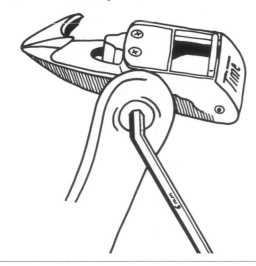

4. Tighten the pedal with the 15mm pedal wrench (Fig. 12.2) or a 6mm hex key (Fig. 12.3). You can do this quickly by turning the cranks backward with a 15mm pedal wrench engaged on the pedal spindle.

SETTING UP CLIP-IN PEDALS

Setting up clip-in pedals involves installing and adjusting the cleats on the shoes and adjusting the pedal-release tension.

There are a number of different mounting platforms for road bike pedals, and your shoe sole must be compatible with your pedal cleats. The original clip-in road bike pedal system was the Look, now used in the majority of pedal systems, which has three M5-threaded holes (Fig. 12.4) arranged in a triangular pattern to accept a three-hole cleat (Fig. 12.9). The original Time pedal system required a flat surface with four smaller threaded holes (Fig. 12.5), and original Speedplay pedal cleats could be mounted on them as well. Original Shimano road bike pedals were made by Look and used the three-hole mounting system, but Shimano Pedaling Dynamics (SPD) began as a system for

mountain bikes with tiny cleats (Fig. 12.8) that were easy to run with and less likely to clog with mud. SPD cleats mount with two side-by-side M5-thread screws, spaced 14mm apart. They screw into a movable threaded cleat-mounting plate behind two longitudinal grooves in the sole (Fig. 12.6). Crank Brothers cleats mount on this system as well. Even though the SPD system was originally meant for mountain bikes, some triathletes prefer it, using an SPD-type single-sided road bike pedal or a double-sided mountain bike pedal so that they can use a mountain bike shoe, which is far easier to walk in than a road cycling shoe.

Shimano's SPD-R pedal (since abandoned) required a shoe having a single lengthwise slot in the sole with an M5-threaded hole at either end moving on a threaded backing plate behind the slot (Fig. 12.7). Now, Shimano's SPD-SL road bike pedals and Ritchey, Time, and Speedplay road bike pedals have moved to the standard three-hole system. Pedal brands not mentioned in this paragraph mount on one or several of these shoe-hole patterns.

Many shoe and pedal manufacturers make adapter plates to fit various shoes and pedals to each other. If you have a favorite pair of shoes, it may be possible to make them work with an unrelated set of pedals.

xii-2 INSTALLING AND ADJUSTING PEDAL CLEATS ON THE SHOES

The cleat is important because its position determines the fore-and-aft, lateral (side-to-side), and rotational position of your foot. If the cleats aren't properly oriented, the misalignment could eventually cause hip, knee, or ankle problems.

1. Put on the shoe and mark the position of the ball of your foot (the big bump behind your big toe) on the outside of the shoe. This mark will help you

PEDAL REMOVAL
AND
INSTALLATION
·
INSTALLING AND
ADJUSTING PEDAL
CLEATS ON THE
SHOES

12.4 **Three-hole (Look) cleat drill pattern**

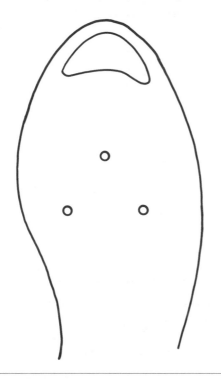

12.5 **Original Time cleat drill pattern**

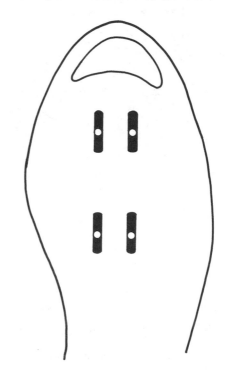

position the cleat so that the ball of your foot will be straight above or just ahead of or behind the pedal spindle. Take off the shoe and continue drawing the line straight across the bottom of the shoe.

2. Grease the cleat screw threads, and screw the cleat that came with the pedals onto the shoe; this step usually requires a 4mm hex key or a Phillips-head or standard screwdriver. Make sure you orient the cleat in the appropriate direction. Some cleats have an arrow indicating forward (Fig. 12.8); if yours do not, the instructions accompanying the pedals will specify which direction the cleat should point, and in some cases, on which shoe an asymmetrical cleat should be mounted. SPD and SPD-R cleats require rubber pontoons on a plate mounted under the cleat (Fig. 12.8). The pontoons guide the small cleat into the pedal. The pontoons are not necessary on a mountain bike shoe as the relieved area in its tread will guide the cleat.

NOTE: *On SPD-R cleats, the pontoon mounts on the rear bolt, pointing back.*

3. Position the cleat. Temporarily place it in the middle of its lateral- and rotational-adjustment range. Setting the fore-and-aft position requires knowing where the pedal spindle is positioned relative to the cleat. Many cleats have a mark on the side indicating the spindle position (Fig. 12.9). If your cleat has such a mark, line it up 0–1cm behind the line you drew in step 1 across the shoe sole. With an SPD pedal, line up the mounting screws 0–1cm behind the mark you made in step 1 (Fig. 12.8). With a Speedplay cleat, place the center of the hole in the middle of the cleat 0–1cm behind the mark you made in step 1. If the cleat has no centering marks and is not SPD, you will have to tighten the screws and set the shoe in the pedal. When the shoe is level, you want the ball of your foot between 0 and 1cm forward of the pedal

12.6 SPD cleat drill pattern

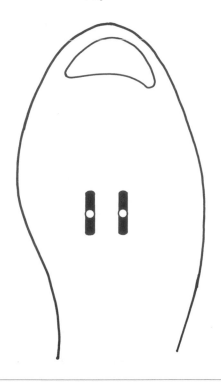

12.7 SPD-R cleat drill pattern

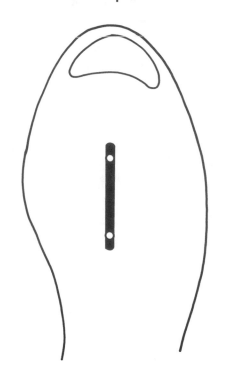

spindle. Putting the ball farther forward is usually helpful to develop power, while high-cadence spinning is usually enhanced with the ball of the foot farther back. If you know which type of rider you are, you can set the shoe as appropriate. Otherwise, split the difference and shoot for the middle of the range. Small feet sometimes do better with the cleat farther forward on the shoe, placing the ball of the foot ahead of the spindle, and vice versa. Mounting the cleat further back also can alleviate metatarsal pain. Make sure you don't put an old-style Time rear cam on a shoe not designed for it, or you will not be able to release by twisting outward.

N O T E : *There are many SPD- and Look-style pedal clones under various brand names on the market. The cleat-mounting and tension-adjustment instructions for SPD or Look pedals generally apply to these models as well.*

12.8 Cleat centered 1cm behind
ball-of-foot line (SPD shown)

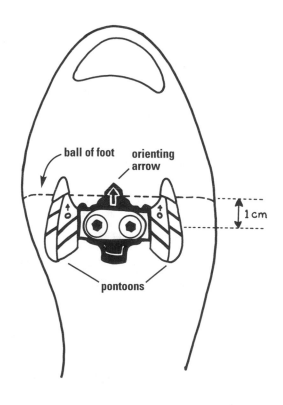

ball of foot orienting arrow

1cm

pontoons

PEDALS

12.9 Look cleat with mark for pedal center

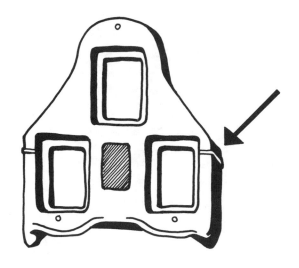

4. Snug the screws enough to prevent the cleat from moving when clipped in or out of the pedals, but don't tighten them fully. Follow the same steps with the other shoe.

5. To set the lateral cleat position, put the shoes on, sit on the bike, and clip into the pedals. Ride around a bit. Notice the position of your feet. Generally, the closer your feet are to the plane of the bike, the more efficient your pedaling will be, but you don't want them in so far that your ankles bump the cranks or the chainstays. Take off the shoes and adjust the cleats laterally, if necessary, to move your feet side to side. Get back on the bike and clip in again. Note that early Time pedals have no lateral cleat adjustment; recent Time models offer it by means of interchanging the left and right cleats.

6. To set the rotational cleat position, ride around some more. If your feet feel twisted and uncomfortable, or if you feel pressure on either side of your heel from the shoe, remove your shoes and rotate the cleat slightly. Most pedals now offer free-float, allowing the foot to rotate freely for a few degrees before releasing. Precise rotational cleat adjustment is less important if the pedal is free-floating. Some pedals have a dial on the back of the clip to set the amount of free-float rotation. Many companies also offer a number of cleat styles having increased or reduced (or eliminated) free-float range. I recommend starting with the greatest amount of free-float angle. You can reduce the float later if you desire. SPD-R cleats come in three styles: one with a wide tip for "fixed" operation and two narrower-tip models for different amounts of free-float. By adjusting rubber bumpers on the pedal body to stick up higher, you can eliminate vertical cleat play. Dura-Ace SPD-R pedals have a 3mm nut on the bottom of the pedal to push the bumper up, and Ultegra SPD-R pedals require removing three screws on the face of the pedal to interchange the two pads with thicker ones.

7. Once your cleat position feels right, trace the cleats with a pen or a scribe so that you can tell if the cleat stays put.

8. While holding the cleat in place, tighten the bolts down firmly. Hold the hex key close to the bend so that you do not exert too much leverage and strip the bolts. There is little danger of overtightening with a screwdriver, but do take care that the blade (or Phillips tip) fits well in the screw slot (or Phillips cross). Push down firmly while tightening to avoid stripping the head of the screw.

NOTE: *If you have a small torque wrench, the recommended tightening torque for most cleat screws is 43–52 in-lbs.*

9. When riding with new shoes or pedals, bring cleat-tightening tools along because you may want to fine-tune the cleat adjustment over the course of a few rides.

CHAPTER 12

225

ADJUSTING

RELEASE

TENSION OF

CLIP-IN PEDALS

12.10 **Release-tension adjustment screw on Look pedal**

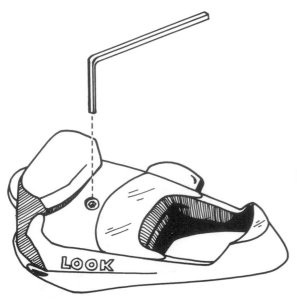

12.11 **Release-tension adjustment screw on Shimano SPD pedal**

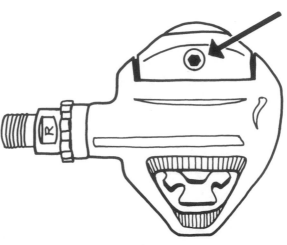

xii-3 ADJUSTING RELEASE TENSION OF CLIP-IN PEDALS

If you find the factory-set release adjustment too loose or too restrictive, you can change it on many clip-in pedals; exceptions are Bebop, Crank Brothers (Fig. 12.21), Diadora, Power, Speedplay (Fig. 12.19), and most Time (Fig. 12.3). Usually the adjusting screws are located on or near the spring-loaded rear clip (Figs. 12.10–11) and are operated with a small (3mm) hex key or a small screwdriver.

1. Locate the tension-adjustment screws. Older Looks have a screw (either slotted or 2.5mm or 3mm hex head) on top of the platform (Fig. 12.10); Look Anatomics and Campagnolo ProFits (Fig. 12.13) have a 3mm hex screw on the side. Look Keos and Shimano SPD-SLs have a 3mm hex screw on the top of the rear clip. Ritchey, Shimano SPD (Fig. 12.11), and SPD-R (Fig. 12.12) have a 3mm hex screw on the back of the clip.

N O T E : *There are many SPD- and Look-style pedal clones under various brand names on the market. The cleat-mounting and tension-adjustment instructions for SPD or Look pedals generally apply to these pedals as well.*

2. To reduce the tension, turn the screw (Figs. 12.10–13) counterclockwise; to increase, turn it clockwise (Figs. 12.10–11). It's the classic "lefty loosey, righty tighty" approach. There usually are click stops in the rotation of the screw. Tighten or loosen one click at a time (one-quarter to one-half turn), then ride the bike to test the adjustment. Many types include an indicator that moves with the screw to show relative adjustment. Make certain that you do not back the screw out so far that it comes out of the spring plate or so far that it can vibrate loose; feel for at least the first "click" to hold it in place.

N O T E : *With Ritchey SPD-style pedals, you will decrease the amount of free-float in the pedal as you increase the release tension.*

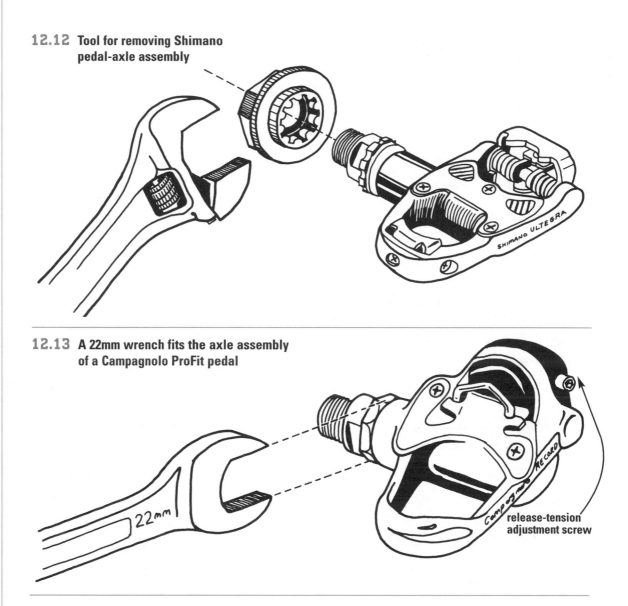

12.12 Tool for removing Shimano
pedal-axle assembly

12.13 A 22mm wrench fits the axle assembly
of a Campagnolo ProFit pedal

release-tension
adjustment screw

OVERHAULING PEDALS

LEVEL 2

Like a hub or bottom bracket, pedal bearings and bushings need to be cleaned and regreased regularly.

There is a wide variation in road bike pedal designs. This book is not big enough to go into great detail about the inner workings of every model. Speaking in general terms, pedal guts fall into two broad categories: those that have loose ball bearings (Figs. 12.14–15, 12.22–24) and those that have cartridge bearings (Figs. 12.16–21).

Many pedals are closed on the outboard end and have a nut surrounding the axle on the inboard end (Figs. 12.12–16). The axle assembly installs into the pedal as a unit and is accessed by this inboard nut. Some axles are held in by a snapring (Figs. 12.17–18). The axle assemblies on older pedal designs (Fig. 12.23) as well as some recent ones (Figs. 12.19–21) are accessed from the outboard end by removing a dust cap.

1. Remove the pedal from the bike (Figs. 12.2–3).

2. Before you start, figure out how the pedal is put together so that you will know how to take it apart;

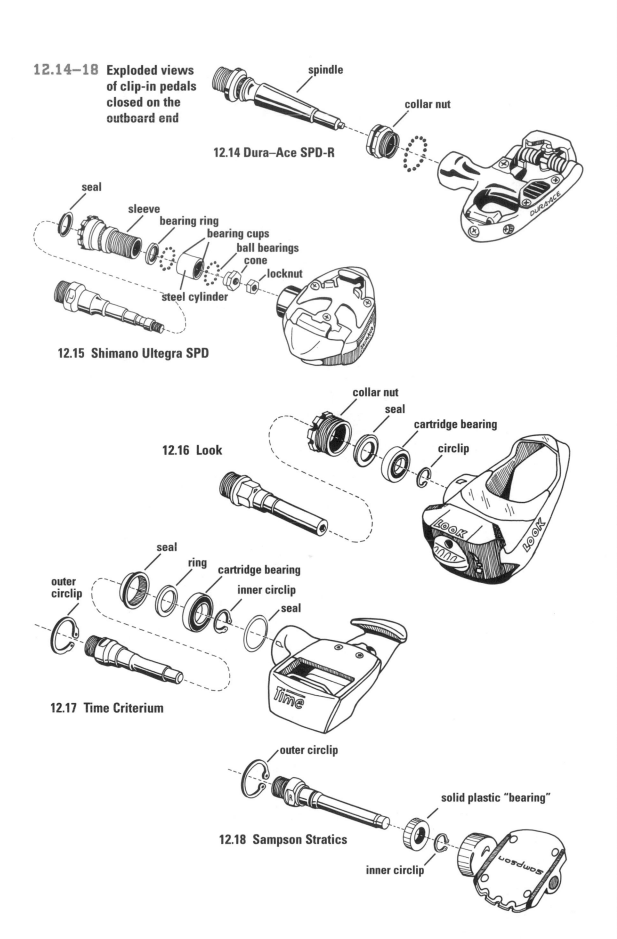

12.14–18 Exploded views of clip-in pedals closed on the outboard end

spindle

collar nut

12.14 Dura–Ace SPD-R

seal

sleeve

bearing ring

bearing cups

ball bearings

cone

locknut

steel cylinder

12.15 Shimano Ultegra SPD

collar nut

seal

cartridge bearing

circlip

12.16 Look

seal

ring

cartridge bearing

inner circlip

seal

outer circlip

12.17 Time Criterium

outer circlip

solid plastic "bearing"

12.18 Sampson Stratics

inner circlip

PEDALS

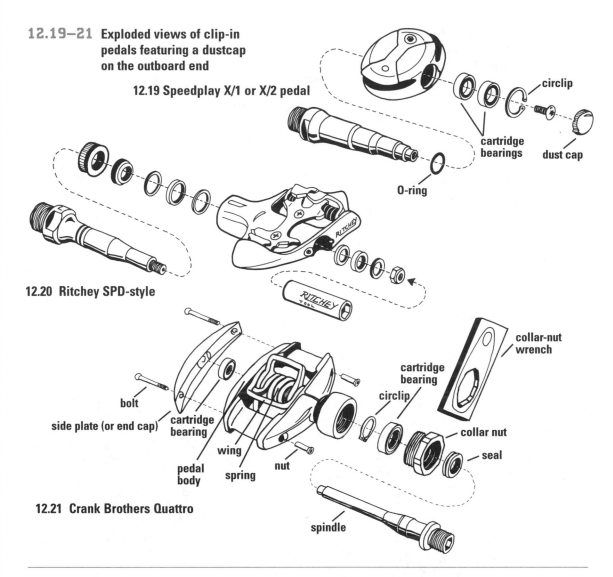

12.19–21 Exploded views of clip-in pedals featuring a dustcap on the outboard end

12.19 Speedplay X/1 or X/2 pedal

circlip

cartridge bearings

dust cap

O-ring

12.20 Ritchey SPD-style

collar-nut wrench

cartridge bearing

circlip

collar nut

seal

bolt

side plate (or end cap)

cartridge bearing

wing

nut

pedal body

spring

spindle

12.21 Crank Brothers Quattro

the following paragraphs and illustrations should help. In a few cases, the workings of the pedal guts may not be clear until you have completed step 1 in the overhaul process.

Most Shimano pedals have two sets of loose bearings and a bushing, which come out as a complete axle assembly (Fig. 12.15). You will see the tiny ball bearings at the small end of the axle (behind the wrenches in Fig. 12.22). Dura-Ace SPD-R (Fig. 12.14) and SPD-SL pedals have a set of ball bearings on each end of the spindle and a set of 6mm-inside-diameter (I.D.) needle bearings (not shown) just inboard of the outboard bearings.

Speedplay X/3 pedals have an inboard 10mm I.D., Teflon bushing, and an outboard 6mm I.D. cartridge bearing. Speedplay X/5 pedals have an inboard needle bearing and an outboard cartridge bearing.

The Campagnolo Record ProFit (Fig. 12.13) pedal has one inboard and two outboard 17mm outside-diameter (O.D.) cartridge bearings.

Look, Diadora, and older Time pedals have an inboard cartridge bearing (19mm, 24mm, and 24mm O.D., respectively) and one or two pressed-in outboard needle-bearing sets (not shown) (Figs. 12.16–17).

Of the newer, carbon-composite-body pedals, Look Keos have a pair of 15mm O.D., inboard cartridge bearings and an 8mm I.D., outboard needle bearing, whereas Time RXS pedals have a 21mm O.D., inboard cartridge bearing and an 8mm I.D., outboard needle bearing.

Speedplay X/1, X/2, and Zero pedals have an inboard pressed-in needle bearing (not shown) and an outboard pair of cartridge bearings (Fig. 12.19).

Crank Brothers Quattros (Fig. 12.21) have two cartridge bearings: a large one on the inboard side and smaller one on the outboard side. This arrangement differs from that of Crank Brothers MTB pedals (Eggbeater, Candy, Mallet), which have one cartridge ball bearing (outboard) and one bushing (inboard). Also, the Quattro does not have a threaded end cap for regreasing the pedal (see §xii-5, step 1 note). This feature was eliminated to increase cornering clearance.

Sampson Stratics (Fig. 12.18) pedals have a 24mm outside diameter (O.D.) solid-plastic "bearing" on the inboard side and a plastic bushing inside the pedal body.

Ritchey SPD-style road bike pedals (Fig. 12.20) have two sets of pressed-in needle bearings, one with an I.D. of 10mm and the other with an I.D. of 7mm.

Power Pedal axles (which only rotate in one direction) are not removable. The bearings are lubricated through the small grease fitting on the bottom of the pedal until clean grease squeezes out of the inboard side.

xii-4 OVERHAULING PEDALS CLOSED ON THE OUTBOARD END

LEVEL 3

1. Make sure the pedal does not have a dust cap or screw cover on the outboard end. If it does, skip to §xii-5. The exception is the Quattro (Fig. 12.21), which has a removable end cap but still is overhauled by unscrewing the inboard

collar nut. Unless you have an old Time, Diadora, or Sampson pedal, remove the axle assembly by unscrewing the nut surrounding the axle ("collar nut") where it enters the inboard side of the pedal (Figs. 12.12–13). You can usually just hold the pedal in your hand and unscrew the collar nut, but you may find that you will want to hold the pedal body in a padded vise while unscrewing the nut. The collar nut is often made of plastic and can crack if you turn it the wrong way, so be careful. Hold the pedal body with your hand or a vise while you unscrew the assembly. The fine threads take many turns to unscrew.

NOTE: *The threads on the pedal body are reversed compared to the crankarm threads on the axle. That means the right-axle assembly unscrews clockwise, and the left-axle assembly unscrews counterclockwise. It's confusing, but like English bottom-bracket threads, pedal bodies are threaded so that pedaling forward tightens the assembly.*

(a) Most Shimano pedals disassemble with a special plastic splined tool (Fig. 4.2, top), as do some Looks and Crank Brothers Quattros (Fig. 12.21). Use a large adjustable wrench or a vise to hold the tool (Fig. 12.12). Most other pedals take a 19mm, 20mm, or 22mm open-end wrench (Fig. 12.13). The collar nut on a Time RXS requires a special tool, but in its absence, the nut is easy to unscrew with a pair of pliers wrapped in cloth to avoid marring the nut's surface.

(b) Campagnolo ProFit (Fig. 12.13) and many Look pedal-axle assemblies unscrew with a 22mm open-end or box wrench; removal of the Dura-Ace SPD-R (Fig. 12.14) and SPD-SL axle assemblies requires a 20mm wrench,

12.22 **Most Shimano axles have a cone and a
locknut, used to adjust bearing play**

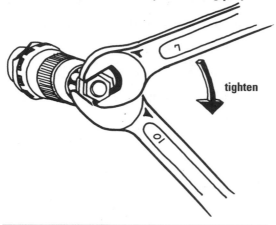

tighten

and Look Keos take a 19mm wrench. Some older Look axles are accessed with a special Look splined tool similar to the one that unscrews most Shimano pedals (Fig. 12.12). Note that original Shimano clip-in road bike pedals are actually Looks with Shimano axle assemblies, and Campagnolo clip-in pedals prior to 1997 (other than an unfortunate attempt by Campagnolo itself in the late 1980s) are also Looks with Campagnolo axle assemblies.

(c) Older Time, Diadora, and Sampson pedal axles are retained by a snapring on the crank side (Figs. 12.17–18). Popping the snapring out usually requires inward-squeezing snapring pliers, but the snapring on a Time Impact requires only a thin screwdriver to remove, once you move the end of the snapring under the little notch in the inboard pedal-body face so that you can pry it up with the screwdriver. There is also a snapring on a Power Pedal, but there is no point in removing it because the clutch bearing and axle assembly are pressed in, and you will not be able to pull them out.

With Time, Look, Sampson, or Diadora, skip to step 3.

2. Once you have removed the pedal body, take a look at the axle-bearing-bushing assembly. You will notice either one or two nuts on the thin end of the axle that serve to hold the bearings and/or bushings in place. Remove the nut or nuts as follows:

(a) If the axle has a single nut on the end, simply hold the axle's large end with the 15mm pedal wrench and unscrew the little nut with a 9mm or 12mm wrench (or whatever fits it). The nut will be tight, because it has no locknut.

(b) If the axle has two nuts on the end (Fig. 12.15), they are tightened against each other. To remove them, hold the inner nut with one wrench while you unscrew the outer nut with another (Fig. 12.22). On Shimano pedals, the inner nut is the bearing cone (Fig. 12.15); be careful not to lose the tiny ball bearings as you unscrew the cone!

3. Clean the parts as follows:

(a) If it is a loose-bearing pedal, use a rag to clean the ball bearings, the cone, the inner ring that the bearings ride on at the end of the plastic sleeve (it looks like a washer), the bearing surfaces on either end of the little steel cylinder (or cylinders, in the case of Look-made Campagnolos), the axle, and the inside of the plastic or aluminum axle sleeve (Fig. 12.15). To get the bearings really clean, wash them in the sink in soap and water with the sink drain plugged; the motion is the same as washing your hands, and results in both the bearings and your hands being clean for reassembly. Blot dry.

CHAPTER 12

231

OVERHAULING
PEDALS
CLOSED ON THE
OUTBOARD END

(b) On a pedal with a cartridge bearing (Figs. 12.16–21), if the bearing is dirty or worn out, it is best to replace it. These units usually have steel bearing covers that cannot be pried off without damaging them, nor can the covers be replaced. Plastic cartridge-bearing covers can be pried off (Fig. 9.29) and the bearing regreased.

(c) Needle bearings (not visible in the figures because they are pressed inside) on Dura-Ace SPD-R/PD-7700 and SPD-SL/PD-7800, Look, Time (Figs. 12.14, 12.16–17), and Diadora can be cleaned with solvent and a thin toothbrush slipped inside the pedal-body bore. The needle bearings usually just need grease, though, because they are well isolated from dirt.

(d) On a Sampson (Fig. 12.18), just wipe down the axle, the plastic "bearing," and the pedal-body bore. Do the same for an inexpensive bushing-only pedal.

4. Lightly grease everything and reassemble the parts as they were, a simple process with bushings, cartridge bearings, and needle bearings, but not so simple with loose bearings!

(a) With a loose-bearing pedal, you have some exacting work to place the bearings on their races and screw the cone on while they stay in place. With most Shimano guts (Fig. 12.15), grease the bushing inside the axle sleeve, and slide the axle into the sleeve. Slide the steel ring, on which the inner set of bearings rides, down onto the axle and against the end of the sleeve. Make sure that the concave bearing surface faces away from the sleeve. Coat the ring with grease, and stick half of the bear-

ings (usually 12) onto the outer surface of the ring. Slip the steel cylinder onto the axle so that one end rides on the bearings. Make sure that all of the bearings are seated properly and none are stuck inside of the sleeve.

(b) To prevent the bearings from piling up on each other and ending up inside the sleeve instead of on the races, grease the cone and start it on the axle a few threads. Place the remaining half of the bearings on the flanks of the cone. Being careful not to dislodge the bearings, screw the cone in until the bearings come close to the end of the cylinder without touching it. While holding the axle sleeve, push the axle inward until the bearings seat against the end of the cylinder. Make sure that the first set of bearings is still in place. Screw the cone in without dislodging the inboard bearings by avoiding turning the axle or the cylinder. Tighten the cone with your fingers only, and loosely screw on the locknut.

(c) Pre-1997 Look-style Campagnolo pedal guts are similar to Shimano, except that the bearing race is machined into the axle (rather than being a separate ring), and there are two cylinders, not one. Orient the cylinders so that their bearing races face outward, and otherwise follow the steps just described.

(d) With Dura-Ace SPD-R/PD-7700 (Fig. 12.14) or Dura-Ace SPD-SL/PD-7800 pedals you needed to push back on the bearing cup (on the end of the 20mm nut that holds the axle into the pedal body) to remove the ball bearings in the first place. Grease the cup and push back on it again to allow enough space

OVERHAULING
PEDALS
CLOSED ON THE
OUTBOARD END

○

OVERHAULING
PEDALS
WITH A DUST CAP
ON THE
OUTBOARD END

between the cup and the cylinder to set each of the 17 balls onto the edge of the cup with a small screwdriver.

5. Adjust the axle assembly. (For Time, Look, Diadora, and Sampson pedals, skip this step.)

   (a) Pedals with a small cartridge bearing and a single nut on the end of the axle, such as Campagnolo Record ProFit (Fig. 12.13), require that you tighten the nut against the cartridge bearing while holding the other end of the axle with the 15mm pedal wrench. Tighten it enough to remove play but not enough to bind the axle.

   (b) On pedals with two nuts on the end of the axle (Fig. 12.15), hold the cone or inner nut with a wrench and tighten the outer lock-nut down against it (Fig. 12.22). Check the adjustment for freedom of rotation, and be sure there is no lateral play. Readjust as necessary by tightening or loosening the cone or inner nut and retightening the locknut.

6. Replace the axle assembly in the pedal body. Smear grease on the inside of the pedal hole; this will ease insertion and act as a barrier to dirt and water. Screw the sleeve in with the same wrench you used to remove it (Figs. 12.12–13).

REMEMBER: *Pay attention to proper thread direction (see note after step 1)! Tighten carefully; it is easy to overtighten, which can crack a plastic nut.*

7. Put the pedals back on your bike, and go ride.

xii-5 OVERHAULING PEDALS WITH A DUST CAP ON THE OUTBOARD END

LEVEL 2

1. Remove the dust cover from the outboard end of the pedal with the appropriate tool. This could

be a pair of pliers, a flat or Phillips screwdriver, a coin, a hex wrench, or a splined tool made especially for your pedals; it's pretty easy to figure out which one is needed to remove the cap. Dig the dust cap out from SPD-style Ritcheys (Fig. 12.20) and Speedplay X/1, X/2, and Zero (Fig. 12.19) with a sharp pick or a sharpened nail (Ritchey pedals first require removal of a 2.5mm hex screw holding down the corner of the dust cap).

NOTE: *Speedplay bearings can be regreased without removing the axle and on newer models without removing the dust cap. On an older X/1 or X/2, remove the dust cap as just described in step 1, insert Speedplay's Speedy Luber grease-injection fitting, and squirt grease in with a fine-tip bicycle grease gun until it squirts out the other end. On newer X/1, X/2, X/3, X/5, or Zero, after removing the screw from the outboard end, pump grease in with a fine-tip grease gun while slowly turning the spindle until you see grease at the opposite end. Crank Brothers pedals other than the Quattro (Eggbeater, Candy, Mallet) have a similar feature, and the screw-in grease adapter (that screws in where the dust cap was and accepts the grease gun tip) comes with every pair of pedals.*

2. Hold the wrench flats on the inboard end of the axle with a pedal wrench, and unscrew the lock-nut with the appropriate-size socket wrench (or box wrench, if there is room for it).

   (a) Ritchey road bike pedals require a deep, thin-wall 8mm socket; Ritchey makes a double-ended thin 8mm socket for the purpose that you can turn with an 8mm Allen wrench in the other end.

   (b) On a Speedplay X/1 or X/2 pedal, remove the TORX T15 or T20 screw on the outboard end under the dust cap (Fig. 12.19) with the

12.23 Loose-bearing "quill" pedal exploded

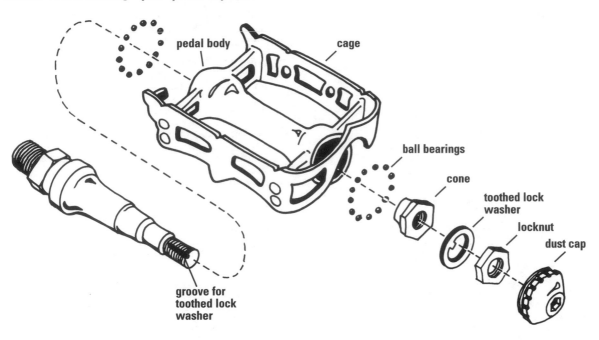

appropriate TORX driver. You may have to heat the bolt with a soldering iron to soften the threadlock compound.

(c) On a Speedplay X/3 or X/5, carefully pry the two halves of the pedal apart with a knife or razor blade after removing the 2.5mm pedal-body screws from either side. Lift the axle assembly out and remove the 9mm locknut from the end of the spindle. Pull the bearings and bushing (all located in an alloy sleeve) and O-ring off the spindle. Clean and grease the parts, and replace the cartridge bearing and bushing if necessary. Reassemble the parts onto the axle and tighten the locknut snugly against the bearing (35–40 in-lbs). When you reassemble the pedal, seal it from water by caulking the inside edges of the pedal-body halves and putting on a new O-ring.

3. Remove the axle. If it is a loose-bearing pedal (Fig. 12.23), hold the pedal over a rag to catch the bearings, then unscrew the cone. Keep the bearings from the two ends separate in case they differ in size or in number. Count them so that you can put the right numbers back in when you reassemble the pedal. The guts should look like Figure 12.23. If the pedal does not have loose bearings (Figs. 12.19–20), the procedure as follows:

(a) With a Ritchey (Fig. 12.20) pedal, once you have removed the 8mm locknut, you can pull the axle out. The pedal has two pressed-in needle bearings inside. Scrub them with solvent and a rag or thin brush, if they are dirty. Removal of bad needle bearings requires a special tool to pull them out.

(b) With a Speedplay X/1, X/2, or Zero pedal (Fig. 12.19), pull the axle out and reinstall the TORX screw in the end of the axle.

PEDALS

12.24 **Dropping in bearings**

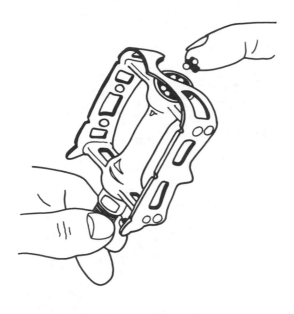

Remove the little snapring from the outboard end of the pedal bore with inward-squeezing snapring pliers. Push the axle back in and carefully push the cartridge bearings out. The cartridge bearings are easily replaceable, but if the needle bearings are in bad shape, you'll have to buy a new pedal body from Speedplay with the needle bearings already pressed in. You can clean them as described for Ritchey pedals.

(c) With Ritchey or Speedplay pedals, dry and grease the needle bearings and put the pedals back together by reversing the process of disassembly. Do not overtighten the Ritchey locknut; remove bearing play but don't bind the axle. Put threadlock compound on the Speedplay TORX end bolt and tighten it snugly (35–40 in-lbs). Then skip to step 11.

4. With a rag, clean the bearings, cones, and bearing races. Clean the inside of the pedal body by pushing the rag through with a screwdriver. If there is a dust cover on the inboard end of the pedal body, you can clean it in place or pop it out with a screwdriver and clean it separately.

5. If you want to get the bearings really clean, wash them in a plugged sink with soap and water. The motion is the same as washing your hands, and it results in both the bearings and your hands being clean for a sterile reassembly. Blot dry.

6. If you removed it, press the inboard dust cover back into the pedal body. Smear a thin layer of grease in the inboard bearing cup and replace the bearings. Once all of the bearings are in place, there will be a gap equal to about half the diameter of one bearing.

7. Drop the axle in and turn the pedal over so that the outboard end is up. Smear grease in that end and replace the bearings (Fig. 12.24).

8. Screw the cone in until it almost contacts the bearings, then push the axle straight in to bring the cone and bearings together; this prevents the bearings from piling up and getting spit out as the cone turns down against them. Without turning the axle (which would cause the inboard bearings to knock the inboard bearings about), screw the cone in until it is finger-tight.

9. Slide on the washer and screw on the locknut. While holding the cone with a cone wrench, tighten the lock nut (similar to Fig. 12.22, but you will be holding the cone with a 13mm or similar cone wrench).

10. Check that the pedal spins smoothly without play. Readjust as necessary by tightening or loosening the cone and retightening the locknut.

11. Replace the dust cap.

12. Install the pedals and go for a ride.

TROUBLESHOOTING PEDAL PROBLEMS

xii-6 CREAKING NOISE WHILE PEDALING

1. The shoe cleats need grease on the tip, or they are loose and need to be tightened, or they are worn and need to be replaced (see §xii-2).

2. Pedal bearings and pedal-body threads need cleaning and lubrication (see Overhauling Pedals in this chapter and §xii-4 and §xii-5).

3. The noise is originating from somewhere other than the pedals (see Troubleshooting Crank and Bottom-Bracket Noise in Chap. 11 or look in Appendix A).

xii-7 RELEASE OR ENTRY WITH CLIP-IN PEDALS IS TOO EASY OR TOO HARD

1. Release tension needs to be adjusted. See Adjusting Release Tension of Clip-In Pedals, §xii-3.

2. Pedal-release mechanism needs to be cleaned and lubricated. Clean off mud and dirt, and drip chain lubricant on the springs and a dry lubricant (like White Lightning) on the cleat-contact surfaces of the clips (Fig. 12.25).

3. The cleats themselves need to be cleaned and lubricated. Clean off dirt and mud, oil the springs, and put a dry chain lubricant or dry grease like pure Teflon on the contact ends of the cleats.

4. The cleats are worn out. Replace them (§xii-2).

5. The clips on the pedal are bent or the guide plates on top of the pedal are worn, bent, broken, or missing. Straighten bent clips if you can, or replace them. If you can't repair or replace the clips, you may have to replace the entire pedal. On Speed-

12.25 Lubricate the springs and cleat contact areas

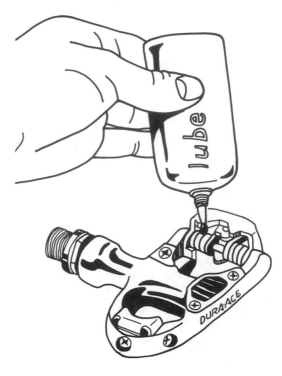

plays, the top and bottom metal plates may need replacing.

6. If it is hard to clip into your pedals, check the metal cleat guide plate at the center of an SPD-type pedal. It is held on with Phillips screws, and they may be loose or have fallen out, or the guide plate can be bent or broken. Tighten loose mounting screws and replace missing or damaged guide plates.

7. If you have small feet, and it is hard to get in and out of a pedal that has a large cleat (Look and copies, Campagnolo) or a large adapter plate, the curvature of your shoe sole may be so extreme that the center of the cleat hits the center of the pedal before the ends have clipped in. The fix may be as simple as removing the little rubber plug from under your Look cleat. You may also need

CREAKING NOISE

WHILE PEDALING

∘

RELEASE OR

ENTRY WITH

CLIP-IN PEDALS IS

TOO EASY OR

TOO HARD

to shim the front and rear of the cleat away from the shoe, or file down the center of the cleat.

xii-8 YOU EXPERIENCE KNEE AND JOINT PAIN WHILE PEDALING

1. Cleat rotational misalignment often causes pain on the sides of the knees (see §xii-2). Loosen and realign your cleats the way your feet want to be oriented when pedaling.

2. You need more rotational float. Consider a pedal that offers more float (or replace fixed cleats with floating ones, or adjust your Look pedals for more float).

3. If your foot naturally needs to tip inward for proper pedaling mechanics, yet your shoe and cleat tip your feet farther out (this correction is built into some shoes), then there is likely to be an increase in the tension on the iliotibial (I-T) band, the tendon connecting the hip and calf. This will eventually cause pain on the outside of the knee. You need to see a specialist because you may need custom orthotics for your shoes to correct the problem.

4. Fatigue and improper seat height can also contribute to joint pain. Pain in the front of the knee right behind the kneecap can indicate that your saddle is too low. Pain in the back of the leg behind the knee suggests that your saddle is too high.

CAUTION: *If any of these problems results in chronic pain, consult a medical specialist.*

SADDLES AND SEATPOSTS

I do most of my work sitting down.
That's where I shine.
—Robert Benchley

After spending a few hours on the bike, you will be highly aware of one component: the saddle. It is the part of your bike with which you are most . . . ah . . . intimately connected. Nothing can ruin a good ride faster than a poorly positioned or uncomfortable saddle.

Position and comfort are also affected by seatpost choice. Triathlon seatposts come in many more varieties than standard road cycling posts to offer a wider range of positioning choices than is needed in road racing. This chapter is mainly concerned with fitting and troubleshooting; to fine-tune your position, see a bike dealer who specializes in triathlon equipment for the most up-to-date saddle and seatpost options.

xiii-1 SADDLES

Bike saddles generally consist of a nylon shell, some foam padding, a cover, and a pair of rails (Fig. 13.1), but variations include extra thick or extra firm padding or high-tech gel inserts; depressions, holes, or splits in the shell to reduce pressure on sensitive areas; lightweight titanium or carbon-fiber rails and carbon or magnesium shells; synthetic leather, Kevlar, or full-grain leather covers. See Chapter 2, §ii–6 about saddle choice.

xiii-2 SADDLE POSITION

Even if you find the perfect saddle, it can feel like a medieval torture device if it isn't properly positioned. Saddle placement is the most important part of finding a comfortable riding position. Saddle position affects your control and efficiency as well. The position of your hands and feet relative to the saddle also influences comfort and saddle choice; with the saddle and bars in the right place, you become a much better rider.

Make sure your seatpost allows you to perform the saddle adjustments shown in Figure 13.2 sufficiently

13.1 Modern Lighweight saddle

PRO TIP

CARBON SEATPOSTS

Carbon-fiber seatposts are susceptible to breakage if the pinch-bolt assembly digs in and cuts some fibers or makes a notch in the post. Some carbon seatposts, like Campagnolo, come with a special binder clamp meant to distribute the clamping force. Unless you have a frame with a built-in binder, make sure you use the clamp if the post comes with one. Without such an angled-slot clamp, reverse the binder clamp, if possible, so that its slot is not lined up with the seat tube slot. Contrary to some urban lore, grease will not damage carbon seatposts but will be counterproductive if you have a problem with the post slipping down. If seatpost slippage plagues you, try using carbon assembly paste on it. Sold variously under the Tacx, Syntace, FSA, and Ritchey Liquid Torque brands, the orange-colored paste contains small spheres that allow the part to be slid, rotated, and adjusted without scratching. Yet it will hold firmly due to pressure of the spheres on the carbon, even when clamped at a lower clamp-tightening torque than you were using to stave off the slippage.

---

to achieve your desired position. See Chapter 3 for a detailed explanation of setting saddle and handlebar position.

xiii-3 SEATPOST MAINTENANCE

A standard seatpost requires little maintenance other than greasing the seat-clamp bolts on installation and periodically removing the post from the frame. Every few months, remove the post, wipe it down, regrease it, dry out and grease the inside of the frame's seat tube, and then reinstall the seatpost (see sidebar about carbon seatposts). This procedure keeps it clean and movable if you want to adjust it. It also should prevent the seatpost from getting stuck in the frame (a nasty and potentially expensive problem), and it will prevent the seat tube on a steel or aluminum frame from corroding from the inside. The procedures for installing a new seatpost and for removing a stuck seatpost are outlined later in this chapter.

Regularly check the seatpost for cracks or bends so that you can replace it before it breaks with you on it.

xiii-INSTALLING A SADDLE

Saddle clamps on seatposts vary widely. Most posts have either one bolt (Figs. 13.3 and 13.6) or two (Figs. 13.4–5) for clamping the saddle.

Single-bolt posts can have the bolt vertical (Fig. 13.3) or horizontal (Fig. 13.6).

Two-bolt posts usually rely on one of two systems. In one, the two bolts work together by pulling the saddle into the clamp (Fig. 13.5). On others, a smaller second bolt holds the tilt angle (Fig. 13.4), while the larger main bolt supplies the clamping force.

Two-position seatposts (Fig. 13.6) are becoming popular on aero bikes. The broad side surface of the

INSTALLING A
SADDLE

°

SADDLE
INSTALLATION
ON SEATPOST
WITH A
SINGLE VERTICAL
BOLT

13.2 Saddle adjustments

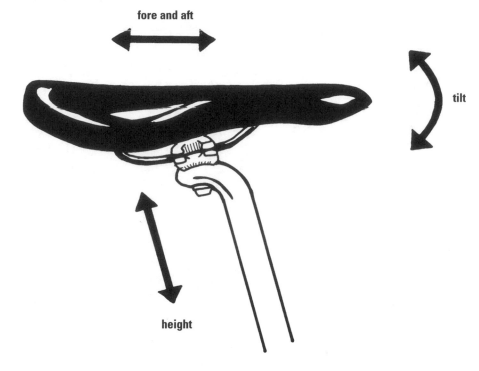

aero post makes it possible to have two positions for the saddle clamp, simulating a shallower and a steeper seat angle.

It's not rocket science to figure out how to remove, install, and adjust the saddle, no matter what kind of post you have, but here are some guidelines that could make a difference. Remember to grease all bolt threads!

xiii-5 SADDLE INSTALLATION ON SEATPOST WITH A SINGLE VERTICAL BOLT

Posts with a single vertical bolt (Fig. 13.3) usually have a two-piece clamp that fastens onto the saddle rails. On most models, moving the clamp and saddle along a curved platform controls saddle tilt. Before you tighten the clamp bolt, make sure there is not a second, much smaller bolt (or "setscrew") that

adjusts seat tilt. If one is present, skip to the next section (§xiii-6).

1. Loosen the bolt until there are only a couple of threads holding on to the upper clamp.

2. Turn the top half of the clamp 90 degrees and slide in the saddle rails. Do it from the back where the space between the rails is wider. You might need to remove the top clamp piece completely from the bolt if it is too large to fit between the rails. If you do disassemble the clamp, pay attention to the orientation of the parts so that you can put it back together the same way.

3. Set the seat rails into the grooves in the lower part of the clamp, and set the top clamp piece on top of the rails (Fig. 13.7). Slide the saddle to the desired fore-and-aft position.

4. Tighten the bolt and check the seat tilt. Readjust if necessary.

SADDLE
INSTALLATION ON
SEATPOST WITH
LARGE CLAMP
BOLT AND SMALL
SETSCREW

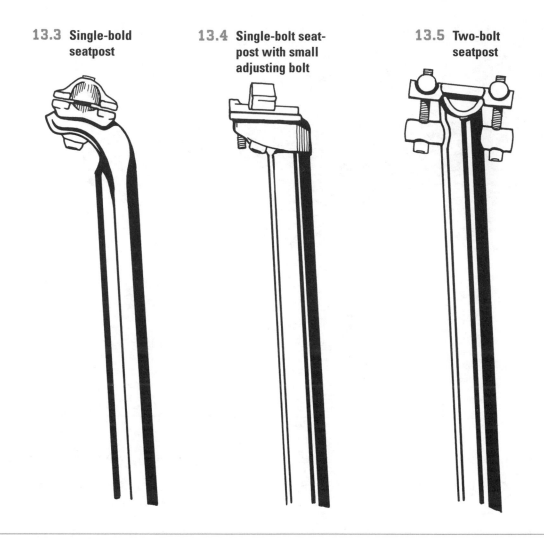

13.3 Single-bold seatpost

13.4 Single-bolt seatpost with small adjusting bolt

13.5 Two-bolt seatpost

xiii-6 SADDLE INSTALLATION ON SEATPOST WITH LARGE CLAMP BOLT AND SMALL SETSCREW

This post type is illustrated in Figure 13.4.

1. Loosen the large bolt until the top part of the clamp can be moved out of the way or removed so that you can slide the saddle rails into place.

2. Set the saddle rails between the top and bottom sets of grooves in the seat clamp. Slide the saddle to the desired fore-and-aft position. Tighten the large bolt.

3. To change saddle tilt, loosen the large clamp bolt, adjust the saddle angle as needed by turning the setscrew, and retighten the clamp bolt. Repeat until the desired adjustment is reached.

CAUTION: *Do not use the setscrew to make the clamp tight! Do not adjust the setscrew unless the clamp bolt is loose!*

NOTE: *On this seatpost type, the setscrew may be vertical or horizontal. On posts with a vertical setscrew (Fig. 13.4), the screw is usually adjacent to the clamp bolt. A horizontal setscrew can be placed at the top front of the seatpost, pushing back on the clamp. With such a setscrew, push down on the back of the saddle with the clamp bolt loose to make sure the clamp and setscrew are in contact. Another type of post has a horizontal tilt-adjusting bolt that passes crosswise through a slot in the seatpost clamp. On this type, the saddle can be fully tightened down, yet the tilt-adjust screw can be loosened and the saddle tipped differently and retightened without adjusting the clamp bolt.*

xiii-7 INSTALLING SADDLE ON SEATPOST WITH TWO EQUAL-SIZE CLAMP BOLTS

This post type is illustrated in Figure 13.5.

1. Loosen or remove one or both of the bolts to open the clamp enough to slide the saddle rails into the grooves of the clamp.

2. Slide the saddle to the desired fore-and-aft position. Tighten down one or both of the clamp bolts completely.

3. Loosen one clamp bolt and tighten the other to change the tilt of the saddle (Fig. 13.8). Repeat as necessary.

4. Complete by tightening both bolts.

xiii-8 INSTALLING SADDLE ON SEATPOST WITH A HORIZONTAL CLAMP BOLT

1. Loosen the bolt shown in Figure 13.6 enough that the clamp pieces will slide laterally outward far enough to allow the saddle rails to drop in. Clip the outer clamp pieces up over the rails.

2. Set the fore–aft position and tilt of the saddle where you want it, and tighten the bolt to draw in the clamp pieces and secure the saddle.

N O T E : *The Cervélo post design (Fig. 13.6) requires that you tighten the draw bolt really tightly and recheck its tightness after the first few rides until you're certain that it's properly seated. One of the rail-support pieces prevents the rotation of the saddle all by itself. It has a*

13.6 **Two-position aero seatpost**

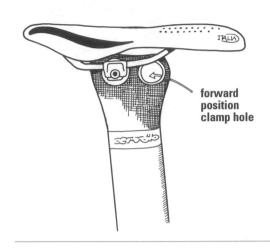

forward position clamp hole

tapered, knurled protrusion that fits into one of the big cross holes in the seatpost. When you tighten the draw bolt, it jams the taper into the hole; but if the bolt is not tight enough, the part can rotate, especially if the saddle is pushed far forward and the rider sits way out on the nose. While having your saddle flip down as you ride is trouble enough, if you ride with it loose and keep pulling the saddle nose back up as it rotates down, you will be using the knurls on the tapered piece like a big round file. They will make the hole bigger, and, since the parts will no longer fit together as designed, you will from then on be plagued with problems holding the saddle in place.

xiii-9 SWITCHING POSITIONS ON TWO-POSITION SEATPOSTS

There are a number of different designs for two-position seatposts, but all of them have two different holes or cradles to hold the saddle-clamping hardware.

1. Unscrew the bolt or bolts and remove the saddle clamp.

2. Push out the plug filling the other hole or cradle, if installed, and insert the saddle clamp and bolt or bolts into the other hole (Fig. 13.6).

SADDLES AND SEATPOSTS

SWITCHING
POSITIONS ON
TWO-POSITION
SEATPOSTS

·

SEATPOST
INSTALLATION
INTO THE FRAME

13.7 **Saddle installation on single-bolt seatpost**

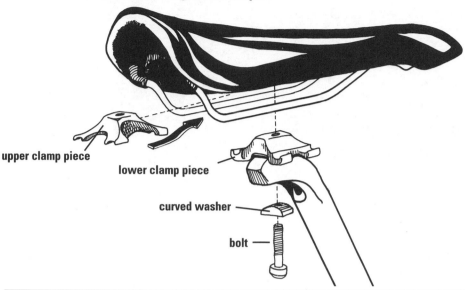

upper clamp piece

lower clamp piece

curved washer

bolt

13.8 **Saddle installation on two-bolt seatpost**

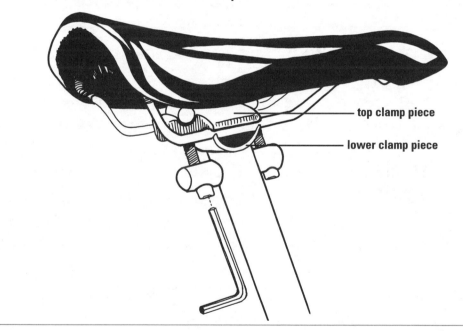

top clamp piece

lower clamp piece

NOTE: *The long head of this post makes it impossible to mount behind-the-seat bottle cages and other carrying accessories if you push the saddle forward when it is in the forward-position clamp cradle. Newer versions have small accessory holes, and you can buy adapters that allow you to mount behind-the-seat bottle carriers directly into those holes.*

xiii-10 SEATPOST INSTALLATION INTO THE FRAME

1. Check for irregularities, burrs, and other problems inside the seat tube visually and with your finger; if there are some, you may need to sand or otherwise clean up inside the seat tube. It may be necessary for a bike shop to ream the seat tube if a post of the correct size will not fit.

13.9 Seatpost installation into frame

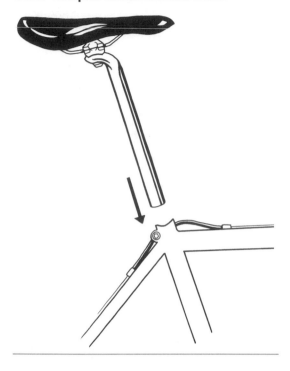

let it dry out. The frequency depends on your riding conditions. With a steel frame, spray oil (or better yet, Frame Saver, which is available in bike shops) into the seat tube to arrest the rusting process. Regrease the post (or apply more assembly paste) on the inside of the seat tube and then reinstall the post.

xiii-11 REMOVING A STUCK SEATPOST

LEVEL 3

You are having this difficulty because you did not follow the important note in §xiii-10. This is a level 3 job; if you make a mistake, you run the risk of destroying the frame. If you're not 100 percent confident in your abilities, go to someone who is—or at least to someone who will take responsibility if he or she screws it up.

1. Remove the seat-lug binder bolt. Sounds easy enough.

2. Squirt penetrating oil around the seatpost and let it sit overnight. To get the most penetration, remove the bottom bracket (Chap. 11), turn the bike upside down, squirt the penetrating oil in from the bottom of the seat tube, and let it sit overnight.

3. The next day, stand over the bike and twist the saddle.

4. If step 3 does not free the seatpost, warm up the seat-lug area with a hair dryer to expand it. Discharge the entire cartridge of a CO_2 inflator at the joint of the seatpost and the seat collar to freeze it and shrink it. (Alternatively, ice the exposed seatpost with a plastic bag filled with crushed ice.) Now try twisting as in step 3.

5. If step 4 does not free the seatpost, you will need to move into the difficult and risky part of this procedure.

2. Unless you have a carbon-fiber seatpost on which you're using assembly paste for carbon parts (see Pro Tip), grease the seatpost and the inside of the seat tube. Grease the seatpost binder bolt. If you are using a sleeve or shim to adapt an undersize seatpost to fit the frame, grease it inside and out, and insert it.

3. Insert the seatpost (Fig. 13.9) and tighten the binder bolt. Some binder bolts are tightened with a wrench (usually a 5mm hex key), and some require two wrenches (usually two 5mm hex keys or two open-end wrenches).

4. After attaching the saddle, adjust the seat height to your desired position. It is a good idea to mark this height on the post with an indelible marker or a piece of tape. This way, when you remove it, you can just slide it right back into the proper place.

IMPORTANT: *Periodically remove the seatpost, invert the bike to drain water out of the seat tube, and*

REMOVING A
STUCK SEATPOST

◦

TROUBLESHOOT-
ING PROBLEMS IN
THE SEAT AND
SEATPOST

(a)　You will now sacrifice the seatpost. Remove the saddle and all of the clamps from the top of the seatpost. With the bike upside down, clamp the top of the seatpost into a large bench vise that is bolted to a very secure workbench.

(b)　Congratulations, you have just ruined your seatpost. Don't ever ride it gain.

(c)　Perform the heat/ice or CO_2 trick from step 4. Grab the frame at both ends and carefully apply a twisting pressure. Be aware that you can easily apply enough force to bend or crack the frame, so be careful. If the seatpost finally releases, it often makes such a large "pop" that you will think that you have broken many things!

6.　If that did not work, cut off the seatpost a few inches above the seat lug and clamp the top of it in a vise. Warm up the seat-lug area with a hair dryer to expand it. Discharge the entire cartridge of a CO_2 inflator down inside the seatpost to freeze and shrink it. Now try twisting as in step 4.

7.　If neither step 5 nor 6 works, you need to go to a machine shop and get the post reamed out of the seat tube. But this only works if you have a cylindrical seat tube; a machinist cannot help with a seatpost that is not cylindrical.

If you still insist on getting it out yourself, you need to sit down and think about it for a while. Will the guy at the machine shop really charge you so much money that it is worth the risk of completely destroying your frame?

Do you still insist on doing this yourself? Okay, but don't say I didn't warn you.

With a hacksaw, cut off the post a little more than an inch above the frame. Remove the blade from the saw and wrap a piece of tape around one end. Hold the taped end and insert the other end into the center of the post. Carefully—very carefully—make two outward cuts about 60 degrees apart. Your goal is to remove a pie-shaped wedge from the hunk of seatpost stuck in your frame. Be careful; this is where many people cut too far and go right through the seatpost into the frame. Of course, you wouldn't do that, would you?

Once you've made the cut, pry or pull this piece out with a large screwdriver or a pair of pliers. Be careful here too. Many home mechanics have damaged their frames by prying too hard.

Once the wedge is out, work the remaining piece out by curling in the edges with the pliers to free more and more of it from the seatpost walls. It should eventually work its way out.

With the post out of the frame, clean the inside of the seat tube thoroughly. A flex hone, sold in auto parts stores (or rented at rental stores) for reconditioning brake cylinders, is an excellent tool for the purpose. Turn the frame upside down, put the hone in an electric drill, and be sure to use plenty of honing fluid or cutting oil as you work. If you do not know how to use a hone, it may be best to take the frame to a bike shop to have the job done or try sandpaper wrapped around your fingers.

Inasmuch as removing a stuck post is so miserable that no one wants to do it twice, I do not need to remind you to grease the new post thoroughly before inserting it in the frame; then check it regularly as outlined above.

xiii-12 TROUBLESHOOTING PROBLEMS IN THE SEAT AND SEATPOST

a. Loose saddle

Check the bolts. They are probably loose. Tighten the bolts and set the desired saddle tilt, after setting fore-

and-aft saddle position (§xiii-2). Check for any damage to the clamping mechanism and replace the post if necessary. If you need help, look up the instructions that apply to your seatpost.

b. Stuck seatpost

This can be a serious problem. Follow the instructions in §xiii-11 carefully when attempting to remove it, or you might damage your frame.

c. Saddle squeaks with each pedal stroke

The problem can come from smooth leather or plastic moving against metal parts or from grit in the rail attachments.

1. On saddles that extend low on the sides, contact between the leather overlapping the saddle shell with the seatpost clamp or rails is a likely culprit. Greasing the contact area will eliminate the noise. Also, roughing up the leather at the contact point will quiet it down, since it is smooth leather sliding on metal that squeaks. Another approach, borrowed from the equestrian set, is to sprinkle the squeaky leather with talcum powder.

2. Also try squirting chain lube into the points where the rails are inserted into the plastic shell of the saddle, in case some grit working at the rails is making the noise.

d. Creaking noises from the seatpost

A seatpost can creak from movement of the clamp holding the saddle. Another possible source is movement of the shaft back and forth against the sides of the seat tube while you ride. Pull the post from the frame and regrease the post and seat tube.

1. Some frames use a collar to adapt the seat tube to a certain seatpost diameter. Remember that the internal diameter of the seat tube is larger below the collar. I have seen bikes that creaked because the bottom of the seatpost rubbed against

the sides of the seat tube below the extension of the collar. You can solve that problem by shortening the seatpost a bit with a hacksaw. If you do saw off the post, make sure that you still have at least 3 inches of seatpost inserted in the frame for security.

2. Similarly, movement between the frame, sizing shims, and the post can cause creaking. Greasing all of these parts well should eliminate the noise.

3. If the creaking originates from the post head where the saddle is clamped, check the clamp bolts. Lubricate the bolt threads, and you will be able to tighten them a bit more.

4. Even when the clamp bolts are sufficiently tight, the saddle rails can squeak in the clamp (titanium rails are especially prone to this). Remove the saddle, apply a thin film of grease to the clamp valleys where they hold the rails, and reassemble.

5. Shock-absorbing seatposts can squeak as they move up and down. Try greasing the sides of the inner shaft. Grease the elastomers inside, too.

e. Seatpost slips down

Tighten the seat-lug binder bolt. If the seat lug is pinched closed and the post still slips down, you may be using a seatpost with an incorrect diameter, or the seat tube may be oversized or has stretched. Double-check the seat tube diameter with calipers or ask your local shop to do so.

Try putting a larger seatpost in the frame, and replace yours if you find one that fits better. If the next size up is too big, you may need to shim the existing post. Cut a 1-inch by 3-inch piece of aluminum from a soda can (you can use an old pair of scissors for this). Pull the seatpost out, grease it and the soda can shim, and insert both back into the frame. Bend the top lip of the shim over to prevent it from disappearing inside the frame. You may need to experiment with various shim dimensions until you find a piece that will go in with the seatpost and will also prevent slippage. Fortunately they're cheap.

With a carbon-fiber seatpost, put special assembly paste for carbon parts on it (see Pro Tip). Second, if you must tighten the clamp more, make sure it is not forcing the corners of the seat tube slot into the seatpost, creating damage and the possibility of breakage. Use an offset-clamp binder or turn the binder around so its slot does not line up with the seat tube's slot (see Pro Tip).

On a titanium frame with an integral seat binder (one that is welded to the seat tube, as opposed to an external clamp), the seat tube will stretch if the binder is chronically overtightened. If the post is slipping because the binder slot has closed up, contact the frame manufacturer for assistance. You may be able to rescue the situation by filing the slot and binder wide enough to keep it from pinching closed (a tedious job, but titanium will yield to a normal metal file). Plug the seat tube with a greasy rag to keep metal filings from falling into the bottom bracket and suspend the frame upside down to encourage the filings to go elsewhere.

By the way, don't try this until you get the go-ahead from the frame manufacturer; attacking the frame in this manner will void the warranty in the absence of explicit authorization. If filing isn't recommended, you will probably have to return the frame to the manufacturer for more comprehensive repair.

CHAPTER 14

STEMS, HANDLEBARS, AND HEADSETS

TOOLS

**4mm, 5mm, and
6mm hex keys**

**32mm headset
wrenches (two)**

hammer

screwdriver

hacksaw

flat file

round file

glue stick

electrical tape

grease

citrus solvent

Optional

**star-nut installation
tool**

**threadless saw
guide**

*I may not have gone where I intended to go,
but I think I have ended up where I intended to be.*
—Douglas Adams

On a bike, you maintain or change your direction by applying force to the handlebar. If everything works properly, variations in that pressure will result in the front wheel's changing direction. Pretty basic, right? Right, but it is the series of parts between the handlebar and the wheel that makes that simple process possible. The parts of the steering system are illustrated in Figure 14.1. In this chapter, we'll cover most of that system by going over stems, handlebars, and headsets.

STEMS

The stem connects to the fork's steering tube and clamps around the handlebar, which these days has one of two standard diameters: 26.0mm or 31.8mm (Cinelli handlebars used to be 26.4mm, and many low-end handlebars are 25.4mm clamp diameter, but you're unlikely to find either of these on a triathlon bike). Stems come in one of two basic types: for (1) threadless (Figs. 14.1–4) or (2) threaded (Figs. 14.5–7) fork steering tubes.

Most high-end triathlon and road bikes now have 1⅛-inch-diameter unthreaded forks, although those took over from 1-inch threadless forks, which were preceded by a century of road bikes with 1-inch threaded forks.

Stems for unthreaded steering tubes (Fig. 14.2) have a clamping collar around the steering tube, and the top headset cup merely slides on and off when the clamping collar is loosened. The stem plays a dual role; it clamps around the steering tube to connect the handlebar to the fork, and it also keeps the headset in proper adjustment by preventing the top headset cup from sliding up the steering tube (Figs. 14.3–4). If you have a 1-inch diameter threadless steering tube (the old standard) and a stem for a 1⅛-inch threadless steering tube (the current standard), you can get a slotted aluminum reduction bushing (normally supplied with a new stem) to allow the stem to be used with the 1-inch steering tube.

Stems for threaded steering tubes (Figs. 14.5–7) have a "quill" that extends down into the steering tube of the

14.1 **Parts of the steering system**

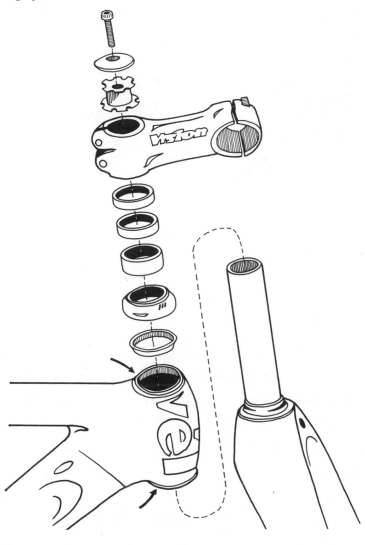

14.2 **Threadless stem**

14.3 **Threadless headset and stem cutaway**

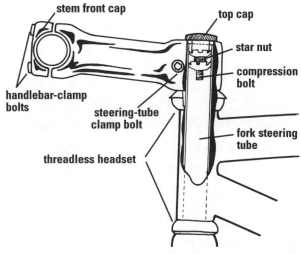

stem front cap

top cap

star nut

compression bolt

handlebar-clamp bolts

steering-tube clamp bolt

fork steering tube

threadless headset

fork and a shaft, or extension, that connects to the handlebar. The stem binds to the inside of the steering tube by means of a conical plug (Fig. 14.5) or angularly truncated cylindrical wedge (Fig. 14.6) pulled up by a long stem expander bolt that runs through the quill (Fig. 14.7).

Traditionally the shaft of a road bike stem that attaches to the handlebar extends out from the fork steering tube at a 73 degree angle so that, when installed on the bike, the extension is horizontal (Fig. 14.7). Stems with angles of 90 degrees and greater, resulting in an upward angle on the assembled bicycle (Figs. 14.3–4), are now commonplace on triathlon and road bikes.

xiv-1 REMOVE CLAMP-TYPE STEM FROM THREADLESS STEERING TUBE

1. Loosen the horizontal clamp bolt(s) (Fig. 14.4) securing the stem around the steering tube.

2. With a 5mm (usually) hex key, unscrew and remove the adjusting bolt (or "compression bolt" because it compresses the headset into the proper

14.4 **Threadless-headset cup held in place by stem**

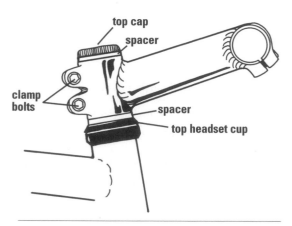

14.5 **Forged aluminum quill road stem with expander plug**

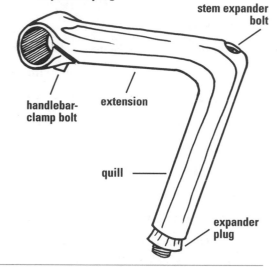

14.6 **Welded quill-type stem with expander wedge**

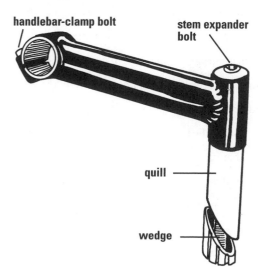

14.7 **Cutaway of threaded headset system, showing expander-plug binding stem inside steering tube**

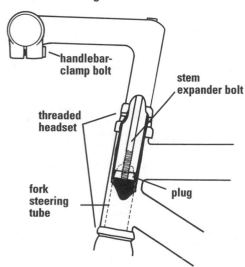

REMOVE
CLAMP-TYPE STEM
FROM
THREADLESS
STEERING TUBE

◦

INSTALL AND
ADJUST HEIGHT
OF STEM ON
THREADLESS
STEERING TUBE

bearing adjustment) in the headset top cap (Fig. 14.8). The fork can now fall out, so hold the fork as you unscrew the bolt.

N O T E : *Some threadless headsets do not use a top cap. For instance, some DiaTech threadless headsets have a collar beveled internally on the top and bottom to adjust headset compression. Without a top cap, as soon as you loosen the stem, the fork can slip out.*

3. With the bike standing on the floor, or while holding the fork to keep it from falling out, pull the cap and the stem off the steering tube. Leave the bike standing until you replace the stem, or slide the fork out of the frame, keeping track of all headset parts.

4. If the stem is stuck to the steering tube and will not budge, thread the clamp bolts in from the other side. Spread the stem clamp by inserting a coin into the slot between each bolt end and the opposing unthreaded half of the binder lug (Fig. 14.9). Tighten each bolt against each coin so that it spreads the clamp slot open wider. The stem should come right off the steering tube now.

N O T E : *If the stem is the type that comes with a single bolt in the side of the stem shaft ahead of the steering tube (Fig. 14.3), loosen the bolt a few turns and tap it in with a hammer to free the wedge. It might require some penetrating oil and perhaps some heat to expand it to free this type of stem from around the steering tube.*

xiv-2 INSTALL AND ADJUST HEIGHT OF STEM ON THREADLESS STEERING TUBE

Installing and adjusting the height of a stem on a threadless fork is much more complicated than installing and adjusting the height of a

14.8 Loosening and tightening compression bolt on threadless headset

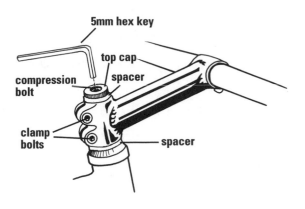

14.9 Spreading the stem clamp to free a stuck stem

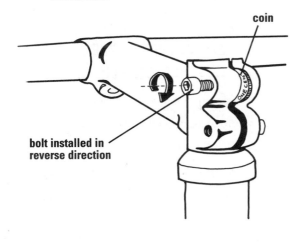

standard stem in a threaded fork. That's why this step is listed with a level 2 designation. Because the stem is integral to operation of the headset (Fig. 14.4), any change to the stem position alters the headset adjustment.

1. Stand the bike on its wheels, so that the fork does not fall out. Grease the top end of the steering tube if it is steel or aluminum, and leave it dry if it is carbon fiber. Loosen the stem-clamp bolts and grease their threads. Slide the stem onto the steering tube.

14.10 **Measuring distance between stem clamp and top of steering tube**

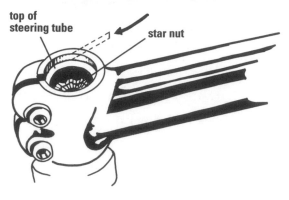

top of steering tube

star nut

2. Set the stem height to the desired level. If you want to place the stem in a position higher than directly on top of the headset, you must put some spacers between the bottom of the stem clamp and the top piece of the headset (Fig. 14.4). No matter what, there must be contact (either directly or through spacers) between the headset and the stem. Otherwise, the headset will be loose.

3. Check the steering-tube length: In order to adjust the threadless headset, the top of the stem clamp (or spacers placed above it) should overlap the top of the steering tube by 3–6mm (⅛–¼ inch) (Fig. 14.10). If it does, skip ahead to step 4.

N O T E : *Most new stems have a 1⅛-inch clamp size, and they come with a simple split shim (a short piece of tubing with a slot down one side) that you can slide over a 1-inch steering tube to make the stem fit on a fork of that size. With this type of stem and shim on a 1-inch steering tube, you can usually use spacers under the stem sized for a 1-inch steering tube, as long as they are wide enough to contact the entire bottom edge of the stem. However, above the stem, you may need to use a spacer and a headset top cap meant for a 1⅛-inch steering tube, in order to push the stem down properly and to aesthetically match the top of the stem.*

SPACERS WITH CARBON STEERING TUBES

If your fork has a carbon steering tube, always place one spacer above the stem (Fig. 14.4). That way, the entire stem clamp is clamped onto the steerer and there is no chance for the upper part of the clamp to pinch the end of the steerer. This is a good idea to do with a steel or aluminum steering tube as well.

If you want to raise your handlebar up high, be careful about using too many spacers below the stem; consult the owner's manual for your fork for recommendations for maximum spacer stack height. It's preferable to use an up-angled stem, rather than a down-angled one with a lot of spacers below it. And of course, make sure the expander plug inside the steering tube (which prevents the stem clamp from crushing the carbon steering tube) is supporting the area under the stem clamp.

4. If the top spacer or the top of the stem clamp overlaps the top of the steering tube by more than 6mm (¼ inch), the steering tube is too short to set the stem height where you have it. If you have spacers below the stem, remove some until the top edge of the stem clamp overlaps the top of the steering tube by 3–6mm. If you cannot or do not wish to lower the stem any farther, you will need a fork with a longer steering tube or a stem with a shorter clamp or a stem that is angled upward more to achieve the desired handlebar height. Stems for threadless steering tubes with clamps of differing lengths are available, as are

stems of varying angles. Replacing the stem is a lot cheaper and easier than replacing the fork.

5. If the steering tube is too long, there are several steps you can take:

(a) If the top of the steering tube is less than 3mm (⅛ inch) below the top spacer or the top edge of the stem clamp (or if the steering tube sticks up above the top of the stem clamp), you have a choice. If you want the option to raise the stem for a higher handlebar position, stack some headset spacers on top of the stem clamp until the spacers overlap the top edge of the steering tube by at least 3mm.

(b) If, on the other hand, you are sure you will never want the stem any higher, you can cut off the excess tube. First, mark the steering tube along the top edge of the spacer above the stem clamp (or the stem clamp itself if you are not heeding my advice to always have at least a single thin spacer above the stem). Remove the fork from the bike. Make another mark on the steering tube 3mm below the first mark. Place the steering tube in a padded vise or bike-stand clamp. By using the lower mark as a guide, cut the excess steering tube off with a hacksaw.

NOTE: *If you are cutting a carbon-fiber steering tube, cut most of the way through the tube from one side, and then turn the fork over and finish by cutting from the other side until the two cuts meet. This will prevent the carbon from splintering, which would greatly weaken the structure.*

(c) In steel and aluminum steering tubes that have already been installed in a bike, there is a star nut (Figs. 14.3 and 14.18) that is inserted inside the steering tube (Fig. 14.10). You screw the compression bolt through the top cap to adjust the headset bearings (but not to retain the headset; the stem-clamp bolts do that). If the star nut is already inside the steering tube and it looks like the saw is going to hit it, you must move the star nut down before cutting. See step 6 for instructions on how to push the star nut in deeper. (Carbon-fiber fork steering tubes have either a glue-in support insert with a star nut inside, or an expandable steering-tube support insert with an integrated anchor for the top-cap bolt [Fig. 14.24]; in either case, the insert must be removed before cutting the steering tube.)

(d) Make your cut straight. Measure twice; cut once! Mark it straight by wrapping a piece of tape around the steering tube and cutting along it. If you are not sure your cut will be straight, start it a little higher and file it down flat to the tape line. If you really want to be safe, use a tool specifically designed to help you make a straight cut; Park Tool's "threadless saw guide" will do the trick. Remember that you can always shorten the steering tube a little more, but you cannot make it longer! Use a round file on the inside of the tube and a flat file on the outside to remove any metal burrs left by the hacksaw or cutter.

(e) When you have completed cutting and deburring, put the fork back in, replacing all headset parts the way they were originally installed (Fig. 14.18). Return to step 1 in this section.

6. Check that the edges of the star-shaped nut are at least 12mm below the top edge of the steering tube. The nut must be far enough down that the bottom of the headset top cap does not hit it once the adjusting bolt is tightened. If the nut is not in deeply enough, you need to drive it deeper into the steering tube after removing the stem, in the case of a steel or aluminum steering tube. In the case of a carbon steering tube, you set the expander plug inside the steering tube under the stem clamp by tightening its bolt with a hex key. This part is a must to prevent crushing the carbon steering tube with the stem clamp.

(a) Driving the star nut deeper into a metal steering tube is best done with the star-nut installation tool (Fig. 4.3, upper right). The tool threads into the nut, and you hit it with a hammer until it stops; the star nut will now be set 15mm deep in the steering tube. If you do not have this tool, go to a bike shop and have the nut set for you. If you insist on doing it yourself, read the next paragraph. Just remember that it is easy to mangle the star nut if you do not tap it in straight.

(b) Pushing the star nut in deeper without a star-nut installation tool requires three steps: (1) Put the adjusting bolt through the top cap and thread it six turns into the star nut. (2) Set the star nut over the end of the steering tube and tap the top of the bolt with a mallet; use the top cap as a guide to keep it going in straight. (3) Tap the bolt in until the star nut is 15mm below the top of the steering tube.

NOTE: *If the wall thickness of the steering tube is greater than standard, the stock headset star nut will not fit in, and it will bend when you try to install it. Even pros sometimes ruin star nuts. It's not a big problem, because replacements can be purchased separately. If yours goes in crooked, take a long punch or rod, set it on the star nut, and drive it all of the way out of the bottom of the steering tube. Dispose of the star nut, and get another.*

If the internal diameter (I.D.) of the steering tube is undersized (standard I.D. is 22.2mm [⅞ inch] on a 1-inch steering tube, 25.4mm [1 inch] on a 1⅛-inch steering tube, and 28.6mm [1⅛ inch] on a 1¼-inch steering tube), you cannot use the stock star nut from the headset for that size. Get a correctly sized star nut at a bike shop or from the fork manufacturer. In a pinch, you can make a big stock star nut fit by bending each pair of opposite leaves of the star nut toward each other with a pair of channel-lock pliers to reduce the nut's width. Now you can insert the nut; be aware that it may not grip as well as a properly sized one.

7. Install the headset top cap on the top of the stem clamp (or spacers you set above it). Grease the threads of the top-cap compression bolt and screw it into the star nut inside the steering tube with a 5mm hex key (Fig. 14.8).

8. Adjust the headset. The steps are outlined in §xiv-14.

14.11   Freeing stem wedge

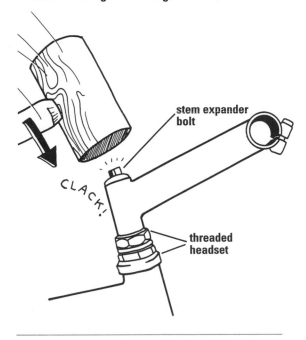

xiv-3 REMOVE QUILL-TYPE STEM FROM THREADED FORK

LEVEL 3

1. Unscrew the stem-fixing bolt on the top of the stem about three turns or so. Most stem bolts take a 6mm hex key. Some stems have a rubber plug on top of the stem that must be removed to get at the stem bolt.

2. Tap the top of the bolt down with a mallet or hammer (Fig. 14.11) to disengage the plug or wedge from the bottom of the quill. If the head of the bolt is recessed down in the stem so that a hammer cannot get at it, leave the wrench in the bolt and tap the top of the wrench until the wedge is free.

3. Pull the stem out of the steering tube.

xiv-4 INSTALL AND ADJUST HEIGHT OF QUILL STEM IN THREADED FORK

1. Generously grease the stem quill, the expander-bolt threads, the outside of the wedge or conical plug, and the inside of the steering tube. If this is the first time you've done this, I know what you're thinking, "Why put grease on something that I want to wedge together?" Don't worry; the grease won't prevent the wedge from keeping the stem tight. What the grease will do is prevent the parts from seizing or rusting together so that you can't get them apart again.

2. Thread the expander bolt through the stem and into the wedge or plug until the bolt pulls the plug or wedge into place, but not so far as to prevent the stem from inserting into the steering tube.

3. Slip the stem quill into the steering tube (Fig. 14.7) to the depth you want. Make sure the stem is inserted beyond its height-limit line. Tighten the bolt until the stem is snug but can still be turned.

4. Set the stem to the desired height, line it up with the front wheel, and tighten the bolt. It needs to be tight, but don't overdo it. You can overtighten the stem bolt to the point that it puts a bulge in the steering tube, so be careful.

xiv-5 STEM MAINTENANCE AND REPLACEMENT SCHEDULE

A bike cannot be controlled if the stem breaks, so make sure yours doesn't break. Aluminum has no fatigue endurance limit, which means that any aluminum part regularly stretched or flexed will eventually fail. Steel and titanium parts repeatedly stressed more than about one-half of their tensile strength will eventually fail as well. Aluminum may fail suddenly; steel and titanium tend to crack first and then tear over time.

What this means is that stems and handlebars are not permanent accessories on your bike. Replace them before they fail on you.

Clean the stem regularly. Whenever you clean it, look for corrosion, cracks, and bent or stressed areas. If you find any, replace the stem immediately. If you crash hard on your bike, especially hard enough to bend the handlebar, replace the stem, the bar, and possibly the fork. Err on the side of caution.

Italian stem maker 3T recommends replacing stems and handlebars every four years. If you rarely ride the bike, this is overkill. If you ride hard and often, every four years may not be frequent enough. Do what is appropriate for you, and be aware of the risks.

HANDLEBARS

I refer generally to both aerobars and standard road drop bars.

xiv-6 HANDLEBAR REMOVAL

a. From a stem with a single handlebar-clamp bolt

Stems with a single handlebar-clamp bolt are shown in Figures 14.2, 14.4–7.

1. Remove the handlebar tape (Fig. 14.12), at least from one side.

2. Remove the brake levers (Chap. 10).

3. Loosen the handlebar bolt clamp (Figs. 5–7). This usually takes a 5mm hex key.

4. Pull the bar out, working the bend around through the stem. If the bar won't budge, or if it will budge but it appears that you will tear up the bar's finish working it out through the stem, or if the bend in the bar will not pass through the stem clamp, you need to open the stem clamp a bit more. On many stems, you can do this by removing the clamp bolt, threading it back in from the opposite side, inserting a coin into the clamp slot, and tightening the bolt against the coin to spread the clamp. (Open-

14.12 Removing handlebar tape

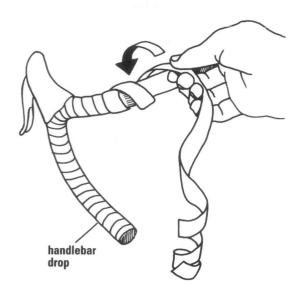

handlebar
drop

ing a stem clamp in this way—but from a steering tube—is illustrated in Fig. 14.9.)

b. From a stem with a removable front stem cap

Stems with a removable front stem cap are shown in Figures 14.3 and 14.22.

1. Completely remove the bolts holding on the front stem cap. There can be two (Fig. 14.3), three, or four bolts, depending on model.

2. Pull off the stem cap, and the handlebar will now drop off the stem. Makes it easy, eh?

xiv-7 INSTALLATION OF COMPLETE AEROBAR: BASE BAR, AERO EXTENSIONS, AND ELBOW PADS

1. If the aerobar has an integrated stem, clamp it onto the steering tube and adjust the headset as in §xiv-2 and §xiv-14. If not, clamp the handlebar into the stem, clamp the stem onto the steering tube; adjust the headset as in §xiv-2 and §xiv-14.

2. Adjust the angle of the base bar (if you have a separate bar clamped into a stem) to the position you like it, and tighten the stem clamp.

STEM
MAINTENANCE
AND
REPLACEMENT
SCHEDULE
.
HANDLEBAR
REMOVAL
.
INSTALLATION OF
COMPLETE AERO-
BAR: BASE BAR,
AERO EXTEN-
SIONS, AND
ELBOW PADS

STEMS, HANDLEBARS, AND HEADSETS

INSTALLATION OF
COMPLETE
AEROBAR: BASE
BAR, AERO
EXTENSIONS, AND
ELBOW PADS

14.13A–E Aero adjustments and aero
extension bend variations

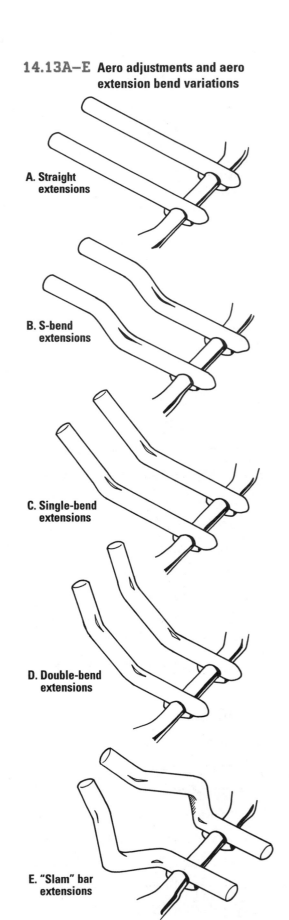

**A. Straight
extensions**

**B. S-bend
extensions**

**C. Single-bend
extensions**

**D. Double-bend
extensions**

**E. "Slam" bar
extensions**

3. Clamp on the aero extensions and the elbow pads. In many cases, the hardware securing the extensions also holds the elbow pads (Fig. 14.15). Some bars allow you to run the extensions underneath the base bar or on top of them; if you have the choice, try them both to see which you prefer. The elbow pads, of course, clamp above the base bar. You will also often have the choice of shape of your aero extensions, be they straight, single-bend, double-bend, S-bend, or the short, radical J-shaped bend of a Slam bar (all shown in Fig. 14.13).

4. Following the positioning instructions in Chapter 3, change the stem length and height if need be, adjust the elbow pad fore–aft, twist, tilt, and width and aero extension width, twist, and reach to your liking, and tighten all of the clamp bolts. If you will be using end plugs in the tail ends of the aero extensions, insert them before you clamp the extensions in place; on many bars, you won't be able to get the plugs in once the extensions are in place.

5. If you have excess length on the extensions, now would be the time to pull them back out and cut them down to the right length. If they are carbon fiber, follow the Pro Tip in this chapter on cutting a carbon steering tube, so that you won't make a hideous cut leaving carbon frayed and peeling back. Clamp the extensions back in place when you're done.

6. Unless the bar has integrated brake levers (as on the book cover), clamp the brake levers onto the ends of the base bar and tighten the bar-end shifters into the ends of the aero extensions.

7. If you are going to run a third brake lever, clamp it onto the right extension, facing forward; see §x-8, Fig. 10.8.

INSTALLATION OF
COMPLETE
AEROBAR: BASE
BAR, AERO
EXTENSIONS, AND
ELBOW PADS

·

INSTALLATION OF
DROP HANDLEBAR

·

INSTALLING A
CLIP-ON AEROBAR
ONTO A DROP
BAR OR
COWHORN BAR

8. Install the cables and housings and route them through or along the bars and frame and to the derailleurs and brakes; see §viii-6 to §viii-12 and §x-4 (and §x-8, if you're running a third brake lever). If you are running the shift cables straight out of the tail ends of the extensions, make sure the cable housing loops you leave entering the frame or cable stops are not so long that they hit your knees.

9. Tape the handlebars (§xiv-11).

10. Check that all of the bolts are tight, and go ride your bike!

xiv-8 INSTALLATION OF DROP HANDLEBAR

1. Remove the handlebar stem-clamp bolt (or bolts), grease the threads, and replace it (them). Grease the inside of the stem clamp, and grease the clamping area in the center of the bar. Grease keeps the parts from seizing over time and also will prevent squeaks from developing.

2. Install the bar and rotate it to the position you find most comfortable. The old-school way was to set a drop bar so that the bottom flat section (aka the "drop"; see Fig. 14.12) was horizontal. Today, pro riders tend to have their drops aimed down and back toward the rear brake or the rear hub, but the setting you choose is entirely a matter of personal preference.

3. Tighten the bolt or bolts that clamp the bar to the stem to the recommended torque—see the torque table in Appendix C. This step is particularly important with expensive, lightweight stems and bars. You can pinch and thereby weaken a lightweight handlebar by overtightening, and the high-strength tubing will crack right by the stem. Light stems

come with ever smaller bolts with ever finer threads, and overtightening can strip the threads inside an aluminum or magnesium stem. If you don't have a torque wrench and you have a light-weight stem with small bolts (e.g., M5 or M6 bolts, which take 4mm and 5mm hex keys, respectively), use a short hex key so that you can't get much leverage. Proper torque is even more important with carbon-fiber handlebars. Also, make sure that there is the same amount of space between the stem and either edge of the front plate on a front-opening stem. Any stem whose clamp gap(s) gets pinched nearly closed when tightened around the bar needs to be replaced, along with the handlebar.

xiv-9 INSTALLING A CLIP-ON AEROBAR ONTO A DROP BAR OR COWHORN BAR

Open the clamps that attach around the handlebar by removing the bolts with a hex wrench.

NOTE: *I will refer to the bike's handlebar when a clip-on is attached to it as the "base bar."*

Clip-on aerobars generally mount on the bulge of the base bar (Fig. 14.14), right next to the stem. If the clip-on you have chosen mounts on the thinner-diameter section of the base bar, you may have to peel back some handlebar tape from the section adjacent the bulge (Fig. 14.12).

For starters, set the clip-on bar level or angled upward slightly. Bolt the clip-on clamps around the base bar (Fig. 14.15A–B). You want the bolts tight enough that the clip-on bar won't slip when you hit a bump or pull on it, but you also don't want to crush the base bar, so make the bolts snug but don't make them scream.

INSTALLING A
CLIP-ON AEROBAR
ONTO A DROP
BAR OR
COWHORN BAR
·
HANDLEBAR
MAINTENANCE
AND
REPLACEMENT
SCHEDULE

14.14 **Installing clip-on aerobars on drop bar**

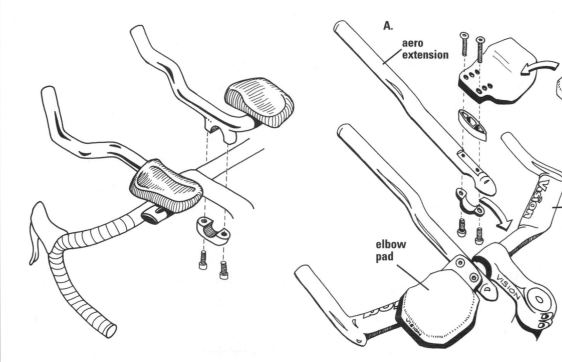

14.15A–B **Installing clip-on aerobars on cowhorn bar**

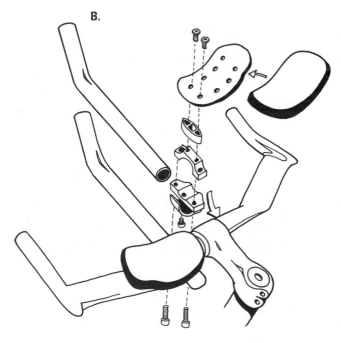

Set the elbow pads in a medium-width position. The pad is often held onto the elbow support with a hook-and-loop fastener such as Velcro; pulling off the pad will reveal the adjusting bolt. Ideally, you want the elbow pad positioned under your elbow or slightly forward of it, and you want the clip-on to be of such a length that your hands grasp the ends comfortably with the elbows on the pads.

xiv-10 HANDLEBAR MAINTENANCE AND REPLACEMENT SCHEDULE

A bike cannot be controlled without a handlebar, so you never want one to break on you. Do not look at the bar as a permanent accessory. All handlebars will eventually fail. The trick is not to be riding them when they do.

Keep the bar clean. Regularly inspect it (under the tape!) for cracks, crash-induced bends, corrosion, and

stressed areas. If you find any sign of wear or cracking, replace the bar. Never straighten a bent handlebar! Replace it! If you crash hard on your bike, consider
replacing the bar even if it looks fine. If the bar has
taken an extremely hard hit, it's a good idea to replace
it rather than gamble on its integrity.

The Italian stem and bar manufacturer 3T recommends replacing stems and bars every four years. As
with a stem, if you rarely ride the bike, this is overkill.
If you ride hard and often, every four years may not
be frequent enough. Do what is appropriate for you,
and be aware of the risks.

xiv-11 WRAPPING HANDLEBAR TAPE

To wrap tape without making a mess, you need both
hands free and the bar rigidly held. Clamping the bike
in a bike stand or holding it in a stationary trainer
should do the trick, but you may need to stabilize the
front wheel between your knees or with a strap around
the down tube and rim or a handlebar holder from
the seatpost to the handlebar. Before wrapping, clean
the bar and inspect it for cracks, crash-induced bends,
corrosion, and stressed areas. If you find any sign of
wear or cracking, replace the bar. I am describing
taping of a drop bar, since it is more involved than taping a cowhorn bar; if you can do this, taping a
cowhorn will be a snap for you.

Tape down any brake and shift cables that are running along the bars in a few places with electrical tape
or, better yet, strapping tape (Fig. 14.16). Shimano STI
levers have brake cables that run beneath the bar tape,
while the shift cables sprout from the lever sides and
remain exposed. Both the shift cables and brake cables
are concealed on Campagnolo Ergopower and SRAM
DoubleTap levers. Tape the cables down where they
will be the most comfortable on your hands. Some

**14.16 Tape cables to the bar before installing
bar tape**

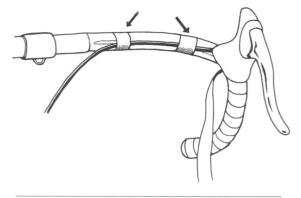

14.17 Wrapping handlebar tape

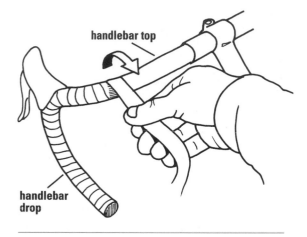

handlebars have grooves in them for the cables; tape
the cables down so that they stay in the creases. Shimano STI brake cables go along the front of the handlebar. Campagnolo Ergopower shift cables generally
go along the front of the bar while the brake cables go
around the back of the bar, but I prefer to route both
the brake cables and the shift cables from the
Ergopower levers along the front of the handlebar.

Generally, handlebar tape has an adhesive backing to preclude the tendency of handlebar tape to
creep and separate. The tape sets usually come with
two short pieces. These are to cover the brake-lever-
clamp bands on a drop bar under the skirt of the rubber lever hood, but you won't need them on an
aerobar. For only taping the grip areas on a base bar

HANDLEBAR
MAINTENANCE
AND
REPLACEMENT
SCHEDULE
·
WRAPPING
HANDLEBAR TAPE

STEMS, HANDLEBARS, AND HEADSETS

and set of aero extensions, you will not need both rolls of tape in the set. For a drop bar, you will need all of the tape.

Peel back the paper covering the adhesive on the tape and start wrapping at the end of the bar. On a base bar or aero extension, start at the end of the bar, just behind the bar-end shifter or brake lever, overlapping the tape end completely on the first wrap. On a drop bar, overhang the tape past the end of the bar by more than about an inch, so that you can push the excess in with the end plug later. Lightweight bars tend to have thin walls and consequently a large inside diameter, and many end plugs will not fit tightly in them. In this case, the extra tape you push in should fill the extra space perfectly.

To have a long-lasting tape job, always wrap from the end of the bar so that each wrap holds down the inner edge of the prior one. Wrapping from the center of the bar and finishing at the ends is a mistake; your hands will constantly peel back the edge of each tape wrap because your hands will push outward on those edges as you ride. The tape will look bad and get torn quickly.

Pull the tape tightly as you wrap, but not enough to break it. Overlap each wrap about one-quarter to one-half of its width (Fig. 14.17). Use as much overlap as you can to increase padding and decrease the chance of the tape slipping enough to reveal the handlebar. The amount of overlap depends on the length of the tape, the width and drop depth of the bar, and the amount you stretch the tape as you wrap.

On aerobars, just wrap where you're going to be gripping the bars, and tape the loose ends down with a few turns of electrical tape. On drop bars, when you get to the bulged section of the bar that clamps into the stem, you should have just run out of tape. If you

have more, you can rewrap part of the bar with more overlap or you can cut off the excess. If the tape doesn't make it to the bulge, you can rewrap part of the bar with less overlap. If you want to end with only a narrow piece of sticky tape holding it down, you can trim the end of the bar tape to a point and hold it down with a single width of electrical tape wrapped around a couple of times. You can follow with the decorative tape piece that came with the bar tape. Otherwise, just wrap around the bar a number of times with electrical tape, going wide enough with it to completely cover the square-cut end of the bar tape. Cut or break the electrical tape so that it ends under the bar.

On a drop bar, push the end plugs into the ends of the bar, using them to push in the extra tape you left sticking past the ends of the bar. Most plugs are now simply that—cylindrical plastic plugs; they can usually be popped in with the heel of your hand.

xiv-12 SETTING STEM AND BAR POSITIONS

Handlebar height and reach settings are very personal. Much depends on your physique, your flexibility, your frame, your riding style, and a few other preferences. This subject is covered in depth in Chapter 3, but here are some brief suggestions.

On the aero (clip-on) bar, you want to find a position that maximizes both comfort and aerodynamic efficiency. The lower and more aerodynamic you are trying to be, the more forward you will want to position your saddle to open up the angle between your torso and your thigh. When setting the reach to the bar, a good rule of thumb is to position your elbow pads so that your ear is over the bend in your elbow. As for width, the narrower the elbow pads, the more aerodynamic you will be. Work on getting lower only after you have gotten comfortable and efficient with a narrow position.

If you stand a lot when you climb, you will want the bar low enough that you can use your arms efficiently when gripping the brake levers and pulling.

HEADSETS

There are three basic types of threadless headsets: standard (aka "external," Fig. 14.18), cupless internal (aka "integrated," Fig. 14.19), and press-in internal with lipped cups (Fig. 14.20). A threaded steering tube gets a thread-on headset (Fig. 14.21).

Road headsets have traditionally come in the 1-inch-diameter size (first threaded and then threadless), but now most road bikes take 1⅛-inch threadless headsets.

The Dia-Compe (now Cane Creek) AheadSet was the first threadless headset (Fig. 14.18), a lightweight system that eliminates the stem quill, bolt, and wedge. The AheadSet connection between the handlebar and the stem is more rigid too. Fork manufacturers prefer threadless headsets because they do not have to thread their forks and/or offer various lengths of fork steering tubes; steering-tube diameter becomes the only variable.

On an unthreaded headset, the top cup or cone and a conical compression ring slide onto the steering tube (Figs. 14.18–20, 14.23). The stem clamps around the top of the steering tube, above the compression ring. When its conical base is pressed into the beveled edges of the hole through the top cup or cone, the compression ring keeps the top cup or cone centered on the steering tube.

A star nut—a nut with two layers of sharp, spring-steel teeth sticking out from it (originally dubbed the "Star Fangled Nut" by Dia-Compe)—fits into a steel,

14.18 Threadless headset

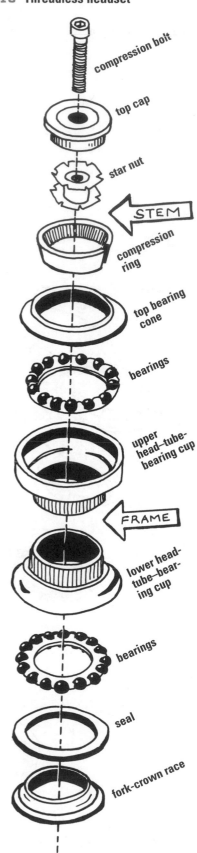

compression bolt

top cap

star nut

STEM

compression ring

top bearing cone

bearings

upper head-tube-bearing cup

FRAME

lower head-tube-bearing cup

bearings

seal

fork-crown race

14.19 Exploded cupless (drop-in) internal cartridge-bearing headset

14.20 Exploded Cane Creek Zero-Stack style press-in internal headset with lipped cups

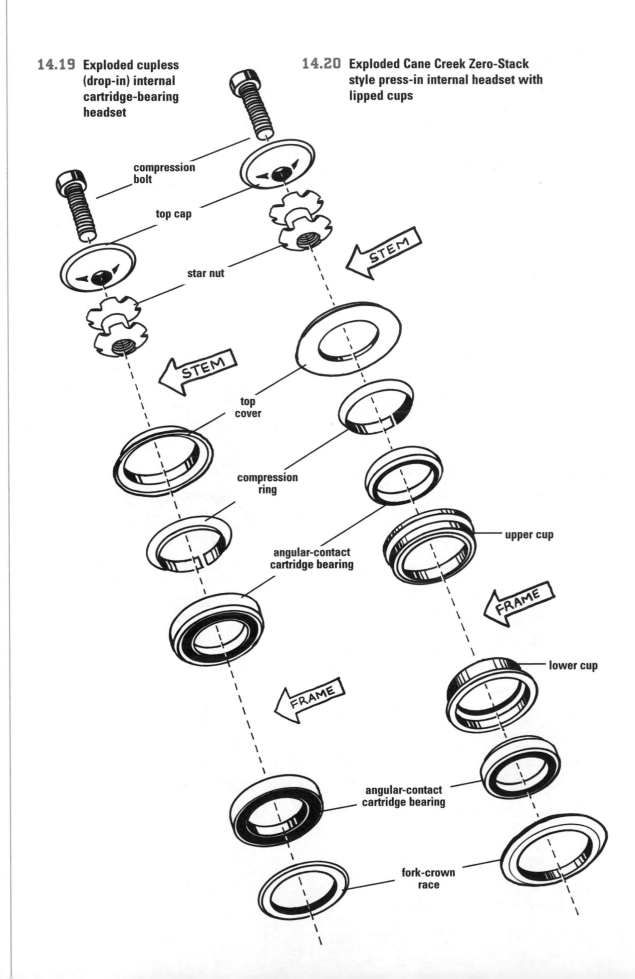

compression bolt

top cap

star nut

STEM

STEM

top cover

compression ring

angular-contact cartridge bearing

upper cup

FRAME

lower cup

FRAME

angular-contact cartridge bearing

fork-crown race

14.21 Threaded headset

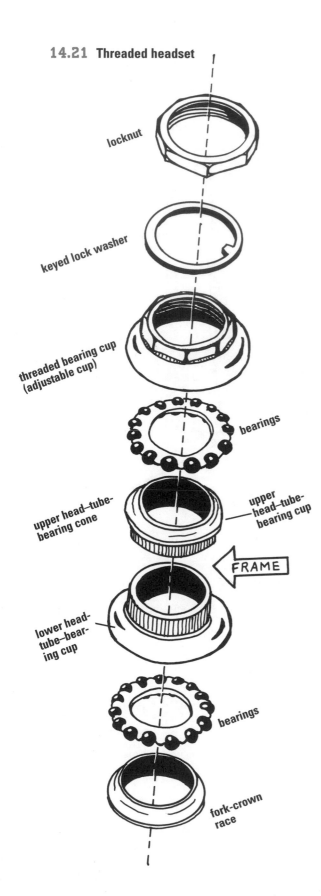

locknut

keyed lock washer

threaded bearing cup (adjustable cup)

bearings

upper head–tube–bearing cone

upper head–tube–bearing cup

FRAME

lower head–tube–bearing cup

bearings

fork-crown race

aluminum, or titanium steering tube and grabs its inner walls (Figs. 14.3 and 14.22). On a carbon-fiber steering tube, an expandable insert (Fig. 14.24) or a glue-in insert with an integrated star nut replaces the standard star nut and serves the dual purpose of protecting the steering tube from being crushed by the stem clamp and anchoring the top-cap compression bolt.

A top cap sits atop the stem clamp and pushes it down to adjust the headset by means of the long compression bolt threaded into the star nut (Figs. 14.3 and 14.22) or into the crush-prevention insert in a carbon steering tube (Fig. 14.24). The clamping force of the stem around the steering tube holds the headset in adjustment (Fig. 14.4).

The latest generation of headset is the threadless internal type, or integrated headset, concealed inside the frame's steering tube (Figs. 14.19–20, 14.22–23). Whereas standard threadless and threadless headsets have bearing cups above and below the ends of the head tube (Figs. 14.18 and 14.21), integrated headsets have bearings seated inside the head tube. Some types of integrated headsets have no press-in cups; the bearings either roll on bearing cups that just drop into the flared head tube and rest on machined shelves within the head tube itself (Fig. 14.23), or the headset simply has angular cartridge bearings that drop into the same style of flared head tube and rest without a cup on those machined shelves within the head tube (Fig. 14.19). Other types of internal headsets have cups with thin flanges that extend out to the edges of the head tube (Figs. 14.20 and 14.22). Otherwise, integrated headsets are identical to and are adjusted in the same way as original threadless headsets.

The top bearing cup on a threaded headset has wrench flats, a keyed lock washer stacked on top of it, and a locknut that covers the top of the steering tube.

STEMS, HANDLEBARS, AND HEADSETS

14.22 Cane Creek Zero-Stack internal headset with press-in cups (cutaway)

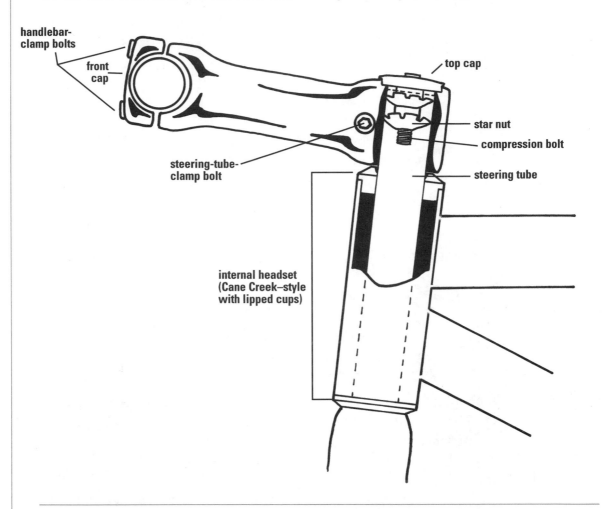

handlebar-
clamp bolts

front
cap

top cap

steering-tube-
clamp bolt

star nut

compression bolt

steering tube

internal headset
(Cane Creek–style
with lipped cups)

That locknut tightens against the keyed lock washer and threaded cup (see Fig. 14.21). Extra spacers may be included under the locknut.

Many headsets—threaded or threadless—use individual ball bearings held in some type of steel or plastic retainer or "cage" (Figs. 14.18, 14.21, and 14.23) so that you are not chasing dozens of separate balls around when you work on the bike. A variation on this (some Stronglight, Ritchey, and FSA) has needle bearings held in conical plastic retainers (Fig. 14.25) riding on conical steel bearing surfaces.

Cartridge-bearing headsets usually employ "angular contact" bearings (Figs. 14.19–20 and 14.26), since normal cylindrical cartridge bearings cannot take the side forces encountered by the bottom bearing of a headset. Each angular contact cartridge bearing (Fig. 9.29) is a separate, sealed, internally greased unit.

xiv-13 CHECK HEADSET ADJUSTMENT

If the headset is too loose, it will rattle or clunk while you ride. You might even notice some play in the fork as you apply the front brake. If the headset is too tight, the fork will be difficult to turn or feel rough to rotate.

1. Check for headset looseness by holding the front brake and rocking the bike forward and back. Try it with the front wheel pointed straight ahead and then with the wheel turned at 90 degrees to the

14.23 **Campagnolo Hiddenset drop-in-style integrated headset system (exploded)**

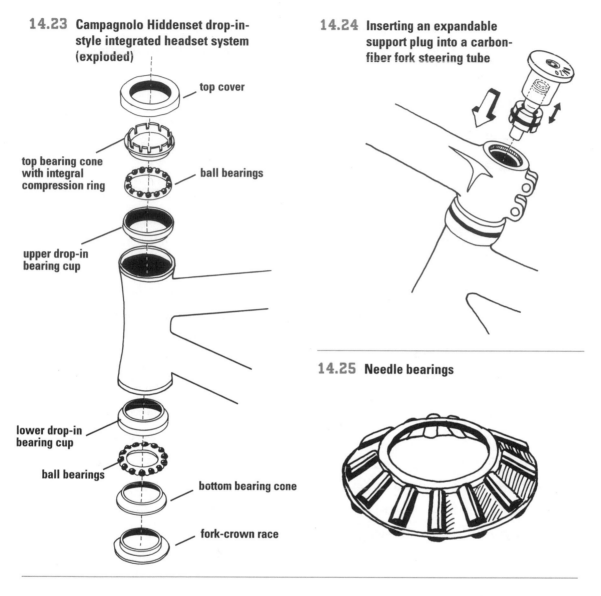

top cover

top bearing cone with integral compression ring

ball bearings

upper drop-in bearing cup

lower drop-in bearing cup

ball bearings

bottom bearing cone

fork-crown race

14.24 **Inserting an expandable support plug into a carbon-fiber fork steering tube**

14.25 **Needle bearings**

bike. Feel for back-and-forth movement (or play) at the lower head cup with your other hand. If there is play, you need to adjust the headset because it is too loose. If the headset is loose, skip to the appropriate adjustment section, §xiv-14 or §xiv-15.

2. Check for headset tightness by lifting the front wheel off the ground and turning the handlebar back and forth. Feel for any binding or stiffness of movement. Also, check for the chunk-chunk-chunk movement to fixed positions characterizing a pitted headset (if you feel this, you need a new headset). Lean the bike to one side and then

the other; the front wheel should turn as the bike is leaned (although some cable housings can resist the turning of the front wheel). Lift the bike by the saddle so that it is tipped down at an angle with both wheels off the ground. Turn the handlebar one way and let go. See if it returns to center quickly and smoothly on its own. If the headset does not turn easily on any of these steps, it is too tight, and you should skip to the appropriate adjustment section, §xiv-14 or §xiv-15.

3. If the headset is a threaded model, try to turn the top nut and the threaded cup by hand. They

14.26 **Lower parts of cartridge-bearing headset**

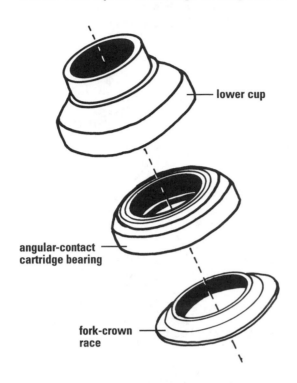

lower cup

angular-contact
cartridge bearing

fork-crown
race

should be so tight against each other that they can only be loosened with wrenches. If you can tighten or loosen either part by hand, even if it passed tests one and two, you still need to adjust the headset; go to §xiv-15.

xiv-14 ADJUSTING A THREADLESS HEADSET

Adjusting a threadless headset—whether it is an integrated type (Figs. 14.19, 14.20, and 14.23) or the external type (Figs. 14.3 and 14.18)—is much easier than adjusting a threaded one. It's a level 1 procedure and usually only takes a 5mm hex key.

a. First steps

1. Check the headset adjustment (§xiv-13). Determine whether the headset is too tight or too loose.

2. Loosen the bolt(s) that clamp the stem to the steering tube.

3. Adjust the headset by tightening or loosening the compression bolt, which runs through the center of the top cap. Be careful not to overtighten this bolt, since it will put too much pressure on the bearings and eventually pit the headset. If you're using a torque wrench, Dia-Compe recommends a tightening torque on this bolt of 22 in-lbs, which is a very low torque. This is a good place to start, but the headset on your bike may require a different torque for proper adjustment.

   (a) If the headset is too tight, use a 5mm hex key to loosen the compression bolt on the top cap about one-sixteenth of a turn (Fig. 14.27). Although this step usually takes a 5mm hex key, on many expander inserts for carbon-fiber steering tubes (Fig. 14.24), the top cap itself is turned with a 6mm hex key.

   (b) If the headset is too loose, use either a 5mm or a 6mm hex key to tighten the compression bolt on the top cap about one-sixteenth of a turn (Fig. 14.27), as just explained for some carbon-fiber forks.

N O T E : *Not all threadless stems are adjusted with the top-cap system. DiaTech threadless headsets have no top cap. Instead, a clamping collar below the stem adjusts headset tension. The stem is first clamped in place. The collar is beveled on the inside from both ends, and it slides down an externally beveled ring above it as you tighten the clamp screw to put pressure on the headset. As soon as you loosen the stem, the headset comes out of adjustment.*

b. Adjustment problems

If the cap does not move down and push the stem down, redo step 2, making sure the stem is not stuck to the steering tube.

Another hindrance occurs if the conical compression ring (Figs. 14.18–20 and 14.23) is stuck to the steering tube, preventing adjustment via the top-cap bolt. Remove the top cap, stem, spacers, and headset top cover first to address this problem.

- With most non-Campagnolo compression rings, which are simply cone-shaped pieces split on one side, you need only tap the steering tube down with a mallet and then push the fork back up to free the compression ring. Grease the ring and the steering tube, and reassemble.

- With a Campagnolo threadless headset (either an integrated Hiddenset—Fig. 14.23—or a standard external one), the compression ring is plastic and is conical on both ends. Its bottom end presses into the beveled hole in the top cone, but its turreted top end is also conical and presses into the hole in the headset top cover that is beveled toward the bottom. Pushing down on the top cover (via the compression bolt pushing down

on the stem) simply pinches the compression ring tighter in its place, rather than pushing it down. Instead, what you must do is flip the top cover upside down (Fig. 14.28) so that the nonbeveled end of its through-hole is against the turreted top edge of the compression ring, and push the compression ring down to preload the headset

---

14.27 Loosening and tightening the compression bolt on a threadless-style headset

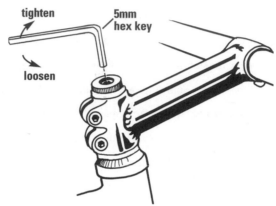

tighten

loosen

5mm hex key

14.28–29 Seating Campagnolo threadless headset

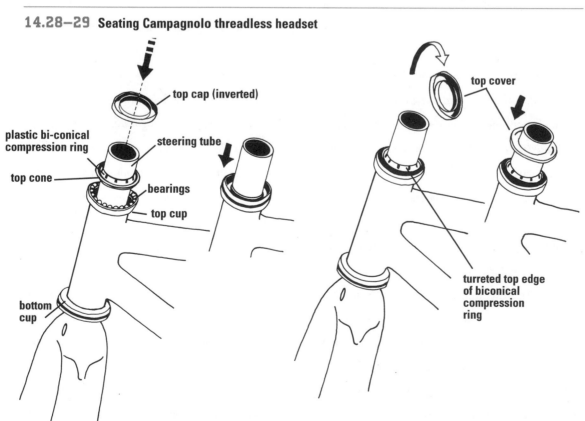

top cap (inverted)

plastic bi-conical compression ring

steering tube

top cone

bearings

top cup

bottom cup

top cover

turreted top edge of biconical compression ring

ADJUSTING A

THREADLESS

HEADSET

·

ADJUSTING A

THREADED

HEADSET

bearings by seating the top cone into them. Then flip the top cap back over (Fig. 14.29), put it back in place, and reassemble the spacers, stem, top cap, and compression bolt.

If neither the stem nor the compression ring is stuck, yet the cap still does not push the stem down, the steering tube may be so long that it is hitting the lip of the top cap and preventing the cap from pushing the stem down. The steering tube's top should be 3–6mm below the rim of the stem clamp (Fig. 14.10) or 3–6mm below the rim of the spacer(s) above the stem. If the steering tube is too long, add a spacer above or below the stem, or use a flat file to make the steering tube shorter. Some top caps have thicker edge lips than others and require more space down to the top of the steering tube to avoid bottoming out on it.

Another thing that can thwart adjustment is the cap bottoming out on the star nut, if the star nut is not installed deeply enough. The highest point of the star nut should be 12–15mm below the top of the steering tube. With metal steering tubes, tap the star nut deeper with a star-nut installation tool, or put the bolt through the top cap, thread it five turns into the star nut, and gently tap it in with a soft hammer; the top cap is used to keep the star nut going in straight. Some top caps have taller center sections than others and require deeper insertion of the star nut to avoid bottoming out on it.

With carbon steering tubes, first loosen the aluminum expander (Fig. 14.24) with a 5mm hex key (Fig. 14.27). Next, unscrew its top cap a turn or two with a 6mm hex wrench. By hand, push the assembly in farther until the top cap stops it, and reexpand the plug with a 5mm hex key. Finally, tighten the top cap down (22 in-lbs of torque is standard) against the top of the stem to adjust the headset.

Once you have fixed the cause of the adjustment problem, return to step 1.

c. Final steps

4. Tighten the steering-tube clamp bolt, or bolts, on the stem. If using a torque wrench, Dia-Compe recommends a tightening torque of 130 in-lbs.

5. Recheck the headset adjustment. Repeat steps 2–4 if necessary. With some integrated headsets, you may need a shim under the top cup so that the edges of the top cap do not drag and scrape on the top end of the head tube.

6. If the headset is adjusted properly, make sure the stem is aligned straight with the front wheel, and go ride.

xiv-15 ADJUSTING A THREADED HEADSET

The secret to good adjustment is simultaneously controlling the steering tube, the adjustable cup, and the locknut as you tighten the latter two together.

NOTE: *Perform the adjustment with the stem installed. Not only does it give you something to hold onto that keeps the fork from turning during the installation, but there are also slight differences in adjustment when the stem is in place as opposed to when it is not. Tightening the stem bolt inside a threaded steering tube (Fig. 14.7) can sometimes bulge the walls of the steering tube slightly, just enough for it to shorten the steering tube and tighten a previously perfect headset adjustment.*

1. Following the steps outlined in §xiv-13, determine whether the headset is too loose or too tight.

2. Put a pair of headset wrenches that fit the headset on the headset's top nut (which I will also call the "locknut") and top bearing cup (or "threaded cup" or "adjustable cup"). Headset nuts come in

14.30 **Offsetting the headset wrenches to loosen the locknut**

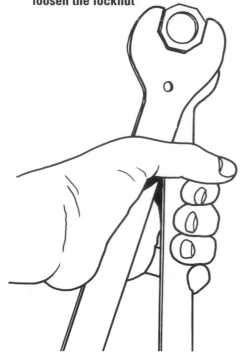

14.31 **Offsetting the wrenches to tighten the locknut**

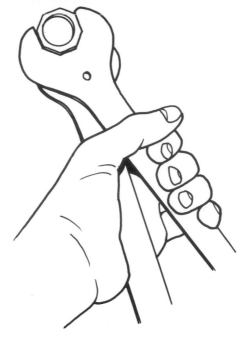

a wide variety of sizes, so make sure you have purchased the proper wrenches. The standard wrench size for a road bike is 32mm. Place the wrenches so that the top one is slightly offset to the left of the bottom wrench. That way you can squeeze them together to free the nut (Fig. 14.30).

N O T E: *People with small hands or weak grip will need to grab each wrench out at the end to get enough leverage.*

3. Hold the lower wrench in place and turn the top wrench counterclockwise about one-quarter turn to loosen the locknut. It may take considerable force to break it loose, because it is generally tight to keep the headset from loosening.

4. If the headset was too loose, turn the lower (or threaded) cup clockwise about one-sixteenth of a turn while holding the stem with your other hand. Be careful when tightening the cup; over-tightening it can ruin the headset by pressing the

bearings into the bearing surfaces and make little indentations. The headset then stops at the indentations rather than turning smoothly, a condition known as a "pitted" or "brinelled" headset.

(a) If the headset was too tight, loosen the threaded cup counterclockwise one-sixteenth of a turn while holding the stem with your other hand. Loosen it until the bearings turn freely, but not to the point where any play develops.

5. Holding the stem, tighten the locknut clockwise with a single wrench. Make sure that the threaded cup does not turn while you tighten the locknut. If it does turn, either you are missing the keyed lock washer separating the cup and locknut (Fig. 14.21), or the washer you have is missing its key. In this case, remove the locknut (the stem has to come out first) and replace the keyed lock washer.

ADJUSTING A
THREADED
HEADSET

·

OVERHAUL
THREADLESS
HEADSET

Put the locknut on the steering tube so that the key engages the longitudinal groove in the steering tube. Thread on the locknut, install the stem, and redo the adjustment procedure.

NOTE: *You can adjust a headset without a keyed lock washer by working both wrenches simultaneously, but it is trickier, and the headset often will then come loose while you are riding.*

6. Check the headset adjustment again. Repeat steps 4 and 5 until the headset is properly adjusted.

7. Once the headset is properly adjusted, place one wrench on the locknut and the other on the threaded cup. Tighten the locknut (clockwise) firmly against the washer(s) and threaded cup to hold the headset adjustment in place (Fig. 14.31).

8. Check the headset adjustment again. If it is off, follow steps 2–7 again. Once it is adjusted properly, make sure the stem is aligned with the front wheel and the stem expander bolt is tight before riding.

NOTE: *If you constantly get what you believe to be the proper adjustment and then find it to be too loose after you tighten the locknut and threaded cup against each other, the steering tube may be too long, causing the locknut to bottom out. Remove the stem and examine the inside of the steering tube. If the top end of the steering tube butts up against the top lip of the locknut, the steering tube is too long. Remove the locknut and add another spacer.*

If you don't want to add another spacer, file 1mm or 2mm from the steering tube. Be sure to deburr it inside and out, and avoid leaving filings in the bearings or steering-tube threads. Replace the locknut and return to step 5.

Wheels Manufacturing makes a headset locknut called the Growler. It replaces the locknut and will not

come loose, even on bumpy terrain. It threads on like a normal locknut and is adjusted the same way. The only difference between a Growler and a standard locknut is that the Growler is split on one side and has a pinch bolt bridging the split. Once the headset is adjusted, you tighten the pinch bolt to keep the locknut from unscrewing.

xiv-16 OVERHAUL THREADLESS HEADSET

These instructions apply to both integrated (Figs. 14.19, 14.20, 14.23) and external (Figs. 14.3 and 14.18) threadless headsets.

Like any other bike part with bearings, headsets need periodic overhauls. If you use your bike regularly, you should probably overhaul a loose-bearing headset once a year. Headsets with cartridge bearings (Figs. 14.26 or 14.32) need less frequent overhaul; some angular-contact bearings can be disassembled and cleaned and some cannot. With those that cannot, if a bearing fails, you either replace the bearing or, if it has press-in bearings (like Chris King (Fig. 14.32) and Dia-Compe's S series, you replace the entire cup (§xiv-20).

Either place the bike upside down in the work stand or be ready to catch the fork when you remove the stem.

1. Disconnect the front brake (see Chap. 10) and unscrew the top-cap bolt (Fig. 14.28) and the stem-clamp bolt, or bolts. Remove the top cap and the stem.

2. Remove the top headset cup by sliding the top cup, conical compression ring (Fig. 14.18), and any spacers off the steering tube. It may take a tap with a mallet on the end of the steering tube, followed by pushing the fork back up, to free the compression ring.

14.32 Chris King–style pressed-in cartridge bearing

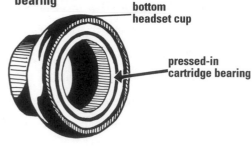

bottom
headset cup

pressed-in
cartridge bearing

3. Pull the fork from the frame.

4. Remove any seals that surround the edges of the cups. Remember the position and orientation of each.

5. Remove the bearings from the cups. Be careful not to lose any. Separate top and bottom sets if they are of different sizes.

6. If the bearings are the type that will not come apart, check to see if they turn smoothly. If they do not, buy new ones. Skip to step 8. Otherwise, clean or replace the bearings:

   (a) With standard ball-bearing or needle-bearing headsets, put the bearings in a jar or old water bottle along with some citrus-based solvent. Shake. If the bearings from the top and bottom are of different sizes, keep them in separate containers to avoid confusion. Blot the bearings dry with a clean rag.

   (b) Some cartridge bearings (Fig. 14.26) can be pulled apart and cleaned. Over a container to catch the balls, hold the bearing so that the beveled outer surface that fits into the cup faces down, and push up on the bearing's inner ring. The bearing should come apart—the inner ring will pop up and out with the bearings stuck to its outer surface. It may take a little rocking of the inner ring

as you push up. If the bearing does not come apart, first pry off the plastic seal covering the bearings with a knife or razor blade, as in Chapter 9, Figure 9.29, and then try again. Wipe the bearings and bearing rings and seals with a clean rag.

7. Blot the bearings dry with a clean rag. Plug the sink and wash the bearings in soap and water in your hands, just as if you were washing your palms by rubbing them together. Your hands will get clean for the assembly steps as well. Rinse bearings thoroughly and blot them dry. Let them air dry completely.

8. Wipe all of the bearing surfaces with clean rags. Wipe the steering tube clean.

9. Inspect all bearing surfaces for wear and pitting. If you see pits (separate indentations made by bearings in the bearing surfaces), you need to replace the headset.

10. Apply grease to all bearing surfaces. If you are using sealed-cartridge bearings, apply grease conservatively.

11. Turn the bike upside down in the bike stand.

    (a) Place a set of bearings into the top cup and a set into the cup on the lower end of the head tube.

    (b) With a Campagnolo or other integrated headset with drop-in bearing cups (Fig. 14.23), place a bearing cup into the seat in the bottom of the head-tube. Place a greased set of ball bearings into the cup, with the bearing retainer oriented properly (see step 11d for tips on determining proper bearing orientation).

    (c) With a cupless integrated headset (Fig. 14.19), set a bearing into the seat in the bottom of the head tube itself. See step 11e regarding orientation.

(d) With loose-ball headsets, make sure you have the bearing retainer right side up so that only the bearings contact the bearing surfaces (note the different upper-cup styles and bearing orientations in Figs. 14.21 and 14.18). If you have installed the retainer upside down, it will come in contact with one of the bearing surfaces, and the headset will not turn well. This is a bad thing, because assembling and riding it that way will turn the retainer into jagged chunks of broken metal. To be safe, double- and triple-check the retainer placement by turning each cup pair and bearing in your hand before proceeding. Many loose-ball headsets have the bearings set up identically top and bottom (Fig. 14.21). The top piece of each pair is a cup, and the bottom piece is a cone; the bearing retainer rides the same way in both sets. Some headsets, however, place both cups (and hence the bearing retainers) facing outward from the head tube (Fig. 14.18).

N O T E : *If there are loose ball bearings with no bearing retainer, stick the balls into the grease in the cups one at a time, making sure that you replace the same number you started with in each cup.*

(e) With angular-contact cartridge bearings, the beveled end faces into the cup (Fig. 14.26) or into the seat machined inside the head tube (Fig. 14.19).

12. Reinstall any seals that you removed from the headset parts.

13. Drop the fork into the head tube so that the lower headset bearing set seats properly (Fig. 14.33).

14. With a Campagnolo or other integrated headset with drop-in cups (Fig. 14.23), place a bearing cup into the seat in the top of the head tube. Otherwise, skip this step.

15. Slide the top cup or cone, with the bearings in it, onto the steering tube. Keep the bike upside down at this point; doing so not only keeps the fork in place, it also prevents grit from falling into the bearings as you put the cup on.

16. Grease the compression ring and slide it onto the (greased) steering tube, so that the narrower end slides into the conical space in the top of the top cup or cone or angular-contact cartridge bearing (Figs. 14.18–20).

N O T E : *On a Campagnolo threadless headset (integrated or external), there is a plastic biconical compression ring inserted into the top bearing cone (Fig. 14.23); it acts like a normal split compression ring, to center the top cone over the bearings. The upper edge of the plastic compression ring is notched like a turreted castle tower in case you accidentally pull it out of the cone and wonder which way it goes back in. Above this part comes the top bearing cover, whose inner edge is beveled for the turreted top conical edge of the plastic compression ring. To preload the bearings, you must first install the top bearing cover upside down (Fig. 14.28) and then push down on it to preload the bearings by pushing the top cone down. If you install the top bearing cover in its standard orientation before the top cone and plastic compression ring are slid down far enough to preload the bearings, the beveled inner edge of the top bearing cover will pinch the turreted upper conical edge of the plastic compression ring in place and not allow it to slide down farther. Once you have pushed the bearing cone down fully in this manner, flip the top bearing cover right side up and put it in place over the cone and compression ring (Fig. 14.29).*

17. Slide on any spacers that were present under the stem.

18. Slide the stem on, and tighten one stem-clamp bolt to hold it in place.

19. Turn the bike over. Check that the stem clamp or the top spacer above the stem extends 3–6mm above the top of the steering tube (Fig. 14.10) and that the star nut is 12–15mm down in the steering tube. If they are, install the top cap on the top of the stem clamp and steering tube, and screw the bolt into the star nut (Fig. 14.27).

20. If the steering tube is too long, remove the stem. Add a spacer or file the steering tube shorter until the stem clamp overlaps it by 3–6mm. If the steering tube is too short, remove spacers from below the stem, if there are any. If there are no spacers to remove, try a new stem with a shorter clamp.

21. Adjust the headset (§xiv-14).

xiv-17 OVERHAUL THREADED HEADSET

Like any other bike part with bearings, headsets need periodic overhauls. If you use your bike regularly, you should probably overhaul a loose-bearing headset once a year. Headsets with sealed cartridge bearings usually never need to be overhauled; if a bearing fails, you either replace the bearing (such as the Shimano shown in Fig. 14.26) or, if the headset has pressed-in bearings (like Chris King, Fig. 14.32), you replace the entire cup. If you have a Shimano cartridge-bearing headset, continue with these instructions. If you are replacing a Chris King or Dia-Compe S headset cup, move on to the instructions for headset removal.

A bike stand is highly recommended when overhauling a headset.

14.33 Setting fork in head tube to seat bearings

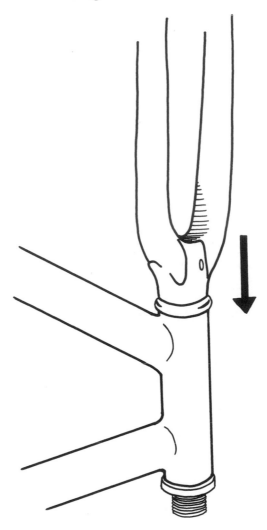

1. Disconnect the front-brake cable (Chap. 10) and remove the stem by loosening the stem bolt three turns, tapping the bolt down with a hammer to free the wedge (Fig. 14.11), and pulling it out.

2. Either turn the bike upside down or be prepared to catch the fork as you remove the upper part of the headset. To remove the top headset cup, unscrew the locknut and threaded cup with headset wrenches: Place one wrench on the locknut and one on the threaded cup. Loosen the locknut by turning it counterclockwise. It's easiest if the

OVERHAUL
THREADLESS
HEADSET

OVERHAUL
THREADED
HEADSET

STEMS, HANDLEBARS, AND HEADSETS

top wrench is angled just to the left of the lower wrench, and you squeeze them together (Fig. 14.30). Unscrew the locknut and the cup from the steering tube. The headset washer or washers will slide off the steering tube as you unscrew the threaded cup.

3. Pull the fork out of the frame.

4. Remove any seals that surround the edges of the cups. Make a point of remembering the position and orientation of each.

5. Remove the bearings from the cups. If the balls are loose, be especially careful not to lose any. Separate top and bottom sets if they are of different sizes.

6. Clean or replace the bearings.

   (a) With standard ball-bearing or needle-bearing headsets, put the bearings in a jar or old water bottle along with some citrus-based solvent. Shake. If the bearings from the top and bottom are of different sizes, keep them in separate containers to avoid confusion.

   (b) With sealed cartridge bearings, check to see whether they turn smoothly. If they do not, buy new ones. Either way, skip to step 8.

7. Blot the bearings dry with a clean rag. Plug the sink and wash the bearings in soap and water in your hands, just as if you were washing your palms by rubbing them together. This helps keep your hands clean for the assembly steps as well. Rinse bearings thoroughly and blot them dry. Let them air dry completely.

8. Wipe all of the bearing surfaces with clean rags. Wipe the steering tube clean, especially the threads, and wipe the inside of the head tube clean with a rag stuck to the end of a screwdriver.

9. Inspect all bearing surfaces for wear and pitting. If you see pits (separate indentations made by bearings in the bearing surfaces), you need to replace the headset.

10. Apply grease to all bearing surfaces. A thin film will do, especially if you are using sealed cartridge bearings.

11. Turn the bike upside down in the bike stand. Place a set of bearings in the top cup and a set in the cup on the lower end of the head tube. Make sure you have the bearing retainer right side up so that only the bearings contact the bearing surfaces. If you have installed the retainer upside down, it will come in contact with one of the bearing surfaces, and the headset will not turn well. This is a bad thing because assembling and riding it that way will turn the retainer into jagged chunks of broken metal. To be safe, double- and triple-check the retainer placement by turning each cup pair in your hand before proceeding.

    (a) Many headsets have the bearings set up identically top and bottom (Fig. 14.21). This way, the top piece of each pair is a cup, and the bottom piece is a cone; the bearing retainer rides the same way in both sets. Some headsets, however, place both cups facing outward from the head tube (Fig. 14.18), so that the bearing retainers are asymmetrical on either end of the head tube. Also, watch for asymmetry in ball size; Ritchey and recent Campagnolo headsets have smaller balls on top than in the bottom.

NOTE: *Stronglight, Ritchey, and similar needle-bearing headsets come with two pairs of separate conical steel rings. These are the bearing surfaces that sit on either side of each needle bearing (Fig. 14.25). You will find that one conical ring of each set is smaller than the other ring. Place the smaller one on the lower surface supporting the bearing: for the bottom bearing, place the smaller ring on the fork-crown race and, for the top bearing, place the smaller ring on the cup on top of the head tube.*

    (b) If you have loose ball bearings with no bearing retainer, stick the balls into the grease in the cups one at a time, making sure that you replace the same number you started with in each cup.

12. Reinstall any seals that you removed from the headset parts.

13. Drop the fork into the head tube so that the lower headset bearing set seats properly (Fig. 14.33).

14. Screw the top cup, with the bearings in it, onto the steering tube. Keeping the bike upside down at this point not only keeps the fork in place but also prevents grit from falling into the bearings as you thread the cup on.

15. Turn the bike upright. Slide on the keyed lock washer (Fig. 14.21). Align the key in the groove of the steering-tube threads. Screw on the locknut with your hand.

16. Grease the stem quill and insert it into the steering tube (Fig. 14.7). Make certain that it is in deeper than the imprinted limit line. Align the stem with the front wheel and tighten the stem bolt.

17. Adjust the headset as outlined in §xiv-15.

xiv-18 TROUBLESHOOTING STEM, HANDLEBAR, AND HEADSET PROBLEMS

a. Bar slips

Tighten the pinch bolt on the stem that holds the bar, but not beyond the maximum allowable torque. With a front-opening stem, make sure there is the same amount of space between the stem and the front plate on both edges of the front plate. With any stem, if the clamp closes on itself without holding the bar securely, check that the bar is not deformed or smaller in diameter than the stem was made to fit, and check that the stem clamp is not cracked or stretched. Replace any questionable parts. You can slide a shim made out of a beer can between the stem and bar to hold it better, but replacing parts is a safer option; there is always a reason why parts that are meant to fit together no longer do! With superlight stems and bars, you cannot just keep tightening the small clamp bolts like you can the larger bolts on heavy stems because you will strip threads and/or cause bar and stem failures.

b. Bar makes creaking noise while you are riding

Loosen the stem clamp, grease the area of the bar that is clamped in the stem, slide the bar back in place, and tighten the stem bolt. Also, sanding the hard anodized surface inside the stem clamp and on the clamping area of the bar can sometimes eliminate creaking. If the bar has a sleeved center section rather than a bulged section, the bar could be creaking inside the sleeve. There's no fix for this; replace the bar.

c. Clip-on bar slips

Tighten the clip-on's clamp bolts.

d. Stem not pointed straight ahead

Loosen the bolt (or bolts) securing the stem to the fork steering tube, align the stem with the front wheel, and tighten the stem bolt (or bolts) again. With a threaded headset, the bolt you are interested in is a single vertical bolt on top of the stem; loosen it about two turns, and tap the top of the bolt with a hammer to disengage the wedge on the other end from the bottom of the stem (Fig. 14.11). With a threadless headset, there are one (Fig. 14.3), two (Fig. 14.4), or three horizontal bolts pinching the stem around the steering tube that need to be loosened to turn the stem on the steering tube. Do not loosen the bolt on the top of the stem cap (Fig. 14.27); you'll have to readjust the headset if you do.

e. Fork and headset rattle or clunk when you are riding

The headset is too loose. Adjust the headset (§xiv-14 or §xiv-15).

f. Stem + bar + fork assembly does not turn smoothly but instead stops in certain fixed positions

The headset is pitted and needs to be replaced.

g. Stem + bar + fork assembly does not turn freely

The headset is too tight. The front wheel should swing easily from side to side when you lean the bike or lift the front end. Adjust the headset (§xiv-14 or §xiv-15, depending on type).

h. Stem is stuck in or on fork steering tube

See §xiv-1 or §xiv-3 and §xiv-5.

Appendixes

APPENDIX A

TROUBLESHOOTING INDEX

This index is intended to assist you in finding and fixing problems. If you already know wherein the problem lies, consult the Contents page in the beginning of the book for the chapter covering that part of the bike. If you are not sure which part of the bike is affected, this index can be of assistance. It is organized alphabetically but, because people's descriptions of the same problem vary, you may need to look through the entire list to find your symptom.

This index can assist you with a diagnosis and can recommend a course of action. Following each recommended action are listed chapter numbers to which you can refer for the repair procedure.

SYMPTOM	LIKELY CAUSES	ACTION	CHAPTER
bent wheel	1. maladjusted spokes	true wheel	9
	2. broken spoke	replace spoke	9
	3. bent rim	replace rim or wheel	n/a
bike pulls to one side	1. wheels not true	true wheels	9
	2. tight headset	adjust headset	14
	3. pitted headset	replace headset	14
	4. bent frame	replace frame	n/a
	5. bent fork	replace fork	n/a
	6. loose hub bearings	adjust hubs	9
	7. low tire pressure	inflate tires	5, 9
bike shimmies at high speed	1. frame cracked	replace frame	n/a
	2. frame bent	replace or straighten	n/a
	3. wheels way out of true	true wheels	9

SYMPTOM	LIKELY CAUSES	ACTION	CHAPTER
bike shimmies at high speed (cont.)	4. loose hub bearings	adjust hubs	9
	5. wheel is too "flexy"	get stiffer wheels	n/a
	6. headset too loose	tighten headset	14
	7. "flexy" frame/heavy rider	replace frame	n/a
	8. poor frame design	replace frame	n/a
bike vibrates when braking	see "chattering and vibration when braking" in Strange Noises		
brake doesn't stop bike	1. brake quick release open	close quick release	10
	2. maladjusted brake	adjust brake	10
	3. worn brake pads	replace pads	10
	4. wet rims	keep braking	10
	5. greasy rims	clean rims and brake pads	10
	6. sticky brake cable	lube or replace cable	10
	7. carbon rims in wet	use aluminum rims or switch brake pads	9, 10
	8. brake damaged	replace brake	10
	9. sticky or bent brake lever	lube or replace lever	10
brake rubs on rim	1. brake misaligned	adjust brake	10
	2. untrue wheel	true wheel	9
chain falls off in front	1. maladjusted front derailleur	adjust front derailleur	8
	2. chainline off	adjust chainline	8, 11
	3. chainring bent or loose	replace or tighten	11
chain jams in front between chainring and chainstay (called chain suck)	1. dirty chain	clean chain	7
	2. bent chainring teeth	replace chainring	11
	3. chain too narrow	replace chain	7
	4. chainline off	adjust chainline	8, 11
	5. stiff links in chain	free links, lube chain	7
chain jams in rear	1. maladjusted rear derailleur	adjust derailleur	8
	2. chain too wide	replace chain	7
	3. small cog not on spline	re-seat cogs	9
	4. poor frame clearance	return to dealer	n/a
chain skips	1. tight chain link	loosen tight link	7
	2. elongated (worn) chain	replace chain	7
	3. maladjusted derailleur	adjust derailleur	8
	4. worn rear cogs	replace cogs and chain	9, 7
	5. dirty or rusted chain	clean or replace chain	7
	6. bent rear derailleur	replace derailleur	8

SYMPTOM	LIKELY CAUSES	ACTION	CHAPTER
chain skips (cont.)	7. bent derailleur hanger	straighten or replace hanger	n/a
	8. loose derailleur jockey wheel	tighten jockey wheel	8
	9. bent chain link	replace chain	7
	10. sticky rear shift cable	replace shift cable	8
chain slaps chainstay	1. chain too long	shorten chain	7
	2. weak rear derailleur spring	replace spring or derailleur	8
	3. road very bumpy	ignore noise; use big chainring	n/a
derailleur hits spokes	1. maladjusted rear derailleur	adjust derailleur	8
	2. broken spoke	replace spoke	9
	3. bent rear derailleur	replace derailleur	8
	4. bent derailleur hanger	straighten or replace	n/a
knee pain	1. poor shoe cleat position	reposition cleat	3, 12
	2. saddle too low or high	adjust saddle	3
	3. clip-in pedal has no float	get floating pedal	12
	4. foot rolled in or out	replace shoes or get orthotics	3
pain or fatigue when riding, particularly in the back, neck, and arms	1. incorrect seat position	adjust seat position	3
	2. too much riding	build up miles gradually	n/a
	3. incorrect stem length	replace stem	3, 14
	4. poor frame fit	replace frame	3
pedal(s) move laterally clunk, click, or twist while pedaling	1. loose crankarm	tighten crank bolt	11
	2. pedal loose in crank	tighten pedal to crank	12
	3. bent pedal axle	replace pedal or axle	12
	4. loose bottom bracket	adjust bottom bracket	11
	5. bent bottom bracket axle	replace bottom bracket or axle	11
	6. bent crankarm	replace crankarm	11
	7. loose pedal bearings	adjust pedal bearings	12
pedal entry difficult (with clip-in pedals)	1. spring tension set high	reduce spring tension	12
	2. cleat guide loose or gone	tighten or replace	12
	3. too much shoe sole curvature	replace shoe or cleat	3, 12
pedal release difficult (with clip-in pedals)	1. spring tension set high	reduce spring tension	12
	2. loose cleat on shoe	tighten cleat	12
	3. dry pedal spring pivot	oil spring pivots	12
	4. dirty pedals	clean and lube pedals	12
	5. bent pedal clips	replace pedals or clips	12
	6. dirty cleats	clean, lube cleats	12

SYMPTOM	LIKELY CAUSES	ACTION	CHAPTER
pedal release too easy	1. release tension too low	increase release tension	12
(with clip-in pedals)	2. cleats worn out	replace cleats	3, 12
	1. maladjusted derailleur	adjust derailleur	8
	2. sticky or damaged cable	replace cable	8
rear shifting	3. loose rear cogs	re-seat and tighten cogs	9
working poorly	4. worn rear cogs	replace cogs and chain	9, 7
	5. worn/damaged chain	replace chain	7
	6. see also "chain jams in rear" and "chain skips," above		
	1. tire rubs frame or fork	adjust axle; true wheel	5, 9
	2. brake drags on rim	adjust brake	10
resistance	3. tire pressure too low	inflate tire	5, 9
while coasting	4. hub bearings too tight	adjust hubs	9
or pedaling	5. hub bearings dirty/worn	overhaul hubs	9
	6. mud packed around tires	clean bike	5
	1. bottom bracket too tight	adjust bottom bracket	11
	2. bottom bracket dirty/worn	overhaul bottom bracket	11
	3. chain dry/dirty/rusted	clean/lube or replace chain	7
resistance	4. pedal bearings too tight	adjust pedal bearings	12
while pedaling only	5. pedal bearings dirty/worn	overhaul pedals	12
	6. bent chainring rubs frame	straighten or replace	11
	7. true chainring rubs frame	adjust chainline	8, 11
stiff steering	1. tight headset	adjust headset	14
tire bulged	1. broken casing threads	replace tire	9
	2. slipped tubular tire	reglue tire and line up valve stem	9
tire pinch flats	1. insufficient pressure	pump tire higher	9
	2. tire diameter too small	replace with larger tire	9
tire valve-stem	1. tube slipped in tire	deflate and slide tire around rim	9
angled sharply	2. slipped tubular tire	reglue tire and line up valve stem	9

STRANGE NOISES

Weird noises can be hard to locate; use this to assist in locating them.

SYMPTOM	LIKELY CAUSES	ACTION	CHAPTER
creaking noise	1. dry handlebar/stem joint	grease inside stem clamp	14
	2. loose seatpost	tighten seatpost	13
	3. loose shoe cleats	tighten cleats	12
	4. loose crankarm	tighten crankarm bolt	11
	5. cracked frame	replace frame	n/a
	6. dry, rusty seatpost	grease seatpost	13
	7. see "squeaking noise," below	see "squeaking noise," below	
clicking noise	1. cracked shoe cleats	replace cleats	3, 12
	2. cracked shoe sole	replace shoes and cleats	3, 12
	3. loose bottom bracket	tighten BB	11
	4. loose crankarm	tighten crankarm	11
	5. loose pedal	tighten pedal	12
chattering and vibration when braking	1. bent or dented rim	replace rim or wheel	n/a
	2. loose headset	adjust headset	14
	3. brake pads toed out	adjust brake pads	10
	4. wheel way out of round	true wheel	9
	5. greasy sections of rim	clean rim and pads	9, 10
	6. loose brake pivot bolts	tighten brake bolts	10
	7. rim worn through and ready to collapse	replace rim or wheel ASAP!	n/a
clunking from fork	1. headset loose	adjust headset	14
rubbing or scraping noise when pedaling	1. crossed chain	avoid extreme gears	8
	2. front derailleur rubbing	adjust front derailleur	8
	3. chainring rubs frame	longer bottom bracket or,	11
		move bottom bracket over	11
rubbing, squealing, or scraping noise when coasting or pedaling	1. tire dragging on frame	straighten wheel	5, 9
	2. tire dragging on fork	straighten wheel	5, 9
	3. brake dragging on rim	adjust brake	10
	4. dry hub dust seals	clean and lube dust seals	10
squeaking noise	1. dry hub or BB bearings	overhaul hubs or BB	9, 11
	2. dry pedal bushings	overhaul pedals	12
	3. squeaky saddle	grease edge of leather	13
	4. rusted or dry chain	lube or replace chain	7

STRANGE NOISES *(continued)*

SYMPTOM	LIKELY CAUSES	ACTION	CHAPTER
squeaking noise (cont.)	5. squeaky seatpost clamps	tighten seatpost clamp	13
	6. seatpost squeaking inside seat tube	shim or shorten seatpost	13
squealing noise when braking	1. brake pads toed out	adjust brake pads	10
	2. greasy rims	clean rims and pads	10
	3. loose brake caliper	tighten brake bolt(s)	10
ticking noise when coasting	1. wheel magnet hits sensor	move computer sensor	n/a
	2. badly glued tubular	reglue tire	9
ticking noise when braking	1. glue on rim sidewall	clean rim with solvent	9
	2. gouge in rim sidewall	sand rough spot	9
	3. high rim seam junction	ignore, or sand seam	9

APPENDIX B

GEAR CHART

These gear tables are in inches and are based on (Table 1) a 700C × 23mm tire (668mm diameter) and on (Table 2) a 26-inch, or 650C × 23mm tire (618mm diameter). Your gear development numbers may be slightly different if the diameter of the fully inflated rear tire, with your weight on it, is not 668mm or 618mm. Unless your bike has 24-inch wheels, these numbers will be very close.

If you want to have accurate gear development numbers for the tire you happen to have on at the time, at a certain inflation pressure, then measure the tire diameter very precisely with the procedure below. You can come up with your own gear chart by plugging the tire diameter (see how to measure it below) into the gear development formula below the chart, or by using one of these charts as a starting point and adjusting them for your tires. For instance, you can multiply each number in the 700C chart here by the ratio of your tire diameter divided by 668mm (the tire diameter we used for 700C). Or, go to Tom Compton's interactive gear chart at www.analyticcycling.com/GearChart_Page.html.

MEASURING TIRE DIAMETER

1. Sit on the bike with the tire pumped to your desired pressure.
2. Mark the spot on the rear rim that is at the bottom, and mark the floor adjacent to that spot.
3. Roll forward one wheel revolution, and mark the floor again where the mark on the rim is again at the bottom.
4. Measure the distance between the marks on the floor; this is the tire circumference at pressure with your weight on it.
5. Divide this number by π—3.14159—to get the diameter.

TABLE 1: 700C WHEELS

CHAINRING GEAR TEETH

REAR HUB COGS	34	35	36	37	38	39	40	41	42	43	44
11	81.3	83.7	86.1	88.5	90.9	93.2	95.6	98.0	100.4	102.8	105.2
12	74.5	76.7	78.9	81.1	83.3	85.5	87.7	89.9	92.0	94.2	96.4
13	68.8	70.8	72.8	74.9	76.9	78.9	80.9	82.9	85.0	87.0	89.0
14	63.9	65.7	67.6	69.5	71.4	73.3	75.1	77.0	78.9	80.8	82.7
15	59.6	61.4	63.1	64.9	66.6	68.4	70.1	71.9	73.6	75.4	77.1
16	55.9	57.5	59.2	60.8	62.5	64.1	65.7	67.4	69.0	70.7	72.3
17	52.6	54.1	55.7	57.2	58.8	60.3	61.9	63.4	65.0	66.5	68.1
18	49.7	51.1	52.6	54.1	55.5	57.0	58.4	59.9	61.4	62.8	64.3
19	47.1	48.4	49.8	51.2	52.6	54.0	55.4	56.8	58.1	59.5	60.9
20	44.7	46.0	47.3	48.7	50.0	51.3	52.6	53.9	55.2	56.5	57.9
21	42.6	43.8	45.1	46.3	47.6	48.8	50.1	51.3	52.6	53.9	55.1
22	40.6	41.8	43.0	44.2	45.4	46.6	47.8	49.0	50.2	51.4	52.6
23	38.9	40.0	41.2	42.3	43.5	44.6	45.7	46.9	48.0	49.2	50.3
24	37.3	38.4	39.4	40.5	41.6	42.7	43.8	44.9	46.0	47.1	48.2
25	35.8	36.8	37.9	38.9	40.0	41.0	42.1	43.1	44.2	45.2	46.3
26	34.4	35.4	36.4	37.4	38.4	39.4	40.5	41.5	42.5	43.5	44.5
27	33.1	34.1	35.1	36.0	37.0	38.0	39.0	39.9	40.9	41.9	42.9

GEAR FORMULA:

Gear development = (number of teeth on chainring) × (wheel diameter) ÷ (number of teeth on rear cog)

To find out how many inches you go with each pedal stroke in a given gear, multiply the gear development by 3.14 (π).

TABLE 1: 700C WHEELS

CHAINRING GEAR TEETH

45	46	47	48	49	50	51	52	53	54	55	56
107.6	110.0	112.4	114.8	117.2	119.5	121.9	124.3	126.7	129.1	131.5	133.9
98.6	100.8	103.0	105.2	107.4	109.6	111.8	114.0	116.2	118.3	120.5	122.7
91.0	93.1	95.1	97.1	99.1	101.2	103.2	105.2	107.2	109.2	111.3	113.3
84.5	86.4	88.3	90.2	92.0	93.9	95.8	97.7	99.6	101.4	103.3	105.2
78.9	80.7	82.4	84.2	85.9	87.7	89.4	91.2	92.9	94.7	96.4	98.2
74.0	75.6	77.2	78.9	80.5	82.2	83.8	85.5	87.1	88.8	90.4	92.0
69.6	71.2	72.7	74.3	75.8	77.4	78.9	80.4	82.0	83.5	85.1	86.6
65.7	67.2	68.7	70.1	71.6	73.1	74.5	76.0	77.4	78.9	80.4	81.8
62.3	63.7	65.1	66.4	67.8	69.2	70.6	72.0	73.4	74.7	76.1	77.5
59.2	60.5	61.8	63.1	64.4	65.7	67.1	68.4	69.7	71.0	72.3	73.6
56.4	57.6	58.9	60.1	61.4	62.6	63.9	65.1	66.4	67.6	68.9	70.1
53.8	55.0	56.2	57.4	58.6	59.8	61.0	62.2	63.4	64.6	65.7	66.9
51.5	52.6	53.7	54.9	56.0	57.2	58.3	59.5	60.6	61.7	62.9	64.0
49.3	50.4	51.5	52.6	53.7	54.8	55.9	57.0	58.1	59.2	60.3	61.4
47.3	48.4	49.4	50.5	51.5	52.6	53.7	54.7	55.8	56.8	57.9	58.9
45.5	46.5	47.5	48.6	49.6	50.6	51.6	52.6	53.6	54.6	55.6	56.6
43.8	44.8	45.8	46.8	47.7	48.7	49.7	50.7	51.6	52.6	53.6	54.5

TABLE 2: 26-INCH WHEELS

CHAINRING GEAR TEETH

	39	40	41	42	43	44	45	46	47	48	49
11	86.3	88.5	90.7	92.9	95.1	97.3	99.5	101.7	104.0	106.2	108.4
12	79.1	81.1	83.1	85.2	87.2	89.2	91.2	93.3	95.3	97.3	99.4
13	73.0	74.9	76.7	78.6	80.5	82.4	84.2	86.1	88.0	89.8	91.7
14	67.8	69.5	71.3	73.0	74.7	76.5	78.2	79.9	81.7	83.4	85.2
15	63.3	64.9	66.5	68.1	69.7	71.4	73.0	74.6	76.2	77.9	79.5
16	59.3	60.8	62.3	63.9	65.4	66.9	68.4	70.0	71.5	73.0	74.5
17	55.8	57.2	58.7	60.1	61.5	63.0	64.4	65.8	67.3	68.7	70.1
18	52.7	54.1	55.4	56.8	58.1	59.5	60.8	62.2	63.5	64.9	66.2
19	49.9	51.2	52.5	53.8	55.1	56.3	57.6	58.9	60.2	61.5	62.7
20	47.4	48.7	49.9	51.1	52.3	53.5	54.7	56.0	57.2	58.4	59.6
21	45.2	46.3	47.5	48.7	49.8	51.0	52.1	53.3	54.5	55.6	56.8
22	43.1	44.2	45.3	46.4	47.6	48.7	49.8	50.9	52.0	53.1	54.2
23	41.3	42.3	43.4	44.4	45.5	46.5	47.6	48.7	49.7	50.8	51.8
24	39.5	40.6	41.6	42.6	43.6	44.6	45.6	46.6	47.6	48.7	49.7
25	38.0	38.9	39.9	40.9	41.8	42.8	43.8	44.8	45.7	46.7	47.7

REAR HUB COGS

GEAR FORMULA:

Gear development = (number of teeth on chainring) × (wheel diameter) ÷ (number of teeth on rear cog)

To find out how far you get with each pedal stroke in a given gear, multiply the gear development by 3.14 (π).

TABLE 2: 26-INCH WHEELS

CHAINRING GEAR TEETH

50	51	52	53	54	55	56	57	58	59	60
110.6	112.8	115.0	117.2	119.4	121.7	123.9	126.1	128.3	130.5	132.7
101.4	103.4	105.4	107.5	109.5	111.5	113.5	115.6	117.6	119.6	121.7
93.6	95.5	97.3	99.2	101.1	102.9	104.8	106.7	108.6	110.4	112.3
86.9	88.6	90.4	92.1	93.8	95.6	97.3	99.1	100.8	102.5	104.3
81.1	82.7	84.3	86.0	87.6	89.2	90.8	92.5	94.1	95.7	97.3
76.0	77.6	79.1	80.6	82.1	83.6	85.2	86.7	88.2	89.7	91.2
71.6	73.0	74.4	75.9	77.3	78.7	80.1	81.6	83.0	84.4	85.9
67.6	68.9	70.3	71.6	73.0	74.3	75.7	77.0	78.4	79.8	81.1
64.0	65.3	66.6	67.9	69.2	70.4	71.7	73.0	74.3	75.6	76.8
60.8	62.0	63.3	64.5	65.7	66.9	68.1	69.3	70.6	71.8	73.0
57.9	59.1	60.2	61.4	62.6	63.7	64.9	66.0	67.2	68.4	69.5
55.3	56.4	57.5	58.6	59.7	60.8	61.9	63.0	64.1	65.3	66.4
52.9	54.0	55.0	56.1	57.1	58.2	59.2	60.3	61.4	62.4	63.5
50.7	51.7	52.7	53.7	54.7	55.8	56.8	57.8	58.8	59.8	60.8
48.7	49.6	50.6	51.6	52.6	53.5	54.5	55.5	56.4	57.4	58.4

APPENDIX C

TORQUE TABLE

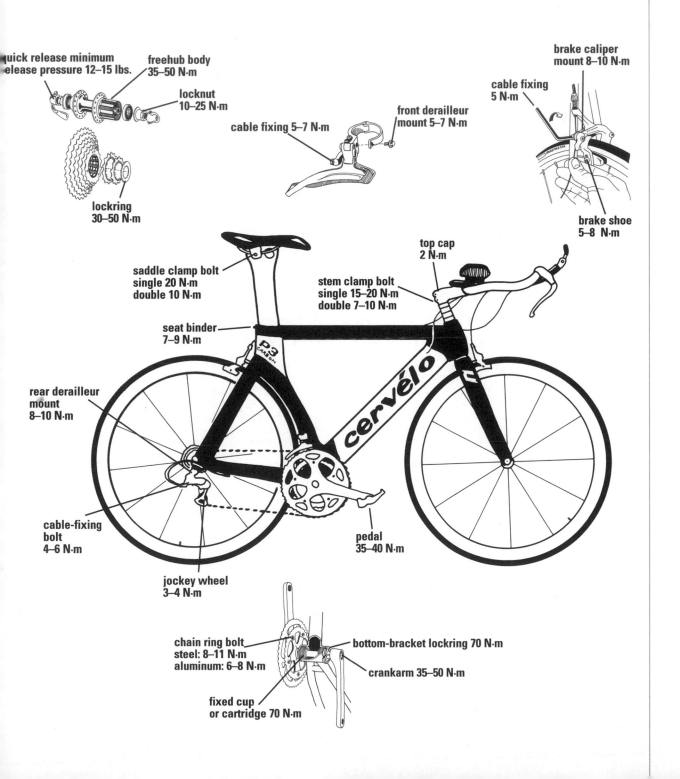

quick release minimum
release pressure 12–15 lbs.

freehub body
35–50 N·m

locknut
10–25 N·m

cable fixing 5–7 N·m

front derailleur
mount 5–7 N·m

brake caliper
mount 8–10 N·m

cable fixing
5 N·m

brake shoe
5–8 N·m

lockring
30–50 N·m

saddle clamp bolt
single 20 N·m
double 10 N·m

top cap
2 N·m

stem clamp bolt
single 15–20 N·m
double 7–10 N·m

seat binder
7–9 N·m

rear derailleur
mount
8–10 N·m

cable-fixing
bolt
4–6 N·m

pedal
35–40 N·m

jockey wheel
3–4 N·m

chain ring bolt
steel: 8–11 N·m
aluminum: 6–8 N·m

bottom-bracket lockring 70 N·m

crankarm 35–50 N·m

fixed cup
or cartridge 70 N·m

One of the single biggest sources of mechanical problems (and breakage risk) is overtightening or undertightening of fasteners, particularly on lightweight equipment. It is great to have the feel for what is tight enough, but many people do not have this, and feel really should only supplement torque measurement. With some parts, particularly today's superlight stems and handlebars, it is incredibly important to tighten them to exact torque specification or you could have a stem or handlebar break while you are riding, which results in an immediate and terrifying loss of control of the bicycle. Even "old guard" mechanics, with their "feel" from years of practice, often overtighten the small, light bolts on lightweight stems.

That said, I also recommend that you develop a feel for bolt tightness. On small bolts, even if you are using a torque wrench, choke up on the wrench so you can feel with your fingers how hard you are twisting it. *Torque = Force × Radius*, and since you are reducing the radius (i.e., the length of the lever) at which you apply the force, you have to apply more force to get the same torque on the bolt, so you are aware of the effort it takes. You don't get this sensation when tightening a small bolt by pulling from the end of a long lever where it takes little force to apply a lot of torque. Don't worry about throwing off the torque reading by choking up, as long as you are pulling smoothly. Most torque wrenches have a spring inside to balance the torque on the square bit drive, and this spring action is independent of hand position (the spring pulls from the end of the wrench, and it is the tension on this spring that determines the reading measured by the wrench, irrespective of where you grab the wrench as long as you don't grab its head).

There is also danger to undertightening fasteners. The handlebar in an undertightened stem clamp can come loose and twist, or an undertightened brake cable can pull free when you really yank hard on the brakes. Also, an undertightened bolt suffers more fatigue during use than one that is preloaded, and thus may break.

The standard method of calculating torque specifications is to load the fastener to 80 percent of its yield strength. When you have a rigid joint, this method works. High bolt preload assures that the fastener is always in tension to prevent metal fatigue in the fastener. However, many bike parts are not rigid, and high torques can overcompress or crush components. This is especially important when you are using parts of different brands, eras, or materials together. For instance, a stem manufacturer's torque specification for a handlebar clamp may not have anticipated that a carbon handlebar would be used, and what would work for an aluminum bar could crush the carbon one. There is no springback in a rigid joint, but if parts flex under tightening (a handlebar is a good example), that flex may provide the preload that the bolt needs at a considerably lower torque setting than if it were bolted through solid steel parts.

Modern torque wrenches usually have a twist knob at the base of the handle to pull tension on the internal spring. You read the torque setting on a vernier scale or against a line on an indicator window on the side of the handle. When the set torque is reached, the head of the wrench snaps over to the side to alert you. Alternatively, a beam-type torque wrench has a needle arm parallel to the wrench shaft that moves across a scale.

You actually need two torque wrenches for working on bikes. The big one cannot measure torques accurately for small bolts. The little one cannot tighten a bottom bracket or crank bolt enough because it does not have a long enough handle, and its scale does not go up high enough.

Using a torque wrench is not a guarantee against a screwup; it simply reduces the chances of one. First, you must make sure that the torque setting you are going for is the one recommended for the bolt you are tightening. The torque table in this appendix includes a lot of bolts, but it obviously cannot include all bolts from all manufacturers, so if you can consult your owner's manual, do it.

Second, lubrication of the bolt, temperature, and a wide variety of other variables will affect torque readings as well. Bicycle bolts generally assume lubrication or threadlock (which provides lubrication before it dries) on the threads, but often not under the bolt head. Lubricating under the bolt head allows the bolt to turn further at the same torque setting than the same bolt without lubrication under the head, and it thus increases the tension on the bolt.

Third, the torque reading will depend on if the bolt is turning or you are starting a stationary bolt into motion, since its coefficient of static friction will be higher than its coefficient of dynamic (sliding) friction. If you try to determine the torque of a bolt by checking what torque setting is required on the handle to unscrew the bolt, you will have estimated a higher torque than the actual one, particularly if the bolt has been in place for some time and has corrosion or dirt around it.

Fourth, the reading on the torque wrench assumes that the wrench head is centered over the bolt; the torque reading will be low if you have a radius multiplying the torque. For instance, measuring tightening torque on a pedal axle (if not using a 6mm or 8mm hex key in the hex hole in the axle end) requires a "crow's foot" 15mm open-end wrench attachment on a torque wrench. The crow's foot creates an offset between the axle centerline and the tool head centerline, which, if lined up straight with the torque wrench, multiplies the torque setting displayed on the wrench handle (i.e., it will make the wrench—the radius—effectively longer). The decimal by which you must multiply the suggested bolt torque to determine the torque setting for the wrench will usually be imprinted on the crow's foot. You must use this torque multiplication factor if you have the crow's foot extending straight out from the torque wrench. However, if you keep the crow's foot at 90 degrees from the torque wrench, provided the crow's foot is short relative to the length of the torque wrench, you can use the torque settings on the wrench (since the hypotenuse and the long side of the right triangle will be close to the same length).

Finally, torque wrenches are not 100 percent accurate, and their accuracy changes over time with wear on the internal spring. Most torque wrenches can be recalibrated at the factory; there will be a bolt attached to the spring that can be screwed in or out to adjust the reading on the wrench to match a known torque. Ultimately, your feel and common sense are also necessary to ensure safety.

It will be worth your while to review §v-16 (in Chap. 5) to help you develop a feel for bolt tightness. Whether or not you have "the touch," a torque wrench is a wonderful thing, as long as you know how tight the bolt is supposed to be.

Listed below are tightening torque recommendations of many bike component manufacturers. Where there is only a maximum torque listed, you can figure around 80–90 percent of that number for the minimum torque.

Most torques are for steel bolts; where possible, aluminum and titanium bolts are described as such in

TORQUE TABLE

the table. Note that it is particularly important to use a copper-filled lubricant like Finish Line "Ti-Prep" on titanium bolts to prevent them from binding and galling; the same goes for installing any bolt into threads in a titanium component or bike frame.

CONVERSION BETWEEN UNITS

The following table is in inch-pounds (in-lbs) and in Newton-meters (N·m) (the latter being the one which I find to be easier to use, since the numbers tend to be nice, round, one- or two-digit numbers). Divide these in-lb settings by 12 to convert to foot-pounds (ft-lbs). Multiply in-lb settings by 0.113 to convert to Newton-meters (N·m). Multiply kgf-cm settings by 0.098 to convert to Newton-meters (N·m).

BOLT SIZES

M5 bolts are 5mm in diameter and take a 3mm or 4mm hex key (except on derailleurs, where they often take a 5mm hex key or an 8mm box wrench).

M6 bolts are 6mm in diameter and generally take a 5mm hex key.

M7 bolts are 7mm in diameter and generally take a 6mm hex key.

M8 bolts are 8mm in diameter and generally take a 6mm hex key.

M10 bolts are 10mm in diameter and on bikes will likely take a 5mm or 6mm hex key (rear derailleur mounting bolt).

The designation M in front of the bolt size number means millimeters and refers to the bolt shaft size, not to the hex key that turns it; an M5 bolt is 5mm in diameter, an M6 is 6mm, and so on, but it may not have any relation to the wrench size. For instance, an M5 bolt usually takes a 4mm hex key (or in the case of a hex-head style, an 8mm box-end or socket wrench), but M5 bolts on bicycles often accept non-standard wrench sizes. M5 bolts attach bottle cages to the frame, and while some accept the normal 4mm hex key, many have a rounded "cap" head and take a 3mm hex key or sometimes a 5mm hex key. The M5 bolts that clamp a front derailleur around the seat tube, or that anchor the cable on a front or rear derailleur, also take a nonstandard hex key size, namely a 5mm. And some brake bolts and chainring bolts take a *Torx* T15 or a T25 key. Conversely, the big single pinch bolts found on old stems usually take only a 6mm hex key, but they may be M6, M7, and even M8.

Generally, tightness can be classified in three levels:

1. Snug (10–30 in-lbs, or 1–3 N·m): small setscrews, bearing preload bolts (such as on threadless-headset top caps), and screws going into plastic parts need to be snug.

2. Firmly tightened (30–80 in-lbs, or 3–9 N·m): this refers to small M5 bolts, like shoe cleat bolts, brake and derailleur cable anchor bolts, derailleur band clamp bolts, small stem faceplate, or stem steerer clamp bolts. Some M5 and M6 seatpost clamp bolts also must be firmly tightened.

3. Tight (80–240 in-lbs, or 9–27 N·m): wheel axle nuts, old-style single-bolt stem bolts (M6, M7 or M8), some seatpost binder bolts, and seatpost saddle clamp bolts need to be tight.

4. Really tight (280–600 in-lbs, or 31–68 N·m): crank arm bolts, pedal axles, cassette-lockring bolts, and bottom-bracket cups are large parts that need to be really tight or they will creak or come loose.

TRIATHLON BIKE FASTENER TORQUE TABLE
(unit conversion factors are at the end of below table)

BOTTOM BRACKETS AND CRANKS	N·m		INCH-LBS	
	MIN	MAX	MIN	MAX
Shimano crankarm fixing bolt (M8 steel)	305	391	34	44
Shimano crankarm fixing bolt (Octalink/Hollowtech)	305	435	35	50
Shimano left crankarm fixing cap (Hollowtech 2)	4	6	0	1
Shimano left crankarm fixing bolts (M5 for Hollowtech 2)	88	132	10	15
Shimano chainring fixing bolt	70	95	8	11
Shimano sealed cartridge bottom-bracket cups	435	608	50	70
Shimano integrated-spindle (Hollowtech 2) bearing cups	305	435	35	50
Shimano loose-ball-bearing bottom-bracket fixed cup	609	695	69	79
Shimano loose-ball-bearing bottom-bracket lockring	609	695	69	79
Campagnolo crankarm fixing bolt (M8 steel)	283	336	32	38
Campagnolo sealed cartridge bottom-bracket cups		619		70
Campagnolo chainring fixing bolt		71		8
FSA M8 steel crankarm fixing bolt	304	347	34	39
FSA M12 steel crankarm fixing bolt	434	521	49	59
FSA M14 aluminum crankarm fixing bolt	391	434	44	49
FSA M15 steel crankarm fixing bolt	434	521	49	59
FSA chromoly Allen chainring fixing bolt		122		12
FSA aluminum Allen chainring fixing bolt		87		10
FSA aluminum Torx chainring fixing bolt		104		11
FSA aluminum bottom-bracket cups	347	434	39	49
Race Face X-type crankarm fixing bolt	363	602	41	68
Truvativ M8 crank bolts, square taper & PS		372		42
Truvativ M12 crank bolts, ISIS		425		48
Truvativ M15 crank bolts, ISIS		425		48
Truvativ M15 crank bolts, Giga X-Pipe		478		54
Truvativ Giga X-pipe left crank bolt	363	416	41	47
Truvativ self extractor ring-16mm hex key required	106	133	12	15
Truvativ English BB cup, 1.37"		363		41
Truvativ Giga X-pipe BB cup	301	363	34	41
Truvativ ISIS overdrive M48 BB cup		602		68
Bontrager crankarm fixing bolts, M15	370	420	42	48
Bontrager sport crankarm fixing bolts, M8	320	370	36	42

	N·m		INCH-LBS	
BOTTOM BRACKETS AND CRANKS *(continued)*	MIN	MAX	MIN	MAX
Bontrager chainring fixing bolt, steel	70	95	8	11
Bontrager chainring fixing bolt, aluminum	50	70	6	8

BRAKES

Side-pull Calipers

	MIN	MAX	MIN	MAX
Shimano caliper fixing bolt (to frame)	70	86	8	10
Caliper fixing bolt-carbon seatstays: Trek, Lemond, Klein	55	60	6	7
Shimano cable fixing bolt	53	69	6	8
Shimano brake-shoe fixing bolt	44	60	5	7
Campagnolo caliper fixing bolt (to frame)		88		10
Campagnolo cable fixing bolt		44		5
Campagnolo brake-shoe fixing bolt		71		8

DERAILLEURS AND SHIFTERS

	MIN	MAX	MIN	MAX
Shimano front-derailleur cable-fixing bolt, M5	44	60	5	7
Shimano front-derailleur clamp bolt, M5	44	60	5	7
Shimano front-derailleur braze-on mounting bolt, M5	44	60	5	7
Shimano rear-derailleur cable-fixing bolt, M5	35	52	3.9	5.9
Shimano rear-derailleur mounting bolt, M10	70	86	8	10
Shimano rear-derailleur pulley center bolts, M5	27	34	3	4
Campagnolo front-derailleur cable-fixing bolt, M5		44		5
Campagnolo front-derailleur clamp bolt, M5		62		7
Campagnolo rear-derailleur cable-fixing bolt, M5		53		6
Campagnolo rear-derailleur mounting bolt, M10		133		15
SRAM front-derailleur cable-fixing bolt, M5		44		5
SRAM rear-derailleur cable-fixing bolt, M5	35	45	4	5
SRAM rear-derailleur mounting bolt, M10	70	85	8	10
SRAM rear-derailleur pulley center bolts, M5		22		3
SRAM rear-derailleur cage-stop screw		13		2
Trek spec for front-derailleur clamp bolt, M5	25	35	3	4

	N·m		INCH-LBS	
DUAL CONTROL LEVER	MIN	MAX	MIN	MAX
Shimano STI fixing bolt (to handlebar)	35	43	4	5
Campagnolo Ergopower fixing bolt (to handlebar)		88		10

HUBS, CASSETTES, AND QUICK-RELEASE SKEWERS				
Shimano hub quick-release lever closing	79	104	8.8	11.8
bolt-on steel skewer		65		7
bolt-on titanium skewer		85		10
nutted front hub		180		20
nutted rear hub		300		34
quick-release axle locknut	87	217	10	25
Shimano freehub cassette body-fixing bolt	305	434	35	50
Shimano cassette cog lockring	261	434	30	50
Campagnolo cassette cog lockring		442		50
Mavic cassette cog lockring		354		40
Trek spec for front-axle nuts (bolt-on hubs)	180	240	20	27
Trek spec for rear-axle nuts (bolt-on hubs)	240	300	27	34

MISCELLANEOUS	MIN	MAX	MIN	MAX
AheadSet bearing preload, M6		22		2
water bottle cage bolts, M5	25	35	3	4
Trek spec for water bottle cage bolts, M5	20	25	2	3
Trek spec for rear-derailleur hanger bolt	50	70	6	8

PEDALS AND SHOES				
Crank Bros. pedal axle to crankarm	301	363	34	41
Shimano pedal axle to crankarm	307		35	
Campagnolo pedal axle to crankarm		354		40
Trek spec for pedal axle to crankarm	350	380	40	43
Time pedal axle to crankarm		310		35
pedal spindle into Truvativ crankarm	186	301	21	34

TORQUE TABLE

	N·m		INCH-LBS	
PEDALS AND SHOES (continued)	MIN	MAX	MIN	MAX
Crank Bros. shoe-fixing cleat bolt, M5	35	44	4	5
Shimano shoe-fixing cleat bolt, M5	44	51	5	6
Shimano shoe spike, M5		34		4
toeclips to pedals, M5	25	45	3	5
Speedplay Frog spindle nut	35	40	4	5

SEATPOSTS AND SEAT BINDERS

	N·m		INCH-LBS	
seatpost saddle rail-clamp bolt, M8	175	345	20	39
cheap steel seatpost band-clamp bolt	175	345	20	39
Campagnolo seatpost saddle rail-clamp bolt, M8		194		22
Campagnolo seatpost binder bolt		88		10
Deda saddle-rail clamp bolt		195		22
Bontrager seatpost with bolt across seatpost head	120	130	14	15
Easton EC90, EC70, EA70 saddle-rail clamp bolts		100		11
Easton EC90 Zero, EC70 Zero saddle-rail clamp bolts		55		6
Easton EA50, EA30 saddle-rail clamp bolts		150		17
ITM K-Sword M6 (for GWS system)	88	97	10	11
ITM K-Sword special bolts (saddle-clamp bolt)	88	97	10	11
ITM Forged Lite All series (alu, alu-carbon, carbon) M7	62	71	7	8
Oval Concepts M6 saddle-rail clamp bolts		133		15
Ritchey saddle-rail clamp bolt: Comp, Old Pro, M8		400		45
Ritchey saddle-rail clamp bolt: WCS, New Pro, M6		165		19
Selcof saddle-rail clamp bolt, M6		71		8
Selcof saddle-rail clamp bolt, M8		177		20
Thomson saddle-rail clamp bolt, M6		60		7
Truvativ M6 two bolt		62		7
Truvativ M8 single bolt		80		9
Trek spec for single bolt using 6mm hex key	150	250	17	28
Trek spec for single bolt using 5mm hex key	80	125	10	14
Trek spec for double bolt using 4mm hex key	45	60	5	7
two-piece seat binder bolt, M6	35	60	4	7
seat-tube clamp binder bolt, M6	105	140	12	16

	N·m		INCH-LBS	
SEATPOSTS AND SEAT BINDERS *(continued)*	MIN	MAX	MIN	MAX
Trek spec for binder bolt for aluminum seatpost	85	125	10	14
Trek spec for binder bolt for carbon-fiber seatpost	65	80	7	9
STEMS				
single-stem handlebar clamping bolt, M8	145	220	16	25
wedge expander bolt for quill stems, M8	140	175	16	20
bar end M6 bolt	120	140	14	16
3T M5 bolts (front clamp, steerer clamp)		80		9
3T M6 bolts (single steerer clamp)		130		15
3T M6 bolts (two-bolt front clamp plate)		130		15
3T M8 bolts (single steerer clamp; expander bolt for quill)		175		20
3T M8 bolts (single handlebar clamp)		220		25
N O T E : 3T specs also apply to Cinelli stems				
Bontrager M8 steerer tube clamp bolts		200		23
Deda M5 steel bolts (bar clamp, steerer clamp)		90		10
Deda M5 titanium bolts (bar clamp, steerer clamp)		70		8
Deda M6 bolts (bar clamp, steerer clamp)		160		18
Deda M6 old-model hidden steerer clamp bolt		130		15
Deda M8 bolts (quill expander)		160		18
Dimension two-bolt face plate bar clamp, M6	80	90	9	10
Dimension two-bolt steerer tube clamp, M6	80	90	9	10
Dimension one-bolt handlebar clamp, M8 bolt	205	240	23	27
Easton EC70, EA30, EA50, EA70 bar & steerer clamp bolts		70		8
Easton EC90 handlebar clamp bolts		70		8
FSA M5 titanium bolts—use Ti prep!		68		8
FSA M5 chromoly bolts		78		9
FSA M6 chromoly bolts		104		12
FSA M8 chromoly bolts		156		18
ITM K-Sword, Uniko, front/rear clamp		97		11
ITM Millennium, Millennium S.O., front/rear clamp	62	71	7	8
ITM Millennium Carbon, S.O. & White S.O., front/rear clamp	62	71	7	8
ITM Forged Lite Carbon, S.O. & White S.O., front clamp		44		5
ITM Forged Lite Carbon, S.O. & White S.O., rear clamp	62	71	7	8
ITM Millennium 4Ever S.O., Forged Lite Luxe S.O. front clamp		44		5

STEMS (continued)	N·m		INCH-LBS	
	MIN	MAX	MIN	MAX
ITM Millennium 4Ever S.O., Forged Lite Luxe S.O. rear clamp	62	71	7	8
ITM Road Racing, Forged Lite Luxe front clamp	106	124	12	14
ITM Road Racing, Forged Lite Luxe rear clamp		88		10
ITM M8 bolts (single-bolt clamp or expander)	150	160	17	18
ITM M7 bolts	106	120	12	14
ITM M6 bolts (bar clamp, steerer clamp)	88	105	10	12
ITM M5 bolts (bar clamp, steerer clamp), 2 front bolts	62	70	7	8
ITM M5 bolts (bar clamp), 4 front bolts	35	44	4	5
ITM aluminum M6 bolts in magnesium stem	44	53	5	6
LOOK stems, all bolts		44		5
Oval Concepts titanium M5 faceplate bolts for alloy bars		84		10
Oval Concepts titanium M5 faceplate bolts for carbon bars		49		6
Oval Concepts M6 faceplate bolts for alloy bars		93		11
Oval Concepts M6 faceplate bolts for carbon bars		53		6
Oval Concepts titanium M6 clamp bolts for alloy steerers		84		10
Oval Concepts titanium M6 clamp bolts for carbon steerers		53		6
Oval Concepts M6 clamp bolts for alloy steerers		93		11
Oval Concepts M6 clamp bolts for carbon steerers		58		7
Ritchey WCS M5 faceplate bolts for alloy bars	26	52	3	6
Ritchey WCS M5 faceplate bolts for carbon bars		35		4
Ritchey WCS M6 clamp bolts for alloy steerers	52	86	6	10
Ritchey WCS M6 clamp bolts for carbon steerers		78		9
Salsa SUL two-bolt face plate bar clamp, M6	120	130	14	15
Salsa one-bolt handlebar clamp, M6 bolt		140		16
Salsa one-bolt steerer tube clamp, M6 bolt	100	110	11	12
Thomson Elite, X2, X4 steerer clamp bolts, M5		48		5
Thomson Elite handlebar clamp bolts, M5		48		5
Thomson X4 handlebar clamp bolts, M5		35		4
Truvativ M5 bolts		50		6
Truvativ M6 bolts-bar		60		7
Truvativ M6 bolts-steerer		80		9
Truvativ M7 bolts		120		14
Trek spec for stem expander	175	260	20	29
Trek spec for handlebar clamp, welded stems	100	120	11	14

	N·m		INCH-LBS	
STEMS *(continued)*	MIN	MAX	MIN	MAX
Trek spec for handlebar clamp, forged stems	150	180	17	20
Trek spec for handlebar clamp with carbon-fiber handlebar		100		11
Trek spec for stem-steerer clamp	100	120	11	14

AERO HANDLEBARS

	N·m	INCH-LBS
Oval Concepts A900 extension-clamp bolts, M5	51	6
Oval Concepts A900 base-bar clamp bolts, M5	51	6
Oval Concepts A700 extension clamp bolts, M6	84	10
Oval Concepts SLAM extension clamp bolts, M5	71	8
Oval Concepts SLAM handlebar clamp bolts, M5	71	8
Oval Concepts armrest bolts, carbon bars, M5	62	7
Oval Concepts armrest bolts, aluminum bars, M5	88	10
VisionTech armrest bolts, M5	70	8
VisionTech extension clamp bolts, M6	88	10
Trek spec for armrest bolts, M5	45	5
Trek spec for extension-clamp bolts, M6	60	7
3T extension clamp bolts, all models, M6	133	15
3T New Ahero armrest-offset arm mounting bolt, M5	80	9
3T New Ahero armrest bolts, M6	106	12
3T Bio Arms handlebar clamp/armrest bolts, M8	177	20
3T Sub-8 and Mini Sub-8 armrest bolts, with riser, M5	71	8
3T Sub-8 and Mini Sub-8 armrest bolts, without riser, M5	44	5

CONVERSION BETWEEN UNITS

The above table is in inch-pounds (in-lbs) and in Newton-meters (N·m) (the latter being the one which I find to be easier to use, since the numbers tend to be nice, round, one- or two-digit numbers). Divide in-lb settings by 12 to convert to foot-pounds (ft-lbs). Multiply in-lb settings by 0.113 to convert to Newton-meters (N·m).

APPENDIX D

GLOSSARY

adjustable cup the nondrive-side cup in the bottom bracket. On a loose-ball-bearing bottom bracket, this cup adjusts the bearings and is removed for maintenance of the bottom-bracket spindle and bearings. On a cartridge-bearing bottom bracket, it tightens the cartridge into the bottom bracket shell. The term is sometimes applied to the top headset cup as well.

AheadSet a style of headset that allows the use of a fork with a threadless steering tube. Also called a "threadless headset." The name is a trademark of Dia-Compe and Cane Creek.

Allen wrench (aka hex key or Allen key) a hexagonal wrench that fits inside a hexagonal hole in the head of a bolt.

anchor bolt (cable anchor bolt, cable-fixing bolt) a bolt securing a cable to a component.

axle the shaft about which a part turns, usually on bearings or bushings.

axle overlock dimension the length of a hub axle from dropout to dropout, referring to the distance from locknut face to locknut face.

ball bearing a set of balls, generally made of steel, rolling in a track to allow a shaft to spin inside a cylindrical part. May also refer to one of the individual balls.

bar-end shifter a shift lever that attaches to the end of a handlebar.

barrel adjuster a threaded cable stop that allows for fine adjustment of cable tension. Barrel adjusters are commonly found on rear derailleurs, shifters, and brake levers.

BB (see "bottom bracket").

bearing (see "ball bearing").

bearing cone a conical part with a bearing race around its circumference. The cone presses the ball bearings against the bearing race inside the bearing cup.

bearing cup a polished, dish-shaped surface inside of which ball bearings roll. The bearings roll on the outside of a bearing cone that presses them into their track inside the bearing cup.

bearing race the track or surface the bearings roll on. It can be inside a cup, on the outside of a cone, or inside a cartridge bearing.

binder bolt a bolt clamping a seatpost in a frame, a bar end to a handlebar, a handlebar inside a stem, or a threadless steering tube inside a stem clamp.

bonk (1) v. to run out of fuel for the (human) body so that the ability to continue further strenuous activity is impaired. (2) n. the state of having such low blood sugar from insufficient intake of calories that the ability to perform vigorous activity is impaired.

bottom bracket (or BB) the assembly that allows the crank to rotate. Generally the bottom-bracket assembly includes bearings, an axle, a fixed cup, an adjustable cup, and a lockring.

bottom-bracket drop the vertical distance between the center of the bottom bracket and a horizontal line passing through the wheel-hub centers. Drop is equal to the wheel radius minus the bottom-bracket height.

bottom-bracket height the vertical height of the center of the bottom bracket above the ground.

bottom-bracket shell the cylindrical housing at the bottom of a bicycle frame through which the bottom-bracket axle passes.

brake the mechanical device that decelerates or stops the motion of the wheel (and hence of the bicycle and rider) through friction.

brake bridge the cross tube between the seatstays to which a rear road brake is bolted.

brake caliper brake part fixed to the frame or fork containing moving parts attached to brake pads that stop or decelerate a wheel.

brake pad (or brake block) a block of rubber or similar material used to slow the bike by creating friction on the rim, hub-mounted disc, or other braking surface.

brake shoe the metal pad holder that holds the brake pad to the brake arm.

braze-on boss a generic term for most metal frame attachments, even those welded or glued on.

brazing a method commonly used to construct steel bicycle frames. Brazing involves the use of brass or silver solder to connect frame tubes and attach various "braze-on" items including brake bosses, cable guides, and rack mounts to the frame.

bushing a metal or plastic sleeve that acts as a simple bearing on pedals, suspension forks, suspension swing arms, and jockey wheels.

butted tubing a common type of frame tubing with varying wall thicknesses. Butted tubing is designed to accommodate high-stress points at the ends of the tube by being thicker there.

cable (or inner wire) wound or braided wire strands used to operate brakes and derailleurs.

cable anchor (see "anchor bolt").

cable anchor bolt (see "anchor bolt").

cable end a cap on the end of a cable to keep it from fraying.

cable-fixing bolt an anchor bolt that attaches cables to brakes or derailleurs.

cable housing a metal-reinforced exterior sheath through which a cable passes.

cable stop (or cable-housing stop) a fitting on the frame, fork, or stem at which a cable-housing segment terminates.

cage two guiding plates through which the chain travels. Both the front and rear derailleurs have cages. The cage on the rear also holds the jockey pulleys. Also, a water-bottle holder.

caliper (see "brake caliper" and "measuring caliper").

Campagnolo Italian bicycle-component company.

Cane Creek American bicycle-component company and originator of the threadless headset. Originally known as Dia-Compe USA.

cartridge bearing ball bearings encased in a cartridge consisting of steel inner and outer rings, ball retainers, and, sometimes, bearing covers.

cassette the group of cogs that mounts on a freehub.

cassette hub (or freehub) a rear hub that has a built-in freewheel mechanism to which the rear cogs are attached.

Cervélo Canadian bicycle company.

chain a series of metal links held together by pins and used to transmit energy from the crank to the rear wheel.

chainline the imaginary line connecting the center of the chainrings with the center of the cogset. This line should, in theory, be straight and parallel with the vertical plane passing through the center of the bicycle. The chainline is measured as the distance from the center of the seat tube to the center of the middle chainring of a triple crank, or, in the case of a double crank, to the center plane midway between the two chainrings.

chain link a single unit of bicycle chain consisting of four plates with a roller on each end and in the center.

chainring a multiple-tooth sprocket attached to the right crankarm.

chainring-nut tool (or chainring-nut spanner) a tool used to secure the chainring nuts while tightening the chainring bolts.

chainstay frame tube on a bicycle connecting the bottom-bracket shell to the rear dropout (and hence to the rear-hub axle).

chain suck the dragging of the chain by the chainring past the release point at the bottom of the chainring. The chain can be dragged upward until it is jammed between the chainring and the chainstay.

chain whip (or chain wrench) a flat piece of steel usually attached to two lengths of chain. This tool is used to remove the rear cogs on a freehub or freewheel.

chase, wild goose (see "goose chase, wild").

circlip (or snapring or Jesus clip) a C-shaped snapring that fits in a groove to hold parts together.

clincher rim a rim with a high sidewall and a "hook" facing inward to constrain the bead of a clincher tire.

clincher tire a tire with a "bead" to hook into the rim sides. A separate inner tube is inserted inside the tire.

clip-in pedal (or clipless pedal) a pedal that relies on spring-loaded clips to grip a cleat attached to the bottom of the rider's shoe, without the use of toe clips and straps.

clipless pedal (see "clip-in pedal").

cog a sprocket located on the drive side of the rear hub.

cogset (see "cassette").

cone a threaded conical nut that serves to hold a set of bearings in place and also provides a smooth surface upon which those bearings can roll. Can refer to the conical (or male) member of any cup-and-cone ball-bearing system (see also "bearing cone").

crankarm the lever attached at the bottom-bracket spindle and to the pedal used to transmit a rider's energy to the chain.

crank bolt (or crankarm-fixing bolt) the bolt attaching the crank to the bottom-bracket spindle on a cotterless drive train.

crank length the distance measured along the crank between the centerline of the bottom-bracket spindle and the centerline of the pedal axle.

crankset the assembly that includes a bottom bracket, two crankarms, chainring set, and accompanying nuts and bolts.

cross three a pattern used by wheel builders that calls for each spoke to cross three others in its path from the hub to the rim. Other common patterns include cross two and cross one.

cup a cup-shaped bearing surface that surrounds the bearings in a bottom bracket, headset, or hub (see "bearing cup").

derailleur a gear-changing device that allows a rider to move the chain from one cog or chainring to another while the bicycle is in motion.

derailleur hanger a metal extension of the right rear dropout through which the rear derailleur is mounted to the frame.

diamond frame the traditional bicycle frame shape.

dish a difference in spoke tension on the two sides of the rear wheel adjusted such that the rim is centered in the frame or fork.

dishing centering the rim by adjusting spoke tension in a wheel.

dishing tool a tool to check the centering of a rim on a wheel.

double a two-chainring drivetrain setup (as opposed to a three-chainring, or "triple," one).

down tube the frame tube that connects the head tube to the bottom-bracket shell.

drivetrain the crankarms, chainrings, bottom bracket, front derailleur, chain, rear derailleur, and freewheel (or cassette).

drop (1) the vertical distance between the center of the bottom bracket and a horizontal line passing through the wheel hub centers (see also "bottom-bracket drop"). (2) the difference in height between two parts, as between the saddle and handlebar. (3) a terrain discontinuity you may or may not want to ride off of. (4) something not to do with your tools.

dropouts the slots in the fork and rear triangle where the wheel axles attach.

dual-control lever a combination brake lever and shift lever integrated into a single assembly

dual-pivot sidepull brake a sidepull brake whose arms pivot at two points rather than one.

DT (aka DT Swiss) manufacturer of spokes, other bicycle components, and tools.

dust cap a protective cover to keep dirt out of a part.

Ergopower an integrated road brake/shift dual-control lever manufactured by Campagnolo.

expander bolt a bolt that, when tightened, pulls a wedge up inside or alongside the part into which the bolt is anchored to provide outward pressure and secure said part inside a hollow surface. Expander bolts are found inside quill stems and some handlebar-end plugs and handlebar-end shifters.

expander wedge a part threaded onto an expander bolt and usually used to secure a quill stem inside the fork steering tube or handlebar-end plugs or handlebar-end shifter inside a handlebar. An expander wedge is threaded down its center axis to accept the expander bolt and is either cylindrical in shape and truncated along an inclined plane or conical in shape and truncated parallel to its base.

feathering adjusting the front derailleur slightly to not rub the chain in cross-gears.

ferrule a cap for the end of cable housing.

fixed cup the nonadjustable cup of the bottom bracket located on the drive side of the bottom bracket.

flange the largest diameter of the hub where the spoke heads are anchored.

fork the part that attaches the front wheel to the frame.

fork crown the cross piece connecting the fork legs to the steering tube.

fork ends (see "dropouts").

fork rake (or rake) the perpendicular offset distance of the front axle from an imaginary extension of the steering-tube centerline (see "steering axis"). Also called "wheel offset" or simply "offset."

fork tips (see "dropouts").

frame the central structure of a bicycle to which all of the parts are attached.

freehub (see "cassette hub").

freewheel the mechanism through which the rear cogs are attached to the rear wheel on a derailleur bicycle. The freewheel is locked to the hub when turned in the forward direction, but it is free to spin backward independently of the hub's movement, thus allowing a rider to stop pedaling and coast as the bicycle is moving forward.

friction shifter a traditional (nonindexed) shifter attached to the frame or handlebar. Cable tension is maintained by a combination of friction washers and bolts.

front triangle (or main triangle) the head tube, top tube, down tube, and seat tube of a bike frame.

goose chase, wild (see "wild goose chase").

handlebar the curved tube, connected to the fork through the stem, that the rider grips in order to turn the fork and thus steer the bicycle. The brake levers and shift levers are attached to it.

head angle the acute angle formed by the centerline of the head tube and the horizontal.

headset the bearing system consisting of a number of separate cylindrical parts installed into the head tube and onto the fork steering tube that secure the fork and allow it to spin and swivel in the frame.

headset cup (see "bearing cup").

headset top cap (see "top cap").

head tube the front tube of the frame through which the steering tube of the fork passes. The head tube is attached to the top tube and down tube and contains the headset.

Hed American component company.

hex key a small Allen wrench.

hub the central part of a wheel to which the spokes are anchored and through which the wheel axle passes.

index shifter a shifter that clicks into fixed positions as it moves the derailleur from gear to gear.

inner wire (see "cable").

integrated headset a headset in which the bearing seats are integrated into the head tube (rather than requiring separate headset cups) and the bearings are completely concealed inside the head tube.

Jesus clip (see "circlip").

jockey wheel (or jockey pulley) a circular, cog-shaped pulley attached to the rear derailleur that is used to guide, apply tension to, and laterally move the chain from rear cog to rear cog.

link (see "chain link").

locknut a nut that serves to hold the bearing adjustment in a headset, hub, or pedal.

lockring a large, thin circular locknut. On a bottom bracket, the outer ring that tightens the adjustable cup against the face of the bottom-bracket shell. On a freehub, the ring that secures the cogs to the freehub body.

lock washer a notched or toothed washer that serves to hold surrounding nuts and washers in position.

master link a detachable, reusable link that holds the chain together.

GLOSSARY

Mavic French bicycle component company.

measuring caliper tool for measuring the outside dimensions of an object or inside dimensions of a tube or hollow object by means of movable jaws.

mounting bolt a bolt that mounts a part to a frame, fork, or component (see also "pivot bolt").

needle bearing steel cylindrical cartridge with rod-shaped rollers arranged coaxially around the inside walls.

nipple a thin nut designed to receive the end of a spoke and seat it in a hole in a rim.

noodle curved cable-guide pipe on a V-brake arm that stops the cable housing and directs the cable to the cable anchor bolt on the opposite arm.

outer wire (see "cable housing").

outer wire stop (see "cable stop").

Oval Concepts Swiss component company.

pedal platform the foot pushes to propel the bicycle.

pedal overlap the overlapping of the toe with the front wheel while pedaling.

pin spanner a V-shaped wrench with two tip-end pins to fit into holes in a lockring; often used for tightening the adjustable cup of the bottom bracket or other lockrings.

pivot a pin about which a part rotates through a bearing or bushing. Found on brakes and derailleurs.

pivot bolt a bolt on which a brake or derailleur part pivots.

preload (bearings) to adjust the bearings to rotate freely without endplay in the axle. This allows them to turn most freely once loaded.

Presta valve thin, metal tire valve that uses a locking nut to prevent air escaping from the inner tube or tire.

quick-release (1) the tightening lever and shaft used to attach a wheel to the fork or rear dropouts without using axle nuts. (2) a quick-opening lever and shaft pinching the seatpost inside the seat tube, in lieu of a wrench-operated bolt. (3) a quick cable release on a brake. (4) a fixing mechanism that can be quickly opened and closed, as on a brake cable or wheel axle. (5) any anchor bolt that can be quickly opened and closed by a lever.

quill the vertical tube of a stem for a threaded head-set system that inserts into the fork steering tube. It has an expander wedge and bolt inside to secure the stem to the steering tube.

quill pedal a pedal with a cage supporting the foot on only the top side, and whose cage plate is a single continuous piece that curves up to a point at the outboard end of the pedal to protect the side of the foot from being scraped on the road (Fig. 12.1). This type of pedal is meant to be used with a toeclip. The cage offset toward the top and curved upward at the outer end also serves to increase pedaling clearance when the rider leans the bike over when riding around a corner, as well as eliminating the excess weight of cage plates extending downward where they would never be used because of the toeclip on the top. A quill pedal will generally also have a tab on its trailing cage plate so that the rider can flip the pedal upright with the toe of the shoe in order to slide the foot into the toeclip.

race a circular track on which bearings roll freely.

rear triangle the rear part of the bicycle frame, including the seatstays, the chainstays, and the seat tube.

rim the outer hoop of a wheel to which the tire is attached.

Ritchey American bicycle and bicycle component company.

saddle (or seat) a platform made of leather and/or plastic on which the rider sits.

saddle rails the two metal rods supporting the saddle; the seatpost is clamped to these rods.

Schrader valve a high-pressure air valve with a spring-loaded air-release pin inside. Schrader valves are found on some bicycle inner tubes and air-sprung suspension forks as well as on adjustable rear shocks and automobile tires and tubes.

sealed bearing a bearing enclosed in an attempt to keep contaminants out (see also "cartridge bearing").

seat (see "saddle").

seat angle the acute angle formed by the centerline of the seat tube and the horizontal.

seatpost the tube (inserted into the frame) that supports and secures the saddle.

seatstay a frame tube on a bicycle connecting the seat tube or the rear shock to the rear dropout (and hence to the rear-hub axle).

seat tube the frame tube to which the seatpost (and usually the cranks) are attached.

sew-up tire (see "tubular tire").

shim a thin element inserted between two parts to ensure that they are the proper distance apart. On bicycles, a shim is usually a thin washer and can be used to space a disc-brake caliper away from the frame or fork or to space a bottom-bracket cup away from the frame's bottom-bracket shell. Shims are also sometimes used to eliminate excess space between handlebars and stems, or stems and steering tubes.

Shimano Japanese bicycle component company and maker of Dura-Ace and Ultegra component lines as well as SPD (pedals) and STI (shifting system).

skewer (1) a long rod. (2) a hub quick-release. (3) a shaft passing through a stack of elastomer bumpers in a suspension fork.

Slime tire sealant consisting of chopped fibers in a liquid medium that can be injected inside a tire or inner tube to flow to and fill small air leaks.

snapring (see "circlip").

socket a cylindrical tool with a square hole in one end to mount onto a socket-wrench handle and with hexagonal walls inside the opposing end to grip a bolt head or nut to turn it.

socket wrench a cylindrical wrench handle with a ratcheting square head extending at right angles to the handle onto which sockets or other wrench bits for turning bolts or nuts are installed. Also called "socket-wrench handle" or simply "wrench handle."

spacer on a bicycle, generally a thick washer, cylindrical in shape, intended to space two parts farther apart. Spacers can be found between the headset and the stem and between the stem and the top cap on a threadless steering tube, or between the upper bearing cup and the top nut on a threaded steering tube. Spacers may also be used to adjust the distance between a bottom-bracket cup and the frame's bottom-bracket shell.

spanner a wrench, in primarily British parlance.

spider a star-shaped piece of metal that connects the right crankarm to the chainrings.

spline one of a set of longitudinal grooves and ridges designed to interlock two mechanical parts together.

spokes metal or composite rods that connect the hub to the rim of a wheel.

spring an elastic contrivance that, when compressed, returns to its original shape by virtue of its elasticity.

sprocket a circular, multiple-toothed piece of metal that engages a chain (see also "cog" and "chainring").

SRAM American bicycle component company. Owner of Sachs, Avid, RockShox, and Truvativ bicycle component companies.

stand-over clearance (or stand-over height) the distance between the top tube of the bike and the rider's crotch when standing over the bicycle.

star nut (or star-fangled nut) a pronged nut that is forced down into the steering tube and that anchors the headset top-cap bolt to adjust a threadless headset.

steering axis the imaginary line about which the fork rotates.

steering tube the vertical tube on a fork that is attached to the fork crown and that fits inside the head tube and swivels within it by means of the headset bearings. A steering tube can be threaded or threadless, meaning that the top headset cup can either screw onto the steering tube or slide onto it, and the stem can either (1) insert inside the steering tube and clamp with an expander wedge (threaded) or (2) clamp around the steering tube (threadless). Also called "steerer" or "fork steerer."

stem connection element between the fork steering tube and the handlebar. An archaic word for stem is also "gooseneck."

stem length the distance between the center of the steering tube and the center of the handlebar measured along the top of the stem.

STI (Shimano Total Integration) an integrated brake/shift dual-control lever manufactured by Shimano.

threaded headset a headset whose top bearing cup and top nut above it screw onto a threaded steering tube.

threadless headset (see "AheadSet").

three cross (see "cross three").

tire bead the edge of the tire that seats down inside of the rim. The bead's diameter is held fixed to established standards by means of a strong, stretch- and tear-resistant material—usually steel or Kevlar. These strands alone are also referred to as the "bead."

tire lever a tool to pry a tire off of the rim.

tire sealant (see "Slime").

toe overlap (or toeclip overlap) (see "pedal overlap").

top cap the round top part of a headset that has a bolt passing through it that screws into the star nut to apply downward pressure on the stem to properly load and adjust the headset bearings on a threadless steering tube.

top tube the frame tube that connects the seat tube to the head tube.

torque the rotational analogue of force. Torque is a vector quantity whose magnitude is the length of the radius from the center of rotation out to the point at which the force is applied, multiplied by the magnitude of the force directed perpendicular to the radius. On bicycles, we are primarily interested in (1) the tightening torque applied to a fastener (this value can be measured with a torque wrench—see Appendix C) and (2) the torque applied by the rider on the pedals to propel the rear wheel and hence the bicycle.

torque wrench a socket-wrench handle with a graduated scale and an indicator to show how much torque is being applied as a bolt is being tightened.

TORX wrench a tool with a star-shaped end that fits in the star-shaped hole in the head of a TORX bolt.

triple a term used to describe the three-chainring combination attached to the right crankarm.

Truvativ a bicycle component manufacturer. Subsidiary of SRAM.

tub (see "tubular tire").

tubular (see "tubular tire").

tubular rim a rim for a tubular tire. A tubular rim is generally double-walled and concave on top. It is devoid of hook sides that constrain the beads of a clincher tire.

tubular tire a tire without a bead. The tube is surrounded by the tire casing, which is sewed together on the bottom. A layer of cotton tape is usually glued over the stitching, and rim cement is applied to the base tape and the rim to bond the tire to the rim (also called "tubular," "sew-up," and in British parlance, "tub").

unicrown a fork manufacturing method in which the fork legs curve toward each other and are welded directly to the steering tube.

welding the process of melting two metal surfaces in order to join them.

wheel base the horizontal distance between the two wheel axles.

wheel dish (or wheel dishing) (see "dish" or "dishing").

wheel-dishing tool (see "dishing tool").

wheel-retention tabs cast-in or separate fixtures at the fork ends designed to prevent the front wheel from falling out if the hub quick-release lever or axle and nuts are loose.

wheelset a pair of wheels for the front and rear of the bicycle.

wild goose chase (see "chase").

wrench a tool having jaws, a shaped insert, or a socket to grip the head of a bolt or a nut to turn it. In British parlance, also called a "spanner."

Zinn author of this book; not to be confused with Zen.

BIBLIOGRAPHY

Barnett, John. *Barnett's Manual: Analysis and Procedures for Bicycle Mechanics.* Brattleboro, VT: Vitesse, 1989.

Bicycling Magazine's Complete Guide to Bicycle Maintenance and Repair. Emmaus, PA: Rodale, 1994.

Brandt, Jobst. *The Bicycle Wheel.* Menlo Park, CA: Avocet, 1988.

Dushan, Allan. *Surviving the Trail.* Tumbleweed Films, 1993.

Leslie, David. *The Mountain Bike Book.* London: Ward Lock, 1996.

Lindorf, W. *Mountain Bike Repair and Maintenance.* London: Ward Lock, 1995.

Muir, John, and Tosh Gregg. *How to Keep Your Volkswagen Alive: A Manual of Step by Step Procedures for the Compleat Idiot.* Santa Fe, NM: John Muir Publications, 1969.

Pirsig, Robert. *Zen and the Art of Motorcycle Maintenance.* New York: William Morrow, 1974.

Schraner, Gerd. *The Art of Wheelbuilding.* Denver, CO: Buonpane, 1999.

Stevenson, John, and Brant Richards. *Mountain Bikes: Maintenance and Repair.* Mill Valley, CA: Bicycle Books, 1994.

Taylor, Garrett. *Bicycle Wheelbuilding 101: A Video Lesson in the Art of Wheelbuilding.* Westwood, MA: Rexadog, 1994.

Van der Plas, Robert. *The Bicycle Repair Book.* Mill Valley, CA: Bicycle Books, 1993.

———. *Mountain Bike Maintenance.* San Francisco: Bicycle Books, 1994.

Zinn, Lennard. *Mountain Bike Performance Handbook.* Osceola, WI: MBI, 1998.

———. *Zinn and the Art of Mountain Bike Maintenance.* Boulder, CO: VeloPress, 1996.

———. *Zinn and the Art of Road Bike Maintenance.* Boulder, CO: VeloPress, 1999.

———. *Zinn's Cycling Primer.* Boulder, CO: VeloPress, 2004.

ILLUSTRATION INDEX

INDEX

ABOUT THE AUTHOR

Lennard Zinn is an avid bike rider, bike frame builder, and bicycle technical writer. He grew up cycling, skiing, whitewater river rafting and kayaking, and tinkering with mechanical devices in Los Alamos, New Mexico. After receiving a physics degree from Colorado College, he became a member of the U.S. Olympic Development (road) Cycling Team. He went on to work in Tom Ritchey's frame-building shop and has been producing custom road, triathlon, and mountain frames at Zinn Cycles since 1982.

Zinn has been the senior technical writer for *VeloNews* and *Inside Triathlon* magazines since 1989. Other books by Zinn include *Zinn and the Art of Road Bike Maintenance* (VeloPress, 2nd ed. 2005), *Zinn and the Art of Mountain Bike Maintenance* (VeloPress, 4th ed. 2005), *Zinn's Cycling Primer: Maintenance Tips and Skillbuilding for Cyclists* (2004), *Mountain Bike Performance Handbook* (MBI, 1998), and *Mountain Bike Owner's Manual* (VeloPress, 1998). Lennard's work can be found online at www.zinncycles.com, www.velonews.com, www.insidetri.com, www.velopress.com, and www.velogear.com.

ABOUT THE ILLUSTRATOR

A former mechanic and bike racer, Todd Telander devotes most of his time now to artistic endeavors. In addition to drawing triathlon-bike parts, he paints and draws wildlife for publishers, museums, design companies, and individuals. Birds are his favorite subject, so he has included a little house sparrow. Todd's work can be found online at www.ToddTelander.com.